With my best regards
Jim Gutstein

Who Is the Dreamer Who Dreams the Dream?

Volume 19
Relational Perspectives Book Series

Relational Perspectives Book Series

Stephen A. Mitchell and Lewis Aron
Series Editors

Volume 1
Rita Wiley McCleary
Conversing with Uncertainty: Practicing Psychotherapy in a Hospital Setting

Volume 2
Charles Spezzano
Affect in Psychoanalysis: A Clinical Synthesis

Volume 3
Neil Altman
The Analyst in the Inner City: Race, Class, and Culture Through a Psychoanalytic Lens

Volume 4
Lewis Aron
A Meeting of Minds: Mutuality in Psychoanalysis

Volume 5
Joyce A. Slochower
Holding and Psychoanalysis: A Relational Perspective

Volume 6
Barbara Gerson, editor
The Therapist as a Person: Life Crises, Life Choices, Life Experiences, and Their Effects on Treatment

Volume 7
Charles Spezzano and Gerald J. Gargiulo, editors
Soul on the Couch: Spirituality, Religion, and Morality in Contemporary Psychoanalysis

Volume 8
Donnel B. Stern
Unformulated Experience: From Dissociation to Imagination in Psychoanalysis

Volume 9
Stephen A. Mitchell
Influence and Autonomy in Psychoanalysis

Volume 10
Neil J. Skolnick and David E. Scharff, editors
Fairbairn, Then and Now

Volume 11
Stuart A. Pizer
Building Bridges: Negotiation of Paradox in Psychoanalysis

Volume 12
Lewis Aron and Frances Sommer Anderson, editors
Relational Perspectives on the Body

Volume 13
Karen Maroda
Seduction, Surrender, and Transformation: Emotional Engagement in the Analytic Process

Volume 14
Stephen A. Mitchell and Lewis Aron, editors
Relational Psychoanalysis: The Emergence of a Tradition

Volume 15
Rochelle G. K. Kainer
The Collapse of the Self and Its Therapeutic Restoration

Volume 16
Kenneth A. Frank
Psychoanalytic Participation: Action, Interaction, and Integration

Volume 17
Sue Grand
The Reproduction of Evil: A Clinical and Cultural Perspective

Volume 18
Steven H. Cooper
Objects of Hope: Exploring Possibility and Limit in Psychoanalysis

Volume 19
James S. Grotstein
Who is the Dreamer Who Dreams the Dream? A Study in Psychic Presences

Who Is the Dreamer Who Dreams the Dream?

A Study of Psychic Presences

James S. Grotstein

THE ANALYTIC PRESS

2000 Hillsdale, NJ London

The chapters in this book have appeared elsewhere and are reprinted here in modified form by permission of their publishers: ch. 1-*Contemporary Psychoanalysis* (1979, 15:110–169) and rev. in *Do I Dare Disturb the Universe? A Memorial to Wilfred R. Bion*, ed. J. Grotstein (1981, Beverly Hills, CA: Caesura Press); ch. 2-Integrating One-Person and Two-Person Psychologies: Autochthony Versus Alterity in Counterpoint. *Psychoanalytic Quarterly* (1997, 66:403–430); ch. 3-Matte-Blanco Today I: Mainly Clinical, *Special Issue of Journal of Melanie Klein and Object Relations* (1997, 15:631–646); ch. 4-*International Journal of Psycho-Analysis* (1978, 59:55–61); ch. 5-*Journal of Analytical Psychology* (1998, 43:4–68); ch. 6-*Journal of Analytical Psychology* (1997, 42:47–60); ch. 7-*Journal of Analytical Psychology* (1997, 42:585–611); ch. 8-*American Journal of Psychoanalysis* (1997, 57:193–218); ch. 9-*American Journal of Psychoanalysis* (1997, 57:317–335); ch. 10-Bion's Transformations in "O," Lacan's "Real" and Kant's "Thing-in-Itself": Towards the Concept of the Transcendent Position. *Journal of Melanie Klein and Object Relations* (1996, 14:109–142.)

Published by The Analytic Press, Inc.
101 West Street, Hillsdale, NJ 07642
www.analyticpress.com

Typeset in Adobe Palatino by CompuDesign, Charlottesville, VA
Indexed by Leonard Rosenbaum, Washington, DC

Library of Congress Cataloging-in-Publication Data

Grotstein, James S.
Who is the dreamer who dreams the dream? : a study of psychic presences / James S.Grostein.
p. cm.-(Relational perspectives book series; v. 19)
Includes bibliographical references and index
ISBN 0-88163-305-4
1. Psychoanalysis I. Title II. Series

BF173.G756 2000
150.19'5-dc21
00-036273

Printed in the United States of America
10 9 8 7 6 5 4 3 2 1

CONTENTS

FOREWORD

Thomas H. Ogden

In reading about this book, and now attempting to speak about it, I feel a bit like humble Dante being guided through the underworld by Virgil. The wonder, the marvel, the splendor, and the terror of the unconscious as portrayed by Grotstein is reminiscent of Dante's portrayal of the underworld in *The Inferno*. Grotstein brings to life for the reader the excitement that Freud must have experienced as the imminence of another order of experience first began to reveal itself to him through his exciting/frightening encounters with the female hysterics who had overwhelmed Breuer. The mystery and the awe became all the greater as Freud followed the trail of his thoughts and feelings in his journey into the underworld of his own mind and body and spirit, an underworld occupied with subjects and objects and invisible presences with their own utterly alien and utterly familiar subjects and objects and history and sense of time and space. Perhaps most important of all is Grotstein's ability to convey a sense of unlimited creative potential of the unconscious; the goal of realizing a greater share of this potential in the analytic experience itself is a pivotal touchstone for the reader's reconsideration of his or her analytic technique.

I will not attempt to present a précis of this book: to do so would require at least twice the number of pages written by Grotstein. With the caveat that any attempt to paraphrase Grotstein is as doomed as an effort to paraphrase a poem, I will discuss a few of the ideas developed in this book. As Frost put it, "Poetry is what gets lost in translation." I would, however, like to offer something of a "Reader's Guide to Grotstein." This is a dense book that, despite its weight, moves very quickly; the writing is enthusiastically brimming over with ideas. This book requires that the reader tolerate a good deal of a feeling of not knowing, of feeling confused and lost. But this difficulty in reading is offset by the fact that the major concepts discussed in this book are revisited in each of its chapters. The return of increasingly familiar, but never static themes has the quality of a recurring musical leitmotif that accrues richness of meaning as the composition proceeds. The book builds toward its final chapter, "Bion's Transformations in O," where I believe the reader will find that the book comes together as more than the sum of its parts.

To turn to the text itself, Grotstein, in his preface, presents his belief that Freud's structural model, involving the interplay of id, ego, superego, and external reality, is a woefully inadequate model with which to attempt to conceptualize the mind. (The Latin terminology introduced by Strachey, despite Freud's admonitions, renders the terms abstract and experience distant.) Grotstein attempts to rediscover the energy and muscularity of Freud's insights by offering a model of the psyche in which there is a phenomenal subject (our conscious experience of ourselves as "I") and an "Ineffable Subject of the Unconscious." The latter term is intentionally ambiguous in that it represents a subject who is a reflection of itself and is known (and knows itself) only indirectly. This is perhaps the central paradox of the book. From the perspective developed by Grotstein, psychological health might be thought of as the degree to which an individual has been able to create a generative tension between the phenomenal subject and the Ineffable Subject of the Unconscious.

Grotstein's discussion, in chapter 1, of the dreamer who dreams the dream and the dreamer who understands the dream represents, to my mind, an important contribution to the psychoanalytic understanding of the phenomenon of dreaming. Grotstein views the mystery of dreaming from the point of view that dreaming is a critical way we have of communicating with ourselves and of processing that unconscious communication in the very act of dreaming. The remembering of dreams and their verbal narration in the analytic setting are secondary and tertiary phenomena. The dreamer who dreams the dream works in concert with the dreamer who understands the dream in their effort to give visual, narrative shape to psychic pain that can be viewed by an internal audience. That audience (the dreamer who understands the dream) understands and bears therapeutic witness to the truth of the experience that is brought to life in the experience of dreaming. This internal therapeutic dialogue, like the stars in the sky, is continuous, but visible only at night (that is, in sleep). The dreamer, never represented in the dream, is the "Ineffable Subject of the Unconscious." In this context, the Ineffable Subject of the Unconscious might be understood as a quality of being that is forever creating metaphoric reflections of itself: Dreams are among its most creative, magnificent, terrifying, enigmatic, unlocalizable creations. It could be said that we are most fully ourselves in the dreaming of the dreams that dream us.

Grotstein's development of the idea of autochthony in the second chapter is a cogent statement of what is most central to the analytic enterprise. "Autochthony," the fantasy of self-creation, is seen as standing in dialectical tension with "alterity," the awareness of the other as a whole and separate subject with an inner life very much like one's own. Autochthony is not a state of being to overcome or outgrow; it is an essential, life-long aspect of experience through which we "personalize" the world by imagining that we created it and that it is a reflection of who we are. Grotstein enriches Winnicott's notion that transitional phenomena are necessary for the infant to accept the separateness of the object and, ultimately, to be able to take part in "object usage." He adds to Winnicott's formulation the important element of an autochthonous (self-creating) phantasy as a healthy unconscious dimension of all object relatedness. Trauma, from this perspective, is the experience of the external world forcing itself on the individual *before the individual has had an opportunity to create it in his own image*; the traumatized individual defensively personalizes the trauma (after the fact) by fantasizing (feeling convinced in the most irrefutable way) that he caused and was responsible for the traumatizing events that overpowered him.

Two important principles of technique follow from this conception of autochthony:

Initially, the analyst's interpretations should address the patient's unconscious fantasies concerning his own responsibility for creating the dangerous (anxiety-generating) situation being experienced (whether within or outside of the analytic relationship. For example, an interpretation might be addressed to the patient's unconscious conviction that his inability to love caused his parents to neglect him in a way that left him feeling terrifyingly alone. The analyst need not concur with the patient's belief that he brought his frightening isolation on himself, but the analyst must recognize the life-preserving, defensive (personalizing) function of the patient's unconscious fantasy that he did so.

The analyst's premature attempts to demonstrate to the patient the "reality" that he or she is not responsible for all that has occurred in his or her own life may undermine the patient's necessary efforts to personalize his world, consequently leaving the patient even more helpless in the face of traumatizing impingements (past and present).

Second, as analysis progresses and the patient becomes conversant with his unconscious autochthonous fantasies (as they have been experienced, interpreted, and rendered manageable in the transference–

countertransference), the analyst's interpretations increasingly address the differences between "persecutors" and "enemies." That is, the analysis becomes increasingly more focused on the differences between persecutory projected aspects of the self, on one hand, and the feelings and behavior of external objects on the other. Grotstein's conception of successful analytic work as a process of turning persecutors into enemies elaborates and extends Loewald's (1960) conception of analysis as a process of turning ghosts into ancestors.

The analytic quest, for Grotstein, involves the voluntary "unconcealment" of private, pain-ridden aspects of self. To achieve this, the Ineffable Subject of the Unconscious and the phenomenal subject join in an effort in which the Ineffable Subject of the Unconscious serves as a metaphorical "playwright of the analytic text." The Ineffable Subject of the Unconscious communicates (in the form of symptoms, dreams, actings-in, actings-out and so on) to the phenomenal subject formerly unexpressed and inexpressible pain. The phenomenal subject brings to the Ineffable Subject of the Unconscious the pain of current life experience (which is saturated with its historical antecedents). The Ineffable Subject of the Unconscious "reworks" current experience, for example, in the form of dreaming, and thus makes it available in its altered form to the phenomenal subject (which is more imbued with capacities for secondary-process thinking and verbal symbolization). This process might be thought of as an internal process of projective identification in which different aspects of the subject make use of one another in creating emotional experience that can be thought, felt, remembered, symbolized, and communicated to oneself and to others. That which cannot be "metabolized" in this manner is manifested in the form of symptomatology.

Grotstein, in chapter 4, discusses the spatial and temporal dimensions of psychological experience. In a lucid and highly original presentation, he proposes that we might think of "inner space" in terms of four different forms or experiences of times and space. The null dimension is characterized by a sense of infinite space and might be thought of developmentally as corresponding to intrauterine experience (which is not "mentalized" since there is no space—or there is infinite space—between subject and experience). Grotstein's description of the experience in the "first dimension" is a vibrant description of the phenomenology of the paranoid-schizoid position. If zero dimensionality is the universe of the point (that is infinite), one dimensionality is the universe of the line: "there is a polarization of spatial [emotional] experience. Mother is either approaching (up the line) or departing (down the line). Moreover, the good mother's departure (down the line) is indistinguishable from the bad mother's approach (up the line)" (p. 92).

The quality of experience associated with the two-dimensional inner space is an experience of emotional thinness and flatness (geometrically represented in fantasy as a plane). Defense takes the form of flattening out of the emotional intensity. Three-dimensional inner space is associated with the qualities of experience of the depressive position: There is a sense of one's own psychological depth, of layered symbolic meaning, of interplay between inside and outside and between oneself and other subjects. Psychopathology is not inherent in any of these experiences of inner space. Rather, psychopathology might be thought of as the breakdown of the generative dialectical tension among these forms of psychic dimensionality. From this vantage point, creativity might be thought of as requiring an ability to remain grounded in three dimensionality while immersing oneself in the possibilities of another form of dimensionality (for example, as Borges does in his imaginative literary excursions into the infinite). Grotstein suspects that experiences of inner space extend into the dimensions beyond three dimensionality in order to account for "the synthesis of component spaces" (p. 97).

It is not possible to discuss in this foreword each of the chapters of this book in detail. In the latter chapters, Grotstein offers rich discussions of the subject of analysis and its internal objects/presences, as well as explorations of the mythology, cosmology, and religious symbology in which the subject finds/creates itself. Instead of attempting to survey that landscape, I will look closely at the final chapter, toward which each of the preceding chapters seems to build. The last chapter is a tour de force that begins with one of the clearest and most inclusive explications of Bion's work that I have encountered. Bion believed that the most basic driving force for human beings was not the Freudian libidinal and aggressive drives or the Kleinian death instinct, but the "truth instinct" (Grotstein's phrase) that involves an ability to achieve a resonance with "O." O is the symbol Bion used to refer to "ultimate Truth," which is unknowable in any direct way. O is beyond words and beyond sensory perception. The infant has a need for Truth that is as strong as his need for food. In early development, the infant projects unbearable (unthinkable) truth into the mother who converts it into bits of knowledge (K), which can be used by the infant for purposes of thinking and feeling that which was formerly unbearable to think or feel. This mother–infant relationship serves as a model for Bion's conception of the analytic relationship. Grotstein explains that transference itself is ultimately directed, through the analyst as object, toward the analysand's own unconscious (the Ineffable Subject of the Unconscious). The analyst in a state of reverie (a state of receptivity free of memory or desire) attempts to live with the truth projected into him by the analysand and, in a sense, "becomes it" before transforming it into symbols (K) that are offered to the patient in the form of interpretations. This is a process of transducing, in Grotstein's words, an infinite or omnipotent unknowable entity into a finite and knowable one.

The process of becoming O represents the achievement, albeit transitory, of the "transcendent position," the individual's gradually developing capacity from infancy onward to tolerate (suffer) and therefore resonate with O, the ultimate realness of anything and everything. Grotstein makes clear that, when he uses the symbol O and the concept of transcendence, he is talking about reaching toward something "beyond" but not necessarily "lofty." Transcendence can be quite quotidian: it might be sensed as an essence of a perception or as a response to a poem or to a conversation. It has to do with our coming into being, our becoming. In other words, the trajectory of transcendence is beyond the structures that defensively imprison us in our subjectivity. From this perspective, the Kleinian paranoid-schizoid and depressive positions might be viewed as strategies that we use to filter the blinding brilliance of O. The paranoid-schizoid "filtering technique" involves the creation of reductionistic binary oppositions (good–bad, victim–victimizer), whereas the depressive position "filtering techniques" involve an evasive use of the complexities of mythic categories played out in "realistic" whole-object relations (for example, the dilemmas of the permutations and combinations of the experience of oedipal jealousy).

The chapter and the book close with a fuller explication of the transcendent position. I will attempt something similar here with the help of a quotation from Grotstein's poetic language: "Transcendence is the mute 'Other' that lies just beyond, around, and within where we are from moment to moment. It is the core of our very Being-in-itself" (p. 301). The transcendent position involves a state of being that is not reserved for mystics who seem to float above everyday life. Transcendence is not a state of being that has left behind the concerns of everyday life experienced as paranoid-schizoid and depressive anxieties; rather, the transcendent position, as I understand it, is a psychological state in which one reaches deeply into everyday life (what other life is there?) and senses something more that saturates and enlivens one's being; it involves experiencing the pain of a beauty that is almost too much to bear.

The great value of the concept of the transcendent position is felt most strongly, I think, when, after having spent some time with Grotstein as he discusses this aspect of the experience of the human spirit and its hunger for coming into being truthfully, one finds the extant concepts provided by Freud's topographic (conscious, preconscious, unconscious) and structural (id, ego, superego) models and Klein's paranoid-schizoid positions a little flat, lacking something of "an imminence unfulfilled" (to borrow a phrase from Borges). In the impossible task of attempting to write about the ineffable, the unknowable, the "something more," Grotstein has made significant strides where few have dared to try (or even thought to try).

PREFACE

Who Is the Unconscious?

The themes of the chapters in this book have occupied my thinking through many years of psychoanalytic practice. Once the chapters were gathered together for publication, some unifying and defining themes seemed to emerge. Searching for a title that would reflect the Ariadne's thread running through them, I realized that I had been trying to address the mystery and ineffability of the self in general and of the unconscious in particular. I found myself attempting to deconstruct the concept of the *subject*, most particularly that which we know as "I," as differentiated from "me" or "self." I began to realize that I wanted to bring psychic entities, the unconscious and its denizens (its internal subject and internal objects), as well as the ego and id, out of the shadows and mists that have enveloped and obscured them in the misleading and deceptive garb of deterministic science, which was Freud's oeuvre, and restore them to their true aliveness.

We psychoanalysts and psychotherapists take these entities so much for granted that we overlook their mystery and wonder. There is a vast difference, for instance, between thinking of an ego, on one hand, and of accepting "I" as the consummate, complex, nonlinear, multidimensional subject, on the other—or between using the construct of the id as opposed to Lacan's (1966) "Other," which I sometimes render as the "second self" or "alter ego" or the "ineffable subject of the unconscious." When the ineffable subject of the unconscious finds an external other who happens to be a psychoanalyst, then the two together constitute what the Greeks called the *psychopomp*, the conductor to the realm of lost souls. Thomas Ogden (1994) calls it "the intersubjective third subject of analysis." In bygone times this entity was known by many names: soul, spirit, presence, or even demiurge.[1]

While searching the literature for background for an earlier contribution on the alter ego or second self, I came across the following advice given to young writers in another age. In 1759, in Edward Young's *Conjectures on Original Composition,* we find: "*Know thyself* . . . learn the depth, extent, bias, and full fort of thy mind; contract full intimacy with the Stranger within thee" (in Cox, 1980). I am searching, in short, for the "Stranger within thee"—and within me—a more vitalistic, animistic, and phenomenological way to address the rich complexity of the mind, one that respects the mind's numinousness, mystery, and infinite possibilities. And I am seeking ways to rescue the id specifically and the unconscious generally from what I believe has been a prejudice—that it is primitive and impersonal, rather than subjective and ultra sophisticated, and constitutes a "seething cauldron." There is reason to believe that the cauldron seethes because it bubbles with infinite creative possibilities and bristles with our indifference to it. One of my aims is to revive the concept of the "alter ego" (second self) in order to restore the unconscious to its former conception before Freud, that of a mystical, preternatural, numinous second self—and then to integrate that older version with the more positivistic conception that Freud gave us.

The unconscious functions with infinite sets and is mediated by "bi-logical"[2] mental processes, according to Matte-Blanco (1975, 1981, 1988), which abound in symmetrizations (self-samenesses) as well as in asymmetrizations (differentiation).[3] In other words, the id and its host, the unconscious, are, upon deeper consideration, characterized by a loftiness, sophistication, versatility, profundity, virtuosity, and brilliance that utterly dwarf the conscious aspects of the ego.

Similarly, when one refers to the ego, its very alienating latinity conceals *its* numinousness and mystery as "I," the subject of experience,

---

1. Plato's name for God, the creator or architect of the world, as distinguished from God as essence. The demiurge figured as the "heretical" Gnostic concept of the immanent God within us, whereas the mystics differentiated between the immanent "God" within us and the "Godhead," the God beyond contemplation.

2. "Bi-logic" is Matte-Blanco's term for a hybrid concept which he substitutes for Freud's primary process. It is conceived of as being situated in varying layers within the unconscious and is characterized by differing proportions of mixtures of symmetrical and asymmetrical logic; i.e., "everything is the same"/"everything is different." At the extreme, the unconscious is characterized by symmetrized infinite sets of selfsameness, i.e., the psychotic state.

3. See chapter 3 for a fuller development of the works of Matte-Blanco and for definitions of symmetrization, asymmetrization, and bi-logic.

especially in its own unconscious reaches.[4] I refer to the "I" that we know as the phenomenal subject and the id, which is really the alter ego to the ego as the ineffable subject. In fact—and this constitutes the major theme of this book—I posit that the unconscious is perhaps as close to the "God experience" as mankind can ever hope to achieve. Bion (1965, 1970, 1992) informs us that the Godhead is utterly ineffable and beyond contemplation and equates it with Absolute Truth, Ultimate Reality, the noumenon, beta elements (unmentalized elements), the thing-in-itself, O.[5] The experience of a presence that is meta-human or preternatural[6] exists as a potentiality in the boundless landscape of the unconscious. I believe that it is here that religious, philosophical, and mystical studies converge with the psychological and the psychoanalytic.[7] This convergence is implied in Plato's concept of The Ideal Forms and in his parable of the cave. Let me cite a passage from Plato's *Republic* in regard to the cave metaphor, a passage that involves a dialogue between Socrates and Glaucon:

> And now, I said, let me show in a figure how far our nature is enlightened or unenlightened: Behold! Human beings living in an underground den, which has a mouth open towards the light and reaching all along the den; here they have been from their childhood, and have their legs and necks chained so that they cannot move, and can only see before them, being prevented by the chains from turning round their heads. Above and behind them a fire is blazing at a distance, and between the fire and the prisoners there is a raised way; and you will see, if you look, a low wall built along the way, like the screen which marionette players have in front of them, over which they show the puppets.
>
> I see.
>
> And do you see, I said, men passing along the wall carrying all sorts of vessels, and statues and figures of animals made

4. Kennedy's (1998) *The Elusive Human Subject* cogently addresses the meaning I am trying to convey.

5. Bion (1965, 1970) uses the term O to designate Absolute Truth or Ultimate Reality, that domain that lies beyond imagination and beyond symbolic reality. It just *is*.

6. By preternatural I do not quite mean omnipotent or supernatural; I mean out of or beyond the normal course of nature; differing from the natural, exceptional.

7. I hasten to inform the reader that this work is not about religion. It uses religion, spirituality, and mysticism, as well as other disciplines in order to obtain different "camera angles" on the "unknown," Freud's real name for the unconscious.

> of wood and stone and various materials, which appear over the wall? Some of them are talking, others silent.
>
> You have shown me a strange image, and they are strange prisoners.
>
> Like ourselves, I replied; and they see only their own shadows, or the shadows of one another, which the fire throws on the opposite wall of the cave?
>
> True, he said; how could they see anything but the shadows if they were never allowed to move their heads?
>
> And of the objects which are being carried in like manner they would only see the shadows?
>
> Yes, he said.
>
> And if they were able to converse with one another, would they not suppose that they were naming what was actually before them?
>
> Very true.
>
> And suppose further that the prison had an echo which came from the other side, would they not be sure to fancy when one of the passers-by spoke that the voice which they heard came from the passing shadow?
>
> No question, he replied.
>
> To them, I said, the truth would be literally nothing but the shadows of the images.

Plato thus presents us with a powerful epistemological metaphor in which there is a fire situated behind a human being facing the wall of a cave. Between the fire and the individual are the Forms, those inherent preconceptions that Bion (1962, 1963) calls "thoughts without a thinker" and that are older than the thinkers who think them.[8] The fire and the numinous figures in front of it constitute the ineffable subject of the unconscious and its inscrutable landscape and workings, one aspect of  which is alpha function (a profound form of meditative intuition; Bion, 1962).[9] We humans realize them from the shadows they cast on the wall

8. Later, I shall differ with Bion somewhat to suggest that the ineffable subject of the unconscious *is* the "thinker" of the "thoughts without a thinker." I use Plato as my resource to suggest that everything is known to that immanent preternatural subject, whose ignominious nom de plume is the id, and to which I shall soon add another name, the "dreamer who dreams the dream."

9. Alpha function is Bion's (1959, 1962) term for an intuitive, nonlinear, nonobjective mental process that approximates Freud's (1911) concept of primary process. According to Bion, the infant is born without it and depends on mother's use of it to contain and "translate" its feelings into appropriate enti-

of the cave. The shadow cast by these "marionette" derivatives of the ineffable subject becomes the phenomenal subject, the self, its object, and the other objects to which the self relates. The shadow of the ineffable I, in other words, is the self, its object, the one that can never be the subject.

PSYCHIC IMAGERY AND PSYCHIC PRESENCES

Transcendentally speaking, the object the infant encounters is not merely a realistic object. That is, it is apperceived (anticipated) by virtue of inherent categories and a priori considerations (including needs, drives, affects, expectations, etc.), all exported by projective identification, which transforms the image of the real object into a phantom (even during moments of extreme trauma). This phantom becomes a compounded, or third, form, a montage, a chimera (hybrid, containing many disparate forms), which ultimately becomes far removed in nature and composition from the original object in reality (see chapter 6). I believe that psychic imagery is the mysterious intermediary (presence) that occupies the internal world both as subject and as object. Psychic imagery also serves as an obligatory link between individuals externally; we relate through the resonating intermediary of our private yet shared images.

My term *psychic presences* is meant to convey the experience of intrapsychic preternatural entities, which present as images or phantoms and which we, in turn, reify as real. These images or phantoms undergo a transfiguration or transmogrification as we progress from the paranoid-schizoid to the depressive position, to use Kleinian terms and concepts. They evolve into symbolic images that designate the "presence of the absence" of the object-person, that is, the presence of the *legacy of the experience with the object* in its absence. Even this status is obsolescent when we evolve to the transcendent position of O, the position in which the need for imagery vanishes altogether and we are face-to-face with Absolute Truth, Ultimate Reality, which are essence and the void (see chapter 10). The idea of a presence in the mind is very close to the older notion of the "numen," as in "numinous" (the numen is the local god of a place).

Intrapsychic life, like interpersonal encounters, is a dance of images—until we achieve oneness with O. In other words, once we "become" O (attain the transcendent position), we serenely realize that

---

ties. In this transaction the infant's feelings constitute the contained, and mother is the container.

everything we "learned" in the depressive position (i.e., all our "transformations in K," Bion's abbreviation for all our knowledge about facts) was but the scaffoldings of necessary approximations or falsifications until we could be ready for O.[10]

I consider the concept of the image to be of consummate importance in our understanding of psychic presences. The term *projective identification* suffered a sea change as it crossed the Atlantic and was torn loose from its strictly Kleinian moorings in unconscious phantasy. Bion's revision of the concept in his container–contained paradigm lent itself deceptively to the American revision. I do not believe, for instance, that the analysand projects into an object per se (if object means an external person). I believe that analysands project into their *image* of the object, and that image is *intrapsychic*. The participation of the real person who is the putative object of the projective identification is separate from, and therefore independent of, that projecting subject. When the analyst is truly influenced by the analysand's projective identifications, this influence involves the counterintrojective and counterprojective invocation of the analyst's own intrapsychic imagery. This occurs in a state of what Ogden (1997) calls "intersubjective thirdness," Mason (1994) names "folie à deux" (or mutual projective identification or "hypnosis"), and Girard (1972) terms "mimesis." Schore (personal communication) and I assign this phenomenon to "intersubjective resonance." My choice of the image as an important intermediary concept was guided by St. Paul's "First Letter to the Corinthians":[11]

> For we know in part, and we prophecy in part.
> But when that which is perfect is come, then that which is in part shall be done away.
> When I was a child, I spake as a child, I understood as a child, I thought as a child: but when I became a man, I put away childish things,
> For now we see through a glass, darkly; but then face to face: now I know in part; but then shall I know even as also I am known.
>
> *[I Corinthians, 13:9–12]*

10. See de Bianchedi (1993) for her contribution on Bion's conception of truth and falsehood.

11. I chose this reference not for its *religious* importance but because of its application to psychoanalytic epistemology. I have not been alone in observing that theologians have been working on problems that correspond to our understanding of the ontological nature of the subject and our epistemological attempts to make sense of the inner and outer cosmos. See Bion (1965, 1970, 1992).

I understand this citation to be an example of the tradition of the mystics, who believe that the spiritual quest is to be able to see clearly, without disguise and through disguise. I also understand it as parallel to Bion's (1965, 1970) concept of "transformation in 'O,'" where we *become* Truth and Real, without knowing and beyond recognizing.

A corollary to St. Paul's Letter is a citation from Virgil's *Aeneid, Book V*:

> The clouds that block thy mortal sight
> I shall remove.

To clear the clouds that block our mortal sight is the psychoanalytic task, but that clearance is deceptive. As the metaphoric clouds clear away outside, our internal vision is all the more opened so that we can then shift from imagery (the object) inward to becoming the subject—in O.

"ROGUE" OR "SUBJECTIVE OBJECTS"

I have come to realize that what we have been calling internal objects are really "third forms," chimerical (hybrid) conglomerations of the *image* of the real object image intermixed with the resulting products from splitting and projective identifications of aspects of the subject. When the object is external, we see what our senses and sensitivities have rendered of our perception of the original object. This rendition becomes a projectively reidentified "subjective object," a psychic entity created by our subjectivity while we think we are perceiving the object as it really is. In other words, what we call perception is more often apperception. Apperception is the falsification or personalized distortion that underlies the illusion of perception. We "perceive" that which we are always already predisposed to encounter.

We forget that we must subjectively "format" the data of our observations with a priori categorizations (Kant, 1787). Just as a film emulsion catches the rays of light and transforms them into corresponding photographic images, so the images we form and internalize are modified by the subjective emulsions of our internal world, which render these data into personalized subjective experiences prior to their ultimate objectification.

The resulting chimerical (hybrid) images are at some remove from their original models, and they become secondary or acquired preconceptions that function like additional filters over our subsequent perceptions, thus rendering them into apperceptions (personalized distortions or "transferences"). We process our experiences from inherent and continuing mental formatting. We and our objects become prisoners, not of the events that transpire between us, but of these subjective transformations and the personalizing modifiers of how we process our experiences.

What have become known as internal objects are, to my thinking, "rogue" or "renegade subjects" ensconced within images of objects. In other words, the agent of intentionality or will of internal objects is always a function of split-off subjects. As Ogden (1986) reminds us, "Internal objects do not think." These internal objects express themselves clinically as primitive, compulsive, relentless superegos, uncontrollable, omnipotent, sometimes impulsive (even addictive) *subjective* objects, or as defective, wounded, or impotent object relics with which we identify.

The concept of the object began to change with Klein's discovery of projective identification and was further modified by the contributions of Fairbairn, Piaget, and others. We have been forced to reassess the true meaning of *object*, a term that, in contrast to *subject*, has a solid ontic (scientific, deterministic) background and lends itself in no small measure because of that provenance to what I believe are serious misunderstandings. Many psychoanalysts and psychotherapists continue to think of the object as the actual other person and to think of the internalized object as the actual external person who is now resident within the mind. It is frequently considered that we "introject" our objects and their values as our own. Freud (1915), referring to Kant, wrote the following:

> The psycho-analytic assumption of unconscious mental activity appears to us, on the one hand, as a further expansion of the primitive animism which caused us to see copies of our own consciousness all around us, and, on the other hand, as an extension of the corrections undertaken by Kant of our views on external perception. Just as Kant warned us not to overlook the fact that our perceptions are subjectively conditioned and must not be regarded as identical with what is perceived though unknowable, so psycho-analysis warns us not to equate perceptions by means of consciousness with the unconscious mental processes which are their object. Like the physical, the psychical is not necessarily in reality what it appears to us to be [p. 171].

I infer that Freud understood that he was borrowing heavily from Kant's transcendental analytic and that the *unrepressed unconscious* is unknown and unknowable and consequently must be treated as if it were Kant's a priori categories. Psychoanalysis is transcendental since it is predicated on the concept of inherent a priori categories with which the individual is constitutionally predisposed to use in anticipating the arrival of the object. Freud's rendition of these inherent categories is the instinctual drives. The phenomenon of transference is also a testimony to this transcendental leitmotif in psychoanalysis (see chapter 6).

PRETERNATURAL PRESENCES WITHIN THE PSYCHE

I wish to reintroduce the term *preternatural* (beyond natural), to which I alluded earlier. Like many others lately, I have been struck by how our psychoanalytic language has flattened and desiccated the essence of the first person pronoun I, the subject and also the object. The ego and the object have become saturated conceptually, and their inherent mystery has all but vanished. I use the word *preternatural* to address the nonlinear complexity of our being alive and human—in the presence of the mystery inherent within others. It suggests exceptional qualities and capacities that we once attributed to gods, messiahs, and mystics.

This meaning of preternatural approximates how I have come to regard the ultimate nature of the subject and the object (the other) and applies to what I consider to be the ultimately sacred architecture of the psyche. It encompasses the human and yet more-than-human capacity we have in our innermost souls to harness infinity, complexity, and chaos and render them meaningful along the variegated dimensions of understanding within the human wave band. The unconscious, particularly the ineffable subject (the id), is like a god, but a handicapped one, because it needs partners in order for its mission to be completed. These preternatural presences include the dreamer who dreams the dream and the mythical author of the analysand's free associations, who are the same.

The concept of preternatural presences came to me as I was beginning to use a clinical technique that I had picked up from my own analyst, Wilfred Bion. His clinical emphasis, which I was late to learn, was not on what I thought I was saying but on the text of what I was saying, that is, on the patterned unfolding of the sequences of my associations. As I slowly recalled what he had imparted, I found myself listening not to an analysand per se (i.e., the person of the analysand who spoke) but to the seemingly depersonified text itself, which, from one point of view, was other than human or personal.

Subsequently, I had difficulties in imparting this technique to supervisees because they felt it was too impersonal. Indeed, it is impersonal in a way. I find that I am listening to an eerie, difficult-to-define, exceptional other, the ineffable subject of the unconscious itself—"speaking" to me through the muffled discourse of the analysand's conscious discourse. This other self is what Lacan (1966) called "the Other" or "the decentered self," that is, the unconscious itself. To me it is the ego's alter ego, and I have called it the ineffable subject of the unconscious, whose nature is preternatural (beyond natural, larger than life), a presence among presences within, encased holographically within an ultimate, internal cosmic subjectivity, the supraordinate subject (see chapter 5).

The concept of preternatural psychic presences presumes a vitalistic, or animistic, demonic (in the positive as well as the negative sense) view of internal mental life. While it is true that the unconscious is a part of our human, personal self, it is nevertheless different. It is both human and more than human (although it was formerly thought to be less than human when the unconscious was considered as an id—"it").

In every absence, from infancy onward, there exists a felt presence (of the object) that either hounds or protects that absence but that certainly occupies it. The sense of presence is bimodal. One presence is the experiencing and contemplating subject itself, which includes the ineffable subject, the phenomenal subject, and perhaps others, which are all compositely located within a holographic supraordinate subject(ivity). This complex subjective presence becomes focused on its other presence, the self, its object of contemplation and reflection, which in turn consists of identified-with presences, that is, internal objects (which I have termed subjective objects since they are estranged, alienated, misrecognized subjects in the disguise of the objects they inhabit).

These objects are subjects at one remove because of projective identification of alienated subjectivities into images of external objects. Our subsequent introjective identifications with these altered images transform them into "familiar within" (dejà vu) or misrecognitions; and, in so identifying with them, we become altered, misrecognized selves. In the psychoanalytic enterprise we psychoanalysts try to name the haunting presences that occupy the absence, and even presence, of the real object and hope that they may ultimately be transformed into benign and realistic presences or returned to their proper owners.

Presence is my designation for the ultimate subjectivity of the supraordinate subject of being, which itself may be a supraordinate presence we ultimately aim to become in an evolution in O (Bion, 1965, 1970), Bion's term for the attainment of our ultimate state of consciousness. The term presence also refers to the ineffable subject, that transcendental (numinous) subject of the unconscious, the phenomenal subject of consciousness and preconsciousness, and the internal—and external (projected)—subjective objects. My choice of the term is also my way of addressing our need to be *present*—and alive—in our own experience and to repatriate our lost subjectivities from the diaspora into which we exiled them.

Years ago, I developed the concept of the background object of primary identification (see also chapter 1). Later I began to realize that this is more a "presence" than an object since it, whether it is unseen (because of its being internal) or visible externally, is sensed as a presence, often a formidable one, not just as an object of contemplation, need, or desire. We are most aware of this entity when we do *not* experience its holding-environment presence securely stationed behind us. The idea of psychic presences seemed to embrace my ideas about both the subject and the object, which are at the heart of this book.

I then began to wonder all over again about the thinking, feeling, and sensing mind to which these presences present themselves, presences that I now believe are larger, more formidable, and often more eerie than life; that is, they are preternatural presences. The mind that houses these preternatural presences is itself a presence of another order, a subjective presence, one capable of considerable objectivity (clear distinction between subject and object) but never loses its connection with its personalness, its subjectivity.

I came to feel that the mind is a subject—no, more than a subject; it too is a presence to be reckoned with. But one cannot reckon with a subject because it is a subject. I realized that from grammar. One cannot, grammatically, objectify "I" in any language. We are reduced to examining the shadow of its presence, as Plato suggested in the parable about the fire, the cave, and the Eternal Forms. In other words, the mind itself is a *holographic* subject, by which I mean that it constitutes a consummate presence totally and seemingly functions in parts as well.

THE INEFFABLE SUBJECT OF THE UNCONSCIOUS AND THE PHENOMENAL SUBJECT OF CONSCIOUSNESS

I picture the psyche/mind, especially "I" and particularly the deeper strata of our I-ness that I call the ineffable subject of the unconscious, as having characteristics like those the ancient Greeks gave to the heroes and heroines who were half-god and half-human. Centaurs and the Minotaur also portray this dichotomy. Even today we attribute to famous personages such as movie stars, national leaders, and sports heroes a kind of quasi-divinity. I have learned from Bion (1965, 1970, 1992) and from Lacan (1966) to think of the real object as a real subject in its own right, utterly unknowable in its ineffable Otherness and preternatural in its ultimate essence. We fail to realize, I am now convinced, how little we are privileged to know about ourselves or about the ineffable subjectivity of others. We can only know *about* them, according to Bion (in transformations in K [knowledge]), which is not the same as achieving ultimate intimacy with them ("become" them [but not as an identification]) in a transformation in O, the Absolute Truth or Ultimate Reality of the Otherness of the other.

Recently, Peltz (1998) addressed the theme of psychic presence from the standpoint of its dialectic with absence and suggested that analysands must develop the ability to experience their own presence in the absence and presence of the analyst in order to be involved in the third area of potential space, where the real workings of analysis take place. In other words, the analysand must become "present" in the experience of the absence and presence of the analyst. It must be apparent that I—and I presume Peltz as well—use the word *presence* here in a sense more akin to Heidegger's (1927) concept of *Dasein* (being here). Since the German language uses the same spelling for the imperative and the indicative mood of the verb, the ineffable subject may be said to be trying to rally the divided selves of its being, including itself, into a rousing unity with the imperative "Be here!" (*Dasein!*).

The qualities of aliveness and humanness require our presence as a subjective self, and we admire those whom we encounter who seem to be present. We feel that we can count on them for authentic interaction. I will try to show that it is the unity of one's ineffable subject and phenomenal subject that ultimately constitutes "being together with oneself," that is, attaining ultimate subjectivity, which is also a goal of psychoanalysis.

I call the inner (unconscious) subject—that is, the numinous ineffable subject—transcendental.[12] This is the term Kant (1787) used for the a priori categories with which we are born and that enable us to anticipate, format, and prepare for new experiences by being able to precategorize them. (Kant actually used the term transcendental subject.) From this point of view, psychoanalysis constitutes a transcendental enterprise. The numinous, ineffable subject originates as a transcendental subject (the unconscious), and it is the individual's transcendent task to "rebecome" that subject (from which it was inchoately separated)—in what Bion (1965, 1970) called "transformations in 'O,'" and which I term the attainment of the transcendent position (Grotstein,

12. The terms transcendent and transcendental may be confusing. The latter corresponds to inborn, a priori categories, according to Kant (1787). The former is best captured by the idea of developing toward or attaining a higher state or a more profound state, for example, of *presence* within oneself. It corresponds to the attainment of a sublimated ideal, which can also be *ontological humility* or unconcealment.

1996, 1997, chapter 10). To put it another way, I believe that the task of psychoanalysis is not the attainment of insight but, rather, the use of insight to attain transcendence over oneself, over one's masks and disguises, to rebecome one's supraordinate subject. This task involves a transcendent reunion with one's ineffable subject in a moment of aletheia (unconcealment).

WHO DREAMS THE DREAM AND WHO UNDERSTANDS IT?

Once, when I was a second-year medical student, I experienced a dream (described in chapter 1). I say "experienced" because I had an epiphany when I awakened from that dream. I knew that, in a way, it was not my dream! Or so I felt at that moment. It occurred to me that the beautiful and awesome dream I had experienced and the dreamer who dreamed that dream were other than I. Someone who was not I was dreaming a wondrous dream while I was asleep! Years later I related this episode to a dinner companion in Jerusalem, Professor Chaim Tadmor of Hebrew University, an authority on ancient Assyrian culture. He was fascinated by my reaction to my dream and informed me that the ancient Assyrians believed that dreams were the language of the gods, that gods spoke to each other through human dreams, and that humans were forbidden from attending to them or remembering them. Dreams, to ancient Assyrians, constituted a divine sexual conversation, and paying attention to them amounted to voyeuristic hubris.

The memory of that epiphany lasted through my analytic training and several psychoanalyses. The meanings of the dream paled in comparison with the mystery of its creation. I realized that we take this awesome phenomenon too much for granted. To say "I had a dream last night" is, in a way, presumptuous. All we can honestly say is, "I was privileged to witness and experience a part of a dream last night. I wish I could have witnessed and experienced the whole dream." In other words, our ability to dream, whether asleep or awake, belongs to a preternatural capacity, one possessed by our holographically and numinously functioning ineffable subject of the unconscious, whose noms de plume are the Dreamer Who Dreams the Dream as well as the Dreamer Who Understands the Dream.

One further point about the ineffable subject is in order: In discussing the unconscious, Freud (1915) stated, "The nucleus of the *Ucs.* consists of instinctual representations which seek to discharge their cathexes; that is to say, it consists of wish impulses" (p. 186).

But then, "It would nevertheless be wrong to imagine that the *Ucs.* remains at rest while the whole work of the mind is performed by the *Pcs*. . . . The *Ucs.* is alive and capable of development and maintains a number of other relations with the *Pcs.*, amongst them that of co-operation" (p. 190).

And, "[We] find that many *Pcs.* formations remain unconscious, though we should have expected that, from their nature, they might very well have become conscious. Probably in the latter case the stronger attraction of the *Ucs.* is asserting itself" (p. 193).

I reason from these citations of Freud that he conceived of the Ucs. as both wantonly discharging in its relentless search for pleasure and relief from unpleasure *and* paradoxically protective of the psyche by actively withholding cathexes from becoming discharged—*out of consideration for the psyche*. As I shall try to show in the following chapters, I believe that the discharging *Ucs.* is not only obeying the ongoing needs of the individual, but also is "discharging" in order to get the attention of the psyche—in dramatic form—of urgent affects and affect scenarios that need to be recognized and processed. On the other hand, the *Ucs.* that retains its cathexis from discharging does so out of a "cooperative" covenant with the psyche to protect it from too much revelation achieved too quickly. Moreover, it is my belief that the *Pcs.* constitutes the "search-engine" of consciousness for the *Ucs.*

SPIRITUAL, ONTOLOGICAL, AND MYSTICAL PERSPECTIVES

In trying to describe psychic presences, I have found it useful to add spiritual, ontological, and mystical perspectives to my thinking. By spiritual I mean those aspects of the ultrasensual, yet still experiential dimension that merit psychoanalytic study, and I hope to show that the psychoanalytic conceptions of subject and object are seriously incomplete without that perspective. The spiritual dimension of presence includes the unconscious capacity for prescience or premonition (Bion, 1992), whereby one aspect of the self seems to be superior in knowledge to our more ordinary self.[13] In addition, that aspect seems to have a quality of unusual authority with its other self. In the premoral stage of infant development, this quality of virtually absolute authority issues

13. As I discuss in chapter 1, the Dreamer Who Dreams the Dream and the Dreamer Who Understands It (each being an aspect of the unconscious) are prescient vis-à-vis the one who witnesses the dream, that is, the waking self.

from archaic internal (subjective) objects situated in "a gradient in the ego." In the later, moral stage, the inner voice of this spiritual quality approximates the deity and relates to guilt as well as to ideals.

Modell (1993), citing William James, addresses the concept of presences as follows:

> James (1902) observed that in human consciousness there is a "sense of reality, a feeling of objective presence, a perception of what we may call something there." It is this sense of presence that may have led the Greeks to ascribe to the abstract order of earth, sky, and sea the presence of a god who is the organizer of what appear to be coherent entities. It is the function of a god to bring order out of chaos. From there, it is a short step to believing that an analogous process occurs within the mind. Chaos is organized by means of a god-like or goddess-like muse [p. 133].

Freud rendered his conceptions of the ego and the id in "scientific" or positivistic terms. It is only with the superego that we get a hint from him of a moral or possibly spiritual entity. On the other hand, Klein's descriptions of the ego, internal objects, the archaic superego, and the death instinct amount to an apocalyptic portrait of the unconscious, one that more approximates the demonic (i.e., the persecutory), preguilt consequences of our primitive intentionality, phantasmal as well as real. Classical psychoanalysis is based on a clearcut division between unconscious intentionality (the drives) and morality (the superego). Kleinians find clinical evidence for primitive superegos that are demonically impulsive as well as compulsive and that, at the same time, seem to impose absolute moral authority over the ego. The Greeks understood this paradox when they portrayed their gods and goddesses as corrupt and corrupting. Spirituality, in other words, is often ignoble, corrupt, and even perverse. The devil himself is a god of a lower pantheon. Jaynes (1976) sees this unilateral hierarchic as the "bicameral mind," a mind that is divided on a gradient dominated by the higher mind. He pictures the infant as being dominated by powerful godlike voices in a state of absolute hypnotic (nonconscious) submission.

By mystical I refer to the capacity that Bion (personal communication)[14] ascribed to the mystics—"being able to see things as they really are—through the filters of disguise." The mystic is also able to see the mysterious that is embedded in the ordinary. The mystic does not

14. Eigen (1998) addresses this theme in his book *The Psychoanalytic Mystic*.

mystify but detects and clarifies. The analyst, without realizing it, is a practicing mystic. The mystical conceptions of the subject can be integrated with a concept that Bion (1962a, b) introduced—alpha function or "dream work alpha."

Bion believed that the infant projects into its mother-as-container for relief, attunement, and understanding and that through her use of her alpha function the mother is able to comprehend the meaning of her infant's cries and signals. He then stated that the infant introjects its mother's alpha function and is able thereafter to begin to think for itself. I have come to believe that alpha function is an inborn given, a Kantian a priori category, that enables the infant to communicate with its mother as an inchoate "sender" to her "receiver" and "processor" function. Correspondingly, it is our analysands' use of their own alpha function that enables them to "send" encoded messages to us as analysts, and it is our intuition (Bion, 1965, 1970, 1992), modified by our correlation of the data with other points of view and with the arrival of the "selected fact" (which gives coherence to the data), that allows us to arrive at an interpretation with our own alpha function ("receiver").

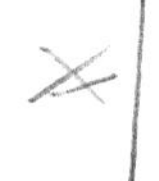

The mystical and spiritual perspectives are older ways of describing our attempts to "divine" the ultrasensual. Following Bion, I have borrowed these perspectives, from the mystics, such as Meister Eckhart (Fox, 1980, 1981b) and from the Gnostics (Pagels, 1979; Bloom, 1983, 1996); today we call these the nonlinear domains of chaos, complexity, emergence phenomena, and paradox. In this regard, I am guided in part by the work of Lewis Carrol (1882), Gleik (1987), Hofstadter (1979), Hoftstadter and Dennet (1981), Hawking (1988), Zohar (1990), Kauffman (1993, 1995), Palombo (1999), and Waldrop (1992), all of whom approach the mystical and the spiritual domains from the perspectives of nonlinear science, mathematics, or both.

THE SIGNIFICANCE OF O FOR PSYCHOANALYSIS

In a series of works on epistemology and ontology, Bion (1965, 1970, 1992) conceived of mental transformations, one of which was the transformation of raw, unmentalized experiences into K (knowledge), initially through the infant's use of mother's reverie and alpha function (patience and intuition), following which the infant could comprehend itself from mother's preliminary "digestion" of the infant's raw experiences. In Bion's terms, this amounts to a transformation from O (unmentalized experiences) into K (knowledge about the self which is to be accepted and integrated). I develop this idea more in chapter 10, but in the meanwhile, I should like to give a preview of what Bion entails in his concept of O. This concept has far-reaching significance for psychoanalysis. Let me summarize for now:

O represents the ineffable, transcendental aspects of the mind, on one hand, and the raw protoencounters or experiences that initially confront the mind, on the other. In classical theory, they can be equated with Freud's conception of the instinctual drives. Bion equated O with Kant's noumena (before they become processed into phenomena), the thing-in-itself, and even with "God," as well as with Absolute Truth or Ultimate Reality. Lacan (1966) similarly talked of the Register of the Real, by which he also meant something beyond imagining and even beyond symbolizing. The Greeks referred to this idea as Ananke (Necessity). In other words, O, in its initial sense, represents cosmic immutability, impersonalness, and utter indifference. Bion tells us, however, that when we are able to allow ourselves to "become O," by which he meant having a capacity to face and to transform into O, then O itself *evolves*, by which I think he meant that we have been able, by countenancing the utter indifference of O, to transform it into our personal, subjective O—by *matching up* with it internally so that our own inner world resonates with the fundamental of the other, like two human tuning forks.

The significance of O for psychoanalysis is, in my opinion, as follows: drives and affects, rather than being the ultimate dreadful content of the repressed, are mere signifiers or mediators for something more profound, ineffable, and incomprehensible. Further, O is not merely localized within; it is omnipresent, within us and in the ether of our externality. More about this in chapter 10.

I end this preface with the question I asked at the beginning: Who is the unconscious? As Maurice Blanchot has mused and as Bion often noted, "Sometimes the answer is an embarrassment to the question." Yet the question must be asked with full premonition about its inscrutability and mystery.

A chance observation in a dictionary by my wife, Susan, provides what I believe is the best way to grasp what I have already stated: "Seminal principle: (Philosophy). A potential, latent within an imperfect object, for attaining full development."[15]

ROAD MAP THROUGH THE BOOK

As the reader proceeds through the chapters of this book, different designations of these preternatural presences appear. In chapter 1, I introduce the Dreamer Who Dreams the Dream and the Dreamer Who

15. *Random House Dictionary of the English Language*, 1966, p. 1297.

Understands It. In chapter 2, I present the "Infant-as-God-the-Creator of its own little universe prior to discovering the universe beyond his creation." In chapter 3, I introduce the "Infinite Geometer," who wields the "calipers of fearful symmetry" and rules over bi-logic and bivalent logical structures. In chapter 4, I present a quasigeometrical version of the dimensions and coordinates of psychic space in which psychic presences dwell.

In chapter 5, I introduce yet another way of talking about these preternatural presences, the ineffable subject of the unconscious and the phenomenal subject of consciousness. In chapter 6, I discuss internal objects as "rogue" or "alien subjective objects" since our identification with them (subjectively) is the source of their haunting and intimidating authority over us within. In chapter 7, I present the myth of the labyrinth and the Minotaur as a developmental staging area for the acquisition of courage, determination, and resourcefulness. In chapters 8 and 9, I develop the theme of Christ as a continuation of the theme of Oedipus, as well as those of Moses, Isaac, Joseph, and other martyrs or would-be martyrs. I present the "Christ archetype" as an aspect of the ego ideal, the hero, the martyr, and the ineffable subject of the unconscious.

In chapter 10, I introduce the notion of the transcendent position, O, the teleological destiny for the supraordinate subject to achieve maturation through and transcendence beyond the paranoid-schizoid and depressive positions.

In all the chapters I am merely presenting differing ways of viewing the ineffable, preternatural, subjective, and ultimately personal essence of "I" in its mystical (more than we thought) relationship to the ineffable O.

ACKNOWLEDGMENTS

As any writer will confirm, it is virtually impossible to be aware of all the individuals who, either by their own works, their personal interactions with the author, or general participation in the atmosphere in which the author participated, may have influenced the author's ideas. For those I have ignored in this acknowledgment, I can only offer my regrets and my apologies, which arise out of amnesia and ignorance. I should like, however, to thank those who I do keenly recall have had a profound influence on this work by their gracious sharing of their thoughts and critiques with me. I, first of all, would like to thank Stephen Mitchell for inviting me to contribute this book and also for his editorial assistance in bringing it to publication. I am very indebted to Dr. Mariam Cohen, and Toby Troffkin for their invaluable in-depth editorial assistance and for their tireless efforts in getting the manuscript ready for submission.

To my friends Thomas Ogden, Allan Schore, and Heward Wilkinson I am indebted for countless moments of precious input that perfuses the entirety of this book. To the late Wilfred Bion and to Albert Mason my debt for professional and personal growth is beyond measure. I am especially grateful to my wife, Susan, for putting up with me and my distractions, for her loyalty, and particularly for her countless, cogent suggestions for the text—and to my children, Laurie and Josh, and their families, for bearing with me. I am profoundly grateful to my patients, each of whom not only has given me a wonderful learning experience for my analytic development, but also has become an integral part of my inner life. I am deeply indebted to my secretaries, Amy Tombor and Johna Barson, who have been loyal, keen, devoted, and diligent in helping to bring this work to publication.

Others whose advice was important in the development of this book include Jane Van Buren, John Lundgren, Harriet Kimball Wrye, Stuart Twemlow, Marilyn Charles, Michael Eigen, Rochelle Kainer, Carol Morgan, Polly Young-Eisendrath, James Fisher, John Stone, Gail Bates, Enid Young, Michael Huber, Paul Williams, Joseph Berke, Roger Kennedy, Joseph Aguayo, Edmund Cohen, Jon Tabakin, William Meissner, John Beebe, Gayle Scott, Ana-Maria Rizzuto, Margaret Fulton, Karen Willette, Joanne Culbert Koehn, M. Guy Thompson, M. Brandon French, and Marcello and Elizabeth Tabak de Bianchedi. There certainly are many others, and I ask forgiveness for not remembering. I am also indebted to Paul Stepansky, Eleanor Starke Kobrin, and The Analytic Press for all they have done to bring this book to publication.

Who Is the Dreamer
Who Dreams the Dream?

Volume 19
Relational Perspectives Book Series

Chapter 1

THE INEFFABLE NATURE OF THE DREAMER

I am, without knowing it, he who has looked on that other dream, my waking state.

—Lois Borges, *The Dream*

This chapter is based on a dream that I experienced—I should now say "witnessed"—while I was in medical school. It occurred shortly after my mother's first heart attack and just before her second, which killed her.

Unlike other dreams I had had before, or have had since, this one seemed in some respects to be about the very act of dreaming. What seemed to be different about this dream was its aesthetic beauty, its spirituality, its otherworldliness, the awesomeness of its presentation, and the experience of its numinousness. I felt that this dream *happened* to me but was not *dreamed*, that is, created, by me—even though it was. The simple truth occurred to me at the moment of awakening that I could not have dreamed this dream, first because I did not generally speak the way the dream's characters did and, second, *I was asleep at the time the dream took place—therefore, I could not have been its dreamer!* I became aware that it was a kind of arrogance to presume that *I* had had a dream. Instead, I felt that I was privileged to have *experienced* and *witnessed* a dream that an "I" I could never know had dreamed! This chapter is my attempt to come to grips with the paradox and mystery of the creation of dreams.

This chapter was originally dedicated to Wilfred R. Bion, whose analysis of my dream was very satisfying; but it is not my purpose here to discuss his analysis of it. What I want to do is explore the *mystery of dreaming*, a mystery that not even Freud solved, and search for that exquisitely elusive, ineffable subject within us who dreams the dream, the one who lurks on the other side of "the dream's navel" (Freud, 1900, p. 525).

When Freud (1900) bequeathed to us his legacy—the psychoanalysis and *understanding* of the dream—patients and laymen generally were so enthralled with this new unraveling of the Linear B of the unconscious that the *creating* of the dream received little notice among scholars; nor did this matter occupy subsequent psychoanalysts. I was naively baffled by the irony that, although we dream every night, we are fortunate if we can remember any portion of our dreams. Why the discrepancy? If we dream every night but are able to recall only minute portions of our potential dream harvest, then why do we dream at all? I concluded that we are compelled to dream in spite of ourselves. Our understanding of dreams is incidental to—or maybe even helpful to—our mental well-being, but the latter ultimately depends on the *fact* of dreaming more than on our being able to understand our dreams.

Lowy (1942) proposed that the benefit we receive from dreaming is in no way dependent on our remembering our dreams and that the benefits of dream interpretation are secondary gains. According to Lowy (cited in Palombo, 1978), dreams link current experiences with past experiences:

> By means of the dream-formation, details of the past are continually reintroduced into consciousness, are thus prevented from sinking into such depths that they cannot be recovered. Those of our experiences which are not at the moment accessible to consciousness are thus kept in touch with consciousness, so that in case of necessity association with them may become easier.
>
> This connecting function of the dream-formation is reinforced considerably by formation of symbols. When this function takes a hand and condenses masses of experiences, perhaps a whole period of the dreamer's life, into one single image, then all the material which is contained in this synthesis is reconnected with consciousness. Dream-formation thus causes not only a connection of single details, but also of whole "conglomerations" of past experience. But this is not all. Through the constancy and continuity existing in the process of dreaming, there is created a connection with this dream-continuity. Which fact greatly contributes to the preservation of the cohesion and unity of mental life as a whole [p. 7].

I understand Lowy to be stating that dreams reinforce long-term memory and help to maintain the stability of mental organization by mediating current experiences and matching them with their past prototypes. He seems to be saying that dreams are the silent service of the mind, that they do not need to become conscious in order to do their work. If this is so, then there must be a creator/transmitter of dreams and a dream recipient who receives and processes the results of the dream work. I designate these as the Dreamer Who Dreams the Dream and the Dreamer Who Understands the Dream, respectively.

Palombo (1978) wrote that dreams occur in narrative cycles over time and are *computational* in their matching functions between current and past information:

> An earlier paper (Palombo, 1976) described an autonomous mechanism of unconscious adaptive ego functioning called "the memory cycle." The memory cycle is a sequence of processes through which new experiential information is introduced into adaptively suitable locations in the permanent memory structure. The most striking hypothesis of the memory-cycle model is that the critical step in the sequence—the step which matches representations of new experiences with the representations of closely related experiences of the past—takes place during dreaming. These new data . . . demonstrate for the first time the precise relationship between the adaptive function of dreaming in the memory cycle, that is, the matching of representations of current and past experience, and the defensive operations of the dream censorship which act to prevent the matching from taking place [p. 13].

On the influence of psychoanalytic dream interpretation, Palombo wrote:

> 1. Dream interpretation appears to have a special efficacy in the building of those intrapsychic structures which restore and renew the incomplete self and object representations acquired during the patient's childhood. This effect results from a synergistic collaboration between the analyst's interpretive activity and the adaptive functioning of dreaming in the memory cycle. It is distinct from, but complementary to, the role played by dreams in providing new data from that part of the patient's memory structure which is ordinarily inaccessible to consciousness.

> 2. The intrapsychic counterpart of the analyst's dream interpretation is a new dream which incorporates the originally reported dream together with the new information supplied by the interpretation. The new dream, which I have called "the correction dream," results in the introduction of the information contained in the interpretation into the precise location in the permanent memory structure which contributed its content to the originally reported dream [p. 14].

Palombo, following Lowy, regarded dreaming as an important cognitive component of the memory cycle and therefore an important element in the organizing function of the ego, one that is necessary for memory integration. Similar hypotheses have been proffered by Fosshage (1997), who speaks of "the organizing function of dream mentation," and by Breger (1977; Breger, Hunter, and Lane, 1971) and Levin (1990). Share (1994), in a carefully constructed piece of psychoanalytic research, finds that dreams can carry the memory of experiences that go back to the first few days of life, and even earlier.

It occurred to me that the production of a dream is a unique and mysterious event, an undertaking that requires an ability to think and to create that is beyond the capacity of conscious human beings. As I began to think along this line, I became dissatisfied with Freud's explanation that it is the dream work (the primary processes) that creates dreams. I wanted to posit a dreamer within, a preternatural Presence. I began to explore the 19th-century concept of alter ego, or second self, as well as the in-dwelling God of the mystics, the Demiurge of the Gnostics, and even the Muses of classical Greece.

The dream I am about to relate, which I had the night before the final examination in pharmacology in my second year of medical school, is different in many ways from my usual dreams. It was this dream that awoke me to a realization that dreams are, at the very least, complex cinematographic productions requiring consummate artistry, technology, and aesthetic decision making. I began to realize that dreams are dramatic plays that are written, cast, plotted, directed, and produced and require the help of scenic designers and location scouts, along with other experts. The stage of the dream can be likened to a container or ground, whereas the play itself constitutes the content or the contained or the figure (as contrasted to the "ground"). In positing two dreamers—the creator/transmitter of dreams and the dream recipient—I am really proposing the existence of a profound preternatural presence whose other name is the Ineffable Subject of Being, which itself is part of a larger holographic entity, the Supraordinate Subject of Being and Agency.

THE DREAM

The setting is a bleak piece of moorland in the Scottish Highlands, engulfed by a dense fog. A small portion of the fog slowly clears, and an angel appears surrealistically, asking, "Where is James Grotstein?" The voice is solemn and awesome, almost eerie. The fog slowly reenvelops her form, as if she had never existed or spoken. Then, as if part of a prearranged pageant, the fog clears again; but now some distance away, on a higher promontory where a rocky crag appears from the cloud bank, another angel is revealed, who, in response to the first angel's question, answers, "He is aloft, contemplating the dosage of sorrow upon the Earth."

The Dreamer Who Dreams the Dream

At the time I had this dream I knew little of Freud and nothing of dream interpretation. I knew only that psychoanalysis existed, that I was drawn to it, and that dreams had meaning. Although the meaning of this dream began to unveil itself in psychoanalysis many years later, I do not want to focus on the meaning of the dream here. Instead I want to call attention to its setting or framework, to its architecture, and especially to its architect or creator.

When I awoke from the dream, I had a strange sense of peace, which I felt contributed to my doing well in the subsequent pharmacology examination, in which I achieved the highest mark. What most arrested my attention then, and thereafter, was the beauty, poetry, spirituality, and mystery of the dream's presentation. I was deeply impressed, mystified, and bewildered. I knew that I had *experienced* the dream—that is, I had *seen* the dream, but I was utterly at a loss to know who *wrote* it. I wanted desperately to be introduced to the writer who could write those lines. I realized all the while that it could not possibly have been me—because *I was asleep at the time!*

It began slowly to dawn on me that my dream was a play or a small portion of a larger play, a narrative conceived by a cunning playwright, produced by a dramatic producer, directed by a director who had a sense of timing and of the uncanny and the dramatic moment, and staged by a scenic designer who could offset the narrative of the dream with a setting that highlighted it to the maximum intensity of feeling.[1] The casting director also had a flair for the medieval and the romantic nature of theatricality.

---

1. McDougall (1985, 1989) similarly conceives of the mind and the body as settings for theatrical productions.

I wanted to be introduced to the producer of the short play. I also wished to be introduced to the casting director. Where did he find those particular angels? I began to want to be introduced to the scenic director who chose the Scottish Highlands. He must have known me very well, because Scotland had been of enormous importance to me in my youth. The setting of Scotland and the use of the word *dosage* were the only aspects of the dream that were familiar to me and belonged to my personal life. Otherwise, the dream was phantastic and mysterious.

The playwright of the dream intrigued me the most and yet most frustrated me because I admired his script but felt so estranged from him. I experienced what Scott (1975) calls the "dreamer's envy of himself." The "I" who wrote that dream was admired, envied, idealized, and unknown to me; he might just as well have been somebody else. He is also known as the alter ego, second self, or Other. This is the preternatural, numinous counterpart to the phenomenal subject to which we are more accustomed.[2] Together, they constitute the *Supraordinate Subject of Being*.

Years after experiencing this dream, I encountered patients who were television writers and functioned as story editors. I was introduced to that sophistication of the writing craft which governs the progress of a play from its inception to its first trial response in the creative mind of the story editor, to its modification based on the criterion of workability, and, finally, to the preview prior to the opening night. What makes a dream workable appears to be the result of complex artistic and effective negotiations within the psyche, in the dream's mixing room, so to speak.

Bion (1962b, 1963), in his concept of the container and the contained, posited that the infant who is contained and the mother who contains him constitute a thinking couple. I believe that Bion's concept can be extended to include a dreaming couple. In other words, mother's breast (Lewin, 1950) or face (Spitz, 1965) can be thought of as a dream-screen container, which welcomes the emergence of the dream on its surface. This process can be understood as an externalization within the self of unformulated dream impressions that, when they appear on the dream-screen, achieve a mythic or phantasmal coherence that satisfies "the dreamer who understands the dream" and therefore makes the process *work!*

Dreams are mercifully disguised to diffuse and suspend the immediacy of toxic meaning and are dramatically vivid, like symptoms, to

---

2. I use the term preternatural to designate a quality of this entity that is best described as beyond natural but not necessarily *super*natural, which to me connotes omnipotence. I employ the term numinous in the ancient sense of the "reigning deity of a place."

attract and fix our attention on their themes. Dreams are like archipelagos. Each dream may be unique and specific in its own right, but under the surface we may glimpse the presence of a continuum, the dream of dreams, which is the mythic fingerprint, the unconscious life theme, the theme of themes, for the dreaming subject. Klein (1960), in a footnote to her *Narrative of a Child Analysis*, suggested that displacement is necessary for the child to be able safely to reveal unconscious phantasies. Perhaps displacement, as Freud (1900) also hinted, is required for the safe exposition of unconscious themes.

An example shows how this story-editor function may work. A patient who was a television writer acted occasionally as a story editor for his show. Once he had to suggest a workable rewrite to an author who was submitting an autobiographical script, but the author refused to submit his story to rewrite. Analogously, in dream work the author presenting the autobiographical reality presents raw, encoded sense data to the dreamer first for "rewrite," which is a way of saying that in dream work the "photographic" reality is transformed into a narrative that has universal dramatic appeal. A safe alteration of the story must take place. Emphases, deletions, and content changes occur in scripts in the external world; in the internal world, the script is mythified, and the elements of the narrative are condensed and displaced through the use of metonymy and synecdoche. Symbols, both personal and universal, serve as transistors to facilitate the change of the ordinary story into a myth.

In the foregoing example, the writer would not submit his story to rewrite, and therefore the story would not work. Why must the story be rewritten in order to work, and what does it mean that a story works? We humans are so composed and disposed that we believe we must first be able to dream a new reality, or, in effect, re-create it in our own mythic ways, to gain sovereignty over it before it can occur. *Thoughts are mental actions, and mental actions are narratives* that must first be tried out or previewed (i.e., thought) before real action is possible.

I believe that this rewrite function is instituted by the Dreamer Who Understands the Dream, one of whose functions is self-reflection (Fonagy, 1991, 1995). When a dream story *is* successfully rewritten, that is, successfully disguised, it still retains the truth of identity implicit in the original story (just as we often recognize almost instantly a friend or relative whom we have not seen for a long time) despite the transformations of age.

The universal myths, for example, the Oedipus complex, the biblical Genesis, the legend of Christ, are condensed narrative prototypes that first emerged in our primal dawn as someone's dream and later conjoined with similar dreams reported by others (Vico, 1744; Coles, 1997; Verene, 1997). As I understand the legend of Genesis, it was important for the God-child, having just been born, to imagine that He created all that His eyes opened to before He could allow for the separate creation of His perceptions (see chapter 2). Gradually, the composite dream was formed and became the myth, and the myth became the prototype and palimpsest for all dreams. The myth offers, furthermore, the reassurance known in the law as the principle of *stare decisis* (let the decision stand)—that there is a precedent to all problems and that the dreamer, if allowed to dream the problems down the vertical axis of Bion's (1977a) grid[3] (the genetic, or, really, *epi*genetic, axis of thinking),

	Definitory Hypotheses **1**	φ **2**	Notation **3**	Atten tion **4**	Inquiry **5**	Action **6**	. . . n.
A β-elements	A1	A2			A6		
B α-elements	B1	B2	B3	B4	B5	B6	. . . Bn
C Dream Thoughts Dreams, Myths	C1	C2	C3	C4	C5	C6	. . . Cn
D Pre-conception	D1	D2	D3	D4	D5	D6	. . . Dn
E Conception	E1	E2	E3	E4	E5	E6	. . . En
F Concept	F1	F2	F3	F4	F5	F6	. . . Fn
G Scientific Deductive System		G2					
H Algebraic Calculus							

Bion's Grid

3. The grid is Bion's way of abstracting mental elements for categorization. The vertical axis of the grid designates the progressive stages of development

can link the external problem to a soluble mythical problem so as to feel hope for a solution.

Ultimately, the Dreamer Who Dreams the Dream is the Ineffable Subject of Being who registers catastrophic changes and transmits them as a dream narrative to the Dreamer Who Understands the Dream for corrective completion. In an analytic hour we can only marvel at the effectiveness of the Dreamer Who Dreams the Dream who organizes the schedule of associative sequences with the problems embedded in that sequence. This schedule of sequences constitutes the organizing principle behind the dream's sacred grammar, which presents associations with seeming randomness (Grotstein, in preparation-a). This organizational randomness, however, is the highly specialized, transformational, generative syntax of the unconscious. Primary process does not quite do justice to the vast sweep of its ingenuity; Bion's (1962b) concept of the alpha function (dream-work alpha) better approximates it, as does Matte-Blanco's (1975, 1988) conception of "bi-logic" (see chapter 3). It is my belief that the organizer of associations is the ineffable subject, a veritable messiah or Cassandra within us.

The Dreamer Who Understands the Dream

As I continued my inquiry into the mystique of the dream, I began to wonder about another member of the theater group, the audience. Freud believed that dreams are nighttime visualizations of wish fulfillments. In my analytic training I accepted that concept until I discovered the object relations theories of Fairbairn and Klein. Even if Freud was right, I began to wonder, who discharges the tension? In other words, who watches the dream to know that it is fulfilling a wish,[4] particularly if the dreamer is asleep? (And Freud did advise us that the purpose of the dream was to protect sleep.) I reasoned that there must be something like an unseen audience in the dream who observes the play, experiences its truths and its messages, and renders an approval that vouchsafes the continuation of sleep. It dawned on me that the dream acts

---

of thoughts from rudimentary conjectures to reflected-upon thoughts. The horizontal axis represents the mind itself and its progression in sophistication in being able to think (about) the thoughts.

4. Freud (1900), as we know, believed that the function of dreams ultimately was wish fulfillment. That may be true, but I believe that we now would consider the likelihood that another prime function of dreams is to mediate the leftover troubling residues of our daily lives which are filled with bombardments of stimuli from outside and evoked feelings from the inside—so as to put them to phantasmal rest, for the moment.

both as an evacuation of the residual daytime tension that threatens our transient escape into sleep and as a reworking of these nighttime accretions of mental stimuli, which become rearranged as narrative, dramatized in theatrical form, and relayed communicatively to an audience who experiences *dramatic communication* in such a way as to experience relief. Now the heldover cares of the day can be put to sleep. *The dream is therapy presented in a dramatic form according to special rules!*

This audience, I reasoned, must be literate, articulate, and theaterwise. Moreover, it must be a most particular critic and have some hidden knowledge of the rules of human drama and narrative. Certain laws must exist by which the framework of dramatic narrative can be stated and portrayed so that therapy can occur. It follows that dreams are arranged by a composite system of subselves, component subjects or nocturnal muses, who speak and arrange the language of poetry, narrative, and drama so that it resonates with a latent story in the audience; it is as if two halves of a mystic symbol which long ago knew each other are rejoining once again. When the potential story existing in the mystic audience dreamer's mind is touched by the narrative spun by the therapeutic dreamer, the two halves of the symbol resonantly come together.

The resonance that occurs with this matching of twins is felt as a "knitting up of the raveled sleeve of care"; that is, a subtext in unconscious phantasy is found that corresponds to the external problem. This correspondence-resonance allows for the experience of a sense of unconscious seamlessness that permits peace of mind to transpire. It can also result in creative problem solving, as in the case of August von Kekule, who discovered the secret of the structure of the benzene ring in a dream and thus opened the door to the discovery of the aromatic hydrocarbons.

The following ideas emerged from my inquiry into the origin of dreaming:

(1) Dreams are dramatic narrations written, directed, and produced by a composite dreamer who is unknown to us, who employs narrative as the instrument of phantasy and myth and uses neurophysiological perception—namely, visualization—to organize the chaotic, fragmented accretions of mental pain left over as residues of yet one more day of existence. What we commonly call a dream is the visual transformation of a never-ending pageant of events in the internal world. Their daytime transformation may be free association or some other manifestation of the unconscious. In short, we never stop dreaming. Dreaming is the absorption and transformation of internal and external sensual data, which, after they have been "dreamed," are ready for mental "digestion" or processing.

(2) There is a dream audience who anticipates the dream and requisitions it from the dream producer in order to recognize its own prob-

lems and resonate with its own hostaged self—a self experienced as having become lost, like Sleeping Beauty waiting to be awakened by the Prince Charming dream, which is forged in the smithy of dream work by the Dreamer Who Dreams the Dream.

(3) Human beings are only pinpoints on the vast surface of cosmic existence and are blessed (or doomed) never to know their true dreamer. It is as if the boundaries of the body-self do not begin to describe, to circumscribe, or to contain the boundaries of the sense of the Ineffable Subject of Being, or, as I would now more properly like to designate it, the sense of I-ness, which seeks its reflection in its selfness. Ultimately, the dream issues from the ineffable and inscrutable O, Bion's (1965, 1970) term for Absolute Truth or Ultimate Reality; coheres into dream language; and vanishes once more back into O's navel. In Plato's cave, the subjects cannot look behind themselves where the fire illuminates the Eternal Forms.

(4) Narrative in dramatic form, as it occurs in dreams, takes place according to certain rhythmic principles that allow it to resonate with the lost mystic hostages of the dream audience.

(5) The dream is a passion play insofar as it is the testimonial staging, performance, and witnessing of the experience of passionate recognition and release. In the rhythmic concordance between the dream actor and the dream audience, the preliminary certification of one's emerging authenticity occurs preparatory to a real certification through experience in the real world. The effect of the audience's certification is to establish a boundary to curtail omnipotent performance and passionate penetrations and, conversely, to authenticate those aspects of the emerging "I" which are worthy of "truth" and realness.

(6) The dream is the quintessence of narrative, cast in the artistic and awesome arrangement of a linear, plot-oriented, sequential story, one that absorbs the passionate outcries of psychic disturbances and perturbations and permits these outcries to "tell their story" in a special and preordained way (according to the laws of narrative) so that the story may be heard. Consequently, the outcries may be forgotten or acted on. Experiences, traumatic experiences especially, are not safe until they have been dreamed, after which they emerge from the first and second dimension to the third dimension of mind (see chapter 3).

(7) The Dreamer Who Understands the Dream is the audience that verifies the passion of the dreamer. In addition to being the requisitioner of the dream, it is also the barrier that contains the dream. It functions as a porous mirror to reflect the passions of the dreamer but also to be influenced by them, much like a mother's relationship to a child. I believe this container-audience-mirror function of the Dreamer Who Understands the Dream corresponds, in Bion's (1977a) grid, to Column

2, the function of which is the antipode of the definitory hypothesis in Column 1 and its obligatory complement (see Figure 1). It questions truth and accuracy, detects omnipotence, and reduces the raw ore of hypothesis to elemental thoughts. If, however, it has become saturated with the passions of its subject of Column 1, it can collude, enviously attack, or greedily purloin the passionate hypothesis for its own perverse purposes, precluding the truthful destiny of the hypothesis in the reifying madness that results. Column 2, in other words, is the Oedipus complex insofar as the latter is a defining barrier, the "law of no," which the child must confront in order to know himself.

The audience is the background that compels the foreground hypothesis to remain in the foreground until it has become sufficiently defined, at which time authentication, correlation, and self-publication are established (Bion, 1970, 1992). The rituals and rites of passage in primitive societies, the requisite 10-man composition for a Jewish religious congregation, the role of a legislature with a president or monarch are everyday vestiges and derivatives of this powerful authenticating function.

As I have portrayed the Dreamer Who Dreams the Dream and the Dreamer Who Understands the Dream thus far, they seem more like the static electrons on the rings surrounding an atomic nucleus in a chemist's diagram than the dynamic, swirling electrons of which the physicists conceive. In all probability, an almost infinite number of highly encoded messages may traverse back and forth between the projecting dreamer (the Dreamer Who Dreams the Dream) and the receiver (the Dreamer Who Understands the Dream), who, in their dynamic, reciprocal output and feedback, finally forge an acceptable dream narrative. In other words, the Dreamer Who Dreams the Dream is the Ineffable Subject of being who, as the registrar of pain, discontent, or sense of endangerment, sends outcries as projected imagistic messages into the containing Dreamer Who Understands the Dream, whose "reverie," like that of the mother of an infant, catches the torment and transforms it into meaning. The internalized mother container and her reverie become the Dreamer Who Understands the Dream.

It is my impression that Bion's concept of maternal reverie includes the maternal capacity to dream or mythify her child's projections, not just handle them realistically. The mother's ability to put the projected pain to sleep is a testimony to her capacity to dream for the infant. The infant then takes in a dreaming couple to correspond to a thinking couple that can put feelings to sleep, think about them, or do both. This function may be the origin of normal repression.

I have suggested that the ineffable subject is the unconscious sensor (not censor) of the dreamer's discontent. What is the role of the former's more conscious colleague, the phenomenal subject? During sleep, the latter participates in sleep as well, whereas the ineffable subject never sleeps. It may be that the ineffable subject originates the dream to protect the phenomenal subject, the guardian of the day. This line of thought would be in accordance with Freud's (1900) theory that the purpose of the dream is to protect sleep. During wakefulness, the phenomenal subject becomes the first-line sensor, who detects danger from outside and relays it to the ineffable subject. Ultimately, the Dreamer Who Understands the Dream can be seen as an arcane representation of the internalized maternal container, which "collects" the narrative urgency and modifies the story until dream solution and resolution are possible.

The Dreamer Who Understands the Dream and the Dreamer Who Dreams the Dream both participate in a holographic paradox of at-one-ment and separateness. They compositely are O, that is, Absolute Truth or Ultimate Reality. They are the background presences for our sense of I-ness. Together they constitute our preternatural or divine or numinous subjective sense of self, the one that is able to experience the Truth of a dream within the dream. In a dream—as previously in prophecies and oracles—symmetry transforms to human asymmetrical experience for a moment. The result is continuing peace of mind, solution of a problem, resolution of a dilemma, a sanctuary with a new lease.

The Dreamer Who Dreams the Dream can normally be thought of as functioning in unity with the Dreamer Who Understands the Dream, allowing the dreamer to possess a sense of continuing identity and at-one-ment with himself. In the analysis of neurotics, this oneness can be seen as the symbolic scriptwriter who writes (determines) the free associations. From another point of view, the Dreamer Who Dreams the Dream and the Dreamer Who Understands the Dream confirm Steele's (1979) notion that "we all have within the language that constitutes us an unknown partner in dialogue" (p. 394). In psychotic illness, on the other hand, it is as if this writer disappears as a single entity and becomes altered, fragmented, and then reconstituted as many disparate, independent "writers" who now create disconnected, loose associations forming a cacophonous argot of the bizarre. Imperceptibly, the "psychotic writers" become the disturbing events themselves, and O, as the sense of agency, evaporates into the mist of the psychotic's maelstrom.

Truth or Reality becomes the new writer in lieu of the individual himself. Psychotic illness, in other words, is a testimony to the departure of the Dreamer Who Dreams the Dream and the Dreamer Who Understands the Dream. One might just as well call psychotic people dreamers who are trying to dream a dream, dreamers who certainly do not understand the dreams, all of them looking for the lost dream and its dreamer.

One can see this phenomenon in the poignantly tragic *Denkwürdigkeiten* of Schreber (1903). His delusional system underwent rapid revisions: at first he was the plaything for sexual abuse by others; then he was persecuted by his psychiatrist, Flechsig; and finally he was being impregnated by God's rays. Obviously, Schreber's delusional system was rewritten by his chaotic "rewrite editor," who I believe was a collaboration between the Dreamer Who Understands the Dream and the Dreamer Who Dreams the Dream. We can see in psychosis the unsuccessful dream function in the unacceptability of the narrative; more to the point, for the narrative finally to become acceptable, the mind must alter itself. *Ultimately, the Dreamer Who Dreams the Dream must find a narrative solution acceptable to the Dreamer Who Understands the Dream, and the two must work together to that end.*

The failure of their harmony becomes psychosis, in which case reconciliation is produced by altering the integral structure, organization, and coherence of the mind itself. Extensive "ad-libbing" or a proliferation of improvisational activity then results until a new psychotic order is established, which submits the Dreamer Who Dreams the Dream and the Dreamer Who Understands the Dream to its new, mad, autochthonous order. The stage of the dream is now situated in the cursorily restored area of past devastations, which Bion (1965) called the domain of –K (negative knowledge on "transformations in hallucinosis," or "alpha function in reverse").

The unsuccessful dream, the nightmare, can be seen as a rent in the symmetry of Perfect Truth. A war between "I" and Self—that is, a war between different aspects of the Background Presence of Primary Identification, the bastion of trust and truth—now seems to undermine the dreamer. If the background presence appears to have been damaged, the dreamer's dreams seem to be too malevolently oracular. The background presence then corresponds to what I have called the experience of the "magus object," that is, one whose language is mysterious, deceptive, and foreboding (Grotstein, 1977a, b; see also chapter 3). It may be a benevolent "Cassandra object," doomed to be disbelieved by one aspect of the person which has been perversely split off and thus has come to be at odds with the dreamer, a development that is often a foreshadowing of psychotic experience.

Freud (1900) said that day residues in the preconscious psychic system are purloined by the instincts, which, like devils, constantly seek human form in order to materialize (the metaphor is mine, not Freud's). In so doing, the instincts effectively offer these day-residue experiences the protection of the repressive barrier. In Bion's terms, the day residues are "beta elements" that are linked with inherent and acquired preconceptions. Freud posited that the amalgam of instinct plus day residue *condenses* in order to achieve sufficient intensity to impinge regressively onto the projection screen of perception—for discharge as a dream. Bion said that this is how sense impressions (day residues) and realized preconceptions are *stored*, awaiting the proper time in the scenario of the unconscious to walk onto the stage of the mind as "alpha elements" (elements of thought available for thinking, dreaming, or remembering).

THE ACTORS

Explanations of the narrative drama of the dream and its literary counterparts must include a discussion of those who perform the play. In an actual play or novel, the characters are created by the author to carry out an artistic intention. They themselves are incidental to the plot unless the focus is mainly on character development. In an actual play, real actors must subordinate their own personalities to their roles and then must project artistic emphasis into those roles. In a television play, the conflict of the hapless actor waiting hungrily to be fed his lines by the writer, who is constantly creating and re-creating him, is quite poignant. The actor is absolutely dependent, like an infant, on his creator and nurturer, the playwright, and the playwright is dependent on the actor to perform his lines. The resentful, envious actor may believe himself to be a fit critic for the playwright's lines and may try to change them to assert his defiant independence. On the other hand, Stanislavski's (1936) "method acting" seems to be based on a Platonic and Kantian notion that all persons contain within themselves the possibility of taking on the role (by identification) of virtually anyone. The unconscious is impressive in its versatility.

The characters in dreams are cast by an uncanny casting director who employs clever techniques—chimerical ones—to produce a composite figure from elements found in all the corners of memory and imagination, elements to be fashioned and honed by the most sophisticated deployment of projective identification and splitting. The finished product is given life. It is as if the dream actors do not know they are actors. We are fortunate if *we* know that they are actors. They occupy mental space, have lines, agendas, purposes, actions, reactions, responses, and the like. The dream is not a dream without them, but we are never the same again because of their cumulative subterranean effect on our psyches.

I am particularly interested in the fate of the contumacious, unpredictable character who is created by the Dreamer Who Dreams the Dream and cast by the casting director of the dream and who, once given life, begins to ad-lib, that is, takes matters into his own hands improvisationally and imagines himself to be the dreamer of the dream. The depressive, forlorn, existential aspects of this capriciously created and perfunctorily dismissed soul were portrayed by Stoppard in his play *Rosenkranz and Guildenstern Are Dead*, and Pirandello dealt with this theme from another angle in *Six Characters in Search of an Author*. I infer that Pirandello's characters had already killed the author by their very birth and were thus orphaned or that they were like "*thoughts without a thinker*," awaiting an author's mind to realize them.

The dream actor is created or requisitioned by the Dreamer Who Dreams the Dream through his casting-director function in order to probe a problem that does not easily "go to sleep." By the dream actor's enacting it internally (or even externally), sufficient separation and objectivity occur to allow the dreamer a "second look" at the problem. Dream acting is experimental action, otherwise known as *thinking*, and it constitutes an experimental probe into a random state of affairs in order to achieve plot resolution. It can be likened to improvisational theater, even though an inscrutable script or scenario exists.

The dream actor who ad-libs has probably been invested with enormous omnipotence in the first place. In his actual performance he upstages the other actors and seeks to take over the whole stage. He attempts to break out of the shackles of the dream in order, like the devil himself, to materialize in the real world and thereby achieve what was denied to him by his imaginative birth. I think this dream actor's appearance heralds psychosis, and the dream in which he is an actor is a psychotic or prepsychotic dream.

The new internal (subjective) objects imaginatively created by projective identification have agendas of their own. Neurotic and borderline psychotic patients believe themselves to be victimized by these "Frankenstein monsters." The key feature of their fear is that they imagine themselves to be characters in the plot of someone else's story. There seems to have been a projective identification of the authorship of the dream (replaying it—the Dreamer Who Dreams the Dream) into an internal object, ultimately the magus (singular of magi), that the object oracularly offers "ultimate truth" to the hapless patient. The magus denotes a sorcerer figure who casts spells on his victims and compels them to follow an enforced scenario from his own life. Fowles (1965) assigned this function to Dr. Conchis (Conscious?) in his book *The Magus*.[5] In personal correspondence,

5. Dr. A. D. Hutter (personal communication, 1996) suggests also that Conchis means "shell" and may associate to the oracular function of women.

Fowles revealed to me that he had been influenced by Jung at the time he wrote the story. He meant the Magus to denote an arcane and archetypal figure who puts his own life story into someone else as the latter's task to master.

The strange task that ensorcelled victims must perform involves an estranged and projected element of their life—on a return trajectory. In the meantime, these hapless victims believe themselves to be impaled on a strange, inexhaustible, and eerie drama. They feel compelled to play it out, though it has no personal meaning for them except for the unconscious guilt that compels them to undertake the journey. It is Kafkaesque. In analysis, as these victims seek to grow, they find themselves confronted, I believe, by a double, a separate personality with a separate agenda that the patients themselves created and gave life to every time they turned their back on their feelings. These doubles seem to be separate human entities who have to be murdered if the patients are to make progress. In classical literature this murder took the form of Orestes' murder of Clytemnestra and Cain's killing of Abel. Perhaps all plots involving parricide belong in part to this theme. It may demonstrate the "other side" of the Oedipus complex. Murder mysteries may also fall into this category.

In psychotic illness, the authorship of the narrative seems to have been obliterated. Neither the dreamer nor the magus is the author of the narrative, responsible for all the complex integrations implicit in dreams. The dream seems to become a chaotic, formless series of disjointed tales looking for an author. The characters in the dream are truly looking for a re-creator, a premise, a director. Psychotic patients no longer fear being abused in someone else's narrative; they now fear being in a narrative that no longer has an author!

THE BACKGROUND PRESENCE OF PRIMARY IDENTIFICATION

I believe that we undergo a sequence of caesuras in which we experience a sense of separation from the object from whom we emerge, that is, from the "background presence, or subject, of primary identification."[6] Freud (1909) hinted at this entity in his paper on family romances, in which he called attention to the child's distinction between (1) the remote and romantic parent and (2) the parent at hand, who is more like the caretaker in the gatehouse of the estate. I see human infants as experiencing themselves as incompletely separated from a mythical object behind them, their background presence, their object of tradition, which rears them and sends them forth.

The Background Presence of Primary Identification is the phantasied and mythical counterpart to Erikson's (1959) concept of epigenesis and the sense of tradition that spawn each individual, the continuity of the sense of cultural or racial identity that ultimately devolves into the individual's personal background. We feel a sense of comfort that someone stands behind us in our effort to face the world. The Background Presence of Primary Identification is a background of safety, as is Sandler's (1960) and Winnicott's (1963a) environmental mother as differentiated from the object mother. It regulates the relationships between "I" and Self ("I"'s first "external" object) and between "I" and its interpersonal objects, much as the placenta did in utero (Beaconsfield, Birdwood, and Beaconsfield, 1980).

This Background Presence evolves from being a coparticipant in the mysterious oneness of primary identification to being a released and backwardly departing soul or spirit of comforting protection; it is ultimately felt as a religious, spiritual, or divine essence or a sense of tradition and background certainty. All this takes place as infants accept separation and find the confidence to use their epistemophilic capacities (designated as K by Bion) in conjunction with libidinal organization (Bion's L) and their inherent, undifferentiated defense organization, sometimes known as the aggressive drive or the death instinct, H. The Background Presence helps to coordinate the K, L, and H focus on all objects of scrutiny so that the sense organs can individually and collectively categorize and conceptualize strange and separate objects to make them familiar.

We may also see an aspect of the Background Presence as ourselves when we *stand behind* our expressed creations and thoughts. We may speak of the phenomenon of the Background Presence of Primary Identification as designating a greater sense of I-ness, one that is preternatural and thus beyond our reach. It is our organizing messianic genius that gives us the free associations descending from a greater Truth than we can possibly have access to, other than through the oracular ambiguities it chooses to offer us.

The Background Presence, in the larger scheme, furnishes the setting of the dream, and the setting of thoughts by day as well. In object representations, the symbolic images of objects are the furniture of thoughts—the tables, so to speak, on which raw thoughts (thoughts without a thinker) are placed to be examined from multiple points of view. The Background Presence becomes the housing and container for these object representations. It guarantees the continuity of space and containment through all transformations of dimension and relationships. It is the principle of continuity, which in religious terms can be called God and in natural science, the guiding principle of natural laws. In Taoism, it can be seen as the unifying, hovering spirit of Oneness that binds all existence. "A finger flicks and a star quivers!" would be the Tao way of expressing this idea. The Background Presence can also be identified with the mystic sense of God (as distinguished from the Godhead) and with the neoplatonic and Gnostic concept of the Demiurge, the active aspect of God that created the universe. The concept of the "God within" (which I refer to as the Ineffable Subject of Being and Agency) has always been heretical in both the Jewish and Christian religions, except for the Kabbalah, the mystics, and the Gnostics (Pagels, 1979).

The Background Presence is also important in the integration of a dream. We take this unifying function for granted when we presume that a dream can be of help in deciphering one's psyche. We presume that the dream represents the product of an intelligence or coherence that has access to memory and hidden emotions and can construct for the dreamer and analyst a narrative that is capable of meaningful decipherment. An intelligence must have conceived the dream from the raw, chaotic elements of experience with a unified purpose and with a unified hand. This unifying function becomes especially apparent when we study the coherences inherent in extended dream associations by a patient. The dreamer, despite numerous resistances, is trying to give us messages by way of associative congeners that keep repeating themselves as if to help and confirm our intuitive sorties. In the sense that the Background Presence is unknowable, it constitutes the "Other," our "alter ego" or "second self." Steele (1979) stated, in effect, that our hermeneutic relationship to ourselves and to objects is basically dyadic insofar as it is both subjective and objective simultaneously. *True empathy is the discovery that our object is also a subject.*

One can consider mental health as requiring a sense of oneness about oneself in continuity with the world within and the world without. Mental illness, on the other hand, involves a perturbation in the sense of oneness and continuity because of a sense of a defective background presence. One does not feel well launched, or well reared, or on stable ground, but, rather, feels existential dread and is vulnerable to anxiety and/or depression or both. Serenity is absent. The sense of continuity is experienced as having been lost or never formed, and in its place is a series of fearful discontinuities forever isolated and estranged from each other. This phenomenon emerges from the painful, primal, pathological splitting of the personality, in contrast to normal, discriminating splitting, and is descended from that primal awareness of being split off from the primal object. It can be spatially visualized as turning one's back on awareness in lieu of accepting it.

The Background Presence, the Dreamer Who Dreams the Dream, offers the dream to "knit up the raveled sleeve of care" of the "I" who needs the dream for sanctuary, for repair, for delay, and for resolution. The "I" normally walks in the benevolent shadow of the all-hovering but unknowable, unseeable, ineffable Background Presence. Psychotic patients, however, believe they have so damaged the Background Presence that they are exiled from the protective grace of its shadow and instead must wander the earth as derelicts without either a dream of hope or a hope of dreaming. Or they may try to restore the Background Presence by pathetically calling on divinity to become the producer of the dream, the sorcerer. Then in some future reincarnation they can be restored to the grace of the dream and drink fully once again from its narratives.

* * * *

After an evening course in cardiopulmonary resuscitation at a local hospital, I experienced the following dream: I am being questioned by an instructor about the procedures I have just learned. Apparently I am hesitant and unsure of some of the techniques, so the instructor first tells me where I am in error and then demonstrates faultless technique. Upon awakening I was struck by how I had been able to represent the perfect instructor. In short, how could I have been so clumsy and so perfect at the same time? In my Scottish Highlands dream, the Background Presence "produced" the setting and ordered the scenario for a narrative having to do with the religious, idealistic, and philosophical implications of a young man's acceptance of the role of physician and his awe at the mysterious power implied in the words *dosage* and *sorrow*. This second dream reveals the Background Presence as the Knower of Truth trying to become manifest through an aperture into the dreamer's awareness as knowledge. Obviously the instructor in the dream understands the techniques of maintaining and restoring life. The student is imperfect and subject to forgetfulness, apathy, disregard. Idealism renders him vulnerable to the Bearer of Truth. In this function, therefore, the Background Presence as instructor serves as a stimulating ego ideal, a presence that wishes to teach and exhort one to pursue Truth.

The K function of the Background Presence, the quest for knowledge in pursuit of Truth, can be seen in many ways. For example, a patient who came into analysis because of his anguish after learning of his wife's affair with another man seriously began to review his past relationships with women. During this period, he chanced upon a previous girlfriend he had known before he was married and had an affair with her. In the past he had had casual affairs with women in distant cities, where his professional work took him, but he assigned no great emotion to any of these affairs. The affair with his ex-girlfriend was different, however. After his affair with her, he pondered the inconsistency of his being able to have an affair while condemning his wife for having had one.

The patient's associations led me to suggest that he was moved to become adulterous with a girlfriend whom he had once loved in order to bring to his attention a phenomenon he had long been enacting without experiencing its significance. I also suggested that, for some reason, he had to commit the phenomenon to action, instead of dreaming about it, to get his attention. He then said that, indeed, he had dreamt about having an affair with this woman and had been disturbed in this dream. He had forgotten the dream until my interpretation. It is my impression that the Background Presence aspect of his "I" acted through the K function (the quest for knowledge) in the dream to no avail, so then it acted through a director-of-action function in waking life to illuminate the problem.

The Background Presence aspect seems to be associated with O, that aspect of Absolute Truth/Ultimate Reality (Bion, 1965, 1970) which is unknowable but approachable through K. O is utterly unknowable. It becomes manifest clinically as symptoms. Bion (1965, 1970) associates it with Plato's Ideal Forms and Kant's noumena, and things-in-themselves. Bion terms the original clinical experience of them "beta elements" (unmentalized elements awaiting "alpha function" to translate them into meaning). The relationship between the thing-in-itself and its transformation, K, can be viewed as a narrative. O can be seen as the Background Presence, exhorting, invoking, or stimulating the Self, its object, to increase its focus and awareness. The exhortation may take the form of symptoms or of spontaneous or determined curiosity.

The awesome, Godlike, arcane, mysterious nature of dreams can be seen in the following case: A young, unmarried woman who dabbled in photography dreamt that she was in her darkroom developing a print. A picture gradually began to form on the paper. She turned the print over and realized that another image, a "ghost," was developing on the other side. She was mystified by this uncanny apparition and wanted to look at it more closely. As she began to look, the dream ended, but not before dream intimations occurred to her that the other side of the print was replete with marvelous and mysterious knowledge about her. In actual fact, this patient had been an orphan and had been reared by a rich, prominent family. The other side of the print seemed to offer her the answers to all her questions about her origins. The dream felt to her like a "divine revelation" frustrated in its aborted epiphany at the ultimate moment. It constituted the "ghost of her analysis."

DREAM NARRATIVE AND THE ORIGIN OF PLOTS

Chomsky (1968) hypothesizes that human beings are born with a capacity for a transformational generative syntax, a capacity for the syntactic organization of the elements of symbolic meaning. Human infants have to wait for the maturity of their symbolic organization to master vocabulary and the rigors of separation, which allow them to make distinctions and integrations of symbols. Vocabulary and semantics are the content within the framework of the syntactic container. The container, from another point of view, must be patient and await the maturity of its counterpart if its own sense of mission is to be fulfilled. I would extend Chomsky's hypothesis of inherited deep structures of grammar to the idea of the inheritability of a tendency toward an instrumentality of narrative (dream) expression.

Pribram (1971) tells us that the human brain is less a discharging apparatus, as Freud believed, than a communicating apparatus in which neurons are busily engaged in rapid, computerlike informational sorties between one another which establish a continuing informational network acting as a single unit. Language is the medium whereby interpersonal communication occurs. Symbolism seems to be the communicative requirement of right-brain organization, which functions according to holistic, space-orienting, contextual, emotional, and visual cues. The holistic symbol seems to be something like a sending beacon that requires amplification, illumination, and informational fulfillment. Semiosis, on the other hand, requires the detailed digital content of left-brain organization, which functions according to syllogistic, linear modes of thinking within the spatial organization of the right-brain directives.

Dreams can be seen as the containers of the content of communication, a content that is constantly being revised and redefined by the container—the symbol—which is making new and varying audience demands on the content. The audience of the dream and the producer of the dream are, therefore, but different aspects of the same symbolic unit. When the audience (the Dreamer Who Understands the Dream) receives the dream from the container/producer, (the Dreamer Who Dreams the Dream), it signals the producer its acceptance, modification, censorship, dream-it-again request. The two are in close contact and relate to "I" as subject and Self as object. The former organizes and produces the form to be viewed as object (self). Another way of describing this situation is to say that the audience and the writer-producer are identical, that they are merely artificial divisions of the primary sense of "I," contemplating itself caught in a moment of communicative intimacy and play, performing the playfully serious task of converting a preconception into perceptual realization and hoping for ultimate recognition. They are Cartesian fugitives arrested momentarily in flight before they can once again return to their pristine oneness.

The setting of the dream helps define the context in which the plot takes place. The setting is the framework, so to speak, but it occurs within the container of another framework, an all-embracing one, just as a play can be part of New York Theater or London Theater. The play is played on a dramatic stage, but the stage itself is in a locale that requires it and anticipates it with dramatic glee. The theatergoing audience and the cultural milieu that spawns it contribute to the background definition and containment that gives the play its purpose, its requisition, and its definition. The audience requires it and will memorialize it. Likewise, the background of the dream can be as important as the foreground, if not more important, depending on the vertex of inquiry.

Isakower (1938) and Lewin (1950) said the mother's breast is the screen on which the dream is projected, and Spitz (1965) offered the notion that mother's face forms the dream screen. These three noted that the dream is a narrative action that needs a surface for proper cinematographic projection and perception. If mother's breast or face is the screen for the projected dream narrative, what is the theater? I suggest that the theater constituting the ultimate containment of the dream narrative, by night as well as by day, and the ultimate author of its framework, is the Background Presence of Primary Identification.

We normally take the dream screen for granted; it is the background that supports our images. But what if the background is our image of a Background Presence we believe to be disfigured or mutilated? The projection on *this* screen would be distorted and even bizarre. What if the screen disappeared altogether, and the dream projection just went out into space? Would it not be the thing-in-itself apocalyptically at large as psychosis?

The narrative is an organizer or framework that functions through analogies or allegories. Its framework allows the thing-in-itself to be transformed into thought, a process that takes place in that emptied space reserved by the infant for the mother in her absence. Once a space can be allowed, narrative fills it up with all the possibilities that can befall the object—and the "I" in isolation. The fact of narrative itself bespeaks the possibility of options, alternatives, dilution of omnipotent tension, and diminution, ultimately, of the Absolute. The narrative allows for the possibility of survival.

Polti (1917), citing Gozzi, Goethe, and Schiller, informs us that all narratives can be classified into 36 distinct plots, which, in turn, may be subdivided into congeners. Without specifying the number of themes, Bettelheim (1976) similarly tried to spell out the various types of myths and fairy tales. I do not know of any study that has tried to classify the themes of dreams into categories. Of more interest to me, however, would be a study of the *relationship* among narrative plots, myths, fairy tales, and dreams.

Further, I would be interested in determining the individual relationships between objects (the characters of the plot) and the essence of the plot. New relationships would reflect universal conflicts between a protagonist and an antagonist with the intercession of the "third Actor," to use Polti's suggestive term. The third Actor gives dimension to the dramatic plot around the conflicts spawned by asymmetry between L, H, and K. L can represent love and need but also the desire to remain unborn; H can represent hatred, aggression, defense, cruelty, or murder but also the concerted efforts of a mother or father to wean or discipline the infant; and K can represent the quest for knowledge and differentiation. L, H, and K are the keyboard of the pianoforte of plot; affects and conflict are the players. L and H are habitues of the paranoid-schizoid position, whereas K emerges from access to the depressive position, and O appears upon entry into the transcendent position.

I believe that my Scottish Highlands dream resounded with a spiritual force, an epic aspect of the dream narrative which contrasts with fairy-tale aspects granting wish fulfillment. The wish-fulfilling aspect is the vertex from which Freud regarded dreams. The organization and ritual of myths and the wish fulfillment of fairy tales offer a space for the instigator of the dream—the irrupting problem—to be thought about more "realistically," considering both internal and external reality. It is as if the narrative cloaks and envelopes the concern with a dressing that can prepare it for eventual internal digestion and external digestion (resolution).

The narrative presents the varieties of plots to organize and unify the data presented to the senses. Plot is therefore an aspect of an inherent structure available for application to chaos, inchoate raw data or data secondarily rendered chaotic through splitting and projective identification in the service of –K. Phantasy is the first epiphany of plot applied to chaotic data from the mythic reservoirs of inherent structural possibilities. Phantasy functions by splitting chaotic data into recognizable qualities of separateness (e.g., pleasurable and unpleasurable).

These elements are then separated into "objects" of convenience. Establishing the separated objects constitutes an act of *creation* of essential phantasies. Our senses create human phantoms ("virtual" images) and then direct them in a narrative so that they behave in a manner destined to subordinate the harmful phantoms to the hegemony of the benevolent ones.

Mental illness can be seen as the belief in the life of the phantoms one has created, yet normal happiness may also have this same ingenuous and awesome origin. Chaos (infinity) is ordered by unconscious phantasy, a process not unlike the "salivation" of food in which the "salivating" mind imparts structure and mythical coherence to its aliment in the form of narrative. The laws of these narratives are the themes or plots in which malevolent or painful objects can undergo felicitous transformations under the tutelage of benevolent objects.

Once chaos is organized by phantasy, the Background Presence is believed by the dreamer to be reinstated again—" God's in His Heaven and all's right with the world!" The mastery of chaos by phantasy then allows for the troubles that determined the chaos—and their descendants—to be thought about by the mind, the organ of thinking (in the depressive position), and remanded to plots and narratives corresponding to the laws of external reality. The premise of each plot is sustained by an agenda that specifically organizes and determines the motivation of the narrative. Life is a theme with many subthemes. When we do not feel together with ourselves, the themes are disparate and disjointed and suffer discontinuities. The narrative is an analogy to the theme. We are all looking for our themes and find them momentarily in the narrative of a dream, or we may borrow the narratives of others (as in plays or novels) to resonate with and to locate our own themes. Our life theme, the Theme of Themes, is, like the Background Presence, unknowable to us. It is analogous to the Order of Things, which psychotics are so driven to reestablish (Schreber, 1903).

An example of this role of mythic narrative can be seen in the analysis of a young woman whose dreams seemed to have a remarkable continuity. All her dreams reflected the process of birth, and the plots of her birth dreams were in the form of sequences of phantasies in which she accounted for her birth in many ways. In her first analytic dream she was on the inside of the "first house I ever lived in." She was there with other internal unborn children, but a man with a knife was on the outside, threatening to enter. Later dreams involved a sequence of phantasies in which she was highborn and special but had to be raised by ordinary parents. She had, in fact, been raised by her grandparents next door to her parents. This dream, however, denoted her omnipotent associations to a sense of divinity.

The other aspect of the dream was her notion that she had created herself without parents. Later, in a dream about homosexual women, she dreamt she had been born from mother but not from father. Still later she was father's child and not mother's. She then imagined she had brought the two parents together to beget her. Finally, she reconciled with the facts of life, surrendered her illusion of control, and accepted the gift of life with all its legacies and hardships.

My Scottish Highlands dream demonstrates a phantasy that the birth of "I" occurs through a mysterious, cloudy vale onto a rugged landscape. The two angels are my first meeting with the breasts of grace. Yet they hint that the sorrow that "I" am to undergo has already been "dosed" as my *moira* (fate).

The birth aspects of dreams function, I have come to believe, to reunite the splits between "I" and Self and between Self and selves and to assist the Self in striving for a sense of continuity from before the caesura to the present time. The Background Presence of "I" is always exhorting itself to return to I-ness after the diaspora it has undergone to acquire K on its circumspect return journey to O. The specific symbolic constructs in the dream narrative attest to this ambiguity and therefore to their own plasticity. For example, a patient with an engineering background dreamt of a Y tube; his associations led me to suggest that he did not know whether the analysis was helping him come together or causing him to split apart. Another patient, a psychotic, dreamt of being Christ on the cross and indicated this posture with his outstretched hands. It became apparent from his associations that he was being crucified for me. His divine chastity and holiness were the models he wanted to impose on my behavior. His crucified, outstretched hands were to keep the analytic couple sexually parted.

ALPHA FUNCTION

Bion's concept of alpha function (dream-work alpha)[7] provides the ultimate, irreducible element of creativity, since it unites the Dreamer Who Dreams the Dream, the Dreamer Who Understands the Dream, the

7. Bion (1959, 1962b) posited that it is the mother's use of her alpha function that allows her to mediate and translate her infant's unmentalized experiences. Successful interchange between her and her infant ultimately results in the infant's introjecting this function for itself. As I argue in chapter 10, I differ from Bion in believing that the infant is born with its own rudimentary alpha function as an a priori given. Thus, it is able to "send" primitively encoded messages (Bion's beta elements) for mother to receive and translate.

Dreamer Who Makes the Dream Understandable, and so on (Bion, 1962b, 1963, 1965, 1970). Bion believed that alpha function (which corresponds to Freud's primary process but is more extensive) processes the data of experience—beta elements, which confront the sense organs—and causes them to undergo an "alpha-betization" (codification) in order to become mentally digestable as elements of thought. This alpha-betization also accounts for the transformation of sense-ible (sensory) experience into sensual imagery (via imagination) and then into dream images that can be dreamed and sorted. It is my impression that Bion meant that the transformation of emotional sense impressions into imagery is facilitated by alpha function's access to inherent and acquired preconceptions, that is, archetypes, which are always pressing to surface but require a sensible experience for a vehicle. Alpha function seems to be able to link experience with the archetypes corresponding to it to produce a mythic dream (narrative) sequence that conveys personal meaningfulness to the dreamer (by day and by night).

Alpha function has at its disposal metonymy, synecdoche, metaphor, and metathesis. Metonymy allows one element to stand for another (e.g., the crown stands for royalty), but it also represents the longitudinal, sequential, diachronic axis of the text. Synecdoche is similar to metonymy and allows for a part to stand for the whole or vice versa (e.g., using London to designate England, or the army to designate a general). Metaphor expresses the associational, vertical expansions that radiate from the concrete image. Metonymy and synecdoche roughly correspond to Freud's conception of condensation but are more variable. Metathesis, which includes condensation and displacement, is the process of decomposition and transposition of elements from one structure or pattern into that of another (e.g., in chemistry, $NaOH + HCl \rightarrow NaCl + H_2O$). Metathesis corresponds roughly to Freud's conception of displacement but also accounts for imaginative resynthesis, in both healthy and abnormal states, which connotes condensation. These four subfunctions of alpha function account for the creation of the elements and compounds of imagery in the mythic reservoir and the mythic streams of the unconscious.

If we consider a portrait artist whose model is O as a paradigm, we could say that O is experienced by his visual sense as beta elements, which are transformed by alpha function into their respective alpha elements. His preconceptive archetypes are the pigments on his palate. His perceptions and his creativity constitute his artistry. Metonymy, synecdoche, metaphor, and metathesis are the ingredients of judgment he uses to select pigments to represent features in various shades, colors, and hues. Ultimately, the strokes he makes belong to the hidden order of art (Ehrenzweig, 1967), which belongs to the ineffable domain of unconscious aesthetic judgement, which may be one of Kant's (1787) inherent (transcendental) categories.

The completion of the work of alpha function lays the foundation for metaphor. Alpha function first transforms O, the chaotic, unmentalized beta elements, into "mythemes" (via the schizoid mechanisms of the paranoid-schizoid position) so that their personal mythical meaningfulness can be understood as a subjective experience.[8] Then these alpha elements can be compared with other experiences. Comparison seems to be the purpose of metaphor. The two tracks are the concrete and the symbolically suggestive. Metaphor begins to emerge when the alpha elements resulting from alpha function proceed laterally on Bion's (1977) grid to undergo comparison, notation, attention, inquiry, and, finally, mental action.

All dreams, myths, and narratives develop through these processes, which not only are the instruments whereby the Dreamer Who Understands the Dream rules on the dream's credibility but also are the elements used by the Dreamer Who Dreams the Dream. All accepted experiences come together in a dual-track metaphor, where one track is the concrete personal meaning of the experience and the other its symbolic significance.

I believe, however, we must take yet another look at the inherent preconceptions. We ordinarily think of the sense impressions as primary and as the initiating elements of creation. A case can be made that the archetypal preconceptions, like Wordsworth's (1798) "unborn babies" or Michelangelo's *Prisoners*, strive and pray for the experiences that can release them from their immemorial marble to be born. *It is as if all our creations are but re-discoveries that experiences release.*

DREAMS AS "DIVINE CONVERSATIONS"

The Assyrians apparently considered dreams to be a secret language between the gods.[9] In the times of Assurbanipal and Tiglath Pileser III, for instance, Assyrian royal inscriptions were written in places inaccessible to the human eye. There was sculpturing in front, but behind the sculpturing were hidden, secret inscriptions. These inscriptions were on clay cylinders inside the walls of buildings. "They were made for the

8. The schizoid mechanisms are splitting, projective identification, idealization, and magic omnipotent denial (Klein, 1946).

9. I am grateful to Professor Chaim Tadmor (personal communication), the distinguished Assyriologist of Hebrew University, for this information.

gods. Dreams were the messages of gods to gods," (Tadmor, 1977, personal communication) said. This secret form of inscription seems to have been taken over by the Jews—perhaps from their Babylonian sojourn—in the form of the sacrosanct writings in their phylacteries.

The notion of a divine language comes down to us from the legend of the Tower of Babel. The omnipotent infant believes himself to possess the god language and resents having to give it up for the earthly language of the mother tongue, which takes at least a lifetime to gain competence in. In this sense, then, the god language is the infant's imagined capacity to confuse his own baby talk with the thing-in-itself and imagine himself to have sway over his cosmos (Grotstein, 1977a, b, 1981a). The infant, in all probability, *is* in contact with a divine language, a language "spoken" by his Background Presence to other aspects of the same presence—a divine parental language, if you will. It is not the language of earthly communication but, rather, the ambiguous, oracular, language of Truth, of O, of Infinity, a grammar that is perfect, a syntax that is absolute, a meaning beyond meaning beyond meaning beyond meaning beyond meaning. This language is the tongue of infinite dimensionality.

The god language can be seen as the ultimate architecture of the dream—the dream by day and the dream by night. It is at one moment the completed connections in the ultimate galaxies of thought—of all the thoughts-without-a-thinker—waiting, like Wordsworth's babies, to be born in thought. Much as in a Picasso painting, where the eye of the face in one perspective is also the head of a figure in another, the "thoughts" are posed in infinite dimensions of infinite possibilities. The dream that is experienced is an infinitesimal portion of this universal hologram. The symbols presented in a dream "talk" to each other in infinite tongues. The "meanings" are meanings beyond meanings. They are a scaffolding for earthly thoughts to be cast upon for redefinition. The "infinite geometer" (see chapter 3), who simultaneously wields the calipers of "bi-logic" (Matte-Blanco's term) and bivalent logic, is another way of representing the ultimate architect of dreaming.

When we analyze a dream, we get the patient's associations, day residues, and memories, and we use the latent and manifest dream associations to reconstruct a possibility of inner thinking, an approximation by analogy, if you will. The actual meaning of the dream is unknowable, because it contains, at the least, all the possible associations forever backward and forever forward in time. The dream is total language beyond comprehension. Comprehension itself is an embarrassment to the near-perfection of the dream. In addition, the perfection and mystery of the dream are penetrated in another way, in the very presentation of the dream itself. The divine language seems to intercede on behalf of the person who experiences the dream. The content and staging of the dream reveal the Dreamer's choice of themes, presentations, and so on, which correspond to the phenomenon of the deus ex machina in Greek plays.

From another perspective, the operant "subject" who presents as the "psychoanalytic object" can be seen as the demiurge (architect, choreographer, dramaturge), not unlike Rhode's (1998) "enigmatic object," who stands astride the infinite and the finite worlds of binary oppositions. It becomes the protagonist of the psychoanalytic drama and must ensorcell the analyst's personal participation in what *appears* to be improvisational drama but actually is scripted by the Ineffable Subject—so that a theme can be played out that authentically represents an untold story about the Self, thus completing an erstwhile incompleted experience. The co-participation of the subjectivities of the analysand and the analyst can be likened to the operation of a Ouija board; that is, the actual agent of the movement of the board is never known for sure (Hunt, 1976). The whole operation of the play devolves from the analysand's own inherent alpha function (dream-work alpha) and its unique interaction with that of the analyst.

THE DREAMER WHO MAKES THE DREAM UNDERSTANDABLE

I believe that the dreamer uses his "sender," the Dreamer Who Dreams the Dream, to convey the autochthonously imaginative creation known as the dream narrative to the Dreamer Who Understands the Dream, an arcane representation of an internal containing object. Together they form (see Bion's Grid, row C, p. 8, this volume) a differentiation between sleep and wakefulness, which facilitates the alpha barrier that Bion (1962a) referred to as necessary for the maintenance of sanity, as well as for forming a protective barrier between the perceptual functions of background and foreground. If the personality of the dreamer is such that he has confidence, thanks to reverie and his use of reverie, that he can postpone his rendezvous with the things-in-themselves, it is because he believes himself to contain an internal *dreaming couple* consisting of a competent mother/container and a spontaneous Self. One partner of this couple is the Dreamer Who Dreams the Dream; the other is the Dreamer Who Understands the Dream. Ultimately, the infant develops confidence in his capacity to "know" his internal and external reality. This tendency normally comes with the gradual dissolution of the hegemony of the omnipotent-thinking couple in favor of a real-thinking couple. The things-in-themselves are at the same time denuded of omnipotence but not of significance.

Gradually, function develops that corresponds to the intrinsic analyst within us all. This function, I believe, is the Dreamer Who Makes the Dream Understandable, the Joseph. He understands that the things-in-themselves are *not* omnipotent but *are* significant and offer necessary perspectives of Truth (O). As a consequence, he tries to utilize the dream narrative to explore the perspectives it casts on the dreamer's daily internal and external mental life for "re-cognition." The "name" of this Joseph-like figure must, like the tetragrammaton, be ineffable and inscrutable, but in recent times the figure has been called the *analyst*. I refer to him as the Background Presence of Projective Identification and as the Ineffable Subject (see chapters 4 and 5). He seems to be the observer who oversees the unfolding of the Scenario and keeps a steady and continuous vigil on it and the agents that seek to interrupt, obstruct, or alter it. In his vigil over and his grasp of the scene of the continuing emotional turbulence and the conflicts they set up, he makes computations or narrational alterations that become the ever-changing directives of the scenario. The Ineffable Subject is the guarantor of its future. He performs many functions, but his most common role is the Dreamer Who Makes the Dream Understandable. His presence and his development is also synchronously reciprocal with the Dreamer Who Dreams the Dream and the Dreamer Who Understands the Dream. That is, the apparent omnipotence of their functions (the god language) tends to reduce the state of respect for Truth and its agents, the things-in-themselves. The Dreamer Who Makes the Dream Understandable—and his partner, the Dreamer Who Is Willing to Have His Dream Understood—form a coalition that seems to mitigate the omnipotent powers who speak the god language. The novelist, the artist, the psychoanalyst today, as well as his close counterpart in ancient Greece, the playwright, generally are the external correspondents to this archetypal function (Entralgo, 1970).

A young female analytic patient once dreamt that she was in my office and was staring at the ceiling. Suddenly a frightening and eerie shadow of an enormous falcon appeared on the spot where she had been staring. She realized that the falcon itself was near but observable only by its shadow. Then she found herself sitting on the floor in the middle of my office with several close friends while I seemed to have disappeared. The group indulged in a religious exorcism of her "possession." The patient's associations to this dream led me to the conclusion that she had come close to experiencing the thing-in-itself, represented as a shadow. The point of dreaming of this shadow of the falcon was that it might not have been the shadow at all but, rather, "it itself!"—the most frightening of all apparitions. The dream was repeated in different transformations in the following weeks.

In one transformation a sinister snake appeared and became her friend and guide. It became associated with the symbol for the medical profession (the profession of her husband as well as of her therapist). Further analysis linked the imagery of the falcon with deadly predatory curiosity, on one hand, and her lifelong persona of apparent superficiality, on the other. The dream of the falcon's shadow seemed to perforate her pretense as a persona and precipitated her involvement in a truer attempt on her part to come to grips with her invasive curiosity and her fear of it.

THE LAMINATIONS OF AWARENESS

I have been using the dream as a specific instance of a consciousness or an awareness within us that is greater than what we have hitherto called consciousness of self. This awareness belongs to a *preternatural self*. The dream is a vent in the shield that separates our two worlds, the outer world of conscious, asymmetrical experience and the inner world of infinite symmetry and inner cosmic vastness. Freud (1900) himself recognized the "dream connection":

> There is often a passage in even the most thoroughly interpreted dream which has to be left obscure; this is because we become aware during the work of interpretation that at that point there is a tangle of dream-thoughts which cannot be unraveled and which moreover adds nothing to our knowledge of the content of the dream. *This is the dream's navel, the spot where it reaches down into the unknown* [p. 25; italics added].

The term *unconscious*, the proper name for this system of inner cosmic vastness that contains "myriad consciousnesses," is therefore an unfortunate one because it belies the awarenesses implicit and inherent in this system. The truth of the matter is that what we call the unconscious is really unconscious *to* us but is itself never unconscious *of* us. I have come to believe that consciousness occurs in laminations of awareness and that these laminations extend in a spectrum from "unconscious" symmetrical awarenesses through preconscious awarenesses, to conscious awarenesses. I also believe that consciousness itself has a bipolar or a bimodal distribution, to use a term coined by Deikman (1971). By bimodal consciousness I mean that our conscious self may have its own conscious awareness, let us say, of both the external world and, to a certain degree, the internal world. The internal world may have many laminations of consciousness, that is, of itself, of other structures, thoughts, and feelings within the unconscious, and so on. Put another way, dreaming takes place in the "mixing room" of System Pcs, originating at its lower frontier, which is juxtaposed to the frontier of System Ucs and epiphanizes at its higher frontier, which is juxtaposed to the frontier of System Cs.

When we focus attention in the act of concentration, we give active conscious awareness to the object on which we are focusing, and we are suspending the background awareness. In other words, when we focus attention, we are lifting the object from its background into the foreground of our attention, but there is still a background attention that is being partially suspended. Analysts encounter this phenomenon, for instance, when we are listening in an analytic hour to patient material and experience two forms of consciousness, a loose background consciousness and a focused foreground consciousness. This phenomenon is also seen, for instance, when we drive a car: we listen to the radio, think our thoughts, and preconsciously watch the traffic without being directly aware of some of these procedures.

Matte-Blanco (1981) said of the narcissism myth that, when Narcissus looked into the River Styx, he saw his unconscious self, his symmetrical twin. Matte-Blanco (1975, 1988) believes that a conscious mind lives in the third dimension of asymmetry, asymmetry being the characteristic of development in real life; symmetry in the mathematical sense characterizes the unconscious and seems to occupy dimensions approaching the infinite. He believes that therefore a barrier between the asymmetrical field of normal living and the "unreal" symmetrical world of the unconscious had to be developed in order to preserve the sanity of the mind. The symmetrical world of the unconscious thus constitutes something of a reservoir of potentiality and creativity, with thoughts being allowed to emerge into asymmetry whenever the subject can tolerate them.

Since the dream has access to the functional primary process (alpha function), it has at its disposal an intriguingly complex capacity for memory storage—the timelessness and spacelessness of the zero dimension (Grotstein, 1978). An infinitude of memories can be stored holographically; that is, each memory byte (to use a computer term) can be stored in the same place, as if an infinite number of ghosts occupy the same body. Dream memory storage therefore avails itself of the vast reaches of its synchronic capacity, made possible by the symmetrical and holographic nature of unconscious functioning. As the dream unfolds, it *seems* to be diachronic, that is, sequential. The nondominant hemisphere of the brain has synchronic and symmetrical capacity, but the dominant hemisphere, in recognizing the dream, experiences it sequentially (*a*symmetrically) because the brain has only three-dimensional space-time (diachronic) capacity. Translation distortion in the retrieval from one mode to the other is enormous. Witness the frustration we all have when we try to remember, let alone repeat, a dream.

Finally, the Siamese twins and quadruplets, those chimerical androgynes of ambiguity, are gathered together by the ballet master of the dream to progress through the highly stylized choreography of the dream scenario. This choreography, the planned steps of the piece, involves the intricacies of expanded and contracted time. This shrinking and expanding of time—often experienced as if Father Time were playing us like an accordion—is accomplished through the instruments of dimension. Whereas we dwell merely in the third dimension—knowingly—in our dominant daily life, by night (see chapter 4) the dream accordion can play us through all the scales on the dual tracks of consciousness. Thus, we experience the logic of the dream in sequential three dimensionality on one track and, on the other track, in the flattened slow motion of the second dimension, in the violent speed of the first dimension, and in the infinite—and infinitesimal—limitlessness of the zero dimension—and thereby experiencing all the choreographic possibilities of space and time.

I-NESS AND HEMISPHERIC MODES OF THINKING

My vision of I-ness and its subsumption of "I" and Self in all possible Cartesian artifactual perspectives is offered as a replacement for what I now believe to be the outmoded psychic apparatus (ego, id, superego) of classical analysis. "I" is always unitary, phantasies otherwise notwithstanding. Yet "I" can be dual as in twinship: "I" → Self (subject to object), "I" → "I" (subject to subject), and so on. Every aspect of ourselves is "I": there is no not-I; id is not "it" but "I."

Furthermore, "I" emerges as both a better and lesser known and knowable entity than has hitherto been thought. I suggest that dreams, phantasies, fantasies, thoughts (thoughts-without-a-thinker) are fashioned by an inspired Presence, a scenarist who seems to cut the primal picture of Truth into carefully partitioned puzzle pieces and then disperses them for our curiosity to retrieve. The coherence implicit in their dispersal is predicated by a "selected fact" that gives them significance and meaning. This selected fact is itself foreordained as the puzzle of Truth is cut, and it is known to the Dreamer Who Dreams the Dream.

Bion (1992) has pointed out that the basic myths of mankind, for instance the myths of Eden, Babel, and Oedipus, all include two important functions: (1) a compunction by a demon to be curious and (2) an injunction by a god against the fulfillment of curiosity. This injunction against curiosity has often been analogized to states of resistance in analysis derived from manifestations of the repressive barrier. I believe that the repressive barrier and the injunction against curiosity have a more profound meaning: there is a natural divide between the functioning of the left-brain mind and the right-brain mind. The hemispheres have two different ways of processing the data of experience. The corpus callosum can be thought of as a metaphoric bridge conveying messages between the two. The repressive barrier is that aspect of the function of the corpus callosum that keeps certain messages from getting across. It conducts selected information and filters out other information. Otherwise, each would destroy the other.

What used to be called the id needs as much protection from what is called the ego as the reverse. The natural barrier between them has much to do with the different dimensional worlds they occupy. Matte-Blanco (1975) demonstrated a difference between bi-logic and bivalent logic as components of two different hemispheric modes of thinking. In short, the nondominant hemisphere functions in the zero dimension with synchronic immediacy (like an infinite vertical orchestra score) while the dominant hemisphere functions in linear, diachronic sequentiality, that is, in the third dimension. The two time-space worlds are incompatible and must be kept apart. This is the intercourse that is so sacred that it must not be known; it must always remain inscrutable.

The act of psychic creation involves the most arcane, most mysterious union between two modes of "being" and of "valuing" the data of inner and outer experience. Their intercourse creates "thoughts." It can never be penetrated. The subject, being ineffable and inscrutable, does not lend itself to objectification but can reveal itself only in "transformations in O," with which we at best can become resonant in the transcendent position.

CONCLUDING REMARKS

The dream is produced by the Dreamer Who Dreams the Dream, a composite of many roles and functions, and is understood by its requisitioner, the Dreamer Who Understands the Dream. The Dreamer Who Makes the Dream Understandable translates the dream for our "understanding," which we use for delay and avoidance of premature confrontations. All three of these Dreamers are functions of "I" and Self in their ultimate, unknowable, preternatural quintessence and awesome excellence. We are fated never to know them, only to be their clients and to walk in their shadow.

The dream is the epiphany of divine conversations between the "ineffable subject" and the phenomenal subject and constitutes a reading of our existence while we are in transit between our once and future being. Narrative is the skilled, artistic, and awesome arrangement of psychic moments into a syllogistic, linear, plot-oriented sequence of events; narrative gathers the outcries from all corners of the psyche and lures them to be dreamed so that their story may be told and forgotten or acted upon, whatever is most needed at the moment. Experiences, generally, and traumatic experience, specifically, are not safe until they are dreamed.

The dream ultimately is a narrative and narrating window into our inner cosmic vastness. Our capacity for self-transcendence ultimately depends on the dosage of sorrow that our minds can tolerate in the unfolding maw of this vastness.

> Our revels now are ended. These our actors,
> As I foretold you, were all spirits and
> Are melted into air, into thin air;
> And, like the baseless fabric of this vision,
> The cloud-capp'd towers, the gorgeous palaces,
> The solemn temples, the great globe itself,
> Yea, all which it inherit, shall dissolve
> And, like this insubstantial pageant faded,
> Leave not a rack behind. We are such stuff
> As dreams are made on, and our little life is
> Rounded with a sleep.
>
> —*The Tempest*

Chapter 2

AUTOCHTHONY (SELF-CREATION) AND ALTERITY (COCREATION)

Psychic Reality in Counterpoint

Keter Ayn Sof shrank and created the Universe.
—The Lurianic Kabbalah

The focus of psychoanalytic theory and practice has gradually shifted from a one-person to a two-person model, leading to more emphasis on the external reality imposed on the subject by the interacting object. While it must be granted that no analysand has grown up in isolation and that two virtually indivisible subjectivities occupy the psychoanalytic setting and thereby inescapably participate in cocreation, the emphasis on intersubjectivity and relationism puts us at risk of returning to Freud's first theory of psychoanalysis, that of actual trauma. The analysand's conscious version of what putatively happened is mirrored and expanded on, and the pathology is assigned to the compulsive repetition of the traumatic event. In other words, an emphasis on (alleged) history is endangering the primacy of unconscious phantasy, that is, psychic creationism. This emphasis also affects the fundamental psychoanalytic principles of the primacy of unconscious phantasy and *psychic determinism* (i.e., one's sense of responsibility for one's self and acceptance of one's life).

My point of view is as follows. The sense of causality in infant and analysand is organized and determined from two distinct perspectives: (1) the actual reality imposed by objects in the external world, a reality to which they felt compelled to comply at their own expense (as emphasized in the works of Fairbairn, Winnicott, and Kohut; and (2) their primary, organizing belief that whatever has happened *to* them originated *from* them, from the point of view of their being the center of their cosmic universe (as emphasized in the works of Freud, Klein, and Bion).[1]

I want to introduce the concepts of *autochthony*—the unconscious phantasy of self-creation *and* of creation of the object—and *cosmogony*, the creation of a world order. These principles (i.e., faculties) belong in the domain of imagination (Britton, 1998) and govern the processes whereby the primitive aspect of the personality, employing primary-process thinking in the form of projective identification, claims an event as personal and thereby makes it that person's own subjective experience, that is, an experience that is "native" to oneself. Autochthony and cosmogony include techniques that people use from infancy onward to *format* and *contextualize* the raw, random (chaotic) data of internal and external events in order to transform them into meaningful personal and subjective experiences. The classical concepts of libidinization and aggressivization (Hartmann, 1939) can be understood as ways of projectively—and then introjectively—personalizing the data of emotional experience by declaring that one cares about or has been personally affected by the events. In other words, one declares that someone or something matters.

Autochthony (from the Greek "born from the earth" or "native to" but used here in the sense of "born from [native to] the self")—solipsistic, syncretistic—is a birth phantasy in which the self is defined by its self-creation, and external objects are understood to owe their origin to having been created by and from the self. Autochthony exists in a dialectical relationship with *alterity*, the awareness of the Otherness of the object and cocreation by it and with it (i.e., the phantasy—and ultimately the realization—of the cocreation and defining of the self *by* external objects, by subjects, or by both). Autochthony designates omnipotent, imaginative self-creationism and the creation of the world of one's objects. It is dialectically counterposed to intersubjectivity and *social constructivism*, the realization of one's dependence on the other and of the absence of omnipotence—a realization that applies not only to one's birth but also to the cocreation with the other of one's personal reality.

Autochthony is the basis of the birth myth set in the time of the Titans, when Gaia represented a divine personification of Mother Earth, and divine or quasi-divine children issued from her.[2] The term has been used by Lévi-Strauss (1958), Jung (1934), and Heidegger (1927) to des-

---

1. Bion, with his concept of container–contained, actually spans both points of view.

2. When Cadmus, the forebear of Oedipus, slew the dragon at Thebes, the

ignate this most primal of universal birth myths, one that is even more primitive than the myth of parthenogenesis (being born from a virginal mother or virginal father); the maternal parthenogenetic myth precedes that of paternal birth, which, in turn, precedes the acquisition of knowledge of the actual act of parental intercourse. Wittgenstein (1933–1935) dealt with the same subject from the philosophical-metaphysical perspective when he wrote on *solipsism*. Such terms as *syncretism* and *sui generis* and such ideas as spontaneous generation, self-creationism, self-referential thinking, ideas of reference, narcissistic thinking, subjective thinking, and imagination all approximate the same concept. Autochthony is present in the idea of something being native to an individual or group and is behind the everyday notion of "taking things personally."

AUTOCHTHONY AND BIRTH MYTHS

Children originally have only one theory of creation, the autochthonous one. As they mature, they develop a second and then a third theory, *parthenogenesis*, in which first mother is the creator without father and then father is the creator without mother. Eventually, they learn yet another theory, that of parental sexual intercourse. Once the infant attains the depressive position, omnipotent creative phantasies are subordinated to the newly accepted realistic basis for being an ordinary, needy mortal who must now respectfully encounter and acknowledge the presence of a world beyond his power to create or control. The world must be effectively adapted to instead, while at the same time the child maintains the hope of having some realistic influence on it. My own imaginative, "Kleinian" rereading of *Genesis* illustrates the concept:

God, the Infant, was born from the depths of His primeval mother, but His Godliness, which represented his primary identification with mother (i.e., infantile omnipotence), helped shield the fact of actual birth. Like all God-Infants, He believed that He had created everything that He opened His eyes to, including Himself first of all, then everything around Him, including His mother and father, Adam and Eve.[3] Being a demanding and therefore commanding God-Infant, He believed that Adam and Eve should be at His disposal and therefore forbade their having sex with one another (infantile attack against the primal scene).

---

dragon's teeth spilled onto the ground, from which, ultimately, sprang the *Spartoi*, the original inhabitants of Thebes.

3. Eve's birth from Adam's rib is another example of autochthony.

As time wore on, however, the God-Infant became more aware of His separateness, and along with this realization He also realized His littleness, helplessness, and vulnerability—and His need for His parents to help Him. At the same time, however, He also became aware that mother, rather than being His solely devoted object, was involved additionally in another relationship—and a passionate one at that—with father. The knowledge of this (sexual) relationship awakened the God-Infant to the fact of the primal scene, which produced a dark shadow on the whole phenomenon of knowing (thus the curse on the snake and the Tree of Knowledge) and terminated forever the illusion of bliss and innocence. The knowledge that mother prefers intercourse with father is the decisive event that ends innocence. With these awarenesses, the God-Infant relinquished the omnipotence and grandeur (Garden of Eden) that shielded Him from the paranoid-schizoid position of persecutory anxiety and demonic travail and entered penitently into the depressive position of reality ("into the land of Nod, east of Eden"). This act of psychological weaning was reinforced by the fiery seraphim, who were forever to prevent His return—though He tries over and over again in his imaginative phantasies to do this by employing unconscious epistemophilic projective identification.[4]

The attainment of the depressive position with symbolic whole-object permanence and constancy allows for the acquisition of a double worldview, the phantasmal, or mythic, and the realistic, and for a transition from a cyclopian to a dual-perspective worldview. From this point onward, the child—and adult—is confronted by the need for interaction with others who are known to be separate subjects in their own right and no longer only objects to take for granted. Each experience with the other constitutes a reminder of one's separateness and of the elusiveness and ultimate unknowability of the other, which is the principle of alterity. What is ultimately achieved is a confirmation of one's subjective sense of agency.

The concept of autochthony was first used in the psychoanalytic literature by Ferenczi (1932) when he distinguished between "the autochthonous and the heterogeneous ego" in defining the difference between the internal and external origins of paranoia due to trauma.[5] Freud established what I am designating as autochthony and cosmogony in his conception of dream work (Freud, 1900) and primary process (Freud, 1911b). His portrayal of libido as primarily discharge seeking unfortunately obscures what I believe is a more fundamental

---

4. I first rendered this portion of *Genesis* in a similar manner in an earlier work (Grotstein, 1981a).

5. I am indebted to Arthur Malin for this citation.

notion, namely, that *libido is creative* as well as *subjectively personalizing* (e.g., endearing, caring, mattering). This notion of imaginative creativeness found its way into Klein's (1946, 1952) concept of unconscious phantasy generally and projective identification specifically, as well as into Winnicott's ideas about object usage (1969a, 1989) and creative play (1971b, c, d). Winnicott foreshadowed my thesis about self-creativeness and autochthony when he stated that the mother must proffer to her infant *the object that he is about to discover at the same time that he creates it!* That is my point: the act of *autochthonous creation* must precede—in order, therefore, to anticipate and thereby prepare for—the *actual discovery* of the whole objects as separate from the self in origin. To put it more familiarly, we must first "dream" (while awake as well as asleep)—that is, imaginatively create and phantasize—our emotional experiences through *primary process*—before we can discover, accept, and own them accountably through secondary process. Thus, autochthony is another way of talking about *imprinting*. Further, we run into this phenomenon when we read a paper or book. I discovered this for myself when I took a course on speed reading. In this exercise one scans the whole paragraph (right-brain formatting) and then creatively reconstructs with one's left brain what one has already scanned.

Freud's concept of *psychic determinism*, the postulate that the ultimate origin of life events lies in instinctual drive expression, exemplifies a "modern" or logical positivistic view of unconscious mental life. The postmodern point of view begins with the semiotic school, particularly with Lacan (1954–1955, 1956, 1966) and his predecessors, Peirce (1931), de Saussure (1966), and Jacobson (1971), each of whom contributed to the "revolution of signs." I derive my concept of the cosmogonic instinct or principle from several lines of thought, including Lacan's (1966) concept that "the unconscious is structured like a language"; Freud's (1900) concept of dream work and the part-instincts, particularly the *epistemophilic instinct* (Freud, 1905); Klein's understanding of the epistemophilic instinct (1928, 1930, 1931, 1945) and her conception of *personification* (1929a); and Winnicott's conception of the subjective object (1969, 1971d), play (1971a, b), and creativity (1971b, c).

I see autochthony and cosmogony as the universal forerunners of and obligatory partners to rational thinking.[6] Freud (1911a) stated that thinking is trial action. The archaic antecedents for this "trial action" can be thought of as a phantasy in which images of objects are created as subjective objects (emanating from the subjective self, which personalizes

6. The idea that the primary and secondary processes are indivisibly operant in rational thinking has been emphasized in the works of Bion (1962a, 1963, 1965, 1970, 1992), Matte-Blanco (1975, 1988), and Dorpat and Miller (1994).

experiences with objects) and then choreographed at the behest of the infant's omnipotent will as a rehearsal for the evolution of formal symbolic thought.

It is my contention that in the transition from the dominance of the one-person model to the two-person model some important aspects of the former have been overlooked. An emphasis on an intersubjective model suggests that psychic reality owes its origin to actual events in the individual's life. The idea that the infant is a tabula rasa is beginning to eclipse the concept of unconscious psychic determinism. I contend that the psychoanalytic treatment of a patient requires that analysts understand how patients *unconsciously* understand their own role in the creation of their life narratives. Patients must examine their beliefs about their unconscious motivations in order to regain their sense of *agency* for the self (Stern, 1985; Moran, 1993) and to be self-accountable.

A universal clinical example may illustrate the importance of autochthony. Many analysands present problems regarding their owning their feelings of neediness and dependency. Very frequently we hear from them that in their childhoods their emotional needs and feelings were ignored or rejected by their parents; they consequently identified with what they felt was their parents' value judgment in regard to their needs and thus became ashamed of them. The "reasoning" was as follows: "If my needs were good, they would have been met. The fact that they weren't met means, ipso facto, that they were not good."

The concept of autochthony seems counterintuitive when one first encounters it. It is implicit in the idea of self-organization (Schwalbe, 1991). Even in regard to social constructivism (Hoffman, 1992, 1994), according to Schwalbe, the individual will coconstruct (take in, accommodate, and assimilate) only that which is true, that is, native, to his nature. We must first create the image of the object or the event we confront in order to personalize it as meaningful to us, thereby making the object or event native to us, that is, personal, or even private. Sometimes this mechanism is confused with envy in the clinical situation when an analysand wishes to "eat privately," that is, he hears our interpretation but doesn't seem to respond to it because of a sense of shame and vulnerability in acknowledging his being the recipient of a "good interpretive meal" rather than being self-sufficient. It is only after time that we realize that the patient *was* affected by the interpretation but had to take it home and make it his own (native to himself) first. Winnicott (1971a, b) clearly understood this when he technically suggested that the analyst should not interfere with the patient's analytic play.

CLINICAL EXAMPLE

A middle-aged female analysand mentioned that when she was depressed as a young girl she would go to the market place in her town and view the sun brightly illuminating the red peppers in the carts in the Italian section. This sight would always cheer her up. "It was my discovery," she proudly informed me.

From a view of psychic development that includes recognition of a cosmogonic instinct, psychopathology can be understood as resulting from a significant intersubjective or interpersonal failure that occurs too overwhelmingly or too suddenly for the infant or patient to have imagined, phantasied, created, or "autochthonized" it beforehand. When this happens, infants/patients surrender to the trauma that they could not have "created" sufficiently beforehand and that thereupon becomes *defined* and re-"created" by the demon object that personifies the trauma. A clinical example may help explain these ideas:

R.G. entered psychoanalysis for marital difficulties. He complained that he felt suffocated by his wife, whom he also accused of being demanding and acerbic. His father had beat him as a child for any minor wrongdoing. His mother was described as apathetic and afraid of opposing the father, traits that prevented her from ever intervening during any of the beatings. R.G. slowly became aware that his wife reminded him of both his angry and demanding father and his uncaring mother. As transference configurations began to develop, he felt that I was too distant, like his mother; at the same time, his own behavior toward me became like his father's toward him, which I interpreted with some effect. My own introjective and projective partial counteridentifications with him were often those of a hapless, bewildered child who looks forward with dread to the next encounter.

During one particular session, R. G. was reviewing his lamentably painful childhood and then plaintively asked, "Why did this happen to me?" I took the question seriously as a vehicle for deeper inquiry on several different psychic levels. What emerged from the patient's associations was an old memory of a long-standing childhood belief that he had not been wanted as a newborn by either parent. He remembered being told that things went bad between his parents as soon as he was born. He also recalled that he felt bad that he had made them both unhappy, particularly his father. In the transference these feelings emerged in such statements as, "I'm not a very good patient. All I do is complain. How do you stand it? Sometimes I think you'd like to get rid of me and get a really good patient." In my inner counterresponses to these statements, I felt as if I were being set up morally to be the villain father, and it felt uncomfortable. It left me little room to be myself and to be able to help him. I felt imprisoned by his powerful masochism.

As the analysis proceeded, R. G. became more aware of his dependency feelings on me in the maternal transference. Protests and persecutory anxieties became more apparent during analytic vacations and breaks. I was able to demonstrate the patient's unconscious voyeuristic phantasies and other unconscious manifestations of his greedy and envious attacks against me. At times he asked to borrow magazines from my waiting room. At other times he would park early in front of my home, where my office was located, in order to "grab a peek" at my wife and children. He developed many phantasies about my wife and children, most of them either idealized or involving envious attacks against them. After a dream he reported in which robbers entered a synagogue and stole the Torah (he was Christian and knew that I was Jewish), I was able to interpret to him that out of anxiety over being separated from me over Rosh Hashanah and Yom Kippur, and because of his envy of my "special inside children," who were fortunate enough to be able to be with me all the time, including holidays, he unconsciously stole into my privacy and personalness, desecrated my "holy" insides, and made himself Jewish by appropriating a Torah.

The interpretation had a riveting effect on the patient. He cried. Then he said, "All I ever wanted was to be loved. I guess my father hated me because I was such a mamma's boy. I was afraid of him and showed it. That must have made him feel terrible." I could confirm this from my own countertransference. In the course of the analysis, R. G. retrospectively came to believe that he had become, out of fear, a disingenuously impassively aggressive, dependent, "false-self" child to both parents and that he had driven them away by his excessive neediness; he also believed that in retrospect he had identified with his aggressor father by masochistically submitting to him. Once he was able to come to this tentative conclusion, he felt relieved. A good portion of the relief came from his being able to explain his own putative participation as unconscious agent in the abuse that he suffered. I say "putative" because this autochthonous revision of his history on his part *is* putative; that is, it is a reconstruction that his primary processes (unconscious phantasies) deemed necessary. This does not mean that his conclusions were correct. After R. G. worked through his phantasies of being confused with each of his parents and with me, he was able to see his father as a separate person; he was able to hate him at first and then to forgive him after realizing that his father could not help himself.

This patient was involved in a marriage in which he had confused his own maternal and paternal superego with his wife and then with me. Underlying all his psychodynamics was his propensity to become confused with his objects by projective identification. He could not effectively express his rage over his parents' behavior because he was confused with them. Only after he was able to achieve and tolerate his separateness in the analysis could he experience and express his rage at objects, whose illnesses he could now countenance because they were at last separate from him. In other words, he could now allow them to be emotionally ill without feeling unduly responsible. This allowed him also to forgive them.

This patient, like all of us, organized the earliest and continuing events of his life under the aegis of the *infantile neurosis* (unconscious phantasies organized in the paranoid-schizoid ↔ depressive positions and the Oedipus complex) *and* what I call the *infantile catastrophic (traumatic) neurosis* (including all traumata to which the analysand believed he had surrendered). I believe that clinical experience reveals that people inherently feel responsible for all that happened to them, no matter how they may defend against this premise with alibis, excuses, protests, and proof of innocence. They take personally the bad things (and good things) that happen to them and consider these occurrences to be their "karma." One reason for this belief is that it satisfies a sense of agency for the self. Another reason, however, is the presence of an archaic superego that colludes with and relentlessly intimidates the subject with guilt feelings for all that happens.[7] Yet here too autochthony is involved: analysands would not feel guilty vis-à-vis their superego if they had not projectively created it in the first place. They must work through the infantile neurosis to achieve psychic separateness from their objects currently and retrospectively before they are able to get a clearer idea of their experiences in the trauma.

When listening to analytic material, we should always wonder where our patients place themselves in terms of what has occurred to them. If, for instance, we hear that a man believes that he has made a bad marriage, we should wonder, first of all, what aspect of himself is being projected into his wife. If we realize that he truly has made a mistake, presumably because of undeniably serious pathology in his wife, we should then wonder why he unconsciously chose her. The same principle applies to reports of child abuse. Analysands who have experienced child abuse, trauma, or other indignities from loved ones or others will almost invariably ask, "Why me?" This is a question we should take

7. The origin of the archaic superego, according to Klein (1940), is in the projective identification from the infant into the parent of hostile, sadistic, demanding, and obligatory wishes. This image of the object, combined with its projected attributions, is then introjected by the infant and becomes an authoritative, judgmental superego within the infant.

very seriously and literally. It leads to the deeper question, "How did I get a mother [or father] like that?" And finally to the deepest question, "What must I have done to mother [or father] for her to be that way to me?" Fairbairn (1940) dealt with this autochthonous perspective when he concluded that the unloved schizoid patient believes that his very *love* must have originally been bad, whereas the depressive feels that his *hate* must have been bad.

It is clinically important for the analyst or psychotherapist always to have the following question in mind when listening to a patient: "What does the patient believe he did to cause these terrible things to happen?" or "What does the patient believe he did to their objects for them to have treated him in this way?" We must allow for the possibility that the patient's belief or hypothesis is an example of a universal autochthonous (i.e., phantasied) assessment by his unconscious sense of psychic agency, rather than an assessment of the facts of what really happened. Patients can truly acknowledge the facts only after they have achieved separation from their traumatizing objects in the depressive position, when, for instance, they can allow for the illness in a parent who is distinguishable from themselves.

CREATIONISM: AUTOCHTHONY AND COSMOGONY AS OBLIGATORY PRELUDES AND ACCOMPANIMENTS TO ALTERITY

Freud (1895) first referred to a distinction between psychic and external (or, in later works, "factual" or "material") reality in his *Project* (p. 373). He again referred to it in *The Interpretation of Dreams* (1900, p. 620), *Totem and Taboo* (1912, pp. 159–161), *Introductory Lectures* (1916–17, pp. 368–369), "The 'Uncanny'" (1919, pp. 244–251), "Dreams and Telepathy" (1922, pp. 217–218), and in *Moses and Monotheism* (1939, p. 76). In the *Introductory Lectures*, he explained the difference as follows:

> Reality seems to us something worlds apart from *invention* [italics added], and we set a different value on it. Moreover, the patient, too, looks at things in this light in his normal thinking. When he brings up the material which leads from behind his symptoms to the wishful situations modeled on his infantile experiences, we are in doubt to begin with whether we are dealing with reality or phantasies. Later, we are enabled by certain indications to come to a decision and we are faced with the task of conveying it to the patient. This, however, invariably gives

> rise to difficulties. If we begin by telling him straight away that he is now engaged in bringing to light the phantasies with which he has disguised the history of his childhood (just as every nation disguises its forgotten prehistory by constructing legends), we observe that his interest in pursuing the subject further suddenly diminishes in an undesirable fashion. He too wants to experience realities and despises everything that is merely "imaginary." If, however, we leave him, till this piece of work is finished, in the belief that we are occupied in investigating the real events of his childhood, we run the risk of his later on accusing us of being mistaken and laughing at us for our apparent credulity. It will be a long time before he can take in our proposal that we should equate phantasy and reality and not bother to begin with whether the childhood experiences under examination are the one or the other. Yet this is clearly the only correct attitude towards the mental productions. They too possess a reality of a sort. It remains a fact that the patient has created these phantasies for himself, and this fact is of scarcely less importance for his neurosis than if he had really experienced what the phantasies contain. The phantasies contain *psychical* as contrasted with *material* reality, and we gradually learn to understand that *in the world of the neuroses it is psychical reality which is the decisive kind* [Freud, 1916–17, p. 368].

This statement represents perhaps the most fundamental canon of traditional psychoanalytic thinking, one with which classical and Kleinian analysts are in absolute agreement. The provenance of psychic reality (unconscious phantasies) has been historically assigned to the discharging (irrupting) instinctual drives by classical analysts and to the unconscious object-seeking drives by those of the Kleinian and object relations schools. The former emphasize infantile sexuality and Freud's (1900) concepts of wish fulfillment and the pleasure–unpleasure principles; the latter emphasize infantile dependency and omnipotence and adaptive, primary object-seeking, behind which lurks the principle of safety and survival.

Recently, Renik (1994) has discussed Freud's (1900) earlier use of the concept of the pleasure–unpleasure principle and his later use of only the pleasure principle (Freud, 1920) and has integrated the idea of adaptive safety (the wish to avoid unpleasure) that was inherent in Freud's original formulation and was lost in the later one. Renik thus assists in bridging the gap between the orthodox and classical schools, on one hand, and the Kleinian and object relations schools, on the other.

According to Freud (1915b), the origin of psychic reality lies in the functioning of the instinctual drives, which operate according to the principle of psychic determinism. Klein (1946, 1955) reiterated the primacy of psychic determinism in her concept of projective identification, whereby, infants, in effect, develop an unconscious phantasy in which they modify their perception and therefore their experience of the object. She failed to use the term *create* but strongly implied it.[8] Bion's (1959, 1962, 1963) concepts of container and contained and of alpha function constitute an interactional elaboration of the creative aspects of projective and introjective identification. According to Bion, the infant, when projecting into mother as container, is initiating the process of meaning; the mother completes this process in her "reverie" owing to her capacity to apply her alpha function (dream-work alpha) to her infant's projective identifications, thereby not only sustaining them but also translating them into operational meaning.

Contrary to Freud's (1905) pronouncement that the ego is first and foremost a body ego, my hypothesis, following Tausk (1919), is that the infant is born as a psyche and claims its body as its own, first by "creating" it by way of identification through projection and then by discovery. Winnicott (1963b, 1969, 1971b,c,d,e, 1989) added his conceptions of the spontaneous gesture, the subjective object, object usage, playing, and the creative act to the general theory of creativity. From infancy onward, Winnicott tells us, we must creatively play with the event-objects that we encounter in order to establish the "play" that we can tolerate. Playing is central to my thesis. In the act of play, we create the event-object as our subjective object of spontaneous illusion in order to establish a cosmogonic order or coherence in the form of phantasy-narrative, which in turn helps establish a sense of personal agency. We then must, through *object usage*, "destroy" the illusional subjective object so as then—and only then—to discover the Otherness of the object, that is, the real object that exists beyond the range of our creationism (and destructiveness). ("Now through a glass darkly, then face to face.") This awareness must await the onset of the object constancy that occurs in Klein's depressive position.

Emde, Kubicek, and Oppenheim (1997) have observed "imaginative reality" during early language development in very young children:

> The authors argue that our thinking about psychic reality is challenged by research observations of the child during the period of early language development. The toddler, at the begin-

---

8. Klein strongly invoked creationism in her work on the epistemophilic instinct (1928), on art (1929b), and on personification (1929a).

> ning of propositional speech, expresses the capacity for "two kinds" of psychic reality. A world of imaginative pretence occurs quite early, and supplements the child's everyday experience. The toddler is not confused by these two experiential worlds and, correspondingly, the use of imaginative activity is strongly supported by caregivers. . . . Imaginative reality refers to a process in which the child makes use of what is familiar in the remembered past in order to try out a world of new possibilities in the present that, to some extent, are oriented towards the future [p. 115].[9]

I consider autochthony and cosmogony to be the fundamental architects of unconscious phantasy, dreaming, and, ultimately, thinking. Together they constitute the larger concept of *creationism*, or *imagination*.[10] The creational (dreaming) functions of autochthony and cosmogony format the mind of infants to help them order their primordial encounter with chaos (infinity) and define the difference, for example, between the event, or stimulus, and the personal experience of it. In trauma, the stimulating event occurs before the victim can "create" it; therefore the victim succumbs to the trauma and turns it into a personified victimizer who thereafter defines the victim-subject. It is as if the victim has (like God) "created" the trauma by making it personal.

Psychic determinism was originally considered to be absolute, since the drives that irrupted into the ego were seen to be the prime determinants not only of intentionality but of all behavior (Freud, 1950, Letter 18, May 21, 1895; Freud, 1905b; Ricoeur, 1965). Freud borrowed the concept of the will, or determinism, from Brentano's (1874) concept of *intentionality*. Three different views of psychic determinism are possible: (1) absolute psychic determinism (the pure intentionality of the drives—or of the putative will of the unconscious beyond the drives); (2) primary autochthony, or relative psychic determinism in which there is personal acceptance by the infant of the drive experience or of the incompletely differentiated outside stimulus that evokes the drive, so that the stimulus is transformed into the infant's own creation to mediate and order its otherwise random or chaotic world; and (3) secondary autochthony,

9. In chapter 10 I suggest that one of the functions of Bion's (1962b) maternal container and reverie is to cocreate imaginative play with the infant in the form of fairy stories and the like.

10. I am prepared to risk criticism for using *creationism*, a term that has been associated with Christian fundamentalism and a literal reading of the Old Testament, that is, with a religio-philosophical belief system that contrasts with Darwinian evolutional beliefs.

in which the infant defends against a realistic traumatic external experience by claiming retrospective responsibility as agent (e.g., Fairbairn's, 1943b, "moral defense"). My concept of autochthony, the creative aspect of projective identification, when considered in conjunction with cosmogony, the creation of a cosmic or worldview, constitutes a relative or modified psychic determinism whereby infants give order and coherence to their chaotic world of internal impulses and external stimuli after the fact. Autochthony borrows from symmetrical logic (see chapter 3) in the wish to extend one's personal subjectivity as a stamp of uniformity on the world in order to make it familiar. It is the underlying common denominator in what Maturana and Varela (1972) term autopoiesis and Schwalbe (1991) terms autogenesis, or self-organization, all of which are ways of expressing a person's attempts to "go-on-being" so as to guarantee self-continuity. It is the basis moreover of constructivism, which, according to Kuhn (1962), is the central notion that scientific knowledge is a human creation.

Alterity, the awareness of the Otherness of the object, which presupposes separation and individuation (Mahler, Pine, and Bergman, 1975), normally enters the psychic reality of the infant when object constancy to use Fraiberg's (1969) term, has been achieved, when the whole object (now a subject) is replaced by an internalized symbolic *representation* of the object (in the place where the object used to be). Its predecessor, the internal part-object (in the paranoid-schizoid position), reflects self–object fusion. The achievement of object constancy represents the arrival of the depressive position[11] (Klein, 1935). Thus, alterity can normally influence the infant to *adjust* to the separate world—or pathologically to *comply* with it as a source of impingement or trauma. The ability of infants to discern the object's effect on them depends on their capacity to be separate and individuated; otherwise, the origin and sense of responsibility for the external trauma from the object is "owned" through default by the infant's creative autochthony and cosmogony.

Classical analysts traditionally interpret the vicissitudes of the expressions of the drives and the ego's defenses against them. The drives are considered to be absolute and peremptory rather than *signals* or *semiotic signifiers of absence* (including distress, as I suggest). Parenthetically, the drives must be differentiated as affective signals of need and distress, on one hand, and as willful declarations of intended

11. Klein (1935, 1940) posited two organizing positions in infancy to account for two respective clusters of infantile anxiety: persecutory anxiety in the paranoid-schizoid position (about three weeks of age) and depressive anxiety in the depressive position (about four months of age), by which time the infant begins to accept its separateness and becomes aware of the object as separate and whole.

action, on the other. I propose that autochthony involves the "ownership" of the drives as a creative forge for ordering—after first creating—the world of objects from projective attributes of the self. Clinically, this revised concept means that the analyst would not interpret the drive or the defense against the drive per se but instead would interpret the patient's own "interpretations" of an unconscious estimation of the maximum anxiety or felt danger (Klein, 1960). To put it another way, the analyst would interpret the patient's unconscious beliefs (phantasies) about the source of the anxiety, including how and why the patient unconsciously believed he had created them. The focus thus shifts from absolute psychic determinism to a consideration of the manifestations of the unconscious belief a patient holds that he is the creator of all things. Yet, paradoxically, the analyst must simultaneously realize that the patient may not have been the actual originator of the trauma.

It is my thesis that all human beings not only experience absolute intentionality as a phantasy but also need to "own" the events that affect their lives so that they may personalize and claim their karma before being able to contemplate that they had no or little control over these events. This is another way of describing the evolution of the process of thinking from the paranoid-schizoid position, in which there is absolute, hierarchical, prereflective "thinking" (e.g., superego to ego) to the depressive position, in which reflective thinking emerges, included in which is the infant's dawning awareness that the object, now separate, also has a separate mind of its own (Trevarthen, 1987; Fonagy, 1991, 1995; Fonagy et al., 1991). Eventually, when the individual becomes an organized self, there develops a paradox in which he believes both that he is and that he is not the author of his intent or desire.

Autochthony and cosmogony are faculties that constitute a prophylactic defense against the impact of trauma and Ananke (Necessity or Fate). The youngest infants experience that they are *fated* by their absolute determinism. As they begin to own their feelings of determinism, they become autochthonous and then feel *destined with desire* rather than *fated from events such as needs* (Bollas, 1989). Thus, infants experience trauma from the occurrence of an impactful event they could not have "created" beforehand; they are overwhelmed by its utter externality, that is, by the complete absence of any personalized, mediating anticipation. By this reasoning, the reliance on autochthony and cosmogony is interposed between the (putative) trauma of peremptory drive irruption (O, Ananke, chaos, infinity) and the intrusion of overwhelming stimuli from the outside; that is, these creationistic, unconscious phantasies mediate those two poles of trauma.

The cosmogonic faculty operates in the infant's attempt to create, first, a *personal* cosmology and, second, an *objective* one. In the case of the former, it can be understood as a function of the need to rationalize and order chaos (randomness, meaninglessness). The cosmogonic faculty involves the use of primary process (particularly dream work) and later of secondary process. Or one can view it as involving Bion's (1959, 1962b) alpha function, which includes both and codifies ("alpha-betizes") the chaotic data of emotional experience into two tiers of meaning. (The first, *myth*, and, *unconscious phantasy*, institute an imaginary narrative unity and order to the chaos; it is succeeded by the second tier of meaning, a *realistic* appraisal.) From this perspective, autochthony, cosmogony, primary process, libido, alpha function (dream work alpha) are equivalent terms for the functioning of what one may also term the *epistemophilic instinct* or *principle*.

Autochthony and cosmogony function within the constraints of *autogenesis*, or self-organization (Schwalbe, 1991; Kauffman, 1993, 1995). The self-creation process is iterated and reiterated along each cycle of progression. The perspective of constructivism [Hoffman, 1992, 1994] also addresses the twin aspects of epistemology, the personal and the objective. In the exercise of autogenesis, autochthony assures subjects that their constructivistic adjustment is not traumatic, that its elasticity allows for the continuation of their selfsameness in change, in contrast to compliance in which their integrity would be traumatically compromised.

My concept of *primary autochthony* applies to Klein's (1946) notion of the infant's worldview during the hegemony of the paranoid-schizoid position when part-objects and part-subjects (egos) constitute the infant's inner reality. *Secondary autochthony* applies to Klein's (1935) notion of the hegemony of the depressive position when whole objects and subjects are operant, although pathological regression secondarily into part-objects and part-subjects may occur. In other words, all psychopathology can be understood as either intrasubjective (primary) or intersubjective (secondary) autochthony, or as infantile catastrophe or trauma.

Exercise of the principle faculty of cosmogony represents a constructivist attempt (solely by the self) to establish a sense of personal cosmic order for the emotional events of life. Integrating the concept of psychic determinism with the principles of autochthony and cosmogony leads to my thesis that absolute psychic determinism constitutes our ineluctable fate or destiny, that which exists before us, persists beyond us, and is relentless and inexorable. It is within "me" and affects "me" but is "not-I." Autochthony represents the infant self's assumption of the source and means of creation like God, of a personal cosmic order; in the process, the pleasure principle becomes attached to the narcissistic capacity to do so. That is, the infant "claims" personal ownership of his drives and becomes an autochthonous, self-determining self with a committed sense of personal agency (Stern, 1985; Moran, 1993). This process represents the infant self's epigenetic progression from fateful passivity and intimidation to active mastery over its destiny, prior to, or even simultaneous with, the acceptance of external reality. Thus, the progression is from "Fate determines me!" to "I am my fate and therefore determine my own destiny!" (Bollas, 1989).

The mind employs primary and secondary mental processes in an integrative effort to register and process (to self-organize and reorganize or construct) the events of daily life, traumatic or mundane, and to consign them to respective worldviews. Primary-process thinking is related to a personal, idiosyncratic, autochthonous worldview, and secondary process to a more objective, interpersonal worldview. The capacity to be sanguine about our objective views of reality (i.e., to take reality for granted) depends in large measure on the cooperative and integrative complementarity of the opposition (not necessarily conflict) between the functioning of the primary and secondary processes. The first worldview is essentially narcissistic (everything is seen as originating from the self); the second is interactive, intersubjective, relational (the other person is seen as ineffably other than the self).

PSYCHOPATHOLOGY AND CLINICAL CONSIDERATIONS

Unfortunately, psychic causality and realistic causality can be confused. Freud's (1905b) first theory of psychic determinism was based on the activity of the instinctual drives. His second theory involved the registration of trauma, which, according to Freud (1920), perforates the *Reitzschutz* (protective shield) and functions thereafter under the control of the repetition compulsion (since trauma is "beyond the pleasure principle"). Classical interpretations about trauma may therefore focus, although not exclusively, on the patient's need to repeat the memory of the putative trauma, which roughly means putting one's personal stamp on the data of experience and then reincorporating it as a personalized experience. From a Kleinian perspective, interpretations may initially focus on how patients *believe that they (autochthonously) caused the trauma in omnipotent psychic reality*. Relational analysts may choose to interpret the experienced *realistic* failures of patients' (whole) objects to protect them during infancy and childhood, particularly in cases of child abuse. Fairbairn (1952) complemented Freud's trauma theory and Klein's theory of projective identification (primary autochthony) with the concept that an imperiled child reacts to trauma by introjectively identifying with the badness of the needed object in order to keep the object good, but Fairbairn (1941) ultimately realigned his views with Kleinian autochthony. He stated in that regard that infants undertake a selective introjective identification with the badness of the needed parents not only out of compliant necessity but also because they believe, in the schizoid position, that their own love was bad from the beginning or, in the depressive position, that their hate was bad. They thereby employ secondary autochthony; that is, they are aware of the actual reality but knowingly have to undergo the fiction of being responsible so as to spare ("launder") their needed objects.

The combination of an emphasis on intersubjectivity (the two-person conception of psychoanalytic treatment) and the increased importance assigned to countertransference phenomena seems to lead to more emphasis on explanations of psychopathology rather than interpretations about psychic reality. It is my belief, consequently, that the one-person model is a necessary complement to the two-person model and that the principles of psychic determinism and psychic reality that inform the one-person model do so normally in terms of autochthony and cosmogony (personal ownership of one's psychic determinism). I advocate a dual-track conception (Grotstein, 1978, 1981a) of psychopathogenesis as follows: (1) The *infantile neurosis* organizes the infant's unconsciously experienced phantasies about its relationship to its primal objects and regulates the dialectic between its "narcissism and socialism" (Bion, 1992; Grotstein, 1995d). (2) *Infantile catastrophe* (Bion, 1962b, 1963, 1965, 1970) occurs with the impact of overwhelming externality when the infant (or even an adult) has not had the opportunity to prepare for the trauma by initially having (autochthonously) created it.

A patient reported that, when he was three years old, he witnessed his father injuring himself in a small accident in the kitchen. The patient heard his father's exclamation of "Ouch!" and immediately retorted, "I'm sorry, Daddy, I won't do it anymore!" This poignant incident can be understood from multiple points of view. Under the principle of *psychic determinism* the boy may be seen as harboring unconscious aggressive wishes toward his beloved father and therefore displacing (projecting) his wishes into his perception of the occurrence. Or, through selective introjective identification of authorship of the event (as described by Fairbairn, 1943b), he may have tried to spare his father from being perceived as wounded. Thus, the child assumed an autochthonous (omnipotent) ownership of the psychic causality of the event and constructed a cosmogonic phantasy to make the event conform to a psychic cosmology that ordered and mediated potentially traumatic random/chaotic events by converting them into personal—and personalized—experiences under the control of his own omnipotent reparative efforts. Consequently, a psychic reality emerges that not only is organized by psychic determinism but also owes its provenance to the child's attempt to "autochthonize" a personal worldview in order to achieve the illusion of mastery, control, personal agency (Stern, 1985), and responsibility. Through these processes we transform the data both of ordinary and of extraordinary (e.g., traumatic) *events* into personal and objective *experiences*. Psychoanalytic treatment can be understood from this point of view as dedicated in part to the reconciliation between the personal and the impersonal points of view.

To repeat, it is not so much that the drives actually determine psychic reality as that infants/patients believe, owing to the creative faculties of autochthony and cosmogony, that they have already created their psychic reality. They have a need to organize the random events of life into a personal scenario of experiences in which they have a subjective sense of agency, because they have assumed a sense of psychic responsibility (omnipotence)! An event (stimulus) is not the same as an experience (psychic response); the former is transformed into the latter first as a psychic reality (primary process, autochthony) and then as a symbolic representation (secondary process, intersubjectivity). There is a parallel difference between an explanation and a subjective interpretation, and I believe that autochthony, whether primary or secondary, is the primary and underlying element in psychoanalytic discourse.

THE DUAL WORLDVIEW OF ALTERITY

The infant is always aware of and is constantly confronted by the presence and existence of the object as other, but its experience of that otherness is far from distinct initially. Infant research studies seem to concur that infants see the object as separate from the perceptual point of view but that they may feel confused with the object emotionally; that is, although they can *perceive* the object as being separate, they *feel* emotionally at one with or intimately connected to the object (as part-object), which amounts to their regarding the object as an obligatory extension—and therefore possession—of themselves. By the time the depressive position and object constancy are achieved, not only is the object—as other—a whole object (actually, subject), but its very autonomy gives rise to the infant's experience of its Otherness. By this time infants, now at the toddler stage, have become self-reflective and are beginning to realize that they have a mind; they can experience that the object too has a mind, and they become aware that they can objectively and subjectively reflect with one aspect of their mind on other aspects, including feelings and the unconscious itself, which Lacan (1966) called "the Other."

The occurrence of trauma in the stage when autochthony predominates is problematic, since the object who may be considered putatively the originator of the trauma cannot yet be considered to be a whole object separate from the infant. In the stage of alterity, however, the infant/toddler/child/adult is able to distinguish the other as separate and is, because of this separateness and though still vulnerable to the pain of trauma, now less vulnerable to "taking it personally." The victim may then either *adjust* (healthy) or *comply* (unhealthy) in a true-self–false-self dichotomy (Winnicott, 1960a). Compliance is achieved by the selective introjective identification of the abusive aspects of the parent (Fairbairn, 1943b) and also by an identification with the aggressor (A. Freud, 1936). The introjectively identified part-parent becomes split into a rejecting and a tantalizingly exciting part-object. These opposing pairs along with the victim's concordant, complementary, and oppositional identifications with them, thereafter constitute the victim's endopsychic (internal) world.

CONCLUDING REMARKS

The sense of psychic agency is related to personally felt responsibility for one's life, that is, to a sense of "owning one's karma." As infants we must first believe that we have created our own personal world; then we claim or "own" (i.e., become the agent for) what we have created; finally, we allow for the external world's impact on us, the world of the separated "Other." To put it succinctly, we as analysts must help patients distinguish between persecutors and enemies. Persecutors are always constituted from the patient's projective assignments to others and therefore always originate within the self. The enemy is never the self but may be clinically confused with the persecutor (which is a transformation of the patient's self). When that distinction is clear, analysands can more sanguinely own what belongs to them, so to speak, and can effectively avoid pathological entanglements with others.

One must first believe that one has autochthonously "created" the world that one discovers or encounters, and then, epigenetically, one must become a self with a continuous "history" who then—and only then—becomes able to allow one's self to be the vulnerable and varyingly helpless recipient of life's experiences. Blame and protest against the world of external objects is often justifiable in fact, but we each must epigenetically and ontologically "earn" our passport to such objectivity—by being sufficiently in touch with a sense of self-responsibility that we are separate from our provisional "enemies" and thus are able to hold them authentically responsible.

Making interpretations to a patient that impute traumatizing ("organizing") responsibility to external objects for his earlier (or even current) life risks the emergence of reifications that collusively establish a manic defense (Klein, 1940) against a personal sense of responsibility for the trauma, thereby foreclosing the patient's capacity to own a sense of internal (unconscious) responsibility as an integral, self-respecting self. *It is the emergence of this retrospective reconsideration by our patients of their own sense of or belief in putative responsibility for their own circumstances (karma), which also becomes psychically retroactive, that warrants our attention to the principles of autochthony and cosmogony.*

Psychic reality can be understood as a twin dialectic, first between primary and secondary (personally felt) psychic determinism and then between internal reality and external reality, which itself constitutes a dialectic between the autochthonous creation of both imaginary and symbolic reality and the Register of the Real. The relationship between autochthony and otherness reflects the ongoing dialectic between intra-subjectivity and *inter*subjectivity. Normal as well as abnormal mental functioning can be understood as the outcome of variations in these multiple dialectical relationships. It is my belief that the only proper subjects for psychoanalytic discourse are primary and secondary autochthony—and that the analyst's only proper intervention is interpretation of the unconscious (autochthonous) phantasies that constitute the patient's psychic reality.

Chapter 3

A FEARFUL SYMMETRY AND THE CALIPERS OF THE INFINITE GEOMETER

The Tyger

Tyger! Tyger! burning bright
In the forests of the night,
What immortal hand or eye,
Could frame thy fearful symmetry?

. . . .

When the stars threw down their spears,
And water'd heaving with their tears,
Did He smile His work to see?
Did He who made the Lamb make thee?

Tyger, Tyger burning bright,
In the forests of the night,
What immortal hand or eye,
Dare frame thy fearful symmetry?

—William Blake, *Songs of Innocence and Experience*

Ignacio Matte-Blanco radically and fundamentally revised the psychoanalytic concept of the unconscious, even attributing the origins of cognition to it. The title of this chapter is meant to suggest that Matte-Blanco the psychoanalyst, although a finite geometer (mathematician), put us in touch with the truer nature of the unconscious and its terrors, with the infinite sets of its components specifically and with infinity (chaos) generally. Thus, the "infinite geometer" is but a poetic way of denoting the Ineffable Subject of the unconscious from mathematical vertex.

Blake's "tyger" can be understood as a preemptive, poetically mystical attempt to animate this infinite terror (which Bion, 1970, designated variously as nameless dread, things-in-themselves, noumena, and O) in order to transduce the chaos of infinity downward to human finite comprehension, toward a contained K (knowledge), a symbolic object that lends itself to the reassurance of contemplation that is suspended, or trial, action.

The word "calipers" refers to Matte-Blanco's (1975, 1988) conception of the interaction of two major modalities of thought, the *homogeneous indivisible mode* and the *heterogeneous divisible mode*, by which he meant the operations of the principles of symmetry and *a*symmetry respectively. The principle of symmetry dissolves differences between distinct identities and is associated with similarities becoming identical, the end result of which would be absolute symmetry, which he termed "absolute indivisibility" (the psychotic state). It also refers to infinity and infinite sets, rather than finite or limited sets. The principle of asymmetry is synonymous with classical Aristotelian logic, the logic of "the excluded middle" (i.e., the logic that if a person is a man, he cannot be a woman; there is no in-between).

Roughly speaking, infinity and symmetry seem to belong to what Freud (1911a) termed primary process, whereas asymmetry corresponds to secondary process. I say "roughly speaking" advisedly because, as we shall soon see, Matte-Blanco innovatively blended elements of symmetry and asymmetry in his concepts of *bi-logic*, which he proffered to replace primary process, and *bivalent logic*, to substitute for secondary process.

An infinite set is the symmetrization (generalization) of a category (e.g., an analysand's mother symmetrizes to the generalized concept of "mother," then to "motherhood," etc.). At the same time, the analysand's mother is a woman who symmetrizes to all women and to ultimate womanhood, and so on. Similarly, she is a human being; thus, by symmetrical or predicate logic, all human beings are the analysand's mother. Ultimately, then, the concepts of mother, woman, and human being become absolutely identical with one another. Asymmetrization, on the other hand, is characterized by the abstraction of generalities into specific categories for classification according to their differences.

A SYNOPSIS OF MATTE-BLANCO'S THINKING

Matte-Blanco (1975, 1988), adhering closely to Freud's (1911b) concept of "the two principles of mental functioning" (the primary processes and secondary process) and to his theory of the unconscious (Freud, 1915b), redefined secondary process as bivalent logic, by which he meant

Aristotelian, or classical, logic. Thus, bivalent logic is mediated by negation and would be one arm of the calipers. (It is important to realize, however, that, while bivalent logic is dominated and organized by the principle of asymmetry, it also mediates comparisons and categories, which involve similarities, or symmetries, as well as differences, or asymmetries.)

Bi-logic, which is associated with the primary processes, is the other arm of the calipers. Symmetry and asymmetry, the two principles that constitute the templates of bivalent logic and bi-logic are ways of categorizing, comparing, and generalizing about objects. In asymmetry, B follows A, but A does not follow B. In symmetrical logic, A could follow B, and B could follow A. Asymmetry is concerned with the differences between objects, symmetry with their similarities and ultimately with their identicalness. Bi-logic, as compared with bivalent logic, is dominated and organized by the principle of symmetry, but, like bivalent logic, it deals with both symmetry and asymmetry. Thus, each type of logic is bimodally represented. Their domination by one of the principles makes the difference in how they operate.

Matte-Blanco summarized Freud's (1915b) characteristics of the primary processes: displacement, condensation, timelessness, absence of negation, and replacement of external reality by internal reality. Further, in symmetrical thinking a part can equal the whole and vice versa. Ultimately, symmetrical thinking becomes infinite sets of categories and infinity itself, or "absolute indivisibility" (which represents the ultimate hypothetical state of symmetry, one in which there exist no differences, one where everything is homogeneous). Psychotics, because of their poor ego boundaries, feel at risk of irresistibly plummeting into this state, as do analysands who experience cataclysmic regression. Absolute heterogeneous divisibility, on the other hand, represents that state of bivalent logic in which everything is absolutely different and there are no similarities, which can also typify psychosis.

Any one element in an infinite set is interchangeable with all others. For example, if the analyst is a man, he therefore belongs to the category of men within the category of manhood, within the category of personhood, within the category of hominids, and so on. As a result, anyone can ultimately be equated with the analyst, as we all too frequently observe in dreams when the dreamer uses displacements. The qualities of reversibility and infinity that characterize symmetrical thinking suggested to Matte-Blanco that the principle of symmetry subtends, and thereby is able to account for, all the characteristics of the primary processes. The unconscious consists only of classes, of infinite sets of classes, according to Matte-Blanco, not of individuals per se.

The unconscious responds to events as sets of signals that it classifies as infinite sets. These sets ultimately become emotions. Thus, emotions are symmetrical, subjective outcomes of symmetrical thinking which reveal themselves through bi-logic. Bi-logic is an expression of the unique combinations of symmetry and asymmetry constituted in stratified layers of the unconscious. The greater the degree of symmetry in a stratified layer, the closer that layer is to the depths of the unconscious; the greater the degree of asymmetry, the closer the layer is to the higher levels of consciousness. Thus, one arm of the calipers of each of the stratified layers consists of bi-logic, which is dominated by the homogenic principle of symmetry; whereas the other arm consists of bivalent logic, which is dominated by the heterogenic principle of asymmetry.

All mental phenomena transpire between the arms of these caliper-modes in a dialectical "dual-track (Grotstein, 1978a). The "Infinite Geometer" of this chapter's title refers to the mystical entity that is suggested in but discreetly omitted from Matte-Blanco's work (except in his 1981 paper). In Bion's formulation, this entity can be understood as the "messiah thought," "God," "O," or even, as I would add, the Platonic and post-Platonic (gnostic) concept of the immanent demiurge within us. This mystic concept (familiar to Meister Eckhart, the 18th-century Dominican theologian and mystic, and to others) is also known as God, the immanent one within us (as opposed to the godhead, which is totally ineffable and inscrutable). Bomford (1990, 1999), himself a man of the cloth as well as a mathematician, elegantly demonstrates the parallels between the traditional concept of God and the psychoanalytic concept of the unconscious. He uses Matte-Blanco's concepts to demonstrate these parallels.

The overriding question is, "Who is it who so deftly and presciently wields these awesome calipers?" Is it the same one who dreams our dreams while we are asleep and who composes and choreographs our patients' free associations? As Rhode (1997) concluded in another context, "A closed system requires an operator that is alien to it, and of a different order from it, in order to enter into a state of transformation" (p. 295). Another way to put the question is to ask, "Who is the geometer who plays the scales of the stratified bi-logic structures in counterpoint with bivalent logic?" The same question could be asked in regard to Ogden's (1994a) concept of the "subjugating third subject of analysis." Since the individual subjectivities of both analysand and analyst are "subjugated" in that mysterious thirdness, how can we envision the inhabitant and operator of that thirdness? (In chapter 1, I suggested a parallel with the mysterious operation of the Ouija board.)

Matte-Blanco, a mathematician as well as a psychoanalyst, could easily stand astride the hard-core ontic nature of psychoanalytic theory and its ineffable ontological aspects. In his original monograph on this subject, *The Unconscious as Infinite Sets* (Matte-Blanco, 1975), he introduced ideas borrowed from set theory and other mathematical theorems to deal with the infinite nature of the unconscious. For Matte-Blanco, the unconscious is infinite in the sense of the potential members of any category or class, a concept that originated with Georg Cantor (1915) and was developed further by Poincaré (1952) but that has been pondered philosophically and theologically since Plato (Knorr, 1982; Murdoch, 1982; Sylla, 1982; Mordant, 1990).

THE IMPORTANCE OF INFINITY FOR PSYCHOANALYSIS

Introducing the concept of infinity into the psychoanalytic lexicon gives us a new paradigm and new perspectives on unconscious mental life.[1] Are the primary anxieties of the unconscious the drives, as Freud proposed, or infinity and infinite sets, as Matte-Blanco suggested? When the concept of infinity is applied to affect theory, particularly protoaffects, the psychotic or borderline experience of affect disregulation becomes more understandable. These patients may not experience affects per se, but infinite protoaffects instead, and are consequently afraid of any stimulus, including the analyst's interpretations, that might induce the release of the reservoirs of these protoaffects. From this point of view, the drives are reduced in importance as unconscious dangers to the ego and are replaced with the fear of unneutralized, ever-proliferating infinity. The drives themselves may even be recast as semiotic signifiers (to use the postmodern idiom) of an even profounder, ineffable signified infinity itself, which Bion (1970) would call O, Lacan (1966) the *Real*, and Ricoeur (1965) *Ananke* (Necessity). Infinity may also be linked with empirical concepts of nonlinearity, such as chaos (Gleik, 1987) and complexity and self-organization theory (Schwalbe, 1991; Kauffman, 1993, 1995), the unpredictable, decentering hidden order of postmodern thinking. Absolute indivisibility (infinite symmetry) plus absolute divisibility (infinite asymmetry) produces chaos, complexity, and emergence phenomena.

Trauma and psychosis are clinical examples of the predominance of symmetrical relations over asymmetrical ones. In trauma, for instance, victims generalize the class of the perpetrator so that the person who traumatized them becomes a whole class (e.g., my father = all men = all mankind). The inseparability of a member of the class from a class is

1. For an interesting and in-depth study of the history of the concept of infinity, see Rucker (1982). For an interesting study of infinity's counterpart, zero, see Rotman (1987).

also typical of psychotic thinking. (For example, a psychotic patient entered a therapist's waiting room and saw the figure of a fish in a picture on the wall. He immediately thought that this fish image was God and then believed that God was giving him a message to leave therapy. The patient was familiar with the symbol of the fish being associated with the origins of Christianity.)

We commonly observe the fear of symmetry in the clinical situation when a patient begins analysis or psychotherapy and enters into ego regression. The fear is usually experienced as fear of losing control, of becoming more dependent on the analyst/therapist, of becoming more helpless and vulnerable.

In the clinical situation we observe the dance between symmetry and asymmetry in various ways. The analysand's successive free associations will be distinguished by the asymmetries of their notable differences, but they will also demonstrate hidden or overt similarities revealing that the unconscious treats them as identical (e.g., a woman in the associations may indicate wife, mother, analyst, lover, etc.). Symmetrical relationships are of importance in yet another way. Each association, from my observations, is linked to its succeeding associations by a symmetrical link; for example, the key theme in the first association will match up symmetrically with its counterpart in succeeding ones. Correspondingly, the analyst listens not only for the symmetries that converge as identities and ultimately as constant conjunctions in the analysand's mind but also for discrete differences that truly make a difference. The analyst's very listening stance is one that seeks to reverberate, resonate, and match with the analysand's state of mind. This matching is effected by symmetrization.

CLINICAL EXAMPLES

The following vignettes illustrate how this paradigm change affects clinical theory and the importance of the dread of infinity.

Example 1: "The Infinite Bizarre Object"

A 43-year-old housewife and teacher informed me in a Monday morning session that, instead of driving home after her Saturday morning session, she had driven southward all the way to the Mexican border and had remained there for several hours. She said this action seemed to relieve her a great deal following her Saturday analytic hour with me. During that session she had revealed that she was feeling that "August is here again" and that she was "going psychotic again." We had frequently discussed her August vulnerability from many angles, including its signaling the end of summer and my vacation, its arousal of memories of her leaving home and of returning to school as a child, and its connection to other dynamic and genetic features.

It turned out that during the Saturday session in question the patient had began to believe that I finally understood her in a new way—that I at last had begun to fathom her secret identification with and idealization of her "mad self" and how she proffered her cooperative "neurotic self" as masque or hostage to me to disguise her alliance with her psychotic self. She had felt exposed and uncontained after the session and was afraid not only of my retaliation but of the retaliation of her own mad self, which she feared would believe that she had betrayed it. Going to the Mexican border gave her a sense of security, because she felt that she was apposing herself against a defining, separating frontier. This act helped tame the infinite chaos that had been set loose within her.

In the early phase of this patient's analysis, another incident had occurred that I was not fully able to understand until I read Matte-Blanco. She was terrified when she accidently became pregnant. The avowed reasons for her terror included fear of having to give up her job (she and her husband depended on her income) and fear that the pregnancy would ruin her figure. I remembered that she had undergone an abortion with an earlier pregnancy with a boyfriend from the past. I asked her if she could feel the fetus within her. She suddenly blurted out, "It's a monster! It has no eyes or mouth! It just throbs! I can't stand it!"

I interpreted to her that she was afraid of this fetus because she was confusing it with the aborted fetus from the past, which she felt had come back to retaliate. I also interpreted to her that she now felt identified with her own mother, who couldn't "bear" her as an infant or child, and that as a consequence of that identification, she felt unable to cope with the enormity of an infant's neediness, with which she identified. I also interpreted that the "monster" fetus reminded her of the bizarre object that had begun to hound and haunt her in early childhood and that had relentlessly pursued her into her adulthood. It was an omnipotent, punitive conscience that would not allow her to have a baby of her own, because she felt she had unconsciously attacked her mother's babies. The patient immediately relaxed and said, "Now it has a mouth and eyes!" She than folded her arms warmly over her abdomen so as to fondly embrace her fetus.

Matte-Blanco's perspective would also suggest that the fetus's transformation into a monster/bizarre object represented the patient's attempt to contain her emerging psychosis (i.e., chaos, infinity, terror, O), which she felt as an inexorable entity beginning to swell inside her, which is the way that Bion (1962b) described the formation of the bizarre object.

After her trip to the Mexican border, the patient reported a dream in which she was conducting a scientific experiment. She had gathered her research findings and was trying unsuccessfully, to "crunch" them in a computer, that is, to submit them to measurement. To her dismay, the data could not be measured. I interpreted to her that she was sad and frustrated that her mad self would not submit to being confined to the limitations of finite measurement, having tasted of boundarilessness. The patient responded, "That's the story of my life. What can I do?"

Example 2: "The Quarantined Object"

A 53-year-old analysand who had suffered with a severe bipolar and an obsessive-compulsive disorder was struck by a hypomanic episode when his wife was diagnosed with breast cancer and had her right breast removed. The analysis seemed successful when he was able to countenance the tragedy that had befallen his wife. A year after he terminated his analysis, he returned with the news that his wife's left breast had just been surgically removed because of the return of breast cancer. His attitude toward his wife had suddenly altered. He began to treat her with indifference and condescension and avoided her sexually. After considerable analysis over his withdrawal from her, it became apparent that he was treating her as a phobic object. The issue of his guilt in putatively causing his wife's cancer emerged. The decisive intervention, however, was my interpretation that he was "quarantining" his wife almost as if she were a repository of nuclear waste that would infinitely proliferate if he were to touch her.

This realization activated a panic reaction in the patient that took weeks to analyze successfully. He recalled that he had abruptly terminated his practice in a distant city upon learning of his wife's first cancer. The unconscious phantasy was that he would split off ("surgically" incise) her cancer, project it into the city where they lived and he practiced, "quarantine" it there, and then escape to the other side of the country. After learning of the recurrence of his wife's cancer, the patient became panicky once more and then "quarantined" the cancer in his wife, who thus became a phobic object.

Example 3: "Fear of Homework"

A 42-year-old single physician consulted me after two apparently failed psychotherapies. She described her mother as a cold "ice queen"—beautiful, removed, and withholding. Her father was a business executive who was frequently away from home; when he was home, he was submissive to the "ice queen." The patient reported that her mother had failed her every time she went to her for advice, for she had no advice to give other than banal homilies. Her father at least had helped her with homework by structuring her time.

The patient's previous psychotherapies had been conducted twice weekly. When I asked why she had never entered psychoanalysis on a four-to-five-times-a-week basis, she suddenly became furious with me. When her fury subsided, I got a picture of a frightened young girl who was claustrophobically anxious about being "pinned down to someone else's schedule" and who was also suffering a fragmentation anxiety about the lack of structure in analysis. She feared that she would not have anything to say and would dissolve or evaporate. She wanted her therapists to give her "homework," that is, something that she could work on herself in between sessions in order to have the comfort of some kind of continuous structure—like the homework structuring conducted by her father, as contrasted to her mother's "hand's off" policy. The patient acknowledged, when I confronted her, that she was afraid of wide-open spaces, of boundarilessness, of infinity.

DISCUSSION

These clinical examples demonstrate how infinity—that is, phantasies of an infinite proliferation of protoaffects or qualities—becomes a profound source of terror. We see this fear in hysteria, in the obsessive-compulsive, bipolar, and borderline disorders, and in psychoses. One of the most troubling problems for schizophrenic patients is their propensity for "overinclusion," the failure of the capacity to gate and prioritize incoming information. Imagine receiving information. Then imagine that each item in that information automatically induces a hypertext link to each component of the information. Then imagine that each hypertext link induces yet another link ad infinitum. That metaphor describes the "overload" of the schizophrenic's psychotic experience, which is not unlike the experience of a patient suffering from an obsessive-compulsive disorder.

In a psychoanalytic hour even with a neurotic patient, it is conceivable to consider that each integer of each free association leads to an infinite moment that is linked temporally in a diachronic (sequential) chain of meaning. A common manifestation of the fear of encountering infinity and infinite sets is in psychoanalytic regression, where there is a backward movement away from the reassuring structures and boundaries that divide entities and objects into definitive categories. Regression seems to be in the direction of primary identification (Fairbairn, 1952; Grotstein, 1994a, b), an archaic state that may correlate with Matte-Blanco's concept of the indivisible mode, a state of absolute symmetry, which is possibly the essence of psychotic confusion insofar as there are no distinctions or separations.

The issue here is one that could be called the relentless proliferation of possibilities or actualities of associations to a member of a class of ideas. Freud (1900) stated that in the unconscious there is no negation. All ideas and potential impulses live side by side without conflict. It is only when they irrupt into consciousness that conflict occurs—because of the encounter with negation, which means that natural boundaries are erected between qualities, thereby establishing differences.

When the symmetrical aspects of bi-logic predominate, as they seem to do in primitive mental disorders, it is as if absolute indivisibility exerts a powerful implosive pull back to primary identification, back to the absolute boundarilessness of the psychotic state. On the other hand, in schizoid, alexithymic, and obsessive-compulsive disorders there is often the reverse: a tendency for absolute heterogeneous divisibility, which creates such detachments, separations, and boundaries that we feel that the patient behaves more like a computer than an animate, emotional person. In the first instance, separation and its consequences are feared; thus, the patient retreats only to default into the disaster of indivisibility. In the second, regressive dependency is the nemesis of these patients,

but they retreat from that anxiety ultimately in the direction of fragmentation. Clinically, most patients seem to evince both trends.

Although the analyst's empathy is of the utmost importance, many patients seem to fear it, allegedly because they do not trust it. Insofar as empathy offers to patients the opportunity for affiliative identification, it may jeopardize for some patients a sense of boundaries and thereby threaten to throw them into the homogeneous indivisible mode.

THE NEW UNCONSCIOUS OF MATTE-BLANCO

Freud (1911b, 1915b) portrayed the unconscious as two-tiered, that included under primal repression and secondary or dynamic repression. In his theory, both primal repression and secondary, or dynamic, repression are ultimately conducted by the ego under the sway of the superego (Freud, 1923a). When Freud (1905b) discussed wish fulfilment and the pleasure–unpleasure principle as subserving the instinctual drives, he suggested that the infant fundamentally aims to achieve pleasure at the cost of unpleasure. For Matte-Blanco, the infant's choice is between an undifferentiated state of existence, which is characterized by absolute symmetry (the indivisible mode), and the reality principle, which predicates the operation of asymmetry, that is, of negation, which reveals the unevenness of reality, with its divisions and differences.

In Freud's theory, unconscious mental life is dominated by the operation of the primary processes, by which he meant principally condensation and displacement, whereas secondary processes are dominant in consciousness. These two are, according to Freud, in an absolute dialectical opposition. Matte-Blanco (1988) altered this picture. His two main principles, symmetry and asymmetry (which correspond, respectively, to the homogeneous or indivisible mode and to the heterogeneous or divisible modes) are inescapably conjoined and operate reciprocally in an irreducible binary opposition (Lévi-Strauss, 1958). Together they constitute the bi-logic structure. These structures exist in an infinite gradient in the unconscious and conscious domains, with each layer or stratification of these domains being one of principally five (for five levels of organization) different bi-logic structures that vary in the proportion of symmetrical and asymmetrical principle they contain. Yet there may be an infinite number of stratifications between absolute indivisibility in the unconscious and absolute heterogeneity in consciousness. In the first stratum, asymmetry is sufficiently in force so that the subject can recognize the distinctions between objects and between himself and other objects. At the other end of the spectrum, in the fifth stratum, symmetry predominates, the mathematical limit of indivisibility of self and objects and objects in general obtains. This state would represent psychosis.

Side-by-side with the homogenic and heterogenic modes in the ascending and descending stratification of bi-logic structures is the *bivalent mode of thinking*, which corresponds to classical Aristotelian logic.[2]

Let me present an imaginative conjecture about how these various entities may be structured. First, imagine an infinite stratification of bi-logic structures, one stacked on top of the other ad infinitum from absolute indivisibility upward to absolute heterogeneity. Also imagine that each bi-logic structure in this infinite stratification is, paradoxically, separated from its adjoining structures and yet at the same time is mysteriously linked with them, perhaps in a Möbius strip of discontinuous continuity. Finally, imagine some preternatural presence, holding the arms of the calipers and at the same time playing the stratified stacks of bi-logic structures and the bivalent logic structure like a hand organ that can be stretched, twisted, and compressed. By so doing, this preternatural

2. I hope that the reader will realize that "side-by-side" and "ascending and descending" are metaphorical expressions.

presence, this "Infinite Geometer," can imaginatively orchestrate all the possibilities of esthetic, ontological, and scientific creativeness and can choreograph all conceivable behaviors.

Bi-logic, in its own right, produces what Freud called the primary processes. For Matte-Blanco, *unconscious cognition* comprises bi-logic structures, in conjunction with bivalent thinking. *The unconscious is a computer!* That is why dreams can be so artfully, thoughtfully, and presciently creative. Let me explain further. Bi-logic, within its own graduated structuring (differing proportions of symmetry and asymmetry), is dominated by the operations of the principle of symmetry despite its containment of some *a*symmetry. Thus, dreams, which obey the laws of the principle of symmetry, do involve of necessity some *a*symmetrical relations in order for some differentiations to be portrayed in the dream.

That bivalent logic contains an aspect of symmetrical logic can be seen as follows. One can visualize this phenomenon in the clinical situation and in the use of computers. In the former one can imagine an analysand uttering a linear succession of free associations to each of which there are innumerable associations with innumerable associations to each of the secondary associations, and so on ad infinitum. In the use of the computer, one only has to imagine an infinity of hypertexts linked to each word of the initial hypertext on any subject.

Bivalent logic, while containing some elements of symmetry (if A equals B, then B equals A; under the law everyone is equal), is nevertheless dominated by the principle of *a*symmetry. Since bi-logic and bivalent logic are each constituted in a binary fashion (i.e., each mode is both symmetrical and *a*symmetrical in differing proportions), they mediate one another. Fundamentally, the ultimate dialectic lies between the principle of symmetry, which governs bi-logic, and the principle of asymmetry, which governs bivalent logic.

The concept that the unconscious can be pictured as an organic or vitalistic computer becomes more credible when we consider the cognitive ramifications of symmetrical logic. Those of us who now use word-processoring computers have come to rely, for instance, on that function which, when summoned, can locate all identical occurrences of a specified set of characters in the text. That ability to locate the "twin" belongs to symmetrical logic. The human unconscious goes several steps further than our word processors, however: it locates not only identities in its matching function but also *similarities*.

Our matching function operates developmentally. An infant uses normal projective identification to attribute aspects of the self to objects of the environment in order to establish bonds of affiliation. Stranger anxiety is affiliation's dire counterpart and follows the first harsh brush with objects that are different. Later, in friendship and especially in love relationships, one witnesses the operation of a mixture of the two. Affiliation or selfsameness (things in common) wrestles with the challenge of difference in that age-old dialectic known as the "war of the sexes."

Using the concept of infinity, one can "mathematize" the idea of love as each partner's desired approximation of the other along the trajectories of an asymptote; that is, each lover seeks his or her object along the arc of an asymptote that reaches the object at infinity. Our concepts of ethics, fairness, and the law may be derived from our desire for symmetry, whereas individuality and achievement can be viewed as associated with asymmetry.

The dialectic between the operation of the principles of symmetry and *a*symmetry can be applied to concepts of early infant development. The conflict between Kleinians and traditional Freudians over the issue of primary object love versus primary narcissism is easily resolvable: they both exist and do so in a dialectical tension in which primary object love reflects the operation of the principle of asymmetry while primary narcissism is a manifestation of the principle of symmetry. Morgan (1998) has recently applied this formulation to the debate between Stern (1985) and Mahler (1968) that pits the concept of symbiosis against that of the initial separateness of the infant. Expressing a Kleinian point of view, Bion (1963) put forth the idea of the simultaneous operation of the paranoid-schizoid and the depressive positions (which he portrayed symbolically as P-S ↔ D), in which the former stands for the operation of the principle of symmetry (and bi-logic structures) and the latter for the operation of the principle of asymmetry (and bivalent logical structures).

PSYCHOANALYTIC CONCEPTS IN THE LIGHT OF STRATIFIED BI-LOGIC STRUCTURES

I believe that Matte-Blanco meant that all human endeavors, interactions, and contemplations inescapably issue from the interplay of similarity and difference in myriad combinations. Symmetry underlies narcissism and subjectivity, whereas object relations and maturity are informed by difference, therefore asymmetry, albeit with descending aliquots of similarity.

For Freud (1911b), the primary processes were associated with unbound cathexes and thus with randomness, whereas secondary process was associated with logical (Aristotelian) thinking. Similarly, Kleinians regard the paranoid-schizoid position as dominated by primary processes and unbound cathexes (particularly of the life and death instincts) associated with such primitive schizoid mechanisms as splitting, projective identification, magic omnipotent denial, and idealization. When Freud's primary and secondary processes and Klein's paranoid-schizoid and depressive positions are reconceptualized in terms of stratified bi-logic structures, a radically complex series of mental operations can be imagined.

KLEINIAN CONCEPTS AND SYMMETRICAL AND ASYMMETRICAL THINKING

We can consider Klein's (1946) paranoid-schizoid position as dominated by the mode of selfsameness or similarities (the principle of symmetry) insofar as infants seek to split off and project away all feelings and disturbances that they feel are "non-self" in order to preserve the illusion of the "purified pleasure ego." Using Matte-Blanco's model, we can envision the paranoid-schizoid position (where primary process, or bi-logical thinking, is predominant), by virtue of the location of its characteristic mode of thinking (in the lower stratified regions), to be a more primitive mode of mental processing that functions to recognize similarities in the object and transform them into identities (from similar to identical). Thus, splitting would split off those elements of self that are felt to be emotionally asymmetrical with oneself. Projective identification would locate similarities in objects or seek to close the gap of separateness between self and object to establish the identicalness of identification. To the degree that some gradually ascending proportion of asymmetry is present, dreaming and phantasying become possible. In other words, primary process *is* a mental processing, albeit of a more primitive kind than secondary process, because it has access to both symmetrical and *a*symmetrical functioning and therefore has considerable latitude.

Klein's depressive position, then, would correspond to the mode of differences (heterogeneity) under the principle of asymmetry. In this position, infants become more aware of and accepting of the reality of their separation from the object, which they then come to realize is different in its Otherness. This new awareness is because secondary process, or bivalent logic, predominates; that is, the proportion of principles (faculties) in the stratified layers of bi-logical structures are tilted more in the direction of asymmetry, and these structures are subordinated to bivalent logic. This new arrangement favors the development of logical Aristotelian thinking, based on the experience of differences.

However, the remaining presence of symmetrical logic (in the bi-logic structures as well as natively ensconced within bivalent logic) allows for the comparison of similarities while also classifying differences. With the rising gradation favoring *a*symmetrical bi-logical thinking, the capacity for *bivalent* logic begins to appear.

Defensive projective identification can be regarded as involving the operation of symmetrization in this way: if the infantile aspect of the personality seeks to invade the object or become the object, the projective reidentification that takes place involves a dedifferentiation of self and object (we are identical).

FREUDIAN CONCEPTS AND SYMMETRICAL AND ASYMMETRICAL THINKING

We may also apply the principle of similarity to Freud's (1920) concept of the death instinct. Hinting at selfsameness, Freud himself associated this instinct with our inevitable return to our origins. It is my impression that the death instinct, as both Freud and Klein conceived of it, is equivalent to achieving selfsameness/similarity (a manifestation of the principle of symmetry) at the expense of difference; the life instinct is equivalent to achieving difference or heterogeneity (a manifestation of the principle of asymmetry). Freud's (1905b) sexual theories, we now realize, valorize difference at the cost of selfsameness/similarity.

The concept of symmetrical–asymmetrical thinking can be applied to the Oedipus conflict, when incest-striving children begin to realize that they must become the "excluded middle" in the relationship into whose midst they wish to insert themselves. In other words, the Oedipus complex is a structuring event in the life of the child in which the predominance of the pleasure principle, which we would now relate to the principle of symmetry (infantile omnipotence) is destined to confront the "law of the father"—that is, negation ("No!"). Thereafter, the child must accept his oedipal ranking outside the parental couple—in bivalent reality—after which time the erstwhile infantile omnipotence surrenders and submerges into the unconscious.

The picture of the unconscious we get from Matte-Blanco is quite different from the one we get from Freud. The latter's "seething cauldron" of forbidden wishes becomes the former's preternatural "spiritual computer," which is the source not only of desire but also of Truth and Justice, in its quest for sophrosyne, "balance."

SCHIZOPHRENIA AND SYMMETRICAL AND ASYMMETRICAL THINKING

Perhaps one of the difficulties in schizophrenic thought disorder may be understood as some kind of error in the ratio of symmetrical to *a*symmetrical thinking in any of a number of the stratified bi-logic structures. Or it may be that there is some disarray in the gradations and the assignment or attribution of graded proportioning. The elliptical thinking that seems to characterize the thought processes of schizophrenics may be due, in other words, to a defect in their ability to order, organize, and integrate the appropriate interrelationships between the principle of symmetry and the principle of asymmetry.

It is almost as if schizophrenic thinking uses both bi-logic and bivalent logic, but both are under the sway of the principle of symmetry. Bion (1963) was aware of this factor in psychotic thinking. He called it "alpha function in reverse," by which he meant that the psychotic portion of the personality had gained possession of the normal thinking processes and was using them in the service of psychosis. The idea that "there is method in his madness" expresses this point.

SYMMETRY AND ASYMMETRY IN THE CLINICAL SITUATION

The dialectic between bivalent (*a*symmetrical) logic and bi-logic (symmetrical) occurs routinely in the clinical situation in our attempts to understand our analysands' utterances. The manifest content of their utterances is understood on one level as obeying the laws of classical (bivalent) logic; but we also seek to understand, at the same time, the bi-logical implications they reveal, for instance, by trying to decode the analysand's manifest content by analyzing the links between successive associations. Each association is a signifier, a hieroglyph; it constitutes its own bi-logical universe, containing both symmetries and *a*symmetries.

For example, an analysand once reported to me, "I was anxious over the weekend but somehow felt relieved when I went rock hunting with some friends." I divided these associations into (1) his being anxious and (2) rock hunting. The anxiety in the first association alludes to my absence, my unavailability to the patient over the weekend. The second association, rock hunting, has the following hypertext link: "Rock" translates into the German *gross Stein* (the patient spoke German), which is close enough to "Grotstein." In other words, an element within the universe signified by the first association matched up with an element in the universe of the second association, which was carefully (unconsciously) selected to give it meaning. Each successive association is a universe of an infinite possibility of meanings. The Infinite Geometer selects those apposite components within each association in such a way that a grammar of structure and meaning mysteriously emerges.

WHO IS THE INFINITE GEOMETER?

A more mystical inclination suggested by Matte-Blanco's work is unstated. The unconscious and conscious minds are described as a complex, harmonious consortium capable of an infinite array of possible combinations. But who is the Infinite Geometer who plays the scales of the stratified bi-logic structures in counterpoint with bivalent logic? Who is the virtuoso who knows all these chords and is able to play this wondrous polyphonic instrument? Is it the preternatural "ghost in the machine" (Ryle, 1949) of German Romanticism, the "God" of the mystics, Plato's demiurge, or Hegel's (1807) "World Spirit"? Or Ananke (Necessity or Fate, reality or circumstance), that is, cultural/linguistic associational anarchy itself?

This question was not posed by Freud or his followers, because Freud inadvertently obscured the question of the *subject* or *agent* of the unconscious and further beclouded it with his formulation of the structural theory, in which increasing hegemony of agency proceeded from the id to the ego. The id was considered to be peremptory and thus without organization or authorship. It was not until Lacan (1966) reread Freud and attempted to "retranslate" his work from its ontic respectability into a more authentic hermeneutic argot that the need for a subject and an agent for unconscious mental life became apparent. Lacan apparently sidestepped the issue, however, by suggesting that the unconscious in a sense is *language* (actually, that it is structured like a language) and is constitutive of the Other. When infants learn to speak, they are "born into the symbolic order of language in the name of the father" (the authority of no). Further, since the unconscious "Other" is indistinguishable from other Others, it is socially commingled with the Others at large and consequently fails to be a strictly private unconscious of the self by itself.

The very concept of the subject of the unconscious involves the notion of symmetry insofar as the subject is ultimately ineffable (not measurable or able to be contemplated), whereas the concepts of self and person, while also borrowing of the ineffable, are felt to be more defined and thus *a*symmetrical.

I have explored the relationships between the concept of the unconscious, Bion's (1965, 1970) "transformations in O," Heidegger's (1927) "Being-in-itself," and my "transcendent position" (chapter 10) and the ineffable and phenomenal subjects of psychoanalysis (chapter 5). O is numinous; it is the Dreamer Who Dreams the Dream *and* the Dreamer Who Understands the Dream" (Grotstein, 1981a). Heidegger's Being, while having an unconscious component, is in the main the more apparent entity that participates in consciousness as the more personally experienced one ("being-in-techne"). I understand Bion's (1965) O, Kant's (1788) thing-in-itself, and Lacan's (1966) Real, along with Cantor's (1915) and Matte-Blanco's concepts of infinity and the new concepts of chaos (Gleik, 1987) and complexity theory (Kauffman, 1993, 1995; Palombo, 1999), as examples of a revolutionary new paradigm about the unconscious.

The drives are no longer the stochastic "prime movers" of the id. The id, instead, is an alter ego with its own sophistication and complexity. The drives are semiotic signifiers and mediators of infinity, of chaos, of the Real, of O, not the signified itself. These drive signifiers *mediate*, not initiate, danger. The infant is potentially born into O but normally never realizes it because mother immediately rescues the infant into her protective blanket of myth (phantasy). The confrontation with O is postponed until the child is ready ("return of the repressed").

The paranoid-schizoid defenses (splitting, projective identification, magic omnipotent denial, and idealization) act as filters against O by guaranteeing selfsameness at the expense of difference. Eventually, the child becomes more tolerant of differences as it enters the depressive position. Once differences and separateness can be tolerated, the child is ready for the transcendent position, which corresponds to Bion's "transformation in O," an objectless state of solitude and serenity (see chapter 10).

I hope to make it clear in this and the other chapters of this book that I am introducing the concepts of *vitalism* and *animism* to describe the preternatural, numinous agent that vitalizes and animates the operation and functioning of our mind/soul/being/subjectivity/identity. Might not Freud (1900) himself have paused to contemplate this mystical dimension when he stated the following (as also stated in chapter 1, p. 32).

> There is often a passage in even the most thoroughly interpreted dream which has to be left obscure; this is because we become aware during the work of interpretation that at that point there is a tangle of dream-thoughts which cannot be unraveled and which moreover adds nothing to our knowledge of the content of the dream. This is the dream's navel, the spot

> where it reaches down into the unknown. The dream-thoughts to which we are led by interpretation cannot, from the nature of things, have any definite endings; they are bound to branch out in every direction into the intricate network of our world of thought. It is at some point where this meshwork is particularly close that the dream-wish grows up, like a mushroom out of its mycelium [p. 525].

This quotation from Freud reminds us that he believed that mental life in general and dreams in particular are dominated by the pleasure principle and that dreams represent attempts at wish fulfillment. Thanks to Matte-Blanco's principle of symmetry, we can now hypothesize that Freud's pleasure principle and the derivative concept of wish fulfillment constitute a particular aspect of the more general principle of symmetry—in which the barriers to pleasure and wish fulfillment imposed by negation in the form of reality and asymmetry are obviated.

INFINITIZATION AND THE DEITY

Matte-Blanco (1981) referred to the relationship of infinitude and the deity in a seldom cited work. (Bomford, 1990, 1999, as mentioned earlier, has also taken up this point.) Voltaire once said that God created man in his own image, and man repaid him in kind. For Matte-Blanco, man is destined, from the mathematical point of view, to be alone at the crossroads of the point (zero dimension; see chapter 4) to create himself as God, to assign God outwardly, to kill God, and then to recognize the God who could not be killed, to recognize God as a *sense* of divinity in himself and in the Other—but always missing the God who cannot be contemplated:

> The rebellion or aggression against the breast, mother, penis, father is "infinitized" at the deeper levels of the mind. . . . A breast, penis, father or mother felt-seen as infinite is isomorphic to the notion of God of more developed thinking. As the deep levels, where everything is infinitized, are always active in all of us, it seems more faithful *to these levels* to refer to the abstract structure of which senicide, . . . parricide and deicide are representatives, and, therefore, to speak of deicide and not of senicide, penicide, matricide, parricide: this is in keeping in more than one way with bivalent logic and with the principle of symmetry, which rules the unconscious . . . [Matte-Blanco, 1981, p. 492].

Continuing on the subject of deicide, Matte-Blanco wrote:

> The strange, surprising, pathetic thing is that, after all, deicide does not exist in either of the two modes: it is an impossible absurdity in bivalent logic (the concept of God is that of an immortal being) and is outside the homogeneous indivisible reality for which no individual, no life or death exists. Yet it is a daily, most present bimodal reality in our life:[3] though it does not exist—is in any of the modes, it is in any and all of us. How? A puzzling suspended animation in midair, somewhere, nowhere, yet *there* [p. 493].

Further on in the same work, Matte-Blanco wrote:

> When we assert ourselves as God and (try to) occupy the whole space we find that the same space may also be occupied by another god: in fact an infinite number of them. . . . Put in other words: there is space for an infinite number of unique gods. This strange absurd formulation must, however, be co-extensive with the clear realisation that we are smaller than anything conceivable: points (which are so small as to have no dimension). Because they have no dimension, points are homogeneous indivisible: the image of *that* which is expressed as infinite. A point, any point, is the unreachable "meeting point" of both modes. Imperfectly expressed: the meeting point of God and nothing[4] [p. 510].

On the nature of God:

> The conception of the two modes of being is full of problems which . . . are fruitful and stimulating. I should like to comment on two of them. . . . Is God an "incarnation" or a representation

3. At this point in the text the author inserts the following footnote: "I employ the term 'bi-modal' to mean something in which both modes of being (asymmetrical or dividing and homogeneous indivisible) are present. This is a more comprehensive concept than bi-logic, of which bi-logic is only a sub-concept" (p. 493).

4. It is of some interest that in the Lurianic Kabbalah one of the meanings of *Keter Ayn Sof*, the innermost and most ineffable of the ten zephirots (emanations, attributes, or powers by which God was believed to manifest himself) is "nothing."

> of the homogeneous unity or is He the homogeneous unity? If the last of these alternative is right, it creates colossal problems, for the concept of homogeneous indivisible reality, *which springs from psycho-analytic observation*, refers to any one of us and to any "piece" of the world. If God is this unity then, considering that psycho-analytic observation has led us to the conclusion that one way of seeing man is as a homogeneous indivisible unity, we must conclude that man is God, i.e., we are controlled with a form of pantheism, which is quite different from self-deification. . . . The only possibility open, and a frustrating as well as a fascinating one, is that of arduous and humble ulterior reflection and effort toward clarification [pp. 510–511].

On maturity, Matte-Blanco wrote the following:

> If somebody is authentic and creative, then he feels, symmetrically, that he is God. If and when he discovers the creativity-divinity of another, he feels annihilated. Then he tries deicide. If *that* God does not die there is no alternative but to accept his existence. A form of politheism is then born in the depths of one's entrails. Maturity means accepting that one is God and at the same time a point, i.e., so small as to have no dimensions, and that the others are also gods and points as well. This is a very difficult achievement; most people remain at the level of self-deification and annihilation of the other. Maturity contains and implicitly expresses the long and detailed story of self-deification, deicide, annihilation, self-deification, birth of two (or more) gods. But the point itself. . . , an O-dimensional space, is mysteriously, in its turn, the "meeting-point" of both modes: the extensive-dividing one, and the indivisible. The point is a wonderful intuitive creation of the human intellect; perhaps mathematics has only begun to explore it [pp. 527–528].

CONCLUDING REMARKS

One of the principal themes embedded in this and other chapters of this book is the notion of an ineffable presence that preternaturally manipulates the metaphoric arms of the calipers of symmetrical and asymmetrical logic. Thanks to Matte-Blanco's contributions, we can speculate—and, of all things, from a mathematical vertex (perspective)—that ineffability is to be associated with the bi-logic capacity; that is, ineffability connotes dimensions that are, in the main, infinite (symmetrical)in their possibilities. Ineffability and its associate, inscrutability, are concepts that seem to bridge, overlap, or even congrue with the notions of the unrepressed unconscious and the deity.

I believe that the unconscious is as close as any mortal is likely to get to the experience of God. Bomford (1996) anticipated me in this belief. In his writings he suggests that the Christian belief in God corresponds in many ways to Matte-Blanco's concept of symmetrical logic. He differentiates between the totally symmetrical God of pure Being and the asymmetrical God as the Creator. If God created mankind, then He is separate and isolated from man and creates images of Himself that are asymmetrically human. Bomford, a theologian and an innovative follower of Matte-Blanco, traces the history of theologians trying to portray the concept of God. The Hebrews and the Christians both opted for the concept of "one God" but ran into difficulties with the idea of a God who is totally abstract and yet interacts with mankind. In other words, Christians and Jews alike were confounded by the Infinite (God as pure essence) and the less than infinite God who deals with finite mankind. Moreover, if God is infinite, He exists outside mankind and is therefore isolated finitely from man. Mathematical logic seems needed if we are to find a new conceptual home for God.

Bomford also points out that in mathematical logic as well as in the logic of the unconscious, each idea automatically designates its opposite. Opposites exist in the unconscious without contradiction. Thus, the existence of God predicates the existence of "no God." This concept leads to what I believe is an inescapable conclusion: mathematically speaking, God is the only legitimate atheist, because only God is capable of contemplating that there is no God. This paradoxical statement has two levels: (1) God, being the Subject of subjects ("Tell them I am that I am"), is incapable of self-contemplation; and (2) God can, however, contemplate His symmetrical counterpart, "no God," as object.

By "no God" I do not mean to be clever or irreverent; rather, this remark is a way of mathematically reconciling what logic tells us is a conundrum in regard to the concept of the deity as well as a conundrum about all entities, human and nonhuman. Every idea, every being, has its negative counterpart, not just its *opposite* (e.g., good versus bad) but its *negative* (e.g, existence versus nonexistence). Mathematically, this idea is contained in negative numbers. The mystics have conceived of the "apophatic language of unsaying" (Sells, 1994) as a way of mediating sacred opposites. When the name of the deity is pronounced, for instance, it must be negated by another saying.

To put it another way, human beings may have created the concept of the deity and elaborated it as a means of coming to grips with the mystical persuasiveness of their experience of the unconscious. Thus, the raw experience of the unconscious would be *absolutely everything* (infinite sets) and *absolutely nothing* (the "black hole" [Grotstein, 1990a, b, c]). This is perhaps the vision that Lot's wife saw when she turned around at the last moment to view what was left of Sodom and Gomorrah after God's sacking of them. Unable to look within because of its awfulness and awesomeness, man translocated his unconscious outward and skyward and called it God, representing both absolutely everything and absolutely nothing—and their *container*. What I am suggesting is that theology, mysticism, epistemology, psychoanalysis, and now mathematics have all begun to converge, revealing pursuit of a common theme—that of the mystifying duality of being.

From the standpoint of psychoanalytic phenomenology, one can begin to understand the wisdom of the Gnostic concept that God (the Creator or Demiurge) is within us as our imaginative, creative unconscious reservoir and is experienced, albeit only indirectly, as the Ineffable Subject of the Unconscious in contrast to its counterpart, the Phenomenal Subject, which is experienced directly. The former lies in a deeper stratum of bi-logic and is therefore immersed largely in symmetry, whereas the latter lies on a higher level and is endowed with more asymmetry.

The long and the short of the psychoanalytic application of these ideas is as follows: every human being is incarnated with *being, subjectivity,* and *agency* (where one is the agent of but not the origin of *causality*),[5] which exist as a trinity within a holographic at-one-ment or indivisible unity. This unity is ineffable and thus largely symmetrical and asymmetrical in part. Ineffability and inscrutability characterize not only our own existence but also that of our others. I refrain from saying "objects" because of the deceptively finite nature of the word. Our others are finite, but their Otherness is ineffably symmetrical in their ultimate unknowability. We humans are doomed to interrelate through the "flashing" of our mutual ineffabilities to each other. In the meanwhile, however, we must be content to live out our lives in the shadow of our inner, ineffable presence and to expect no more from our others as we encounter them along the way.

5. Causality proper is in the domain of the ineffable, i.e., God. See Wilkinson's (1998) discussion of phenomenological causality.

Chapter 4

INNER SPACE

Its Dimensions and Its Coordinates

Freud offered us two major constructs with which to grasp the mind. The first is that of the mind as a topographical series of continuous yet discontinuous landscapes known as the Systems *Ucs* (unconscious), *Pcs* (preconscious), and Cs (conscious) (Freud, 1915b). The second construct, the structural theory, presents the mind as a psychic apparatus consisting of id, ego, and superego (Freud, 1923a). The psychic apparatus sits astride the topographic construct so that all three components share the space of the System *Ucs* and System *Pcs*, whereas the id and the superego do not occupy the space of System Cs. I use the word space to introduce the theme of this chapter. The mind can be thought of as being characterized by *spatial* as well as *temporal* dimensions or coordinates, and these dimensions or coordinates can be plotted on a polar-coordinated graph. In other words, individuals dwell in time and space categorizations within which all human activity is transacted. Time and space are, according to Kant (1787), primary categories that format our experiences.

Mathematical theory can be thought of as the shadow of object relations in different dimensions. My aim in this chapter is to relate what psychic dimensionality might look like at various stages of cognitive-emotional development to the worldview (*Weltanschauungen*) of individuals at those stages.

Psychic space is an important metaphoric concept of mind that has many implications worthy of psychoanalytic interest. Psychic space encompasses all psychic content, which includes not only internal objects (i.e., self-representations and object representations) but also representations of events and relationships. It is my belief that a relationship exists between (1) the mind and its contents and (2) certain spatial considerations. I further believe that the study of the development and expansion of one's sense of dimensionality and of psychic space is of clinical and theoretical importance in psychoanalytic thinking. Put succinctly, it is my contention that all psychopathology can be thought of as conditions or states in which the patient experiences a sense of being trapped within a psychic space that is characterized as the zero, first, or second dimensions. Effective psychoanalytic or psychotherapeutic interventions function in part to help the patient out of his entrapment by demonstrating convincing alternative perspectives that help him to believe that he indeed is not trapped, that alternatives (the attainment of the third dimension of length, width, and height) exist.

Further, I postulate the operation of a psychical "dual-track" principle (faculty) in which the mind may become, normally and transiently, partially dissociated in order to achieve *self-reflection* (Fonagy, 1991, 1995) and *intersubjectivity* (Trevarthen, 1974, 1979, 1980, 1983, 1987, 1988, 1991; Trevarthen and Hubley, 1978; Stern, 1985, 1989) and be able to "mind" the mind of another. In self-reflection, the mind may divide itself and contemplate what it is feeling, considering, or experiencing, whereas intersubjectivity enables one to consider another point of view and empathize with it ("trial identification"). I just referred to the idea that a correspondence exists between psychopathology and a patient's experience of feeling entrapped in dimensional states. Reality can generally be conceived of as being spatially defined in three dimensions: length, width, and height. Unconscious phantasy can be conceived of as occupying the first dimension (either/or; no in between), thus leading to the experience of entrapment. The experience of being in the first dimension is that of having no margins in width or depth. Thus, one feels trapped in a worldview in which there is no choice other than either/or—for example, if the good mother is present, then the bad mother is absent—and the reverse. There are no shades of gray. Everything is absolute (see Table 1).

I should like to add that psychopathology can also be thought of as a condition in which the patient experiences himself as being dominated by an absolute single (cyclopean)[1] track. Psychoanalytic and psychotherapeutic interventions function not only by helping patients to emerge into the third dimension, but also by allowing them access to a mental/emotional dual-track (stereoscopic) perspective in which

1. It is interesting that, in the traditional Jewish myth of the "evil eye," the demon is conceptualized as cyclopean, that is, one-eyed. The obvious "cure" for its evil would, then, be the application of another eye, so that the demon could see things in stereoscopic perspective rather than in demonizing absolutes.

Table 1 The Dimensions of Psychic Space

	Metaphorical Expression of Dimensionality	Mathematical Expression of Dimensionality	Stages in Development of Psychic Dimensionality	Clinical Expressions of Psychic Dimensionality
Null Dimension	infinite space; timelessness	a dot on a Cartesian polar-coordinated graph	fetal existence (total symmetry); newborn (no self–object differentiation)	thinking is solipsistic, concrete, syncretistic, narcissistic; primary-process thinking; fusion–confusion; psychosis
First Dimension	polarized space; acutely specific time	a series of points on a graph (i.e., a line)	infant becomes aware of and accepts separation; polarized domain of symbiosis	persecutory anxiety of Kleinian paranoid-schizoidposition; fear of having feelings; acute sense of time; "time warp" of the traumatic event
Second Dimension	flatness; rhythmicity and cyclicity of time	a plane	self object differentiation; internalization of objects	objects and experiences are felt as flat; "shallow" (conventional, sterile) personality and relation-ships; affective flatness; regressive depressive apathy
Third Dimension	depth; reality	3-dimensional space	Kleinian depressive position; part-objects become whole objects; internal objects become object representations	objects are viewed in depth and with depth; symbolic thinking; projective identification more like displacement

they can self-reflect (I $\leftrightarrow$ self) and therefore have access to multiple alternatives.

Creativity may be understood in part as requiring that one aspect of the mind stay anchored, as it were, in the third dimension (i.e., depth—both concretely and metaphorically) of reality, while another aspect of the mind experiences *zero dimensionality* (i.e., infinity). For instance, this split may be what took place when Einstein, presumably anchored in the third dimension, contemplated being on the tip of a light beam projecting into outer space, after which experience he was able to formulate the laws of relativity.

In other words, psychopathology, considered from the point of view of psychic dimensionality, is a state of mind in which there is only one view: *no alternatives exist*. And there is no way out of one's dilemma—one is trapped in a cyclopean nightmare. Mental health can be understood, consequently, as the capacity to exist in a three-dimensional worldview with a dual-track mind, so that alternatives to one's dilemmas exist and so that, if they do not, one can at least mourn their absence. Perhaps one of the curative factors in psychoanalysis is the analyst's function in providing differing perspectives and lifting the analysand above an entrapping worldview of absolutes into a higher dimensional view of other possibilities.

VISUALIZATIONS OF PSYCHIC SPACE IN THE PSYCHOANALYTIC LITERATURE

Tausk (1919), Federn (1932), Schilder (1933), Isakower (1938), and Spitz (1965) all considered the importance of the boundaries surrounding the psyche. Tausk called attention to the flattening of the images of the self and its objects and the disordered spatial relations in schizophrenic deterioration. Federn emphasized the dissolution of ego boundaries in psychosis, and Schilder called attention to the importance of the vestibular apparatus and its role as an organ of balance in mediating dimensionalization and orientation in inner and outer space. A psychic space is implied in Isakower's notion that the dream must be experienced as a projection onto a screen surface, which he thought of as the image of the breast; Spitz suggested that the screen is mother's face. Piaget (1956) introduced fundamental distinctions between perceptual space and intellectual space and, at the level of intellectual space itself, between sensorimotor and representational space.

Bion directly addressed the issue of psychic space by defining its components as the container and the contained, each having a separate genesis. He associated the container with the maternal caretaking functions that, through reverie, intuition, and empathy, absorb the content of infantile projections (unmentalized protofeelings and sensations) and "translate" them into useful thoughts. Bion (1970) later conceptualized "transformations in O, with O designating the inchoate experience of "the deep and formless infinite," infinity (infinite sets), or chaos itself. Thus, when mother as container (mind) absorbs her infant's projections, she transforms them from O, chaos, infinity (the infinite dimension), downward to binary oppositions, such as "good object" and "bad object," which the infant can tolerate and understand. These binary designations represent the result of a maternal transduction from the infinite dimension to the first dimension of finiteness and inchoate understandability—on their way to the third dimension of reasonableness. She thereby not only transduces these inchoate "furies" into understandable needs, but also virtually "exorcizes" her infant's demons.

Bion (1962b, 1963) also postulated a distinction between *thoughts* and the *mind*. The latter had to be created in order to think the "thoughts without a thinker." Thus, Bion distinguished between mind as "container" and a thought as that which is "contained." Mind generates thoughts, which originate as unmentalized or unthought. Thus, it is important in clinical assessment to determine the dimensional status and maturity (capacity for higher or lower dimensionality) of the mind-as-container as well as the dimensional maturity of the thoughts-as-content that are not only being thought but also being thought about (reflected upon). The mind of a young child witnessing a primal scene or even a real Holocaust may be so immature that the mind-as-container traumatically withdraws from thinking about the event and postpones processing it; such an event then becomes a traumatic memory that may be scheduled for a later "return of the repressed." However, traumatic memory is not like other memories that can be repressed. It is "remembered" in the zero dimension; that is, it becomes, in Matte-Blanco's (1975, 1981, 1988) terms, an "infinite set" (i.e., "symmetrized," without boundaries in either space or time and without end).

Bion also suggested that the psychotic portion of the personality can misuse alpha function (the capacity to think) by appropriating it from the normal personality; this misuse is "alpha function in reverse," which I associate with the negative first dimension, that is, the "demonic" negative space of reversals (Bion, 1962b). Bion also postulated the notion of "transformations in hallucinosis," which are "psychotic transformations in 'O'." Although he left the difference unclear, it is my impression that psychotic transformations involve (1) the absence of a counterbalancing dual track which includes the third dimension of reality, and (2) the presence of -K, the concept of the lie or the delusion, which is another way of referring to "alpha function in reverse."

Matte-Blanco (1975, 1981, 1988) approached the concept of psychic space from the perspective of the principles of symmetry and asymmetry.[2] In applying mathematical principles to the psychoanalytic concept of the unconscious, he reduced the importance of the drives and instead valorized the idea of infinite sets and of infinity itself. As we learned in chapter 3, he portrayed the unconscious as regulated or mediated by an ascending–descending series of stratifications or layers of bi-logic structures, which can be thought of as binary-oppositional modules[3] with varying and reciprocal degrees of symmetry and *a*symmetry. Recall that at the deepest portion of the unconscious the module may be totally symmetrical, at which point there is "absolute indivisibility," that is, a total lack of distinction whereby everything (and everyone) is equated with everything (and everyone) else. At the highest point of utter consciousness, the module is dominated by total asymmetry, or "absolute divisibility," where there are no similarities, only differences.

The important point here is that Matte-Blanco conceived of the unconscious as stratified progressively in the direction of infinity. In terms of Bion's concept of the container and the contained, we could say that infinity is, paradoxically, the unbounded container of infinite sets of all categories. If infinity were not the container, then the content of the unconscious would be *random* rather than *chaotic*—states of chaos include a strange attractor that gives a hidden coherence to what otherwise would be randomness or pandemonium. Thus, the infinite container of the System *Ucs.* may be thought of as the "strange attractor" of its chaos (i.e., infinity, symmetry). Perhaps both Freud's (1923a) conceptualization of the id as a "seething cauldron" and Klein's (1933) conception of the death instinct reflect the feared irruption of infinity into a finite mind.[4]

Meares (1984) has suggested that psychic space has an ontological dimension, that it exists as a "virtual space" between the ego and the self, and that, as we develop more associative linkages with objects, our sense of space expands. Meares emphasizes the language of relationship in terms of inner space:

---

2. I must once again thank the late Professor Ignacio Matte-Blanco for his kindness long ago when he helped me with some of the conceptions in this present work (as well as in another, as yet unpublished work, on the dual-track theorem).

3. Lévi-Strauss (1970) coined the term "binary opposition" to designate a structure in which opposite, dialectical qualitites were constantly conjoined.

4. The reader is referred to Rucker's (1982) in-depth history of the development of the concept of infinity.

> The language of a relationship can alter one's sense of space. One's sense of inner space expands when an other elaborates or makes links to the flow of one's associative thought. This is a function of empathic language. Someone who successfully uses such language is "close." . . . Conversely, someone who communicates exclusively through logic and linear thought is usually considered "remote." These observations suggest that, at least in a figurative sense, there may be an inverse relationship between the magnitude of inner space and the sense of distance between oneself and the other [p. 170].

In yet another conceptualization of psychic space, Wisdom (1962) distinguished between two classes of internal objects: *nuclear objects* and *orbital objects*. Using this spatial metaphor, we can envision narcissism, for instance, as an inner condition in which orbiting caretaking objects constellate around a nuclear self that contains identificatory (internal) objects. The orbiting objects constitute a *spatial perimeter* or *container* for the self. Object love, on the other hand, could be pictured as the reverse, that is, as self-representations orbiting around the object, where the self is a perimeter and container to the object. In all probability the matter is even more complicated. A dimensional concept beyond the third is required in order for us to contemplate the simultaneity of the self with its orbiting objects while it orbits around the object, so that each object has two separate relationships to the self, stationary and orbiting. These spatial functions involve consideration of the dimensions of polar-coordinated space, which is the spatial representation of the objects of the senses.[5] Thus, the self and its objects can be regarded as existing in the null, first, second, and third dimensions in regard to space and time.

THE FUNCTIONS OF DIMENSIONALITY IN INNER SPACE

For mental content to be experienced, there must be a space between it and its container (object) and a perimeter around it. The spatial and tem-

5. I am limiting my thesis to the application of Euclidean plane geometry to psychic phenomena, but I should like to mention Thom's (1975) "catastrophe theory." Thom posited that any two variables in an equilibrium of a single entity can be plotted to give a third-dimensional ("morphogenetic") model, the roof of which is flat and smooth when there is a state of perfect equilibrium but which develops characteristic "catastrophe cusps" in states of disequilibrium. The implications of this theory for psychoanalysis are far reaching and must be reserved for a later contribution.

poral distances between self and object, and object and object, constitute, along with the perimeter, the functions of dimensionality in inner space. The concept of the dissolution of ego boundaries in psychosis must involve some understanding of spatial shifts. Patients feel, think, and behave in ways that suggest that they have a concept of their inner and outer space and frequently are aware of disturbances in their sense of space. Claustrophobia, agoraphobia, acrophobia, the landscape of dreams, the feeling of being "beside oneself" are but a few examples. Our theory must help us conceptualize the space and the surfaces, in which feelings and thoughts, like the toys of play therapy, can be examined, rotated, tested, joined to other thoughts, and so on. This space is thus a workbench of thinking. Without this space, there is concreteness or even psychosis.

We understand this idea when we invoke the idea of figure and ground, in which an object can be seen to be standing out from its background. If we see the background as the container that frames the figure in the foreground and that *defines* it, we can see that the characteristics of the space are important to the mental content. We exist and think in spatial terms. We seem to correlate external spatial phenomena with a template of inner space mapping that corresponds to this external space. Space, then, becomes the context and perspective for thought and the road map of experience. Thoughts and feelings, like armies, must have room in which to maneuver, and the room for maneuvering can determine the solution to the problem being considered. A patient, for instance, may be depressed and at the same time very anxious about his depression. The depression and the anxiety about it require at least two separate spaces of internal mental consideration: the *raw experience* per se and the *reflection* on the experience.

THE ONTOGENESIS OF PSYCHIC DIMENSIONALITY

My concept of the origin and development of the sense of space borrows from the infant development studies of Bower (1971, 1974), Trevarthen (1974), Boston (1975), and Emde, Gaensbauer, and Harmon (1976). Their findings reveal a sophisticated development of perception and motivational cognition at an earlier time than had been thought possible. The ability to experience space is subsumed under Kant's (1787) transcendental (primary, inherent) categories (before experience and anticipating experience). This capacity was considered by Hartmann (1939) to be a primary aspect of ego autonomy. It seems to emerge from the inchoate sensations on the newborn's skin, which "awaken" its sense receptors into its functions as a surface, as a boundary between self and nonself and as a container of self. Disorders of this phenomenon have been described by Bick (1968) and Meltzer (1975) as "adhesive identification." I have described the normal development of this phenomenon as "cohesive identification" (Grotstein, 1981a). Ogden (1989a) refers to these early sensory boundary experiences as constituting the "autistic contiguous position."

I presume that the fetus is in a state of equilibrium or harmony with its environment—and in a state of total symmetry mathematically. Hypothetically, if one were to touch the periphery or surface of the fetus at several points and then project these individual points onto a Cartesian polar-coordinated graph, the result would be a single point on that graph, a point representing the sum of all the points, because of the total symmetry. When all the projected points converge to a single point, the null (zero) dimension (of infinity or total symmetry) has been attained. To put it another way, since the fetus is surrounded by a watery moat, any point of impact on the surface would be evenly (symmetrically) distributed. As the newborn is exposed to experience, the phenomenon of asymmetry begins to develop, and the points on the surface of the newborn's skin would be projected onto polar-coordinated space as a series of points now extended into a line, thereby achieving the first dimension. Further development allows the line to expand to a plane (the second dimension), and finally the third dimension gives depth to the plane, each transformation connoting steps in maturation and development.

The psychological states associated with this spatial progression can be described experientially and clinically. A single point on the Cartesian polar-coordinated graph is associated with concretistic and syncretistic thinking. All events are coming toward and emerging from the point. It is the reference point of solipsistic (autochthonous) or narcissistic thinking. States of fusion-confusion emanating from projective identification typify the universe of the point. There is no differentiation. The container of psychic space and the contained are identical. The single point describes the domain of primary process and of the experience of psychosis. There is no space for the maneuvering of thoughts. Consider the following clinical example: A patient recalled that as a young child, she had heard her father arguing with her mother, running down the stairs, getting into his car, and starting the motor. In her memory the motor turned over and over endlessly, whereas, in actual fact, it took a second, after which he drove off, never to be seen again. The patient had trapped her father in a time warp by collapsing the dimensions of psychic time-space from the third dimension to the null dimension of infinity and timelessness.

Following birth, two separate vicissitudes of development of the skin-boundary phenomena seem to occur: (1) differentiation into a sophisticated sensory apparatus for perception and (2) dedifferentiation by way of projective identification, with a resulting elimination of awarenesses of perceptions and boundaries. These two function harmoniously or conflictually as a dual-track system of infantile development (Grotstein, 1977a,b). The development of awareness and toleration of the gap, the space in distance and time, between the departing and returning of mother constitutes the *"baptism" of the awareness of space.* Infants who can "contain" this space in the absence of their objects can initiate and expand the sense of space and can therefore become (and maintain being) separate. They can perceive some separated aspects of experience, which they can then begin to represent symbolically.

Without separation in time and distance there can be no concept of psychic space and therefore no perception and certainly no representation. In order to represent or be represented, the self must be separated from the object, and only then can it re-present it. An object representation can exist only as an object of an already differentiated self-representation contemplating it. In other words, the self must allow the object to be separate (that there be a space between them) in order for the object representation to be a container for the self, that is, symbolization.

As infants begin to accept their awareness of separation, their experience of their universe becomes that of a line (a series of points) on a polar-coordinated graph. But development of a newborn's self-awareness, which is stimulated by growth and experience, is uneven. The points of impact are random, and the registration of these points is experienced as an asymmetrical expansion of the self. Geometrically, the asymmetry causes the point on our metaphorical Cartesian polar-coordinated graph to become a line. The universe of the line leaves no margin for ambiguity. There is a polarization of spatial experience. Mother is either approaching (up the line) or departing (down the line). Moreover, the good mother's departure (down the line) is indistinguishable from the bad mother's approach (up the line). The line is the polarized domain of symbiosis descriptively and of the persecutory anxiety of the Kleinian paranoid-schizoid position phenomenologically. If the infant is empty or hungry, then the breast is considered to be full, and vice versa, thereby predisposing the infant to feelings of envy. It is a closed, hydraulic-like system that emphasizes quantitative considerations rather than qualitative ones. Patients living in this domain are afraid to show their feelings for fear of losing body contents. This hydraulic concept applies to the landscape of unconscious phantasies: in the Kleinian way of thinking, a good breast departing is experienced as being identical with the arrival of a bad breast.

As further development takes place, differentiation between self and object begins to occur. This incipient differentiation causes the line to expand to a plane. In this dimension objects and experiences are felt as two dimensional, flat, without depth. This is the *Weltanschauung* of the storybook heroine and hero, and of cartoon figures. One can observe it in the depressive apathy of regressed patients and in schizophrenic affective flatness. Patients living in this domain seem to lack depth to their personalities and do not perceive the world about them and the relationships they encounter in any depth. Personalities living on the planar surface are conventional, clichéd, and sterile. Catastrophe is encountered when one slips off the plane and goes over the edge; in practical terms, this phenomenon can refer to unexpected changes in one's experiences.

Consider the following clinical example of the phenomena of the planar dimension: An adult schizophrenic patient made mention of a time in childhood when her father was driving the family on a Sunday afternoon, and she feared he would drive over the horizon. Associations to the event led to the recovery of sensuous oedipal feelings for him. Another patient dreamed that, as she crossed the street to my office building and looked up to the ninth floor, where I was located, the street began to narrow to the size of a small tunnel and began to feel flattened. Her anxiety about her forthcoming hour with me had caused her in her dream to leave the third dimension of space and to be pressed into the second dimension of flatness. She feared regression.

A 47-year-old businessman who entered analysis because of depression had an almost total amnesia for events occurring before age nine. His mother was hospitalized with tuberculosis for two years when he was a year old and again when he was nine years old. His free associations were often visual and spatial in their orientation. For instance, he represented his amnesia spatially as a large, flat surface underneath a thin blanket. On one occasion he described his reaction to a car accident. He realized that he could have been killed, but he had no emotional response to the accident. He had isolated the incident and had *flattened* out his feelings about the accident, as it were, by stripping the event of meaning, thereby taking away from it the depth of its significance. He realized in the next moment that he had two time frames about the event and therefore two realities, one reality in which he was safe and the other in which he was in great danger. This patient then began to realize that his capacity for detachment in general was due to his ability to flatten out the significance of the events in his life. By going into the second dimension he was able to rob traumatic events, including the absence of his mother, of their significance. On another occasion, while associating to recollections of his father worrying about his own business affairs and of the recent loss of his wife, the patient's mother, this patient had an image of himself floating helplessly and timelessly in space. There was an absence of taste, smells, sensations; he was in a state of sensory deprivation. He then saw something tubular, like a barber's pole, which was pretzel-shaped and winding like a double helix, with a bright greenish cast to it. Now he also experienced a ringing in his ears and sensed that the space in which the image was cast was greyish and milky. His associations to this image led me to interpret to him that he fled from the anxiety of his father's grief over losing his wife and worrying about his business by going inside an image of the breast, where he found himself in a state of sensory deprivation (null dimension).

Infants develop a sense of space and time virtually from the beginning. At first they may fight the awareness of space and time expansions and limitations, but gradually they learn to accept them, at first transitionally. Eventually, the development of potential or transitional space (Winnicott, 1951) begins to supersede the struggle against time and space awareness in the paranoid-schizoid position and allows the toddler to experiment or "play with" time and space so as to master them. When development then proceeds to the Kleinian depressive position, the spatial container of the mind achieves a view of its objects *in* depth and *with* depth (contents). This is the domain of the third dimension, the dimension of maturity. The object and the self are separated and therefore separate from each other; independent and multiple origins of causality can now be entertained. Part-objects now become whole objects; in other words, internal objects become object representations. This is the domain of symbolic subject and object representability and symbolic thinking and reflection.

CLINICAL AND THEORETICAL CONSIDERATIONS OF PSYCHIC DIMENSIONALITY

When Tausk (1919) described the anatomy of the "influencing machine,"[6] he detailed the flattened appearance of the patient's anatomy projected into it. In acute and chronic schizophrenics and borderline patients, one more commonly finds concrete perceptual abnormalities such as rising feelings, narrowing of the body, and other body-distortion feelings. Neurotic claustrophobic patients experience a *metaphoric*

---

6. Tausk (1919) found that chronic schizophrenics developed a delusion of an "influencing machine," which represented a projected or detached and dehumanized alien aspect of their bodily organs and their mind and which controlled their thoughts and bodily functions.

("as if") closing of the space they are in, but psychotics experience the *actuality* of it. It is my belief that psychotics are literal about their perceptual relationship to space because of a defect in their capacity to organize and represent space; they cannot experience space per se. Their difficulty is caused not only by a regressive disorganization of ego boundaries and the ego apparatus of reality testing but also by a dismantling of the function of the vestibular apparatus, a phenomenon alluded to by Federn (1932) and Schilder (1933). Normal and neurotic patients are able to rectify their disturbed perceptual images (thanks to intact vestibular functioning), a capacity that manifests itself as secondary elaboration and secondary revision, which is the mind's way of reassembling disjointed images into a coherent gestalt.

The regressive elaboration of the null, first, and second dimensional states is governed and overridden by the compensatory rectification of secondary elaboration and revision. I recall a schizophrenic patient who informed me that after a particular session in the fourth year of treatment he had walked outside my office building, turned a corner, and suddenly become "aware of the third dimension." Everything and everyone he encountered seemed different. They were "fuller," "rounder." It was only then that he realized that he had been imprisoned in a more lowly dimensional *Weltanschauung* all his life.

Elsewhere (Grotstein, 1977a, b) I have developed the thesis that a dual-track system, mentioned earlier in this chapter, is involved in infantile development. One track, that of the differentiated infantile self from birth, proceeds alongside another, undifferentiated track, and the former assists the latter in completing its development. One can also understand the dual track as the initially independent existence of the two cerebral hemispheres. In infants, the right hemisphere seems to be operant from the very beginning, whereas the left hemisphere is relatively nonoperant at first (Schore, 1994).

This dual-track system seems to be operant in psychic space as well; two dimensions operate simultaneously. For instance, in cases of regression in the service of the ego the normal ego maintains the third dimension while the regressing ego can return to the second, first, and null dimensions experimentally. Sleep is another example; people who experience hypnogogic terror seem almost to believe themselves to be falling from the well-ordered space of the third dimension into the infinity of spacelessness of the null dimension. In psychosis, however, the dual track merges into one, and consequently the stability of the third-dimensional foothold is lost. Psychosis can also be thought of spatially as mental content without a container, one of the functions a mental hospital can supply for a psychotic patient.

PSYCHIC DIMENSIONALITY AND PROJECTIVE IDENTIFICATION

Projective identification is a phenomenon of the first and second dimensions and is made possible by the dual-track nature of symbiosis. In the process of projective identification, the infant wants either to undo an already established separation between the self and the object by relying on the other track, which still experiences nonseparation, or to expel unwanted aspects of the self by projecting them into an object that is perceived to be a special and permanent container for expelled self contents. Projection cannot take place in the null dimension, because there is no self–object differentiation to allow projection *from* and projection *to* (Grotstein, 1981a). Thus, the psychotic state may involve projections that were formed earlier, when the personality was in a higher dimension; or the currently psychotic person may form projections only because of some residual nonpsychotic aspects of the personality that offset the full psychotic attainment of the null dimension.

There is yet another way of accounting for the operation of projective identification in psychosis, however. Tausk (1919) implied and Federn (1932) explicated the idea that in psychosis a decathexis of the ego boundaries occurs as the psychotic person withdraws and disembodies. In so doing, psychotics seem to withdraw into an inner fortress, as it were, leaving behind the residue of their former selves, including their sense organs, all of which then become indistinguishable from the surrounding objects, which then seem to take over the former self. What seems to be identification through projection is really disidentification by withdrawal (Grotstein, 1995a, in preparation-a).

Projective identification that does occur in the third dimension is closer to displacement because of the person's awareness of the nature of the relationship to the object. Objects in the third dimension are symbolic as well as representational and therefore lend themselves to displacement, not projection. That is to say, projective identification represents an unconscious phantasy in which the subject invades an object or expels unwanted content into an object from whom the self is *not totally* separated. Displacement in the third dimension, on the other hand, depends on the memory of experiences with objects from whom one has already been separated. In addition, such states as empathy and intuition involve projective identification in the third dimension of psychic space.

THE PSYCHIC APPARATUS AND DIMENSIONALITY

The ego, insofar as it is a separate entity (an "I," according to Freud, 1923a) is in the third dimension. The id, which is symmetrical until experience modifies it, is in the null dimension. Repressed experiences of the dynamic or secondary unconscious, which may be related to both ego and asymmetrical id, exist in the first and second dimensions, if not also in the third. The superego is in the first, second, and third dimensions depending on its level of maturation. There is a problem, however, when we speak of a self-representation *within* the ego from the spatial point of view. The self-representation designates the ego as well as the id and superego. Difficulties in defining the differences between self, sense of self, ego, and self-representation borrow from the optical paradoxes of psychic space. I suggest that self is the object reflection of Freud's *das Ich* ("I") and can be viewed from the instinctual, moral, rational, and subjective viewpoints. Furthermore, the concept of the split brain allows us to look on all phenomena both from the rational point of view (left brain) and from the subjective point of view (right brain) and helps us regard the space of the psychic apparatus variously as the *emotional space*, the *rational space*, and finally the supraordinating and uniting *ultimate space*, which stereoscopically mediates the first two. The ultimate space is the sense of self; its components are the vertices of consideration.

I believe that the *sense of self* is the I → Self reflection in which both aspects are made up of contributions from the *sense of emotional space* and the *sense of rational space*. The *sense of moral space* may, for instance, combine the emotional and the rational. The *sense of unconscious space* comprises the primary, uncommitted (symmetrical) aspects of emotional space in addition to those aspects of "ego" experience (asymmetrical) destined to be dedimensionalized for mental storage and postponement. It may also include elements of the *sense of rational space* and the *sense of moral space*. There may be a *sense of negative space* (Bion, 1965) beyond repression and beyond projective identification, which seems to be cursorily improvised as an internal mock-up of the external world in an attempt to obliterate the self's relationship to the external world in favor of this malevolently psychotic one. This is the space of perversely reconstituted psychosis. *Transitional space* may be an ad hoc spatial arrangement, an intermediate area between self and object in which experiences such as psychoanalytic transferences occur.

All these senses of space may exist variously from the null through the third dimensions. The *ultimate space*, the sense of self, may have to extend into dimensions beyond the third, in order to account for the synthesis of its component spaces. All growth and maturation can be seen as expansions of the sense of the *ultimate space* of the self. The dimensions of psychic space thus are perimeter reflections of the self's relationships to its objects in the internal object-object representational axis. The coordinates of psychic space are the objects themselves, which have a complementary relationship to the perimeter, all under the aegis of a plastic, shifting, and evolving container–contained dichotomy.

THE DIMENSIONALITY OF TIME

In the zero dimension, time (like space) is infinite. One of the terrors of patients suffering from psychosis, melancholia, or similar conditions is that they cannot endure time gaps (e.g., those between analytic sessions), either because they cannot partition time without dissociating or splitting off from it or because they cannot represent it symbolically in terms of object faith and trust (object constancy and permanency). Thus, the melancholic feels trapped in a "black hole" in time without end. Hell is conceptualized as an eternity of suffering. Panic sufferers similarly say that while they are in the state of panic they believe it will last forever.

The psychoanalytic concept of traumatic fixation predicates a time factor, a virtual arrestment of one's being. A trauma becomes inscribed both in forever, or infinite, time (zero dimension) and in acutely specific time (first dimension), creating the phenomenon known as a *time warp*. Parenthetically, the zero dimension is also a way of describing the locale of Bion's (1965, 1970) O, or emotional turbulence.

The timelessness of the zero dimension continues into the first dimension and "shares time," so to speak, with a sharpened or acute sense of time.[7] There is not enough time to be with the needed objects when they are present, and, conversely, when they are absent, there is too much time before they return—if ever ("Mommy is *never* coming back!"). The maturing toddler who needs to be put on a schedule has begun developmentally to recognize time in the second dimension. Toilet training institutes the awareness of time *rhythms*, which help the toddler with object constancy. Rhythm predicates cyclicity and thus return of the object. In pathology, however, an apathetic or a schizophrenic patient may feel the flattening of time and of all other experiences as well.

A patient's dream exemplifies cyclical time: "I was in a church parking lot. Then I saw a large movie screen. A Bergmanesque movie was

---

7. It should be borne in mind that time and space are primary Kantian categories, along with causality.

playing. It was in black and white. A girl with blonde, braided hair says, 'At the end of the road there'll be a new beginning.' Then she's out of the black-and-white movie and with me in person in the dream and repeats what she said in the dream." This analysand is trapped in a time warp. He is in love with two women. One seems to be the woman of his future life, the other of his past life; but his future life is the future of the child he seems identified with, and he has considerable bitterness about his past life and cannot proceed to his future life until his past life is compensated for by the second woman, who seems to represent the irreplaceable compensation. One is reminded here of Nietzsche's (1889) concept of "eternal-return."

In the third dimension the dual track makes itself felt in terms of time. One may patiently exist in sequential time, while "at the same time" contemplating past time, future time, or timelessness. In addition, one can allow oneself to remain in what Heidegger (1927) ontologically referred to as the "forever present time" in which *Dasein* exists.

CONCLUDING REMARKS

In this chapter I have introduced an ontic (mathematical) concept to measure or survey the landscapes of psychic space and time. In chapter 3, I employed the metaphors of calipers and the geometer to suggest that there is a knowing yet unknowable presence in the unconscious, the ineffable subject, who, like a geometer, wields the calipers of the two principles of logic (that of spatial and temporal symmetry and that of spatial and temporal *a*symmetry) to give the phenomenal subject all the possibilities inherent in the space-time continuum–discontinuum (the spatiotemporal perspective of Matte-Blanco's "bi-logic"). Let me add yet another metaphor: that of the musical hand organ, which I introduced earlier. With one hand on spatiotemporal symmetry and his other hand on asymmetry, the Infinite Geometer can wield the metaphoric hand organ—by pulling, compressing, and bilaterally twisting—and can choreograph all the dimensions to the music of time and space, thereby releasing all their inherent possibilities into creativity. This is how dreams are dreamed, art created, and lives lived.

Chapter 5

PSYCHOANALYTIC SUBJECTS

An underlying theme of the entirety of this work is the idea of psychic presences.[1] The idea of a psychic presence borrows heavily from the olden schools of vitalism and animism and yet seems to convey the emotional immediacy of the presence of the essence or being of something or someone. In the past the words ghost, spirit, or soul were used, but those designations are too suggestive of spirituality and the supernatural and thereby elude what I am trying to convey.

In this chapter, however, instead of the expression psychic presence I use the more familiar terms subject and subjectivity to refer to a topic that has captured the interest of thinkers in every field and in every age. By presenting various thinkers' views on the topic of subjectivity (i.e., one's subjectiveness or "subjecthood" or essence), I am acknowledging connections with the disciplines of mythology, religion, spirituality, philosophy, metaphysics, and linguistics in order to show the awesome dimensionality and ramifications of this concept for psychoanalysis.

CONSTRUCTS OF SUBJECTIVITY IN RELIGION, PHILOSOPHY, AND MYTH

My aim in this chapter is to be more suggestive than conclusive about the significance of parallels between various disciplines in regard to the concept of subjectivity. I wish to share my sense of amazement about what I believe are striking similarities between the psychoanalytic concept of the *unconscious*, the ontological and philosophical concepts of

1. It was Roy Schafer (1968) who first coined the term *presence* when he described primary-process presences (pp. 82–139).

subject and *being* (as distinct from ego or self), and the mystic-religious notion of *God* and the *Demiurge* (as distinct from the Godhead), especially in terms of the mystic tradition of Meister Eckhart (Fox, 1981a; Sells, 1994; Webb and Sells, 1995), the Gnostics (Pagels, 1979), and the Lurianic and Zohar Kabbalah (Scholem, 1976).

Subjectivity is the quintessence of Platonic ineffability; that is, we can get only a glimpse of the shadow that the subjective "I" casts on the walls of the cave as its "selfness." In his attempt to clarify the concept of subjectivity, Descartes proffered the idea of subject and object, a dichotomy that was recognized and respected by Aristotle, St. Augustine, Kant, Fichte, Schelling, Hegel, Schopenhauer, and Brentano. St. Augustine, according to Modell (1993), defined self-consciousness as a "private self" and viewed this inner or private self as a source of spirituality and authenticity. Kant (1787) spoke of the "transcendental subject" as the "I who thinks," yet he distinguished between a "metaphysical self" and a "personal self," according to Cassam (1997). (This distinction seems to be in line with my categories of the Ineffable Subject and the Phenomenal Subject, respectively.) However, Kant equated the transcendental with a priori capacities and distinguished it from the "transcendent" (speculative).

Husserl (1931, 1962) posited the concept of the "transcendental Ego," which is not a part of this world, in contrast to the idea of the man who is capable of self-experience in everyday life. I take the former to be Husserl's way of designating what I am calling the Ineffable Subject and the latter to be the Phenomenal Subject of quotidian experience. Wittgenstein (1921) argued that the philosophical self is not the human being, not the human body or the human soul, with which psychology deals, but rather the metaphysical subject, the limit of the world—not a part of it.

A revival—beginning with Husserl and continuing through Heidegger, Sartre, and current psychoanalytic intersubjective theorists—of the beliefs of the mystics seems to be ocurring in which the subject–object dichotomy (and the mind–body dichotomy) is seen as merged, like conjoined twins. That is, each element of the pair is somewhat distinct from the other, yet both are considered to emerge from a common source; thus, each is relative to the other. Within of this postmodern view, we are prevented from considering the subjective uniqueness and unity of the mind without blending it with the subjectivity of the world of so-called objects from which it emerges. (To use the figure–ground paradigm, we would say that, although the figure emerges from the ground, it nonetheless remains a part of that ground, and the ground continues in it. In other words, the ground behind the figure continues in the figure, even when the figure obscures the ground's presence.) I think it is only reasonable to consider both philosophical points of view as valid, just as in physics it is sometimes better to conceptualize light by using wave theory and at other times more helpful to use quantum theory. Thus, a dual-track concept is necessary to understand certain phenomena that would otherwise be fated to be significantly obscured.

In myth, subjectivity has been associated not only with individuality but also with narcissism, as opposed to a socially interacting self. The narcissistic aspect of subjectivity may have originated with Cain or with Prometheus and coursed through medieval times as Machiavellianism (Wilson, 1995), as opposed to quixotism. In ancient Egypt, subjectivity was shared with a second figure, Ka, which was believed to accompany one throughout life and even survived one's death; it was thought of as a protective divine spirit, not unlike the *paraclete* (advocate of or intercessor for human beings in their relation to God) of Christian theology.

SUBJECTIVITY AND BEING

The concept of being has been explicated in ontology and phenomenology, most prominently in the contributions of Dilthey (1883), Husserl (1931, 1962), and Heidegger (1927, 1968). (It has not as yet become significant in the psychoanalytic lexicon, but deserves to be, in my opinion.) This chapter is not the proper forum to do justice to the richness of the idea of being, in Heidegger's (1927) sense of *Dasein*; here I wish only to be tangential to but respectful of it. I think the concept of being is congruent with Heidegger's concept of *aletheia* ("unconcealment"), which I render as "raw ontological experience"—realness, or naturalness—or, in Ogden's (1997) terms, aliveness or humanness. Perhaps the relationship between subject and being is as follows: the subject must own a sense of responsibility for its being—for being itself—and must never veer from maintaining the importance of its being.

Heidegger (1927), in his emphasis on the meaning of being, put it this way: "I not only exist, I exist meaningfully" (p. 193). He associated values with dimensions of being. Values are subjective, whereas Truth is objective. Heidegger united them. Thus, values give truth to subjectivity and subjectivity to Truth. He stated that "fundamental ontology" must precede all distinctions between fact and value; thus, the factor of subjectivity is primary. In other words, being, meaning, existence, and subjectivity are all a priori concepts. To the concept of meaning I should like to add that of *mattering*, which I deem to be more subjective and personal. In other words, our being *matters* to us, and therefore has *meaning*.

SUBJECTIVITY AND AGENCY

The concept of agency presents a paradox.[2] Consider the example of learning to drive in a special automobile that has two operating steering wheels. The subject steers one wheel, and Fate/God/Ananke (Necessity) steers the other.

The paradox of human agency is reflected in the Hebrew *midrash*, from which the following statements are taken: "One is the agent of action but not the origin of action." "Do not give up acting but give up the fruits of action. Creation is God's—one is acting something that has already been decided."

This passage reminds me of von Kleist's (1810) concept of the pure, passive grace that characterizes the movement of a marionette, which is both immobile and captivating to the puppeteer. As in the relationship between the hypnotist and his subject, each seems to control the other, one passively and the other seemingly actively. From the *midrash* we derive the idea of agent as representative of action originating elsewhere (i.e., in the sense of a talent agency representing a client). As I proceed, I hope to show that there is a distinction between the ineffable subject as essence of being—and as agent or architect of its development. Yet at the same time, they can be considered as two varying phases of its holographic unity.

CONSTRUCTS OF SUBJECTIVITY IN PSYCHOLOGY

Subjectivity in Early Psychoanalytic Theories

That the notion of subjectivity is not explicated in the works of orthodox, classical, Kleinian, object-relational, or interpersonal contributors owes much to a *Zeitgeist* that was seemingly dominated by a positivistic, deterministic propensity with which the leaders of psychoanalysis, beginning with Freud, were preoccupied in their efforts to establish a scientific foundation for psychoanalysis and thus achieve credibility and acceptance by a skeptical and cynical nonanalytic environment. Thus, early psychoanalysts gave us what Heidegger (1962) referred to as an ontic (materialistically scientific) reading of human motivation, as compared with an ontological (existential, where the question of one's being

2. The Aristotelian concept of *entelechy* comes close to the meaning of agency. Aristotle spoke of *entelechy* as the condition of a thing whose essence is fully *realized*. In other philosophies it has been thought of as a vital force that directs an organism toward self-fulfillment.

matters) reading. The validation of the connections between psychoanalysis and epistemology, philosophy, linguistics, and ontology, among other disciplines, had to await another age, which is now arriving.

The idea of the subject seems in retrospect to have been implied in Freud's (1905b) theory of infantile sexuality, the function of the libidinal drives, and the action of cathexis. One also sees a prefiguration of the psychoanalytic subject in the works of Melanie Klein when she focused on the clinical construct of the "infant of analysis," the model of a virtual infant in the analysand's unconscious, which reveals mental pain to the analyst during free association. Furthermore, the concept of the subject is implicit in Klein's (1940) conception of the depressive position, in which infants begin to replace their narcissistic image of the object in favor of one emphasizing mother's separateness, wholeness, and uniqueness. And when Klein (1955) discussed the use of projective identification by the protagonist in Green's (1947) novel *If I Were You . . .*, she clearly noted, as did the author himself, that the protagonist became progressively further removed from himself with each new proxy use of another's life; indeed, he behaved as if he were demoniacally possessed, Klein and Green both observed.

One model of subjectivity and its relationship to agency comes to us from Tausk (1919) and his study of the origins of the notion of an "influencing machine" in schizophrenics. In the final form of the illness, patients experience a sense of transitivism, in which they feel totally passive and *subject* to the control of a seemingly externalized (projected) influencing machine, which originally constituted their own mind and body organs. In their deteriorated disembodiment, in other words, they regressively recapitulate the origins of their assumption of their being. Tausk believed that an infant is born as a psyche that has the task of discovering its putatively alien body and then owning it (both of which it accomplishes by way of "identification through projection" followed by "introjection"), following which it claims it. Before it claims it, however, the body and its parts are like marionettes to the psyche (see von Kleist, 1810), which it manipulates as strange effigies, a phenomenon that returns in reverse in the final stages of an untreated schizophrenic psychosis.

Subjectivity in Contemporary Psychology

Piaget's Concept of Subjectivity Piaget (1968) differentiated between the *individual subject* and the *epistemic subject* (a differentiation that is the provenance of Lacan's concept of subjectivity):[3]

3. I am indebted to Polly Young-Eisendrath for supplying me with the reference to Piaget on subjectivity.

> Structuralism calls for a differentiation between the *individual subject*, who does not enter at all, and the *epistemic subject*, that cognitive nucleus which is common to all subjects at the same level. . . . Now after such precipitation of the "me," the "lived," from the "I," there remains the subject's "operations," that which he "draws out" from the general coordinations of his acts by reflective abstraction. And it is these operations which constitute the elements of the structures he employs in his ongoing intellectual activity.
>
> It might seem that the foregoing account makes the *subject* disappear to leave only the "impersonal and general," but this is to forget that on the plane of knowledge . . . the subject's activity calls for a continual "de-centering" [splitting] without which he cannot become free from his spontaneous intellectual egocentricity. This "decentering" makes the subject enter upon, not so much an already available and therefore external universality, as an uninterrupted process of coordinating and setting in reciprocal relations. . . . The *subject* cannot, therefore, be the *a priori* underpinning of a finished posterior structure; rather, it is a center of activity. And whether we substitute "society" or "mankind" or "life" or even "cosmos" for "subject," the argument remains the same [pp. 141–142].

The Contributions of Infant Development Research Infant development research has also addressed the issues of agency and subjectivity. Stern (1985, 1989), for example, has suggested that, as infants develop from an emerging self into a core self, they acquire a *sense of agency* as the felt originator of their motivations.[4] Trevarthen (1979, 1980, 1987, 1988, 1991) has posited a *sense of intersubjectivity*, through which infants acquire a sense not only of their own subjective being but also of mother's subjectivity. Baron-Cohen (1995) has written about the infant's acquisition of a *sense of mindedness* (self-reflection), as compared with "mind blindness" in oneself and others, and Fonagy and colleagues (1991) have discussed the *capacity for self-reflection* (i.e, the capacity to recognize one's own sense of mindedness) as well as the capacity to recognize that others have independent minds that need to be interpreted. All such contributions have anticipated the "subjective revolution"

4. Lacan (1953–1954) distinguished between the ego's capacity to be an agent, on one hand, and the Subject in and of the Unconscious on the other, the former belonging to the Imaginary Order and the latter to the Symbolic Order.

(which includes an interest in the concepts of self-reflection and intersubjective reflection), or what Bollas (1989) called the *age of subject relations,* in postmodern psychoanalytic thinking.

Subjectivity in Contemporary Psychoanalysis

Among today's psychoanalysts, the concept of subjectivity arose seemingly independently of other disciplines as a legacy of the countertransference literature and ultimately devolved into the postmodern concept of intersubjectivity (Dunne, 1995; Gabbard, 1995). It is notable in the works, for instance, of Bollas (1989), who argued in favor of a "subject relations theory"; Kennedy (1996), who advocates the concept of "subjective organizations"; Borch-Jacobsen (1982, 1996), who has examined the concept of the subject from the perspective of mimesis; and Moran (1993), who integrates subjectivity and agency. Lacan (1966) and his followers have even sought to formalize the concept of subjectivity itself, especially that which is resident within the analysand, as the psychoanalytic subject "*of* and *in* the unconscious," that is, as the one who inhabits—and even haunts—the unconscious.

Subjectivity has also begun to surface in postmodern psychoanalysis as narcissism, in the analysand, and as countertransference, in the analyst. It is implicit in the new concept of intersubjectivity and has reached its apotheosis in Ogden's (1994a, 1997) concept of the "intersubjective third subject of analysis" (which I call the covenant), a concept that itself follows upon the earlier works of Jung (1966) and Tresan (1966), both of whom posited the notion of the subjective third in the transference situation.[5] Ogden's "analytic thirdness" is the dialectical chimera, as it were, of the intersubjective interaction of the analysand's and analyst's respective subjectivities; that is, the quality of subjectivity inheres not only in each of the two participants but also in the relationship itself. In other words, the interrelationship is itself a subject. I myself regard the subjugating subjective third subject as a twinship of

---

5. I am indebted to Arno Goudsmit, Nathan Schwartz-Salant, and John Beebe for these references. I use the term *covenant* to enlarge upon Ogden's important formulation of the "analytic third subject" so as to convey the fact that every relationship, whether between two or more individuals or between internal subjective objects, is always characterized by an implied and unconsciously mutually accepted agreement as to the rules of engagement. I originally came across this finding in the work of Opie and Opie (1959), who found that the latency-age schoolchildren they studied needed no referees or applied rules for their playing together. They made up their own rules and stuck to them. Klein's unconscious infant of analysis can also be thought of as a "third subject."

subjectivities in which that of that of the analysand normally predominates over the subjectivity of the analyst so that the former can direct the analytic play, as it were, since only the analysand's subjectivity knows where the body is buried, so to speak.

The "subjugating intersubjective third subject of analysis" owes its origin and operation, in my opinion, to the following considerations. Among the infant's attachment repertoire in attempting to seek it's mother's bonding with it is its capacity for *appeal*, which depends on the success of the projective transidentification[6] of its plaintive condition to its mother. A more forceful variety of appeal appears in the mechanism that Klein (1946) termed *magic omnipotent denial*, which has to do with the infant's unconscious phantasy that, through anal masturbation, it invades mother's body from the rear and takes possession of the mother, her breasts, or both. This unconscious phantasy resembles the actions of the hypnotist, the puppeteer, or the ventriloquist insofar as one person seeks to possess and manipulate the actions of another who is under his thrall. When the other person enters into an actual hypnotic thralldom (mimesis, folie à deux, collusion) with the dominating or subjugating one (considered to be the incubus or the succubus in medieval times), perhaps the inroad into the vulnerability of the subjugated one lies either in the latter's (1) own unconscious desires and urges to be dominated, taken care of, or "analyzed" by his analysand, or (2) in the analyst's superego itself, which may be all too eager to collude with another, external critic to enclose the analyst within its guilt-producing, persecutory pincers. In other words, when anyone criticizes us, it is as if the game is two against one, or really two against none if we give over our "power of attorney" to the critical ensemble. In chapters 8 and 9, I hint at this potential guilt in the analyst as a proxy guilt. There also may be a third vulnerability in the analyst that allows him to become subjugated. That vulnerability is the analyst's unconscious and conscious desire to facilitate the progression (not just the progress) of the analysis. Projective transidentification can also be understood as the hypnosis or folie à deux (mimesis).

An interesting perspective on subjectivity was stated by R. Pinheiro (1996, personal communication):

> By opening up the gap or space between my image and myself, such that I realize I am, not my image, I can begin to dis-identify from images, from narcissism, and in this way my self as

---

6. Projective transidentification is the term I (Grotstein, 1999c, d) suggest for those aspects of projective identification that seem to have an interpersonal or intersubjective impact. I use it to distinguish it from projective identification proper, which to me is strictly an intrapsychic phantasy.

> "subject" may emerge. . . . The self as "subject" lives through negation of the self as image. . . . Although we suffer from "castration"—the "cut" that makes a "hole" or "gap" between subject and object (or subject and image)—such "castration" at the same time liberates us from narcissistic capture by the image [via e-mail].

Benjamin (1995), in a thoughtful review of subjectivity, stated:

> The term subject . . . refers to . . . a locus of experience, one that need not be centrally organized, coherent, or unified. Yet it can still allow continuity and awareness of different states of mind, can still feel more or less alive, can be more or less capable of recognizing or feeling the impact of the other. . . . Psychoanalysis has to retain some notion of the subject as a self, a historical being that preserves its history in the unconscious. . . . Even if the subject's positions are "constructed," psychoanalysis must imagine someone who does or does not own them. . . . And precisely because psychoanalysis claims that something else that is not-I (not ego but It) speaks, that the self is split and the unconscious is unknown, It must also be considered to belong to the self. And this idea of an otherness within, an unconscious, unavoidably both transforms and preserves . . . the idea of a transhistorical, essential self: not a Cartesian ego, not even all ego, but still a being separately embodied, and in that sense an individual psyche [pp. 12–13].

I am in total agreement here with Benjamin.

Subjectivity and Agency

Subjectivity and agency have lain concealed behind their more modern counterparts psychic determinism and the functions of the id, ego, and superego. (In olden days, such ideas as entelechy—or, later, conation—connoted the idea of motivation, or agency.) Lacan (1966) referred to a sense of agency, however, and assigned it to the ego, differentiating it from the sense of the psychoanalytic subject of and in the unconscious and the concept of desire. The concept of personal agency has been recently formalized in infant development research by Stern (1985, 1989), Trevarthen (1979, 1980, 1988), and others. Moran (1993) explores the relationship between the subject and the concept of agency in psychoanalytic writings and picturesquely points out that the id seems to have been portrayed in psychoanalysis as a homunculus. Her ideas on this subject are pivotal:

> *Subject* refers specifically to the one who speaks to the analyst, and the term *agency* to the notion of the determination or control of thoughts, words, and actions. . . . In his work Freud lost sight of the importance of the issues of subject and of agency and consequently ultimately proposed a topography of the mind unattached to any subject. . . . Freud imputed agency to the apparatus. Thus he located the concept of agency apart or separated from the concept of the subject within the psychoanalytic framework of thought that he developed [pp. 4–5].

Moran identifies "a crucial problem that consistently blights Freudian theory: namely, the confusion surrounding Freud's theoretical presuppositions regarding the nature of human agency. . . . For example, who wills defense?[7] Is it the ego, the subject, or is the ego synonymous with the subject?" (p. 21). She suggests that there is a discontinuity between the nature and functions of the subject and of agency and that they can be reconciled by the concept of "structuration," by which she means that there is a mysterious overlap between subject and agency in which one cannot tell whether a phenomenon originates in one or the other.

Westen (1997) has recently proposed a revision of Freud's theory of motivation by relegating the hegemony of motivation to the affects, a revision that is in keeping with the concepts of Bowlby, Sandler, Kernberg, Lichtenberg, and others:

> The model presented here . . . views feelings as the instigators of motivated behavior, whether those feelings stem from activated drive states (as in the subjective experience of hunger, or the subjective state of sexual arousal) or a history of learned associations between representations and emotional states. Human motives reflect the interaction of a brain tuned to certain affective frequencies and an environment, including a cultural environment, that affords a spectrum of experiences with potential motivational significance [p. 529].

Westen's revision of the psychoanalytic theory of motivation finds its apotheosis in Lichtenberg's (1989, 1992) theory of motivational systems.

---

7. Here Moran is referring to one of the great conundrums in Freud's theory—that of the source of agency in "counter-will."

I conclude from my reading of Westen and Lichtenberg that the concept of agency or intentionality is virtually isomorphic with affects.

Meissner (1993, 1996) rigorously assigns agency to the unconscious and subjectivity to consciousness. He is equally rigorous in questioning the current use of the term *intersubjective*; he prefers *interpersonal* instead. His belief is that individuals can observe neither their own subjectivity (only their self-as-object) nor the subjectivity of the other, which also is only an object to the observing subject.

According to Ogden's (1994a, 1997) theory of thirdness, relationships between people are mysteriously controlled by a third, intangible relationship, a haunting subjectivity that eerily controls and mediates the felt experiences and motivations of both parties without either being certain of the true origin of motivation or experience. We are determined even as we believe that *we* determine. Similarly, Lacan (1966) said that the ego speaks and does not know that it is spoken-by the Other through it. But Stern (1985), Moran (1993), and others use *agent* in the sense of the originator of action. Thus, we see that the term agent is controversial!

Much of the difficulty in arriving at the concept of a psychoanalytic subject and a sense of agency for the self may be due to a confusion in psychoanalytic theory between the use of Freud's topographic model (1915b) and his structural model (1923a), a confusion that Gray (1982) and Busch (1996) cogently addressed. Rangell (1969, 1971, 1990) anticipated the need for a psychoanalytic concept of the subject and agent by ably integrating Freud's two models in his concept of the "decision-making function of the ego," a function that has roots in the conscious, preconscious, and unconscious aspects of the ego. Furthermore, Moran (1993) has pointed out that Freud (1894) hinted at the concept of agency in his notion of the "anti-will," the resistance.

I believe that Rangell's concept of the decision-making function of a multifaceted ego paves the way for a fundamental reconsideration of the psychoanalytic conception of the unconscious. One such reconsideration is found in the work of Matte-Blanco (1975, 1988; see also chapter 3). If we were to place Rangell's and Matte-Blanco's ideas together, we might arrive at a hypothesis that would unite the topographical and structural models. For example, we might conjecture that the ego and the id are constantly conjoined alter egos (combined dialectical structures) of one another along the gradient of the Cs.-Pcs.-Ucs. axis.

Thus, the polarity of primary process versus secondary process would be replaced by a progressive series of changing ratios between the symmetrical and the asymmetrical modes of thinking throughout (see chapter 3). The contrast between bound and unbound cathexes may also have to be modified from their polar opposition to the concept of a gradient. One of the derivative ideas of this theme is that one can no longer think of the id or ego in isolation from one another (or, for that matter, from the ego ideal and the superego). Indeed, one can imagine that the Ucs.-Pcs.-Cs. gradient contains "structures" consisting of each of them in varying valence ratios. I expand on this idea later in this chapter, when I propose a revised conceptualization of the unconscious.

Subjectivity, Decision-Making, and the Sense of Psychic Responsibility

In Freudian theory, a sense of subjectivity seems to have been attributed generally to the ego, especially because of its identifiable personal tangibility. Unconscious intentionality was attributed to the id and its drives, but it was usually pictured as impersonal as well as unruly, peremptory, primitive, and chaotic. Further, when Freud (1915b) stated that the unconscious lacks structure, I think analysts assumed that it also lacks "personality." Yet the unconscious (the id) is also the locale of the creation of dreams—while we (the ego) sleep. What appears consequently to be primitive and chaotic from one viewpoint may be, paradoxically, sophisticated beyond our ken. I think that Lacan's (1966) concept of the "decentering of the subject" addresses this paradox.

It seems that every component of the Freudian psychic apparatus—the ego, id, and superego (and ego ideal)—can be conceived of as being "cyclopean" (having one perceptual field), that is, as an incomplete entity that must seek the verdict of the other subjectivities internally and objects externally in order to express, fulfill, and inform itself. Bion (1962b, 1963, 1970, 1992) suggested as much in his concept of "common sense" and the "consultations" with other faculties that are required to achieve a consensus. Thus, the subject *in* and *of* the unconscious (Lacan's, 1966, phrase) may be thought of as blind, like Tiresias, the seer in *Oedipus Tyrannus*; the ego, for its part, is incomplete without the subjective ratification and notarization of the unconscious. The superego, like the judge in Genet's *Balcony*, is sent into anonymity and desuetude if there is no potential criminal to judge.

I believe that each aspect of the mind is a component of an overall, collective sense of subjectivity, which holographically expresses our sense of being (*Dasein*). Whereas the passive aspect of the subject inheres in its "beingness," the active aspect of the subject consists of the sense of psychic responsibility (Rangell, 1990) and agency, collectively and individually, in every aspect of the self in terms of intentionality, decision-making, and responsibility. This division between passive and active aspects of the sense of subjectivity is suggested in Winnicott's (1963b) original concept of the "being," as contrasted with the "doing," infant.

The Psychoanalytic Object New concepts of subjectivity underlie our contemporary views of the analysand and the analytic situation itself, leading us to ask, "What is it that we psychoanalysts analyze?" I believe there is a universal phantasy that we each have a person within us, a homunculus nested (like a Russian doll) within us; in postmodern terminology such an entity might be called a "virtual self," or one who exists in our phantasy. It has been intuited by writers, especially in the 19th century, as the alter ego or "second self." In Edgar Allen Poe's (1845) "The Story of William Wilson," the second self is a mysterious guardian angel. The protagonist in Oscar Wilde's (1890) novel *The Picture of Dorian Gray* outwardly remains impervious to aging while his hidden portrait reveals not only his aging but the degeneracy that his character is undergoing over time. Thus, the subject, the inner person, may be understood as a barometer of our inner affective and ontological authenticity. It designates the ongoing experience of a self-reflective, feeling being.

In his papers on technique, Freud (1912) advised analysts to obtain an analysis for themselves. His rationale for this recommendation was directed less toward their psychopathology than toward convincing them that there really is such an entity as the unconscious. I think we still share Freud's wonderment about the presence within us of this paradoxical (strange yet familiar) self, "the Stranger within Thee" (Edward Young, 1759, cited in Cox, 1980), the one we have learned about in our own analysis and elsewhere. "Where id was, there shall ego be," said Freud (1933, p. 80), but must the id truly yield to the ego? Moreover, why does the id not have a more personal name than "it"? I am suggesting that the id is really the alter ego and that it expresses itself to us subjectively as the Ineffable Subject of Being.

Groddeck (1923), who, along with Nietzsche (1883), introduced the idea of *das Es* as the mainstay of the personality, wrote, "If we like, we can think of life as a masquerade at which we don a disguise, perhaps many different disguises, at which nevertheless we retain our proper characters, remaining ourselves amidst the other revelers in spite of our disguise, and from which we depart exactly as we were when we came" (p. 18). The unconscious, whether considered topographically or structurally, constitutes a personal isomorphic subjective structure. It is an ineffable construct whose modulus of elasticity allows for transformative changes—but only within the limitations inherent to its basic character or nature. This subjective structure is self-defining; it therefore self-organizingly personalizes and subjectivizes all experiences. It remains loyal to its basic code of uniqueness.

We psychoanalysts seem to follow Plato's metaphor of the cave by intuiting the subjectivity within our analysands by the shadow that the mystical fire behind them casts on the wall of the cave. Knowing (learning about) ourselves is the positivistic/deterministic goal of ontic psychoanalysis. Bion (1965, 1970, 1992), on the other hand, believed that the goal of psychoanalysis is being able to resonate with (be in touch with) our inner sense of O (which I understand to be our inner sense of authenticity, or subjective I-ness), that is, with the subject in and of the unconscious (Lacan, 1966), with the authentic subject of undisguised experience, the natural progenitor of the true ("being") self (Winnicott, 1960a, 1963b). Ogden (1994) has proposed the "intersubjective subjugating third subject of analysis" (or, for short, the "subjugating third subjectivity," or "the subjugating third"), which is formed by the mutual unconscious projective identifications of the analysand and analyst, each having projected his own subjective elements into the third area (potential space), including subjectivity (being-ness, personification), omnipotence, intentionality, and agency. This new invisible entity is felt by its creators to have taken on a life of its own, one that omnipotently directs and controls each of them; they are therefore unwitting "ventriloquists" for this mythic, preternatural homunculus.

Jung's (1966), Tresan's (1966), and Ogden's (1994a, 1997) concept of the subjective thirdness of the analytic transference–countertransference relationship corresponds to a standard Kleinian technique, namely, that of attempting to locate the "analytic infant"—a virtual infant, as it were—who constitutes the true subject of analysis. Bion (1963), for his part, while also dealing with the analytic subject (but not by that term), believed in the necessity of studying not only the "psycho-analytic object" but also "psycho-analytic elements":

> Psycho-analytic elements and the objects derived from them have the following dimensions:
>
> 1. Extension in the domain of sense.
> 2. Extension in the domain of myth.
> 3. Extension in the domain of passion.
>
> An interpretation cannot be regarded as satisfactory unless it illuminates a psycho-analytic object and that object must at the time of interpretation possess these dimensions [p. 11].

By psychoanalytic object I understand Bion to mean the unconscious theme that the analysand maximally presents for understanding and interpretation. Using my own terminology, I would say that the analysand's Ineffable Subject speaks to his Phenomenal Subject, who feels—through sense (noticing), myth (unconscious phantasy), and passion (caring)—reflexively through the analyst/container. The content of the message constitutes the analytic object. That is, the analytic object becomes the ongoing theme which the "subjugating third subject," who can otherwise be thought of as the dramaturge or choreographer of the passion play of the analysis, presents to both analysand and analyst for them to play out, to understand, and to interpret.[8] To me, the "subjugating third subject" predicates the presence of a quasi-sublimated directorial aspect of the patient (which originates through the use of projective transidentification and magic, omnipotent denial [Klein, 1946], who constitutes the subjective director of the analysis.[9] The analyst's counteridentification occurs in his role as container (Bion, 1962b), in the form of empathy, reverie, intuition, and "dream-work alpha." In this role, the analyst shares the analysand's pain-as-analytic-object by "day-dreaming" the analysand; that is, the analyst takes the analysand into his preconscious, where the pain is deciphered through the use of sense, myth, passion, and intuition.[10]

Lacan (1966) was perhaps the first to bring the importance of the psychoanalytic subject to our attention in his epochal "rereading of Freud." His conception of the "subject *in* and *of* the unconscious" has become a highly evocative idea in its own right. He also posed a radical revision of the psychoanalytic concept of the unconscious. In brief, he posited that the unconscious, rather than being inherent and self-emerging as in Freud's (1915b) conception, is instead automatic, linguistic, external (cultural), interpersonal, decentered (from the self), and constitutive of the Other,[11] the ego's twin. It is structured as a language

---

8. The analysand being dramaturge or choreographer, his or her portion of the "subjugating third subject," constitutes a subset of the Gnostic Demiurge, the preternatural force or deity within. Its nom de plume is the Dreamer Who Dreams the Dream (see chapter 1).

9. Projective transidentification is my recently proposed term to designate those aspects of projective identification that *seem* to be interpersonal, as distinguished from projective identification proper, which to me is basically an intrapsychic phenomenon (Grotstein, in preparation-a).

10. Parenthetically, the analyst's counteridentification, as just described, is a *trial*, or *partial*, identification; a total identification is abnormal. The kinds of counteridentifications are (1) concordant, (2) complementary, and (3) oppositional. The first two of these counteridentifications have been proposed by Racker (1953, 1957, 1968) and the third by me (Grotstein, 1995a).

11. Lacan's (1966) use of the terms "Other" and "other" may be confusing to the reader. My own understanding is that the Other is the decentered (from the ego) subject of the unconscious but also designates the quality of Otherness of the other. When the infant is born, according to Lacan, it believes that it has lost, not the object, but a part of itself, which it later confuses with the object,

and speaks through the ego as its veritable channel to the interpersonal other. Indeed, Lacan (1966) went so far as to say that the unconscious *is* language. The subject in and of the unconscious, on the other hand, is that which one signifier represents to another signifier.

Put briefly, the Lacanian subject is a transient evanescence that appears in the interstices of chains of signifiers as language is evoked by desire and in the resultant establishment of meaning the subject disappears. The Lacanian subject has a very short half-life, and in the brief moment in which it appears it experiences a lack, which nominally is the other and ultimately is the other's desire. It is not to be confused with *being* or "I" or self. It is as if the subject, for Lacan, were a device that language requires to become spoken or thoughts require to be thought, after which it disappears by "slipping under the signifier." Lacan also emphasized the essential fragmentation of the self and proclaimed that each aspect of the personality emerges and remains incomplete (each is characterized by a lack and thus is "subjected" to a desire for its respective other). Consequently, the ego, superego, and the unconscious all remain incomplete over a lifetime and rely on others (internal objects) within the self as well as the Other within the self (the unconscious) and other objects that are external to the self for survival.

Moreover, the Ineffable Subject needs to empower the Phenomenal Subject as its agent/procurer so that it can comb the landscape of external reality for objects of experience that can conveniently lend themselves as displacement signifiers to correspond as "stand-ins" for noumena (beta elements) that have become activated in the forge of the unconscious by the Ineffable Subject.

Explicit in Lacan's considerations of the subject is that while it is in and of the unconscious, it plays no part in System Cs. topographically or in the ego structurally, the latter of which he considers to be the subject's "false self'" and its "symptom" (Lacan, 1966; Weber, 1990; Boothby, 1991; Fink, 1995). According to Fink's interpretation of Lacanian theory:

> The subject is conceptualized [by Lacan] as a stance adopted with respect to the other's desire (the mother's, etc.), insofar as that desire arouses the subject's desire, that is, functions as object a [autre].[12] The subject comes into being as a form of attraction

---

the other. Once the infant descends into the symbolic order of language in the name of the father, it becomes aware of its cut-offness from its own Other (the intersubjective origin of language in its own unconscious and from the Otherness of the other, the objects toward whom it experiences desire.

12. I conceptualize the origin of infants' perceptions of the other's desire as being due in part to their projective identificatory attribution of their own

> toward and defense against a primordial, overwhelming experience of what the French call *jouissance:* a pleasure that is excessive, leading to a sense of being overwhelmed or disgusted, yet simultaneously providing a sense of fascination. . . . Subjectivization—making the alien jouissance one's own. "One takes the causal alterity upon oneself, subjectifying what had previously been experienced as an external, extraneous cause, a foreign roll of the dice at the beginning of one's universe: destiny" [Fink quoting Lacan]. . . . Thus, Lacan's version of *Wo es war, soll Ich werden* is that "I am caused by another but must assume my own sense of agency as an 'I' who is and who shall be. I must own my destiny" [p. xii].

Lacan's version of the psychoanalytic subject appears to be linguistic—or, more precisely, semiotic—in derivation, since it emerges only as the infant encounters language. Although Lacanian theory seems to differentiate between subject and being (which I equate), it seems to equate the subject with a sense of agency insofar as the sense of subjectivity is seen to emerge as soon as *jouissance* (the instinctual drives) is encountered. At first the drives and the whole content of the id is "Other" to the developing being, who then must claim its decentered self as his own, that is, must subjectivize his experience—from within as well as from without—in terms of being made a subject (of desire) by the other (the other's desire for his desire, in the Hegelian sense).

Lacan's conception of the subject has a lot in common with Piaget's (1968) notion of the epistemic subject, which is that aspect of the infant self which can avail itself not only of its inherent capacity to acquire information as sensorimotor schemata but also of its ability to assimilate and accommodate to data from the external world. The following explanation of Lacan's concept of the subject is from Evans (1996):

> The fact that the symbol of the subject, S, is a homophone of Freud's term *Es* (see Id) illustrates for Lacan the true subject is the subject of the unconscious. In 1957 Lacan strikes through this symbol to produce the symbol $, the "barred subject," thus illustrating the fact that the subject is essentially divided [p. 196].

I gather from this citation that Lacan identified the subject (ultimately) with the id, that he both united and disunited the subject of the

---

desire into the object, a factor that also plays a significant role in the consequences of the mirror phase.

unconscious with the subject in the ego, and that he ultimately assigned subjectivity to the id and agency to the ego.

PROPOSAL FOR A REVISED PSYCHOANALYTIC CONSTRUCT OF SUBJECTIVITY

Redefining Subjectivity

I find the definition of the word subject vague and elusive no matter where it is used—whether in ancient philosophy, modern philosophical studies, or current psychoanalytic discourse (either as *subject* itself or in the term *intersubjectivity*). Heidegger (1927), for instance, distinguished between the concepts of "being" (*Dasein*) and "subject," but I am not really sure how he differentiated them. For me, one of the clearest definitions is that of Matte-Blanco,[13] who believed (1) that subjectivity emerges when the mind becomes aware of itself in the act of perceiving and responding to an object and (2) that errors by the self are the markers that reveal the presence of the subject, whose subjectivity is predicated on patterns of asymmetrical thinking within the organization of symmetrical thinking. Although Bion never addressed the concept of the subject formally, Matte-Blanco's idea clearly expresses Bion's notion of subjectivity as it is used in his concepts of reverie, intuition, and the abandonment of memory and desire (which Bion deemed necessary for one to listen to oneself listening to the other).

I believe that the psychoanalytic concept of the subject is inclusive of the whole personality and of its putative component selves. Following Tausk (1919) and Federn (1952), I believe that the infant is born as a yet-to-be-embodied psyche, which soon enough becomes confronted with the intrusive neediness and demandingness of its "psyche-soma" as well as with the intrusive vicissitudes of the object world. As soon as the psyche accepts its sense of obligation or covenant to live its life (i.e., accepts responsibility for its subjectivity), it is born as a "subject of being." That is, it accepts its lot of being subject to Ananke (Necessity), which one can think of as Freud's (1933) concept of chaos (inclusive of the drives), Bion's (1962b, 1963) concept of "nameless dread,"[14] and Matte-Blanco's (1975, 1988) conception of the unconscious as infinite sets.

The following is my own definition of subjectivity, one that goes back to basics. The derivation of the word subject, from the Latin mean-

13. I am grateful to Carole Morgan for this reference to Matte-Blanco.

14. Bion's "nameless dread" includes minus K (–K), beta elements, inherent preconceptions, the "deep and formless infinite," and O.

ing thrown under, expresses the quintessence of experiencing oneself in the ontological act of experiencing (i.e., experiencing oneself experiencing). *Experience* here is best conceived as a reflexive verb, as in (to paraphrase Descartes) "I experience, therefore I am!" By agreeing to experience the event-object confronting me as "object," I, the subject, sample and prepare for the strange new event-object by anticipating its nature with inherent a priori categories (Kant, 1787) that I have at my subjective disposal. That is, I autochthonously "create" it (see chapter 2) in order to make it familiar (native) so that I can counter and countenance its strangeness. In so doing, my "I" has transcendentally (Kant, 1787) transformed a perception into a subjectivized apperception, which is later objectified as a symbol. (Bion, 1962b, would say that I have submitted the event-object [beta element] to alpha function.)

In this formulation, then, the subject comes into being when it experiences a lack, a lack that originates at birth when fetal completeness and perfection are shattered by the act of birth and the newborn is "thrown under" (into) the breach of experience and engaged to the death (i.e., for a lifetime) with the minions of the Real (with infinity, chaos, Ananke, beta elements, noumena, things-in-themselves, O). These minions of the Real conflate with the newborn subject's experience of "need" to become "demand," as the primordial subject accepts and claims its needs as its own. These needs qua demands become *desire*, and forever after the subject will be defined by its desire, by its lack, which once was the "other" (the other aspect of its erstwhile perfect self) that became separated from it. (The subject may very well be what Freud the hermeneutician, not the determinist, had in mind when he conceived of libido theory and cathexis, if we consider that these concepts include such subjective or personal features as caring, mattering, and meaningfulness and therefore define the subject by his desire and by his hate.) The rent-asunder other, who is always confused with the object, is indistinguishable from and responsible for being the object of desire, which fact distinguishes the subject as the one who experiences because he desires the object in order to complete a lack and thereby restore his erstwhile perfection. I have already posited that two subjectivities exist (as aspects of a Supraordinate Subject of Being and Agency): the Ineffable Subject and the Phenomenal Subject. What characterizes each of these subjectivities is an incompleteness that reminds each of its need for the other and for the external other.

Developmentally, the infant may be constituted as a subject from the very beginning as an emerging self (Stern, 1985, 1989) as it becomes "subjected" to the experience of being and needing. The infant thus comes into its "ontological own" as a subjective being at the very dawn of experiencing experience—before it becomes a subject of (subjected to) language in the latter part of the second year of life, according to Lacan (1966).[15] According to Trevarthen (1979, 1980, 1988), it enters into the experience of intersubjectivity, which begins about four months of age, the time that Klein (1940) assigned to the onset of the experience of the depressive position, Mahler (1968) to "hatching," LeCours (1975) to the beginning of myelination of the corpus callosum, and Winnicott (1971a) to the beginning of the capacity to play. I suggest that this pivotal developmental moment in the toddler's life may herald the onset of that subset of intersubjectivity which is now called "self-awareness" and "awareness of the mindedness of others" (Fonagy, 1991, 1995; Fonagy et al., 1991; Butterworth et al., 1991). In other words, the infant/toddler is no longer cyclopean in its world view. It now comprehends that mother is a subject in her own right and constitutes another, separate, autonomous world of subjectivity and objectivity. I suggest that this is the time when the infant/toddler becomes "aware of the importance of its being," to use a phrase from Heidegger (1927) and reconcilingly begins to accept its sense of being a subject, that is, subjected to Ananke, Necessity.

Since infants are born subjective in the sense of being subjected to the transitivistic (self-referential) experiences of inchoate neediness and chaos from within themselves and of uncertainty from outside, perhaps we can attribute a primal unconscious sense of subjectivity to newborns, who upon recognizing the vulnerability of their new-found sense of emerging subjectivity in turn impart subjectivity (personalness, humanness) to all their phantom creations by projective identificatory attribution and assignment. This possibility was suggested by Tausk (1919):

> The projection of one's own body may . . . be traced back to the developmental stage in which one's own body is the goal of the object finding. This must be the time when the infant is discovering his body, part by part, as the outer world, and is still groping for his hands and feet as if they were foreign objects . . . this object finding within's one's own organs, which can be regarded as parts of the outer world by projection, must be preceded by a stage of identification with a narcissistic libido position, and it is necessary to assume two successive stages of identification and projection. . . . I am, then, assuming the exis-

15. Perhaps Lacan postdates the dawn of subjectivity to the time of language acquisition because he seems to subscribe to the concept of primary narcissism, which predicates infantile at-one-ment with mother and thus no separate subjective life of its own. Klein early on did away with with primary narcissism as did infant developmentalists later (Stern, 1985).

> tence of these two successive phases of identification and projection in object finding and object choice within one's own body [pp. 72–73; italics added].

My reading of Tausk is as follows: infants first discover and then claim their body through projective identification, which constitutes owning a sense of agency for it and bequeathing extended personal subjectivity to it. (When infants dissociate and projectively reidentify split-off aspects of their painful being, then "renegade" or "rogue" subjects are set up in objects, which when internalized are experienced as "alien subjective objects." I elaborate on this idea in detail in chapter 6.)

Subjectivity not only dares to risk being the authentic sense organ for experience (i.e., for *being*) but becomes active by subjectivizing experiences as its own personal repertoire and finally links up with its sense of *agency* (intentionality, will, desire, conation, entelechy) to seek and to react to experience—all the while remaining true to its nature. Subjectivity in action can be seen in infants as they lick an object with their spittle—to make it their own personally (subjectively) experienced property—prior to attempting to swallow it.

Since our subjectivity is a function of our "agreeing" to experience ("throw ourselves under") whatever internal or external happenings come our way (as in an arcade game in which the road is experienced as coming toward the driver rather than the other way around) in order to claim and maintain our aliveness and humanness, it is always in a state of flux. We allow experiences to happen to us and also allow ourselves to be affected by them. As we defensively withdraw from experiencing our experiences, we forfeit the integrity of our subjectivity and, by inescapable default, our aliveness.

It is my belief that "world spirit"—that is, Hegel's (1807) *Geist*—appears to shrink (or to become decentered as the unconscious) as the infant accepts its self-in-the-world and becomes branded and claimed by personal and also social subjectivity. That is, one's own unique and idiosyncratic fingerprint or sign converts the universal into the personal. To become a subject, then, means to allow oneself to be subjected to life and to claim oneself out of the maw of the cosmic universal.

Thus, subjectivity emerges in every gap of our security with objects—from and before birth. It is the first experience of the rent in our feeling of seamlessness. The subject, in its overarching supraordination, is compositely "I." Self is its shadow and object. Identity is its administrator. Soul is its ancient name and its spiritual dimension. Entelechy is its vitality. The subject both passively experiences its being and actively initiates adventures in order to mediate the infinity (or chaos, nonlinear complexity, Real, O, Ananke) that confronts its lack.

The Holographic Subject

We unconsciously experience ourselves to be occupied by both an ineffable, preternatural subjective presence (I refrain from suggesting an omnipotent object)—what I call the Ineffable Subject—and its more tangible counterpart, the Phenomenal Subject, whose presence we regularly experience in the quotidian reaches of our daily life as the feeling and thinking self we claim to know, ultimately as our sense of being (our *Dasein*), or our self. The quintessence of subjectivity is the harmonious, complementary cooperation that transpires between these two (which is not to say that there are not a virtually infinite number of component subjectivities within us).

It is as if we as conscious subjects metaphorically sit on the lap of a more awesome subjectivity within and behind us, one that dreams our dreams (see chapter 1), originates our thoughts and feelings, and teleologically pursues and choreographs our lives (see chapter 2). Together, these two subjectivities, the interpersonal Phenomenal Subject and the private, awesome Ineffable Subject, are part of an overall supraordinate subjective organization or sense of I-ness (what I call the Supraordinate Subject of Being and Agency).[16]

I employ the terms ineffable and phenomenal to designate the deeper and the more surface subject, respectively. Yet even this distinction is misleading. I really imagine the subject to be a unitary, holographic entity that includes different *faces*—the ineffable face, the phenomenal face, and other (as yet undesignated) faces—of its existence on different plateaus of unconsciousness ↔ consciousness.

In short, I am arguing, following the lead of Matte-Blanco, that one cannot speak of the id ("it," "the Other I") without intimately including the ego (the realistic "I") in progressively varying conjoint proportions. That is, the id and the ego operate like progressively graduated conjoined twins: they are, paradoxically, separable and inseparable at the same time, in differing reciprocal proportions. This idea was hinted at but left undeveloped in Hartmann's (1954) concept of the undifferentiated matrix from which both id and ego develop. I suggest that the id and ego be conceptualized as mysteriously entwined together (and the same with the superego) by virtue of their inherent holographic nature. The question of unconscious versus conscious, or of id versus ego or superego, becomes moot when one imagines the mind in terms of a topographic gradient of varying structural combinations of ego and id. This gradient reflects an infinite stratification not only of combina-

---

16 I borrowed the terms private and interpersonal from Modell's (1993) cogent contribution on the self.

tions of "bi-logic" and bivalent thinking but also of subjectivity, agency, and being (see chapter 3). Thus, we can consider there to be a virtually unlimited number of discrete subjectivities, which at the same time are holographically unified.

In addition, by employing Matte-Blanco's concept of the dialectical (binary) structure of "bi-logic," I conjecture a counterposing of a holistic or ultimate sense of a subjectivity of being with an ultimately objective decision maker; between them is interposed a composite agent, composite connoting that it claims responsible agency for its unconscious motivation and seeks to integrate it with its known capacity for decision making (prioritization). In chapter 3, I typified this construction as the calipers of the Infinite Geometer, in which the data of subjectivity are dialectically poised between "bi-logic" and bivalent logic, that is, between the operation of the principles of symmetry and asymmetry (Grotstein, in preparation-a). Further, applying Ogden's new model of the "intersubjective third" in a way that he does not propose, I suggest that a third subjectivity can also exist intrapsychically as a bridge-covenant between the Ineffable and the Phenomenal Subjects. In short, they need each other.

Stern (1985) proposes that we divide self-experiences into a "social self," a "private self," and a "disavowed self" (p. 229). My concept of the Ineffable Subject would correspond to his private self, the Phenomenal Subject to his social self, and my concept of "rogue subjective objects" (see chapter 6) to his disavowed self, and to Winnicott's (1960a) "true self." My ideas are also compatible with Modell's (1993) distinction between the "private self" and the "social self," categories that derive from Winnicott's (1963b) private "being self" and his social "doing self." Modell (1993) stated the case exactly as I see it when he wrote, "The private self is . . . a paradoxical structure that frees one from dependency, yet requires the other for its continued existence" (p. 78), suggesting, following Winnicott (1958), that the capacity to be alone depends on the presence of the object, at first externally and later, internally.

My proposed model of holography—what I call the Supraordinate Subject of Agency and Being—combines several concepts from the works of others. I am applying Matte-Blanco's model of binary oppositions to the layering of this Supraordinate Subject. That is, I posit not only that the subject is holographically unitary but also that it is multilayered, from the phenomenal and tangible manifestations of its upper, conscious, reaches to deeper and deeper strata of varying ineffability in the unconscious. That is, the Supraordinate Subject includes a primary nonreflective (cyclopean) level, a primary (developed) reflective level, a dynamic personal (secondary) level, the various levels of the preconscious, and so on. To posit the existence of this supraordinate psychoanalytic subject that is both holographically holistic and at the same time separated into layers and dispersed multiple functions, I am also using Rangell's (1969, 1971, 1990) "decision-making function of the ego," which has roots in the unconscious, preconscious, and conscious topographies and Bion's (1965, 1970, 1992) alpha function and intuitionistic thinking. Mitchell (1997) has discussed this as the phenomenon of "multiple selves."

The Ineffable Subject may seem omnipotent and omniscient, but it is actually helpless and blind. It is like Hermes, who was cursed (because of his gossiping) and rendered speechless by Apollo, reduced to being a messenger; like Cassandra, who was cursed (for rejecting Apollo's advances) to have foresight but not credibility; and like Tiresias, who was cursed by Hera with blindness for stating that women enjoy intercourse more than men do. Characterized by the same handicaps—speechlessness, incomprehensibility, blindness—the unconscious subject requires the Phenomenal Subject, as its duly constituted partner, to express its opinions. At the same time, the Ineffable Subject, for its part, gives deeper and broader meaning and significance to what it receives from the Phenomenal Subject. The ancient Greek concept of the oracle seems to have prefigured the idea of the Ineffable Subject.

The cooperative functioning of the Ineffable Subject and the Phenomenal Subject may be coopted and sabotaged by rogue, or renegade, subjects (see chapter 6), which constitute internalized pathological organizations (Rosenfeld, 1987) or psychic retreats (Steiner, 1993). Our sense of being (and, by derivation, our sense of subjectivity) is compromised by an incompleteness that is due not only to the lack of fulfillment of our teleological destiny through maturation (Schou, 1997) but, more especially, to a lifetime of projective identification—a partial self-ostracism—by which one's subjectivity becomes progressively alienated from the original subject's putative design. In other words, the projecting subject becomes progressively deadened as the ostracized self is exiled and pathologically reorganized as strange yet familiar objects or demons, internally and externally ("rogue subjective objects"). From this perspective one can say, "The shadow of the subject falls upon the object," in contrast and complementary to Freud's (1914b) original statement.

A paradox in regard to the Ineffable Subject must be mentioned. One view of it might be that it has no function other than pure existence. Winnicott (1963b) seemed to suggest this notion of pure being when he posited the private "being infant" who relates to but does not communicate with ("because no communication is necessary," according to Winnicott) the holding-environment object. Here Winnicott shows the profundity of his mystical and ontological vision. He, the master of paradox, stumbled onto one of the profoundest of religious paradoxes: that of the conception of God as pure being as opposed to God as the active creator of the universe and of mankind. Plato was concerned with this issue and coined the term *Demiurge* for God the architectural creator in contrast to the God of pure Being. The Gnostics and mystics heretically thought of a differentiation between a God within and the Godhead beyond (Bion, 1970; Pagels, 1979; Fox, 1980, 1981a; Sells, 1994; Webb and Sells, 1995). And of the 10 sephirot (the emanations or powers by which the Creator was said to become manifest) in all the versions of the Kabbalah, the inner and most hidden one, Keter Ayn Sof, is pure Being (the others become progressively more imminent and revealed to mankind, by popular demand, as it were). Thus, even Jewish mystics, obsessed as they were with the doctrine of the *Shma* ("God is One"), felt the necessity to classify Him into 10 sephirot.

These reapportions of God closely apply to the mysterious nature of the subject, I believe. I say "closely" because, as I argue later, I believe that we have inferred God from the projective identification of our own unconscious in the form of our inner subject(s).[17] It is my impression that what I am calling the Ineffable Subject has at least two functions: (1) pure being and (2) ineffable or oracular communication and agency, as in dreams, free associations, parapraxes, jokes, and symptoms.

Redefining the Unconscious

Freud stated that the System Ucs. lacks consciousness. I take this to mean that it thereby lacks the capacity for self- reflection and is also deprived of the asymmetrical portions of bi-logic. If that is so, how does the System Ucs. "think" (as in dreams, symptoms, free associations, art, etc.)? That is, how does primary process process? In his topographic model Freud positioned System Ucs. as counterposed to System Cs. and then interposed System Pcs. between them, with the latter thus having two frontiers, one between each of the other systems. I believe that, while this tripartite structuring is valid, it is also misleading insofar as it pictures the three segments as equal partners in the sequence Ucs. ↔ Pcs. ↔ Cs. I picture System Pcs. as overlapping and interpenetrating Systems Ucs. and Cs., and I believe that System Pcs. is the true mediator (agent) that initiates and activates unconscious subjectivity (being), impulses,

17. If we use Ogden's (1994a) concept of "the subjugating third internal subjectivity," we can imagine two subjects interacting together, with the product of that interaction being a consummation of their subjectivities which acts synergistically (more than the sum of its parts) as a divine and awesome subjugating third Subject, "God."

affects, and thinking (the primary processes, "bi-logic") in the internal world and modulates stimuli arising in System *Cs.* from the outer world.

I have come to believe that System Ucs. is overvalued. A careful rereading of Freud (1915b) has persuaded me that System *Ucs.* is, by and large, inert within its own domain. It is, I believe, the extensive involvement of the lower region of System *Pcs.* that activates System *Ucs.* and releases its fateful cargo whereas the upper region of System Pcs. interacts extensively with System *Cs.* to help mediate the irruptions from the deeper chamber. It follows, consequently, that the Ineffable Subject would be the numen[18] that is situated at the System *Ucs.*-System *Pcs.* frontier and that the Phenomenal Subject would be located at the System Pcs.-System *Cs.* frontier. (We could just as easily think of the unconscious, topographically as well as structurally, as the `ultimate self," and the conscious and preconscious self as the "proximal self." What is critical, however, is to be able better to define the relationship between different subjective selves, all of which are paradoxically connected and yet seemingly disconnected.)

I believe that System *Ucs.* constitutes our inner unlived potential. Like the marionette (von Kleist, 1810), the idol, the doll, the toy, or the creation, the unconscious represents the unlived, the Ideal Form essences within us, the "life of the beautiful." The unconscious comprises the mythical, the Real, the transcendental (the computer's formatting code). It is the transcendental contribution to the "unrepressed unconscious" that is meant by Plato's Eternal (Ideal) Forms, Bion's inherent preconceptions, Kant's a priori categories, and Tomkins's (1978) inherent affects.[19] This is the substrate for the generation of meaning. As Modell (1993) put it, "Strictly speaking, psychic structures can never be personal; since they can never be experienced, they can only be said to generate experience" (p. 145). I am suggesting that what we call the dynamic unconscious is actually the result of activation of System *Ucs.* by System *Pcs.*, the "search engine" of the psyche.

The unconscious is transfinite. The beautiful essence is incapable of living in the actuality of experience. Thus, the dialectic here is one

18. The "numen" is the local deity of a place. Here it designates the agent or decision-maker.

19. From my researches into the work of Kant (1783), I have come to appreciate the difference between his use of "transcendentalism" and the "transcendent." The former designates the a priori categories with which human beings are natively equipped to anticipate and format the data of sensory experience. From that standpoint, psychoanalysis is a Kantian transcendental enterprise. "Transcendent," on the other hand, is characterized by "speculations that are unwarranted by logical reasoning;" which I take to mean either imagination, phantasy, intuition, or faith.

between essence and experience. The unconscious begins to breathe life when it is touched by the tendrils of System Pcs. and, in that luminous act, becomes the Ineffable Subject. This implies that the Ineffable Subject has a lack, is incomplete. It needs the object and its phenomenal subject (of raw experience), its other(s) in order to experience itself as a subject in its own right and to have its ineffable and inscrutable essence transduced into known and shared experience via the alpha function of the container (Bion, 1962b), which is both the object and the Phenomenal Subject. In other words, the registrar of caring and mattering, and thus of aliveness and humanness, is a composite of the Ineffable Subject and the Phenomenal Subject.

THE PSYCHOANALYTIC SUBJECT/OBJECT: CLINICAL CONSIDERATIONS

I view the analysand as a composite (Supraordinate) subject, that is, one whose subjectivity is both ineffable—as the subject of subjects, not unlike the Gnostic sense of the God within us (Pagels, 1979)—and phenomenal, as it becomes incarnate in the clinical situation, whether consciously or preconsciously. The Phenomenal Subject experiences and expresses the pain that is transduced to it by the Ineffable Subject, who initiates the inchoate cry as the silent martyr of agony (and joy). The Phenomenal Subject becomes the more conscious registrar of agony and experiences the not so silent symptomatic distress that finds its way into the patient's sense of emotional pain and is expressed in free associations and dreams. In its incompleteness as the voiceless initiator of distress signals, the Ineffable Subject needs the Phenomenal Subject, its registrar, who in turn is equally incomplete and must rely on a synchronicity with its ineffable counterpart.

It remains the unalterable aim of every psychoanalyst, no matter the persuasion, to "reach the patient," by which phrase it is generally assumed that the analyst wishes to reach that aspect of the patient whose inner reservoir of feelings is incompletely known to him or her, that lies hidden behind the defenses. The task of analysis, consequently, is to help the analysand achieve *aletheia* ("unconcealment"). It is my belief that the unconcealed self is the Supraordinate Subject of Being, which includes the Ineffable Subject and the Phenomenal Subject.

Perhaps we can say then, that the analytic quest is not so much for insight alone but for the patient to become freed up enough to risk unconcealment of the true self, that is, the self-conscious, pain-feeling, abject, ontological self, the one that the poultice of analysis is designed to draw to the surface.

I believe that the Ineffable Subject and the Phenomenal Subject demonstrate, in their roles as agents, a particular propensity whose uniqueness appears most dramatically yet subtly in psychoanalysis. Together they represent dramaturgy in the theater of the Real. Let me explain. Whereas the essence of Freud's theory of psychoanalysis is that of the irruption into consciousness of the drives from the unconscious, Lacan (1966) and other postmodernists after him conceived that the "motor" that drives psychoanalysis is information (Bowlby, 1969), signification (semiotics, as opposed to discharge), or communication. If we take communication as our basis, we may hypothesize that the Ineffable Subject is the ongoing generator of our experiences and of how we feel about them. The Ineffable Subject thereby becomes the dramaturge, the author/playwright of the analytic text; it seeks to dramatize—through pantomime, charadelike maneuvers, dreams, or symptoms—the quintessence of the emotional pain we may not fully recognize that we feel. The Phenomenal Subject becomes its ambassador-with-portfolio, its registrar of agony and joy, and its analytic representative at large. In other words, the Phenomenal Subject feels the pain of object encounter and relays it to the Ineffable Subject, who silently reworks it (dreams it), and retransmits it back to the Phenomenal Subject. In our clinical work we see the dramaturgical function of ad hoc component subjectivities that improvisationally (or so it seems, though this is not really the case) interact in order to dramatize the presentation of hidden traumatic situations and narratives to the analysand's consciousness. In other words,as analysts, we know the truth of Hamlet's words, "The play's the thing/ Wherein I'll catch the conscience of the king."

What the Ineffable Subject cannot adequately process, it represents to the Phenomenal Subject as the *analytic object* (Bion, 1965), that is, the symptom. This analytic object, the as-yet-unmentalized, uncompleted experience of emotional pain (Bion called the elements of such experience, variously, beta elements, things-in-themselves, or noumena, O) is the Ineffable Subject's nom de plume, its envoy. Because of the analysand's capacity to develop a transference neurosis, his Phenomenal Subject is able to receive and experience the unmentalized elements of experience and present them in turn to the analyst-as-container, who, through reverie, intuition, and wisdom, is able to transform them into useful knowledge (Bion's "K"). These are then returned to the Ineffable Subject, where they reenter the iterative, spiralling cycle of O so that the mythic stream of the unconscious can resume its eternal flow. One can hypothesize that psychopathology represents an incompletion in the iterative transformational cycle of $O \rightarrow K \rightarrow O$ and that one of our goals as psychoanalysts is to introduce our analysands to a self-reflection of, and repetitive contact with, their subject of being (rather than to enable them merely to understand themselves) so that with each recertification from this pilgrimage into a subjective solitude of being they emerge ever-more self-transcendent, that is, ever-more accepting of their being (*Dasein*), their subjectivity, their experiences, and their psychic responsibility for them. I believe this being "at one with the experience" is what Bion meant by "transformations in O." That, to me, is the quintessential goal of analysis.

A Kleinian analyst might define psychopathology as the unfinished transformation of internal (subjective) objects (paranoid-schizoid position) into symbolic whole-object representations (depressive position). To put it more simply, one might say that psychopathology means that we have oversubjectivized an experience (taken it too personally, so to speak) and have not been able to get past it. In Matte-Blanco's (1988) terms, we have taken it too symmetrically and not asymmetrically enough (we are not separate enough from it). It follows, then, that in psychopathology—especially when it is presented as the patient's sense of being victimized, persecuted, or manipulated by internal objects (superegos)—the internal objects are but the envoys of the Ineffable Subject, who—much like an oracle—seeks dramaturgically to pantomime the meaning of the pain in encoded terms for us first to experience and then to "translate." The Ineffable Subject continues pantomimically to present the analytic object (the unmentalized pain) until we "get it"!

I should like to posit that a considerable portion of the task of analysis is to decode *alienated subjectivities* (i.e., "rogue subjective objects" in the form of projectively identified internal objects; see chapter 6). I believe, first of all, that every person feels identified with his internalized objects and, second, that these internalized objects are compounded hybrids that always include split-off subjectivities from the original projecting subject (self). Thus, an internal object always consists of aspects of the subject as well as images of the external person as object. (Following an interpretation, an analysand wittily remarked, "Oh, I see. My superego is really myself in drag!") In other words, what are called internal objects are really "subjective objects" (Winnicott, 1967) or, when they are split off and projected or reintrojected instead, "rogue subjective objects" (or "rogue subjects," for short). These internal and external rogue subjects may become chronic enclaves of resistance; they acquire an existence of their own because of projective attribution, dissociation, and the acquisition of an independent sense of subjectivity, agency, and autonomy, an existence that remains extraterritorial to the original subjectivity of the projecting subject. I believe that these attributes characterize Rosenfeld's (1987) "pathological organizations" and Steiner's (1993) "psychic retreats."

In some cases these rogue subjects—actually, exiled stunted subjectivities—seem to perform a charadelike drama in which the patient's conscious ego is confronted, for instance, with persecutory, superego-like objects. That is, these alienated subjects of the original ego appear in disguise and dramatize *their* persecution to the ego that alienated and projected them into seeming oblivion. Now they return from the dark side of their exile and, like the Count of Monte Cristo, seek repatriation, vengeance, and recognition for their betrayal. It is as if the subject of analysis metamorphoses from its holographic unity into its constituents by transforming itself into each of the character-personages in this theater of the unconscious, with the result that, between each of the members of the endopsychic cast, a moment-to-moment transpires that in many ways resembles the serial of our daily life on the network of quotidian of reality.

The Patient's Quest

My interest in the concept of subjectivity arose simultaneously from my reading of the postmodern literature on this idea and from clinical material from patients. Patients themselves sometimes express their quest for unconcealment of their true subjectivity, that is, their desire to find and reunite with their true self (what I call the Supraordinate Subject of Agency and Being). For example, an elderly analysand who was contemplating his forthcoming death made the following comment: "I do not fear death. I only fear the pain that may usher it in. They say that our true nature is always unknown to us—until the very last moment of our lives, when the true self is really revealed in its totality and mystery. That experience may be worth the pain."

Another analysand, a middle-aged woman who had just become divorced, experienced her "subject-self" in another way. Relieved to be finally free of her uncaring husband, she remarked that she would miss the sexual intercourse, for it was when she climaxed that her inner self seemed to be released and momentarily rejoined with her. Her next association was to "visitation rights" in regard to her children, but I interpreted to her that sex itself was for her a "visitation rite"; I was thinking to myself that the meeting of one's true self must be what Heidegger (1962) meant by *aletheia* (unconcealment) in terms of "being." Perhaps, too, it is what Lewis Carroll (1871) had in mind in *Through the Looking-Glass and What Alice Found There*. From this perspective we might say that an analysand uses his analyst as his own personal mirror so that his inner subject, his soul, may find its reflection—and be contacted anew. Separation from one's analyst consequently becomes separation not only from therapy and the therapist but also from access to one's inner subject. Thus, analysis provides analysands with "visitation rites" (and "rights") with their inner subject.

After relating a dream, another patient suddenly wondered, "What is the *dream's* unconscious?" (That is, what is unconscious in the dream to the dreaming subject?) I was tempted to counter with "the dreamer's consciousness" but instead, following a lead from Bion and Lacan, suggested that the dreamer's unconscious while he is in the dream is not consciousness (symbolic reality, i.e., the Register of the Symbolic [Lacan, 1966]); it is the Register of the Real itself (Lacan, 1966), O (Bion, 1965, 1970).

Another patient stated, "Someone in me places barriers in front of me as I proceed in life and succeed in my work. How does he know how to do it?" My partial interpretation to him was, "One you seems to be cleverer than the other you, and you may then feel that it is worth your while to identify with the power of this grim, ominous, omniscient aspect of yourself, even if it costs you the pain of being its depressed and hopeless victim." This interpretation evoked an interesting response from the patient: he stated that when he felt good about himself, he believed that a guardian angel was looking out for him and that when things were bleak he felt that he was cursed by a devil on his shoulder. His response to my interpretation was one of the influences that resulted in my reconceptualizing the nature of internal objects. I had been accustomed to thinking in terms of the presence of bad (or even sadistic or evil) internal objects that function generally as archaic superegos. Now I think that the superego itself and the ego ideal are generally normal, no matter how seemingly distorted or malicious they may appear to be, and that what we see in pathological situations are the "barnacles" of the patient's projective identifications, which obtund the appearance and expression of the normal superego and ego ideal. The seeming destructiveness toward the self by these archaic superegos and ego ideals is but a dramatic portrayal of uncompleted object experiences in the psychodrama of analysis which can become known only through the charade of the roles that they play ("Now do you get it?"). The unconscious, in its role as the Ineffable Subject, can be thought of as a dramaturge as well as actor, when all is said and done, in a drama that seems to be a very serious passion play.

Clinical Example 1

The epiphanic discovery of his own alter ego occurred in a patient after a puzzling dream. In this dream the patient and his wife were walking down one of the narrow streets of a medieval walled city in the Italian mountains. The patient looked up to the balcony of the second floor of a building and saw a man who was looking down at him in a warm, smiling, and familiar way, although he was a stranger to the patient. The patient experienced a sense of déjà vu. Immediately, he found himself holding a filled martini glass, which he tried to hide from view. In the next moment the "familiar stranger" had come down to the street and whispered into the patient's ear, "Sinuses."

During free association to the dream, the patient recalled taking a highly enjoyable vacation trip to the Italian mountain region and experiencing a spiritual uplifting after visiting a number of shrines, churches (including the Vatican), and the Italian countryside in general. The patient, who had recently become aware of his growing problem with alcohol, suffered from chronic prostatitis, which was exacerbated by his drinking problem. Being a physician, he had developed the interesting idea that prostatic fluid seemed to be almost identical to the fluid in his sinuses and nasal passages, a theory about which he considered writing a paper for the medical literature. He came upon this theory when he experienced prostatitis and later compared it with how he felt when he became ill with sinusitis.

In both conditions he experienced an "inner sensation" of a distinct kind of malaise. At the same time, he did not take his theory too seriously: he had never heard such an idea mentioned by other physicians, and there was no mention of it in the literature. The point of his associations was that the sinus-prostate connection was known only to him. He was puzzled by the warmth and friendliness of the stranger in the dream who also knew of this connection. Indeed, on several nights preceding the one in which he experienced this particular dream, he had threatening dreams in which a menacing, criminal-type person was stalking him.

I interpreted to the patient that the warm, friendly stranger in the dream was felt to be his alter ego, his other self, who, though seemingly a stranger, was strangely familiar, knew him well, and wanted to help him with his alcohol problem. This stranger also represented me; I was intimately associated with this stranger, since he and I were felt to be the ones really involved in his analysis whereas he, the "analysand of record," seemingly looked on impassively. I went on to say that in reality I had not known about the patient's drinking problem until he reported this dream to me. I therefore concluded that his analytic (Ineffable) subject appeared in this dream in the form of a friendly advisor who knew about his drinking problem and could help and whose presence in the dream represented his own call for help.

I recognized the similarity of the word martini to the name of his father, with whose alcoholism he was unconsciously identified, and interpreted the medieval walled city as a symbol of his medieval, formal, scholastic, nonhuman self, which was all too self-enclosed, omniscient, and remote. The Italian countryside, I suggested, represented his new-found passion for things Italian, with which he associated warmth, graciousness, openness, and humanness (cherished qualities he had only begun to develop in the analysis).

The patient seemed greatly relieved by my interpretation but was also puzzled, not so much by the interpretation itself but by its implications. He felt relieved at being able to realize the existence of an uncanny presence within him that served as a silent but all-knowing sentinel, one who was there to help him if only he had the humility to summon it. The patient, who was very well versed in psychoanalytic concepts, had an idea about the unconscious as a seething cauldron comprising such wicked impulses as greed, envy, and destructiveness. It was a refreshing surprise to him that this "other," this "analytic subject" who was able to help him, was also there in his unconscious. The patient was especially sanguine about the idea that this friendly advisor knew him so thoroughly, especially his shadow side, and yet still wanted to help him.

I then interpreted to the patient that a seething cauldron was what his unconscious felt like when the infantile aspect of his personality could not tolerate the awareness of its need for help from another—whether his mother or his father in the past or his analyst in the present—and that the helpful external other is connected with this helpful aspect of his inner self. Now, by his having asked me for help for his alcoholism (through his unconscious subject), his own felt (conscious) sense of self (his subjectivity) was rejoined with his "inner advisor self." Thus, the original view he had formed of his internal world was one in which he felt the presence of the other as a demon who was sometimes evil and sometimes demanding, critical, and proscribing; that demon, I suggested, represented the personification of his own unrelenting, untamed infantile side. In our relationship, I further suggested, this infantile side of him was shown by his fear of trusting me lest I look down on him, shame him, ridicule him, or have unreal expectations of him. I reminded him that he would often say to me, "I hate to have you look over my shoulder." (This patient, by the way, also felt continually persecuted by authority figures in the workplace.)

The patient was silent for the longest moment, then began to weep. "You mean that there is hope for me . . . I have had a helper inside me all this time and have fought him, and that you and he are linked up and don't give up when I'm angry, nasty, resistant, and off the wagon?"

The tenor of the analytic moment in which this material emerged allowed me the courage—and I hope the wisdom—to make the following interpretation:

> The demonic you, the stalking conscience in the previous dreams, is but the other side of this paraclete other in the latest of your dreams.[20] Each side helps. One side shows you your projected self, as if to say, "I'm you! Do you get it?" It is also the one who makes you fearful and ashamed of asking for help for your alcoholism. It is as if you must accept your feelings of shame and allow them to be overcome by an awareness of the need for help in order to reduce the feelings of being persecuted by the cruel other. But the cruel other is you at one remove, altered, disguised, and reversed; and it menacingly demands that you recognize it. The more you unconsciously demonize it as your scapegoat, the more persecutory and retaliatory it is felt to become—and yet, at the same time, more sacred. Thus, your ever-increasing guilt feelings.

The patient responded, "You mean my unconscious is performing a passion play to save me by flashing my own disowned wickedness in front of me . . . for me to reown?" He then broke down in tears of profound relief.

This patient had had dreams prior to this one in which the image of a bleeding child would appear. It was this recurrent image that helped me to intuit that the analytic subject is the one who, like the ego ideal (Freud, 1914) with which it may be identified, helplessly feels the psychic pain. This painful and pained image it must relay in code, to both the Phenomenal Subject and to the analyst, as the "psychoanalytic object" (Bion, 1965); that is, the Ineffable Subject must speak through the analysand in ambiguous, pantomime-like, free associations that must be deciphered.

Clinical Example 2

A married career woman in her early 50s, the mother of three children, entered analysis with me claiming that she was suffering from "midlife crisis." She related the following story during an analytic session. In New York City on business, she decided to take a walk after breakfast one morning. While walking down a street that was familiar to her, she suddenly became aware of another woman, much younger and more beautiful than she, walking toward her from the opposite direction. Their eyes met for a moment, then each continued walking.

20. The patient was Catholic and had mentioned the paraclete (advocate) in an earlier analytic session.

The analysand admitted feeling haunted by and obsessed with this other woman and her gaze. Her associations revealed her belief that the woman was her double, an almost exact double of her 30 years earlier, when she first went to New York to become an actress. She then associated to how she had been plagued by self-doubts and self-consciousness all her life and her terrible feelings that she had been a failure in her previous marriage and in her acting career. Of relevance here is that the analysand was an only child who had been inconsistently reared by an impulsive, tempestuous mother who often beat her.

I interpreted to the patient that she regarded the woman she had encountered in New York as her lost self, the "innocent" one whom she felt she could not hold on to because it was not safe to do so. She had always felt bad for having to desert that self and was now feeling extremely sad and lonely, because of her encounter with what seemed to her to be her double, for a former self that somehow seemed to be still waiting somewhere to be found. The analysand was deeply moved and began to feel hopeful. She reported how she was taking such good care of her husband and children, how much she appreciated them, and how well off she now was in her life. Subsequent analytic work focused on the retrieval of her lost subject.

Intersubjectivity

In my "trial subjective counteridentification" with the analysand who dreamed of a friendly stranger in an Italian walled-city, I had been developing feelings in which I resented his not using my help (although he actually was) in controlling his alcohol problem. During many of his sessions I found myself drifting into a reverie (in which I was in a virtual fugue state) as I thought about an unfinished work of mine on the alter ego. I soon realized that my distraction was my way of trying unconsciously to help my patient by forceful example (magic omnipotent denial with projective identification). My reverie into my unfinished work on the alter ego turned out to be quite relevant to the analysand as well.

Evidently, in my fugue state I had become like a puppeteer in my attempt to manipulate the analysand for his own good. Then I realized that the analysand was the original puppeteer, that he had been unconsciously manipulating me to manipulate him—or, really, to understand him—so as to help him quit drinking. The denouement of my "alter ego reverie" followed suit. In that reverie I began to think about William Goldman's *Magic: A Novel*; the tales of E. T. A. Hoffmann, especially *The Lost Reflection*; Oscar Wilde's *Portrait of Dorian Gray*; and von Chamisso's *Peter Schlemihl's Remarkable Story*, about a man who sold his shadow to the devil. In Goldman's novel, the protagonist is a ventriloquist who enters into a folie à deux with his dummy, who gradually becomes the ventriloquist's "dominator." When finally the ventriloquist kills the dummy, he suddenly dies too. The other novels, which are from the last century, also present a demonic second self that eventually gains control over the pathetic protagonist who has created it. I began then to realize not only that the analysand's story was about projective identification, magic omnipotent denial, and folie à deux but also that it represented a hidden agenda in the analysis.

I gradually came to believe that forces were operating in the analysand's preconscious mind as if a puppeteer (shades of von Kleist!) or a ventriloquist were seeking omnipotently to manipulate and control me and my interventions so that I would become more supportive and symmetrical with the patient's state of mind (the alcoholic does not like to drink alone). There was another voice and pressure from within him that authentically wanted me to know about his condition and to help him by "calling him on it." The vision of the helpful man in the dream who knew so much about him represented a mixture of a manipulated, collusive me coexistent with another me and with an aspect of the patient who did know and who wanted to help him without his being persecuted by guilt feelings.

In this analysis, a subjugating intersubjective third (Ogden, 1994a, 1997) force (or covenant) had been established by which the analysand and analyst had each unconsciously felt controlled. It was as if the mythical construct of a "subjugating third" had been mutually created as a virtual third, a folie à deux that seemed unconsciously to control both the analysand and analyst. I wondered how this virtual third had acquired its power and authority in the analysand.[21] While pondering this question, I could not help thinking of how group psychology develops and also how we create the God image, which, in turn, controls us. Then I realized that the omnipotent, manipulating, and controlling qualities assigned to the subjugating third represent a coalescence of the original sources of these veritable puppeteers and ventriloquists in each of the participants of an analysis. Put another way, the subjugating third amplifies the unconscious relationship between the superego and the

---

21. As I stated earlier in this chapter, I believe that the intersubjective third, subjugating or otherwise, is irreducible to two separate but collusive entitites: the extended or projected subjectivity of the analysand and of the analyst. But, in normal analytic situations, the subjectivity of the analysand is always predominant since only the ineffable subject of the analysand (the Dreamer Who Dreams the Dream and the Dreamer Who Understands it) has any inkling of the unconscious agenda that the analysis must undergo.

ego of both the analysand and the analyst so that ultimately the analysand can use the leverage of the unconscious relationship between the analyst's superego and ego, that is, the analyst's own unconscious infantile neurosis, to manipulate the analyst.

I thought then that I had come across the roots of the group analysis that now seems to define postmodern analysis. Its future role in couples therapy can only be eagerly anticipated. It is almost as if in therapy there is an invisible Ouija board over which each participant exerts some control without being aware of the participation of the other(s), thereby lending a mysterious sense of agency to the instrument in its own right. Thus, the agency of control in Ogden's third intersubjective subject is ineffably located mysteriously among the three "participants," but particularly between the two real subjects.

By group analysis I mean that the psychoanalysis of an individual today represents an intrapsychic, intersubjective analysis. In each participant there exists a moiety, or portion of a whole entity, that becomes operant when the analysis begins. The moiety in the analysand develops a transference so as to resonate with its counterpart in the analyst. This situation is not unlike sex. Plato anticipated this phenomenon in his concept of the Androgyne—the part from which we are dissociated at birth and for which we spend a lifetime looking. This concept also speaks to Lacan's (1966) concept of the splitting of the subject at birth.

Thus, in psychoanalysis we see a resurgence of "psychic sexuality," in which both analysand and analyst consist of unconscious puppeteers or ventriloquists who seek the truth and yet also attempt to collude against the progress of the analysis. The analysand's "subjective moiety" seeks and unites with that of the analyst to form the "subjugating intersubjective third." Each participant initiates the control and continues the act of unconsciously controlling the other despite the illusion that the subjugating intersubjective third has assumed control. The subjugating intersubjective third is like a relay system, a satellite disk, as it were, that represents the condensation of the unconscious controlling maneuvers of each participant and also represents a Ouija board model in which authorship of motivation is denied to each participating individual subject.

I should like to make one further comment about the concept of the subjugating third. Insofar as it is operant as a manipulating or controlling (even if analytically informative) force, I believe that this third subject is the equivalent of what Mason (1994) terms folie à deux or mutual projective identification (mutual hypnosis) and what Girard (1972) terms mimesis. A designation other than subjugating third is required, in my opinion, to encompass Bion's (1970) concept of reverie and transformations, or evolutions, in O. What Bion's concept refers to is not situated in the mutual force field created by the subjugating third; instead, it approximates the idea of "meditative surrender."

SOME PHILOSOPHICAL AND MYSTIC-RELIGIOUS CONSIDERATIONS

What I am about to discuss is obviously highly speculative, and my justification for entering into this subject is based in large part, but not exclusively, on clinical inferences over time. It is my impression that the epiphanic religious experiences that I have witnessed in psychotic patients in the hospital and in outpatient treatment (and also in nonpsychotic patients) have relevance to this general theme of religious experiences. One frequently finds in the subacute and chronic stages of psychosis that the patient experiences religious delusions, either of *being* God or of being subjected to God's will, oftentimes in a sexualized way, as in the Schreber case (Schreber, 1903; Freud, 1911a; Sass, 1994; Lothane, 1995). After quoting a passage from Schreber's (1903) *Denkwürdigkeiten*, in which Schreber admits to finding it "incomprehensible . . . that other humans beings should have existed at that time apart from myself" (p. 125), Sass (1994) writes:

> The stance of passive concentration gave rise . . . , in perfect accord with Wittgenstein's analysis of solipsism, to a pervasive sense of subjectivization, of experiencing experience rather than the external world, to a feeling that, as Schreber puts it, "everything that happens is in reference to me.". . . As Wittgenstein often pointed out in his later writings . . . , it is nonsensical to doubt immediate subjective experience and impossible to argue . . . about notions like solipsism [pp. 40–41].

My reading of what Sass and, through him, Wittgenstein are saying is as follows: The psychotic exemplifies absolute, unmediated solipsism, which presents as total subjectivity since the links to objects that would mediate this absoluteness have been dissolved through decathexis and have fallen back on the subject. Absolute solipsistic subjectivity *is* the experience of either being God or being "Godly" (having intimate relations with the deity). This conception is reminiscent of the Hindu, Gnostic, and Kabbalistic theories of the origin of God. In the Hindu and Kabbalistic myths, God shrank in order to create the universe, leaving aspects of Himself behind as His creations. The Gnostics believed that God was the ultimate being but that the creator of the universe was that manifestation of Him known as the Demiurge (the craftsman). Meister Eckhart and other mystics believed in the copresence of God the ineffable Being and the Godhead, that aspect of God within human beings that was left behind at Creation (Fox, 1980, 1981a; Sells, 1994). In the mystical experience that Bion (1965, 1970, 1992) designated as "transformation in O," one may find oneself identified with either Absolute Truth or Ultimate Reality, which the psychotic may (mis)interpret as God.

It is my belief that this sense of the Ineffable Subject of the Unconscious, which I attribute to the unconscious, closely approximates one's experience of the deity, especially when this subjectivity is conceived of as a projective identification of the most ineffable aspect of oneself into another domain (e.g., heaven). This is not to say that God does or does not exist. His own ineffability precludes our questioning His existence any further. That venture constitutes "epistemic incest," a common tendency of psychotics.

Since God is ineffable and inscrutable (never an object of contemplation), then the only way He can be known is through the projective attribution of some essence within us that is proximate, that is, through the ineffability of our unconscious (or, more specifically, of the Ineffable Subject of the Unconscious). Herein lies a problem that has beset religious thinkers since the beginning of the God concept. Is God located in heaven—extraterritorial to earth—or does He permeate our existence both inside and out? The Gnostics and the mystics, following Zoroaster, conceived of two gods, one that was *immanent* (within the human being) and one that was *transcendent* (beyond the human being). The Gnostics, following Plato, came to think of God the ultimate Being as well as God the creator of the universe, that is, the Demiurge, the agent, and decision maker (Pagels, 1979; Bloom, 1983, 1996). Yet if God is the Ultimate Subject and if it is a universal law that every subject is incomplete and thus subject to desire, then perhaps we can hypothesize why God created mankind. He may have needed mankind "to desire His desire" so as to ratify and notarize His Ultimate Being. Why would this be so? In chapter 3 I discussed the paradox that God may be the only legitimate atheist because only He knows for sure that He does not exist. This paradox, that it takes the existence of God to negate God, belongs to Matte-Blanco's (1975, 1988) concept of "bi-logic" and the existence of infinite opposites in the unconscious.

It may very well be that the unconscious, while not really being the same as the Godhead, may be as close to God (the Demiurge that dwells within us as a direct descendant of the Godhead) as any mortal may ever be.

THE INEFFABLE SUBJECT AND THE EGO IDEAL

I cannot close this chapter without a brief note about a possible relationship between the ego ideal and the Ineffable Subject of the Unconscious. Freud (1914b) stated that, as the infantile ego was subjected to the experience of frustration after birth, it surrendered its grandiosity (omnipotence) to the ego ideal, which became positioned thereater in a gradient in the ego. It is my contention (as I develop in chapters 8 and 9) that the ego ideal is that aspect of the Ineffable Subject which reflects the latter's teleological (premonitory) function as the guardian of the individual's future.

CONCLUDING REMARKS

In this chapter I emphasize the importance of the concepts of subjectivity, agency, and being in arriving at a more ontologically valid understanding of the elusive meaning of I-ness. I conceive of subjectivity as being intimately interconnected with pure being (*Dasein*) and with conscious *and* unconscious agency. The term subject, in all its meanings, suggests the ultrapersonal dimensions of our being and doing in the world, where being and doing (agency) are as ineffable as the subject with which they are intimately associated. Translating my conception of the psyche into Freudian terminology, I am saying that subjectivity, agency, and being suffuse and interpenetrate all the structures and functions of the psychic apparatus and each level of the Freudian topographic model.

I have tried to give the reader a sense of the striking similarities between various disciplines with respect to the concept of subjectivity. One might say that agency (the drives of Freudian psychoanalysis) presents as *doing*, phenomenology as *feeling*, ontology as *being* and *reflecting*, and spirituality as *transcending*. (All these may be considered within the embrace of Husserl's, 1962, concept of *transcendental subjectivity*).

Subjectivity is not only the personal sense organ that is receptive, or sensible, to internal as well as external objects of sensation but also the numinous spirit that both haunts and empowers narcissism. It develops as infants accept a sense of responsibility for themselves and their unconscious and conscious sense of agency and intentionality, thereby accepting their being-in-the-world (*Dasein*). Although subjectivity becomes manifest in the infant's aliveness and humanness as it becomes a soul or spirit of vitality (being a subject because it has allowed itself to be "thrown under" or into the breach of experience, or the "actual"), it still remembers the perfection and infinity of its fetaldom, when it shared its oneness with the essences of the Eternal Forms of Plato.

In this chapter I have sought to enfranchise System *Ucs.*, particularly that component of it known as System *Pcs*, with a subjectivity that I designate as the Ineffable Subject, which is activated by the *Ucs.-Pcs.* frontier of System *Pcs.*[22] The Ineffable Subject's more conscious counterpart, the Phenomenal Subject, which is activated by the *Pcs.-Cs.* frontier of System *Pcs.*, is the one we generally refer to when we use the word subjective. It is the Phenomenal Subject that philosophers, ontologists, infant developmentalists, and postmodern psychoanalysts (particularly those espousing intersubjectivity) seem to describe and that Ogden (1994a, 1997) has in mind in his innovative concept of "subjects of analysis."

Whereas the Ineffable Subject is numinous, the Phenomenal Subject is secular, manifest, incarnate, palpable. I consider these two subjectivities to be holographically and holistically part of an overall ultimately indivisible subjectivity—the Supraordinate Subject of Being and Agency—which is both holistic and divided. That is, although the Supraordinate Subject overarches the Ineffable Subject and the Phenomenal Subject and is inclusive of them, it can be understood in its own right to holographically include an ineffable as well as a secular (more tangible) aspect. I further hypothesize that this overall subjectivity, which is both ineffable and phenomenal, occurs in an infinite, vertical layering of the psyche, thereby imparting structural and topographic complexity to the concept of the subject as well as to the concepts of agency and being. From a holographic point of view, subjectivity *is* being, and it "colonizes" by symmetrizing its objects of experience.

In this chapter I also suggest that the inner subject can undergo specific self-division in order to construct psychic dramas, as in dreams and phantasies, to capture the attention of the analysand and analyst for analytic processing.

Finally, I hypothesize not only that the unconscious is indivisibly constituted by id *and* ego but also that it is, in its ineffability as subject and agent, the progenitor of the human experience of the deity, which experience is then projected upward into the more exalted region of Heaven. Human beings not being able to contemplate the Godhead, confuse their own unconscious with the mystical God, which/who is the Ultimate Subject and therefore utterly uncontemplatable. God, in

---

22. Hamilton (1996) and Kantrowitz (1997) have written about System *Pcs.* in terms of the analyst's experience of the analysand.

other words, constitutes the ultimate Subjugating Intersubjective Third Subject of our creation.

I believe that the time has come for psychoanalysts to employ the concepts of being, subjectivity, and agency because of their phenomenological explicitness and eloquence. Furthermore, I believe that subjectivity, agency, and being are inseparable components of "I"-ness. They are useful tools in ontologically complementing—maybe even replacing—the ontic view of the psychic apparatus and thereby approximating the "language of experience" (Bion, 1965, 1970, 1992). With them, one can begin to grasp the complexity of human beings, who are haunted by and subjected to a strange yet familiar preternatural self in their psychic realm while all the while they desperately attempt to become their own agent in this inner cosmic melee.

Chapter 6

INTERNAL OBJECTS

The Chimerical Monsters, Rogue Subjective Objects, and Demonic "Third Forms" of the Internal World

The emergence of the concept of intersubjectivity and its offspring, subjectivity, demands that we rethink our notions of the object. An internal object is often thought of as if it bore a one-to-one relationship with its counterpart, the external object. Actually, they are quite different. The object loses its pure status as an object for the subject as soon as the projecting subject infiltrates its image of the external object (individual, person) and merges with it (from the projecting subject's point of view) through projective identification. The object's image thereupon becomes "subjectified" (autochtonized, made "native" to it) by the projecting subject (see chapter 2).

On the other hand, a projecting subject may unconsciously seek to possess or merge with another subject (for example, mother). In the depressive position mother has been transformed from a part-object to a whole object and, being considered separate and unique in her own right, achieves the status of a subject in her infant's mind. By projecting into her subjectivity, the infant reduces (dehumanizes) her as subject back to part-object, upon which action she loses *her* subjectivity (for the infant).

Furthermore, the term external object belies the mystery and uniqueness that inhere in the subjectivity and Otherness of the so-called object. In analysis we are offered the opportunity to deconstruct what and whom we really mean when we refer, say, to "mother." We learn that in analysis that the person of the analyst, the mother, or father is known *about* but never truly known.

I object to the term object, particularly internal object, because of what I believe are the logical-positivistic limitations of the concept. Jung was an inspired medievalist, but Freud's *Weltanschauung* seems to have been constrained by the notion of a fixed firmament, a world view inspired by the Enlightenment and whose founding father was Descartes. It was Hegel (1807), however, to whom much of the credit must go for our psychoanalytic notion of the object. When Freud discovered (really, *re*discovered) the unconscious, he blended the logical positivistic notion of absolute science and the German Romantic conception of the mysterious preternatural powers of Nature. The result was a lexicon of ontic, mechanistic, dehumanized entities such as "drive" and "object," rather than "homunculi," "chimerae," "monsters," "demons," "angels," "ghosts," or "revenants."

It is my belief that the function of objects, when internalized, is to become "carriers of O," that is, mediators of the infant's "nameless dread" until it is able to accept its relationship to O (the ineffable) through "K" (knowledge about itself and the world of real objects) (in chapter 10). In other words, the infant must "exorcise" its premature experience of nameless dread into "carriers" or "container objects," which derive originally from the infant's experience of mother-as-container. The internalized object must ultimately be processed through iterative reexternalizations until they become "cleared," that is, when the subject is mature enough to reclaim his projected subjectivity back from the object and thereafter be able to internalize, not the object per se, but the legacy of his experience with the object, thereby releasing the object and expanding the horizon of his own subjectivity.

BAD OBJECTS DO NOT TRAVEL; ONLY GOOD OBJECTS DO

Before I continue the discussion of the concept of the object, I should like to comment on one of its significant clinical aspects. Clinicians have long recognized that people who had rearing experiences with good objects are more secure than those whose primary experiences were with bad objects. When this phenomenon is more carefully scrutinized, we generally find that the experience of believing that one contains good objects inside one (the *legacy* of good-object experiences) offers one a feeling of being *blessed* and of being protected at a distance from the locale of the good object. Not so with bad-object experiences, where the sense of *curse* obtains instead. One aspect of the latter phenomenon could be understood as: the worse the actual primal object actually was, the more the subject felt compelled to identify with it at the expense of its own ego, thereby feeling too impotent to leave home. A corollary of

this reasoning would be that the unfortunate subject unconsciously perceives the object's distress and tries to "cure" the object by fusing with it. At the same time, the subject may believe, thanks to unconscious autochthonous phantasy, that it was originally responsible for the damage to the object.

THE IMPACT OF SUBJECTIVITY AND INTERSUBJECTIVITY ON THE CONCEPT OF THE OBJECT

Postmodernism has introduced the concept of relativism and dialectics into psychoanalytic theory and practice, especially in the considerations of subjectivity and intersubjectivity (Lacan, 1966; Stern, 1985; Trevarthen, 1991; Natterson, 1991; Moran, 1993; Ogden, 1994b, 1997; Muller, 1996; Orange, Atwood, and Stolorow, 1997). Moreover, the importance of the drives has been reduced in favor of affects; and chaos, complexity, and "emergence" theory[1] (Gleik, 1987; Waldrop, 1992; Kauffman, 1995; Palombo, 1999; Holland, 1999) have emerged from the natural sciences and linked up with recent psychoanalytic developments—particularly Bion's (1962b, 1963, 1965, 1970, 1992) concepts of alpha function (dream-work alpha), alpha and beta elements, infantile catastrophe, and transformations and evolutions in O; Lacan's (1966) Register of the Real; Matte-Blanco's (1975, 1988) ideas of infinite sets, infinity itself, bi-logic, and bimodality (Rayner, 1995), and Dennett's (1991) and Damasio's (1994) neuroscientific refutation of the mind as a "Cartesian theater."

Cognitive science proposes that the mind functions by way of parallel processing; thus, any thought or image is a virtual thought or image, not one screened on an inner theater. For instance, when we observe ourselves dreaming, we are undergoing complex rectifications and illusions about witnessing and experiencing a dream that only seems to be presented to us. In other words, we only imagine (dream) that we dream the dream! Matte-Blanco (1975, 1988), speaking from a mathematical perspective, described the unconscious as existing and operating beyond the capacity of consciousness to contemplate. These hypotheses go a long way in discrediting the notion of the mind as a

1. Emergence theory supersedes chaos and complexity theory. As Holland (1999) thinks of it, emergent phenomena transcend the nature of the object from which they emerge. One cannot predict or anticipate them by examining the parts that give rise to them. Each part gives rise to something more than itself.

three-dimensional "bag" containing objects or as a theater in which objectified scenes are witnessed.

These new ideas free the object from its constraint to the drives and instead portray the drives, along with the affect container that now encompasses them, as merely signifiers, that is, as signifying messengers of a profound ineffable signified, the infinite, ineffable, chaotic, yet chaotically ordered, unconscious itself. The monstrous forms that the appearance of internalized objects take can be understood as the individual's subjective (imaginative) attempts to encompass, contain, account for, and mediate unconscious infinity, chaos, complexity, emergence phenomena, beta elements, things-in-themselves, noumena, Ideal (Eternal) Forms, or O, or the "Real"—concepts that transcend the drive-driven objects of logical positivism and invoke imagery from a much earlier epoch.[2] In other words, individual subjects initially personify the data of their personal experiences as internalized, alien subjectivities incased in images of objects (Klein, 1929).

CLINICAL VIGNETTE

RB is a 63-year-old, recently married (for the first time) businessman who was in a previous analysis for over 20 years. His presenting complaint in both analyses was difficulty in establishing and maintaining a deep and enduring relationship with a woman. RB is Catholic by birth and by early school education. His ne'er-do-well father left his mother and him shortly after his birth and visited him only occasionally. He described his mother as a vacuous, narcissistic, highly demanding, immature, and very insecure woman who placed many household demands on him from early on and would punish him severely for any shortcomings. She insisted that he sleep in bed with her until his adolescence, whereupon he left home and lived sporadically with his maternal grandparents and also with an aunt, as well as at home. He suffered from attention deficit disorder as a child (but did not know this until recently) and consequently performed poorly in school. He nevertheless became an autodidact by teaching himself a great deal about literature, the arts, movies, music, and philosophy, however, so that today one cannot detect his humble beginnings from his manner and content of speech and presentation. He appears to be a well-educated, cultured, poised, and unusually worldly and knowledgeable person.

2. The term devil, which is derived from the Greek Word *Dia-bolos*, literally means "scattered asunder." Thus, the devil became the incarnation of chaos, whereas God became the incarnation of the coherence that mediated chaos.

His way of courting women followed a pattern. He would become an obsessed voyeur when he chanced upon a beautiful woman. Over the years, he pursued women who were famous beauties, models, singers, or movie stars, many of them married at the time. His manner was so suave that none of the women resisted him. He would become very excited in the pursuit; his voyeurism became heightened, and he would then stalk the woman. His interest was clearly specular; he loved gazing at the women's legs. Their personalities were much less important to him. He would find a way to approach each woman and appeal to her—always successfully. No sooner would he be successful than he would become claustrophobic and immediately feel bored, trapped, and apathetic and start planning his escape. Once he got to know a woman, he would become frightened and have dreams of female monsters attacking him. Women became demonic; he felt he could not trust them. It was easy to see that his perception of them bore a direct relationship to his experience with his seductive mother, without a father around to regulate the oedipal boundaries. My interpretations to him in that regard however, were of little avail.

Not too long after he began his analysis with me, he met a young artist. No sooner did she enter his office than their eyes met, and they both began to weep. "As if we had been waiting to meet each other all our separate lives," he romantically but poignantly remarked. She was half his age, but she also fell hard for him. Unbeknown to me until sometime later, he had in the meanwhile consulted his former analyst, who allegedly warned him about his inability to be in love with a woman and also about the "May–December" nature of the relationship. Upon analysis of this duplicity it became clear that the patient distrusted me because I did not oppose his relationship to this woman. I mainly analyzed his claustrophobic resistances to his experiencing intimacy with her, whereas his former analyst was felt to have really understood him insofar as the latter believed that the patient could not sustain an intimate relationship with any woman. This "belief" alerted me to the presence of a powerful negating superego with him.

Analysis of his claustrophobia became pivotal in his being able to live with and ultimately marry this woman. She too gradually became a monster for him in his dreams. For instance, in one dream he was attending a movie and witnessed a scene in which a woman seduced a man, stabbed him with a knife, and then emerged from the screen and came over to him in the reality of the dream. She appeared very friendly, coy, and seductive. Then she turned into a vampire, and he woke up in terror.

His associations to the dream centered on his fear that he could not satisfy his new wife and also on his sense of disappointment in her because of her lack of breeding and her poor use of English. I interpreted to him that he unconsciously attributed (projected) his own abject infantile neediness into her, where it became monstrous, vampirelike, and insatiably demanding. Moreover, since he had contempt for his own needy self, he also transferred this quality to her as well. His disapproval of her lack of breeding and poor use of English was a projective identification into her of his own erstwhile uneducated self. Thus, she was devalued on one level and frightening, possessive, and demanding on another. The patient was surprised that everything he feared in his wife came from his own self-assessment, but he gradually came to accept this interpretation.

Ultimately he came to realize that *he* was the monster, that is, a split-off and projected aspect of his cruel sadistic self ("rogue subjective object") that had become merged with cruel and demanding images of his mother. Joined up with this image was a second image, that of a greedily devouring, insatiable, vampirelike monster, which was a residue of his split-off, needy, infantile self. These figures ("rogue subjective objects") combined to become a monstrous superego, sometimes female and at other times male. It was his male superego that would characteristically attack either me or the relationship between us as he made progress in the analysis. He consulted with his previous analyst, whom he had professed to me to distrust, so as to be able to externalize this superego figure. The analysis of his creation of his "orphan" (rogue)-subjective objects allowed him to make progress. He and his wife have now been married for seven years and still seem very happy with each other. They and her three children from two previous marriages seem to be a happy and functioning family.

The analysis of his claustrophobia, though significant, was only the beginning of a long journey into his labyrinth (see chapter 7). At times when he reported difficulties with his wife or her children or with work, he would frequently say, "It's a nightmare!" I understood that dealing with difficulties in his everyday life were often nightmarish for him because the unpleasant events resonated with a deeply hidden, inner, infant subjective self that had become lost and detached from the rest of him as he grew up. He recalled that occasionally he would renounce pleasure and joy and would retreat into himself to appear hidden from others. On these occasions he would frequently use cave imagery. He would talk longingly about how he liked to hide in metaphoric caves of isolation so that he would not have to bother with people. He associated this retreat with the idea that he had, in his own words, made a Faustian bargain[3] (Blomfield, 1985; Ogden, 1997; see also chapters 8 and

3. Recall the patient in chapter 5 who believed that he had once made a fatal Faustian bargain.

9) with the devil to foreswear all pleasure and joy. He would look forward to contacting women or purchasing luxury yachts or cars but would not be able to consummate acquiring them with pleasure. He had to get rid of them instantly.

He became obsessed with antique cars and yachts and would excitedly trace their lineage from the factory or from the yachting company that built them. He became knowledgeable about all the previous owners and other specifications about yachts. As soon as he owned the cars or boats, however, they suffered the same fate as the women. He become a well-respected amateur yachtsman and classic car collector. Analysis revealed that he had become fixed on these items as an unhappy child who sought relief by reading the yacht and automobile advertisements in the *National Geographic* magazines of the time. And, too, his absentee father had been an automobile salesman. They and the caves represented safe enclosures for self-healing.

Dreams involving vampire and monster imagery helped me understand that he felt like a vampire in the sense that his desire for a person, career, or luxury item conferred a curse on that object because, allegedly, of the felt badness of his all-consuming neediness. He frequently related to me that he had been terrified of ghosts as a child but, of course, had not actually encountered any. Following the pattern of Fairbairn's (1940) conception of the schizoid personality's dilemma, it was his very *love* that was felt by him to be bad. Things or people he loved quickly lost their value as they became involved with him or fell into his orbit of malinfluence. He could not take in anything good from the experiences and thus felt empty inside. He was stimulated to long for someone and then could not tolerate the contact. The origins of this agonizing frustration were partly oedipal since he had slept in the same bed with his mother until almost puberty and his father had left his mother in his infancy. More important, however, he experienced his mother as harsh, demanding, uncompromising, and unfair. To want something was to want something from an enemy. He therefore withdrew from the *personal* desire for another person. He retreated into romantic fantasy and learned to desire *images* of desirable women, actually as part-objects—legs.

He had loved his maternal aunt, who had always been good to him and who had beautiful legs. Like the vampire, he lived in the virtual world of the second dimension (Grotstein, 1978a, chapter 4) in which the realness of the object is flattened out into romantically promising images in phantasy—*that dare not see the light of day in reality!* He would unconsciously extract the goodness or beauty from these women, dismantle these qualities from them, and then reassign them to his hobbies. As a collector he was in control.

He had been significantly depressed after a brief tour of duty in the army, and during this time he fell in love with a woman whose family would not allow him to pursue her, allegedly because of the difference in their backgrounds. He accepted this verdict painfully, stoically, and resignedly, as if an aspect of him inwardly concurred.

Analysis of this depression with resignation led us to his belief that he had "signed a Faustian bargain" never again to be in love or attempt to find pleasure. Since that time he had limited his pleasure and excitement to the obsessive pursuit of acquisitions—the classic cars, yachts, women—and on acquiring them he would lose interest and expediently trade the cars and yachts to others. His voyeuristic eye could pursue them in the phantasy of the future, but he had to release them on possession.

One of his former girlfriends, perhaps the most brilliant and insightful of all of them, understood this difficulty. One day when he was reading a yachting magazine in her presence, she approached him sexually, and he gently rebuffed her. She thereupon said, "You'd rather think about me than have sex with me!" This insight helped him see that he was unable to relate to human beings as persons but rather acted like a vampire who extracted the person's essence and assigned it to an internal, phantasmal image with which he could masturbate in the privacy of his metaphoric cave.

The two-dimensional nature of his experience was revealed when he described some of the elegant women he had dated. While he was talking about them, I visualized a highly stylized magazine picture with symmetrical romantic images of people and seamless backgrounds. When I mentioned this image to him, he remembered that since childhood his inner life had been spent in the romantic seamlessness of movies and magazines. The interpretation of "vampire" struck him to the core. He realized that he had become an existential, nightmarish predator who stalked his prey but could not enjoy them because of his unconscious guilt feelings and their connection to his Faustian bargain. In short, he was demoniacally possessed, seeking release through the analysis and his marriage, on one hand, and proof of loyalty to the dark force (the devil, who was also related to his father) on the other.

He was also obsessed with maintaining contact with elementary and high school friends, both male and female, in an attempt to return to the unlived life of his past. Once, when he was in his early 20s, he attended a party where he "gazed across a crowded room" and met the eyes of the most beautiful woman he had ever seen! They talked for a long time, and although she was soon to be married to a man who was also at the party, she secretly proffered her telephone number to him. He was so overcome that he lost it. They both were scheduled to leave the city in a few days. He frantically asked everyone he knew at the party if they knew her and her telephone number but to no avail. He cursed himself for his carelessness and his fate. He felt tantalized and tormented, and she haunted him for years. About 30 years later he was thinking of her when he suddenly remembered that she had been born and raised in a small California town not far from Los Angeles.

He hired a private detective to conduct an intensive search for her and learned that she was still alive, married to her original fiancé, and lived *two blocks from him on the same street!* He screwed up his courage, went down the street to meet her, rang the doorbell, and was greeted by a beautiful young woman who at first appeared to be the original woman at the same age as he had remembered her—but it was her daughter. She informed him that her mother had died only the week before![4]

The patient's obsessive sentimentality about his childhood and adolescent years and about even casual acquaintances reflected his attempt to catch up with lost years, which he had failed to experience because of his emotional dissociation. These persons had become images or signifiers of his needed objects of an even earlier time, that is, his mother, aunt and grandmother. This pattern was also related to the "vampire" aspect of his personality. Whatever he truly desired rapidly lost its value as soon as he acquired them or began living with them. Like a vampire, he stalked his prey, attempted to desire and to possess it, and then the excitement would vanish. The desired object represented a deceptive "undead ghost" because he believed that in his infantile and childhood depression he had killed the connections to the object whose loss he could not tolerate. The dead object became the "*undead ghost*" that beckoned, excited, tantalized, and rejected him—each time mocking him because he was marked by fate never to enjoy fulfilment. When he was able to begin tolerating losses in the analysis and to understand the process of mourning, the lost object became a *spirit*, one that seemed to make him happy as it accompanied him.

DISCUSSION

In traditional psychoanalytic thinking, the term object represents a "Cartesian exile" or "fugitive" reduced to the lowly status of a literal, concrete puppet or icon that has escaped from a deeper and more

4. Surely this portion of the case material demonstrates Jung's (1966) concept of *synchronicity*.

hidden inner cosmic order, one that paradoxically both defines this hidden order and is reciprocally defined by it (Grotstein, 1981b). The term object, in other words, misses the eery, mysterious quality of the relationship between the subject and "third forms." In the dazzling light of the Enlightenment, preternatural spirits, presences, angels, and demons, along with their cosmologies, were bleached into apparent oblivion. These designations waned, and their remains were reminted in the alchemy of a newer, "scientific" lexicon. Nevertheless the spirits that occupied their successors (i.e., "internal objects") continued to haunt our minds.

The term object emerged in the wake of Descartes's distinction between *res cogitans* and *res extensa*. Once a separation could be made between a thinking (or perceiving) self, on one hand, and the object of its contemplation, on the other, the concept of the object of thought and perception evolved. The object became a fundamental fixture in physics, medicine, and other sciences, designating a concrete, measurable—and therefore definable—entity. The Cartesian distinction can be portrayed as subject → object, in which the arrow represents a unidirectional transformation. Hegel (1807) portrayed the relationship with reciprocal arrows, subject ↔ object, a reciprocity that is illustrated in his dialectic of "The Master-Slave" allegory (Kojève, 1934–35). The concept of dialectics implies a hidden order or covenant between the *thesis* and its putative oppositional "adversary," *antithesis*. A reciprocal, active ↔ passive aggressive situation undergoes an endless series of dialectical shifts and transformations. In dialectical encounters, an inexorably defining thirdness seems to initiate, create, and choreograph the encounter and in turn is transformed by it—the ultimate result being an existentially fateful "return bout"—on its way to a reconciling synthesis, which, when attained, is fated to become the next thesis to its antithesis in an endless series of iterations.

This endlessly cycling vortex of dialectical tensions represents the closed world of the mind, of the secondary or personal unconscious, the absolute linear world of persecutory anxiety, the world that mathematically (polar-coordinated space) is defined as the domain of the first (linear) dimension (see chapter 4). The pure object *and* the pure subject are altered by their mutual encounter of combative "desire for the other's desire" and by the power to express and/or negate (withhold) that desire. Hegel (1807) said, " Human desire must be directed toward another Desire" (cited in Kojève, 1969, p. 5). We might today restate it as, "Man seems to desire the subject as object but really desires the subject's desire for his own desire—so as to vouchsafe his own desirability." The hypnotist becomes the desiring victim of his hypnotee—and the reverse.

THE INFLUENCE OF DIALECTICS AND CONSTRUCTIVISM ON THE OBJECT

Hoffman's (1992, 1994) concept of constructivism and Ogden's (1994b, 1997) concept of dialectical intersubjectivity predicate that the subjective self of the analysand emerges anew through continuous iterations of change through its interaction with the subjectivity of the analyst. In other words, each participant inexorably modifies, determines, and defines the ever-changing subjectivity of the other. Thus, the object cannot be located as a static noun since it is ever-changing in the mysterious alchemy of mutual interpenetration with the subjectivity of the other.

THE DIALECTICS BETWEEN OBJECT AND SUBJECT

The subject and the object engage in two dialectics. One is the defining difference between them. "I am subject only because you, the object of Otherness, are *not* me; therefore you, by being different *from* me, define me." In this instance, the object that defines the difference is a whole object and therefore a subject in its own right; it is the latter's ineffable otherness that defines the original subject who engages with it. This subject–object differentiation occupies a great deal of the philosophical literature and has been referred to by Descartes, Kant, Hegel, and others.

The other dialectic is that of contemporary psychoanalysis. In regard to the importance of the ego–object differentiation the object relations perspective contrasts with that of the intersubjective perspective, which holds, following Husserl (1931), Heidegger (1927), and others, that an individual is a subjective "Being of Beings" emerging from a matrix of other subjectivities so that in every interaction a common intersubjectivity organizes and determines the interaction of the participating subjects. This concept of a primordial universal pool of subjectivities inheres in Lacan's (1966) concept of the universal pool of language, which organizes the unconscious of every person and doubtlessly descends directly from Hegel's concept of the "World Spirit."

A dual-track conception (Eigen, 1983; Bucci, 1985; Grotstein, 1986, in preparation-b, see also chapter 4) is needed to bridge these dichotomous conceptions. An infant may initially relate as a subject to the mother-as-breast object because of the limitations of its intersubjective capacities at the beginning of its life. Trevarthen (1979, 1980, 1987, 1988, 1991) believes that infants develop the rudiments of intersubjective capacities and "other-mindedness" at approximately four months of age, the time when Klein (1935) suggests that the infant begins to attain the depressive position and Mahler (1968) observes that "hatching" occurs. I posit that there are two internal worlds in regard to the other, one having to do with the internalization of the object qua object, considered in the classical Freudian, Kleinian, and Fairbairnian theories of internal object relations; and another having to do with what Jacobson (1964) refers to as the object-representational world, the domain of symbolic, evocable representations of objects (in which the subject has undergone successful mourning for the departed object). *The intrasubjective world of intersubjective relations* would begin with the onset of an infant's attainment of intersubjective capacities at the threshold of the depressive position.

"INTERNAL OBJECTS" AS SIGNIFIERS OF EXPERIENCES

Psychoanalytically, the object is a way of talking about how we signify or encode and contain our experiences of events in the inner and outer worlds by a concretizing personification of the impact on us, and therefore within us, of all persons and events. Internal objects can be understood in at least two separate ways: (1) internal objects, as concrete personifications of experiences, constitute the imagined architecture of our internal world; and (2) internal objects can acquire sovereignty over our psyche at any given moment as we find ourselves (unconsciously) identifying with that internal object and behaving as if we are in hypnotic subjugated thralldom, spell, or trance—*becoming* it at that moment or enacting the scenario or agenda that it subjugatingly compels us to follow. From the Kleinian point of view, we *are* and we *become* what we believe we have done to our objects (because of projective, followed by introjective, identification with the object), and therefore our phantasies about the content and disposition of our inner objects become a critical statement of the true sense of worth of our inner being. Klein (1932) used the term object to designate all an infant's sensations and experiences, including its experience of its own body parts. Thus, feces, genitals, eyes, mouth, teeth, and the like constitute "part-objects." Hinshelwood (1997), in his review of the "elusive concept of 'internal objects'" in the history of the British Psycho-Analytical Society, points out that Klein and her followers, on one hand, and Anna Freud and other classical analysts, on the other, understood and used the concept of objects differently:

> My reason for preferring this term to the classic definition, that of "an object installed in the ego" is that the term "inner object"

> is more specific since it exactly expresses what the child's unconscious . . . feels about it. In these layers it is not felt to be part of the mind in the sense . . . of the super-ego being the parents' voices inside one's mind. This is the concept we find in the higher strata of the unconscious. In the deeper layers, however, it is felt to be a physical being, or rather a multiple of beings, which . . . lodge inside one's body, particularly inside the abdomen [p. 885].

Then:

> The internal mother, alive and revived, is not just a replica or representation of the external mother who is dying. The independent life of the internal object—a live mother and a live finger—contrasts with the reality. This very concrete hallucination is a specific indicator of the inner life, as distinct from the external one [p. 886].

Ultimately, the object becomes our way of assessing our internal inventory. We consist of objects, and these objects either bless us or curse us.

INTERNAL SUBJECTIVE OBJECTIVE OBJECTS AND CATASTROPHIC CHANGE

One can infer that Bion (1963) hints at a reciprocity existing between the infant's experience of "catastrophic change" and an opportunity for gradual transitionalization (Fairbairn, 1951; Winnicott, 1951; Brown, 1987) in terms of development. The infant is confronted with the task of "learning from experience" by employing "alpha function" (its own and mother's) to discern the "elements" that it needs, separating them from the object that supplies its needs, be able continuously to mourn its experience with the object and thereby enable the object to be "released" to its own separateness and subjectivity. In other words, the infant must find the object, use it, and then release it as it separates from it. It can undergo this protocol if the object that is found and used can be transformed from the erstwhile security of its concrete presence to a satisfying enough image of it in its absence so that the infant can then begin to store legacies of its useful and fulfilling experiences with the objects-as symbolized memories. The more the infant can become able to appreciate the goodness and meaningfulness of the actual experience with the object, the more its legacy appreciates in the infant's internal world. The infant identifies with this legacy and thereby develops a sense of identity based upon this appreciation. The infant's relationship to the goodness of the internalized legacy is known as a blessing, whereas its negative counterpart, the result of a legacy of bad experiences is known as a curse.

BACKGROUND OF THE CONCEPT OF THE OBJECT

The idea of the object descends from Freud's (1905) original concept of instinctual drives and their need for an object to facilitate discharge, but the object-relations schools of psychoanalysis modified the concept. Mitchell (1981), reviewing the history of concept of the object in the works of Klein and Fairbairn, emphasizes Klein's belief that the drives are tightly bound to internal and external objects from the very beginning, whereas Fairbairn emphasized the primacy of the external object. Klein (1930) stated, "The child's earliest reality is wholly phantastic" (p. 238). Mitchell (1981) interprets Klein's theory of drives (desire) as inherently implying the object of its desire. In other words, an image is attached to the desire from the beginning.

Klein (1921) applied the term object to all basic experiences. In the paranoid-schizoid position, whatever was experienced was experienced as an object, not only in the grammatical sense but especially in the psychic sense; that is, the infant's hunger could be understood as an "internal devouring breast." In the depressive position, the object is symbolized in its absence so that true thinking can take place by virtue of one's being able to maneuver internal symbols. The whole object of the depressive position is equated in many ways with "object representations."

Infants (as subjects) treat their needed ones (mothers, fathers, nannies) as objects, actually, part-objects. Mother, though a person, is not considered by the infant to be a fully separate individual (person, subject) in her own right until the infant has achieved the depressive position (object permanency and constancy). Consequently, the infant seems to regard its mother as someone (or something) that exists solely for its needs alone and is thus *its* object. That is, the infant may *perceive* itself to be separate from the object but simultaneously may emotionally *conceive* that the object is an extension of it. This form of thinking has been termed egocentric (Piaget, 1923a, b, 1924, 1926), prereflective (Fonagy, 1991, 1995; Fonagy et al., 1991), or cyclopean and is characteristic of Klein's (1946) paranoid-schizoid position.

I have used the term autochthonous to designate the infant's unconscious phantasy that it creates itself, its parents, and the world to which it progressively opens its eyes before coming to realize, in the reflective stage of intersubjectivity (the depressive position of object permanency and constancy), that another world exists and is occupied by external *subjects* who are separate from the infant and who existed before the infant (see chapter 2). The infant may be *perceptually* separate from its mother, but, because of its immaturity and vulnerability and because of the availability of the unconscious phantasy of projective identification (Klein, 1945, 1955), it can *emotionally* imagine itself *not* to be separate, that is, as connected to its mother like psychical conjoined twins. The infant is thus both separate and not separate at the same time or alternately, depending on its point of view at the time. This conjoined twin image derives from the dual-track theorem (Grotstein, 1981a, in preparation-a; see also chapter 4) and reconciles Winnicott's belief that "There is no such thing as an infant; there is only the infant and its mother," with infant development findings, as presented by Stern (1985), that the infant is separate from the very beginning.

As the infant moves into the depressive position, the mother may remain an object of need; but as she begins to attain the status of whole object, she begins to be transformed into a *subject*,[5] a person with ineffable individuality and personal mystery. The conflict in the infant's mind between its perception of mother as object and as subject is what the Oedipus complex ultimately is about. Put another way, the infant's subjectivity constrains it to conceive of its mother as object, as Winnicott (1969) suggested in his concept of the "subjective object." Later, when the infant achieves some *objectivity* about mother, it comes to realize that she is a *subject* (objectively perceived).

CHIMERICAL MONSTERS OR ROGUE SUBJECTIVE OBJECTS: DEMONIC THIRD FORMS OF THE INTERNAL WORLD

When the image of mother-as-object is internalized by the infant, child, or adult, this image is altered by the phantasied effect of the latter's projective identifications. The image of mother-as-object is transformed into a hybrid chimera[6] by being intermixed with aspects of the infant's projectively reidentified *subjectivity* (within the image of the object). When

5. That is, transformed in the infant's eyes. Mother has been a subject all along.

6. A chimera is an imaginary monster that is compounded of incongruous parts. The Sphinx of Thebes is an outstanding example.

this "subjectified object" image is then internalized by the infant, it undergoes the additional process of introjective identification, both in the ego and in the superego (Freud, 1917; Grotstein, 1981a, 1994b, 1995a, 1998b). My thesis is that people phenomenologically fear objects legitimately when the latter are truly dangerous enemies. On the other hand, people experience persecutory anxiety in regard to "rogue subjectivities," that is, "subjectified" objects; or, more accurately, they fear the return of their own projected (alienated) subjective parts. In other words, the subject experiences persecutory anxiety in regard to its projected, alienated self ensconced in the object.

From the Kleinian point of view, one develops into (by introjective identification) what one believes one has done to (modify) the object (by projective identification). What one has done to the object is resubjectified with, by, and as oneself, both positively and negatively, as one's iterative, ongoing sense of complex, self-organizing subjectivity. One of the profound pains an infant experiences in the depressive position is not only the awareness that it believes it has wounded the object as object but also its growing awareness that it has wounded the object as *subject*. It begins to dawn on the infant that the object it has been using has been a feeling subject all along.

This secondary alienat*ed*, and alienat*ing*, subjectivity is experienced not so much as an "object" but as a subjective, strange yet familiar distortion—a demon or monster, alien, misbegotten chimera, or homunculus. These entities may be internal or external, although the externally feared one may not be consciously *perceived*, only *experienced* as such. A person fears not only the fearsomeness inherent to other persons but also the negative attributes that we projectively—subjectively—attribute to them or that their provocations selectively release into our awareness from our inherent repertoire of preconceptual possibilities (Bion's, 1963, "memoirs of the future"). We may properly *fear* the other as our natural, pro tempore *enemy*, but we feel *persecuted* by how we believe we have unconsciously altered the other with our projective attributions. One of the tasks of psychoanalysis is to help our analysands differentiate the persecutor from the enemy, and this task is accomplished by helping them recognize their lost subjectivity as the persecutory moiety of the object.

Klein, like Fairbairn, thought of the object as the natural complement to the infant's impulses and feelings. She thought that, through projective identification, the infant—or the infantile portion of the adult personality—would reidentify either its ego, id, or superego into the image of the object and thus transform it (Klein, 1946, 1955). Upon reintrojection, this projectively altered object is internalized in two tiers of the personality: (1) concordantly as a superego object (i.e., if the infant projected a "greedy" portion of its id, then the returning object would be "insatiably demanding"), and (2) as a complementary identification with the object (i.e., the object of the infant's "greedy" attacks is installed via introjective identification as a "mutilated object" in the ego) (Grotstein, 1981a, 1994c, 1995a).

"OBJECTS DO NOT THINK"

The issue of *subjectivity* and *agency*[7] (which to me are indivisible; see chapter 5) is important when considering how we experience the effect of internal objects on us. Ogden (1983), in his discussion of the internal object as an amalgam of projected self and object, asserts that "*if internal objects are thoughts . . . then they themselves cannot think, perceive or feel, nor can they protect or attack the ego*" (p. 229; italics added)—to which I add that *only subjects do*. Internal objects, insofar as they are direct representations of external persons, do not think. Their influence on us is preconditioned by the omnipotence and intentionality of the subjectivity that we projectively attribute to the object. We become influenced by a self-induced hypnotic state of thralldom in which a superego subjective object casts a spell on a subjective object within the ego and in which we are doubly identified, in the superego and in the ego. It is as if a dominant superego subjective object had become a ventriloquist or puppeteer for another subjective object in its spell.

The apparent capacity of internal objects to influence, think, or direct us is due to the power of omnipotence, agency, intentionality (motivation, will), and subjectivity with which we repersonify them and projectively attribute to them externally and internally. Even when external objects traumatize and manipulate victims in the real world, they speak internally with the voice of authority, which the victim subjectively surrenders to them! The voice we turn over (projectively reidentify[8] into the object) is our own sense of agency as subjects, or, put another way, our "power of attorney." One aspect of this internal transfer(ence) of power of agency is that of the "Faustian bargain" (Blomfield, 1985; Ogden, 1997; see also chapters 8 and 9).

---

7. See Moran's (1993) in-depth monograph on the relationship between subject and agency in psychoanalysis, to which I referred in chapter 5.

8. When projective identification is employed defensively, the projecting subject initially *de*identifies with the projected aspect of itself as it *re*identifies that portion of itself in its image of the object (Grotstein, 1994c, 1995a, 1999c, d).

"ROGUE SUBJECTIVE OBJECTS"

Internal objects (or, as I like to call them, internalized "rogue subjective objects") constitute *psychical presence*, a *third force* within the psyche (third in regard to the subject and the external object as the first two). Since they result from splitting, projective identification, and introjective identification and all the transformations those processes entail, internal objects must be thought of as third internal entities, paralleling another thirdness, Ogden's (1994b, 1997) "intersubjective third." The "subjugating" quality of his "subjugating intersubjective third subject" owes its provenance to the analysand's own subjugating (demanding) id and superego, in addition to those of the analyst.[9] The subjugating superego subjective object, in turn, results from the projective identification, pathologically, of the "greedy," willful, omnipotently demanding aspects of the analysand's (and the analyst's) infantile personality (id) into the object. On reinternalization, it is installed as a superego within the analysand. The normal counterpart of this "greedy" self is that aspect of the Ineffable Subject of the Unconscious (chapter 5), otherwise known as the Dreamer Who Dreams the Dream (chapter 1). The Dreamer Who Dreams the Dream becomes, with uncanny prescience, imaginativeness, and versatility, the "playwright/director" of the seemingly improvisational theater that constitutes the psychoanalytic session and bewitches the analyst's subjectivity to participate in the play in whatever repertory role it feels should be played out at the moment. The stage for this theatrical performance is potential space (Winnicott, 1951, 1967).

The subjugating as well as the submissive qualities of these third forms owe their origin to Klein's (1946) schizoid mechanism of magic omnipotent denial, but they can also be understood as following the spontaneous techniques of play, as conceived by Winnicott (1971a), and that can be understood as being subtended by dreaming, phantasying, projective identification, autochthony, cosmogony, imagination, personification, and illusion (chapters 1 and 2). An infant can thus phantasize that it can magically (action at a distance) enter mother's body and control it at will, like a puppeteer.

The projected (subjective) attributes from the projecting subject are felt (by this projecting subject) no longer to be relocated in the self as subject but ensconced in the object-as-object. As derivative subjects,

9. In regard to the subjugating third subject, one cannot help being reminded of the medieval demonological notion of the *incubus* and *succubus*, who sexually invaded innocent souls while they were asleep.

however, these translocated subjects retain their *personifications* (Klein, 1929a) and their power of *omnipotent agency* (or intentionality) and enter into a conflict with the original subject, which disidentified from them. In other words, the discarded and ostracized orphan, alien, feral, or rogue subjectivities continue to identify as subjects with the original ostracizing subject and seek repatriation with the same violence with which they were expelled—in the form of persecutory anxiety, or as Freud (1915b) termed it "the return of the repressed." Their return is, in turn, just as violently counterrejected by the initially projecting subject, creating the internal status of a virtual Armageddon; thus, they become infused with a sense of persecutory and personalized agency, omnipotence, and intentionality whose provenance was the originally projecting infantile subject.

Let us now consider the fate of these alienated subjectivities after the subjectified object has been internalized. The original projecting subject is now haunted by internal ghost-monster-demons toward which there is an eery feeling of déjà vu.

KLEINIAN AND FAIRBAIRNIAN OBJECTS

Freud (1917) gave us the first map of the unconscious world of internal objects. The narcissist who cannot bear mourning the loss of a needed object denies his loss by splitting the image of the object and internalizing it in two tiers. A sadistic aspect of the object is internalized within the ego ideal (later superego), and another aspect, an impoverished one, is internalized in the ego.

Virtually the entirety of Klein's and Fairbairn's considerations of object relationships are in large measure derived from Freud's formulation. According to Klein, the quality of sadism was projected (concordantly) by the narcissistic infant into the object before internalization so that it became a sadistic superego upon internalization. At the same time, since the narcissistic infant believes that in phantasy its sadism *has* damaged the object, a damaged aspect of the object is also internalized—in the ego—and identified with. Klein's internal objects are made up of an amalgam of projected aspects of the infant-subject and the object-as-object, which are thereby transformed into altered, hybrid third forms with the emphasis placed clinically on the original subject's projections as their motive force.

Fairbairn, on the other hand, pictured the internal world as filled with rejecting and exciting objects that authentically derived from objects in the infant's world who were realistically intolerable but absolutely needed (Grotstein, 1994b, 1998a) and who, upon internalization, were divided into images of rejecting and exciting (tantalizing) objects. Thus, Klein pictured the objects as altered by unconscious phantasy, and Fairbairn pictured them as real objects whose badness is so critical that they had to be internalized in order to be controlled, along with aspects of the original ego which split off in order to maintain their relationship with these bad, though needed, objects.

Although Fairbairn's endopsychic structure can represent both his and Klein's versions of object relations, the two writers differ over the issue of the primacy of reality versus the primacy of phantasy. Fairbairn dealt with the infant's realistic need to comply (as a false self) with a real mother or father who is absolutely needed yet who is also realistically intolerable. Klein's infant deals with the mother or father as altered by projecting identification. Both points of view are valid complementarily (Grotstein, 1994a, c, 1998a) and can be reconciled with my concept of autochthony (see chapter 2), that is, the infant's egocentric belief that it caused the mother to be bad—before it enters the depressive position, where it can see her as separate and can then feel freer to hate, process, and even to forgive her (Grotstein, 1994b, 1998a).

"INTERSUBJECTIVE"—AND "INTRASUBJECTIVE—THIRDNESS"

Ogden (1994b, 1997) applies his concept of intersubjective thirdness to the relationship that develops between the two (external) participants of analysis. I believe that his concept can be applied to the relationships between internal objects as well. In Fairbairn's terms, a secret agreement or "covenant" seems to be in place among all the endopsychic participants. It is as if there were a folie à deux or collusion between the central ego (CE), on one hand, and its two split-off subjects, the antilibidinal ego (AE) and libidinal ego (LE), to stay repressed and doubly repressed respectively in order to preserve the stability of the supraordinate, original subject (Original Ego). In this role, the CE, in conjunction with its ideal object (IO), represents a "subjugating superego." At the same time, there seems to be a hidden agreement between AE and LE for the former, in conjunction with *its* partner, the rejecting object (RO), to be a more primitive "subjugating superego to the libidinal ego and *its* partner, the exciting object (EO), which in turn "agrees," albeit reluctantly and painfully, to be subjugated and tormented.

A LEXICON OF SOME OBJECTS AND THEIR IMPLICATIONS

Subjective object: Winnicott (1969b) thought of the subjective object as one that the toddler creates as an illusion in potential space, juxtaposed against the image of the real (external) object. The toddler must use and destroy this self-made image as if it were indistinguishable from the real object. The real object, on the other hand, must persist without retaliation. The need for the destruction of (the image of) the object has been alluded to by many theorists, but the putative reason behind the alleged destructiveness has never been clarified to my satisfaction. To me, it seems that the rationale for the infant's need to encounter and destroy the image of the object (not yet realizing that it is but an image) is, first of all, to break out of the series of "yolk sacs" or primal claustra by which it feels encapsulated. In other words, these destructive impulses may be rituals whereby the infant breaks through its "egg shell." Second, the infant—and the adult—needs progressively to destroy the illusory image of the object that interposes itself between it and the subjectivity of the object in the Real. This principle is mindful of St. Paul's "First Letter to the Corinthians," in which he mentioned, "Now through a glass darkly, then face to face . . ." (*I Corinthians*, 13:12). The dark mirror must be broken over and over again for us to be able to discover and rediscover ourselves and the soul of our needed others. This principle of "breakthrough" is what underlies the subtheme of Oedipus and of the sphinx.

The concept of the subjective object and of object use gives us an interesting picture of the origins of transference. Winnicott (1969) seems to have been describing Klein's (1946, 1955) mechanism of projective identification but in a way that is closer to Fairbairn's (1941) concept of identification. Winnicott placed the subjectively created, illusional object in potential space, apart from the real object, while Klein would see a perceptual and conceptual confusion between what the infant or toddler creates and the real object. This dichotomy is of some importance in concepts of transference. Ogden (1994b) retains Winnicott's (1967) concept of potential space and there locates a bivalent subjective object, that of "the analytic third," (combined subjectivity [-ies]) that represents the composite projected subjectivities of the analyst and the analysand). During the course of the analysis it is experienced as a "subjugating subjectivity," Ogden's innovative way of designating what may also be called "the transference–countertransference neurosis" (Grotstein, 1994b, 1995a).

Mnemic object: Bollas (1992) defined this as "a particular form of subjective object that contains a projectively identified self experience, and when we use it, something of that self state stored in it will arise" (p. 21).

Transformational object:[10] Bollas (1992), in reaction to the conception of object as a container of projections, described the transformational aspects of an object as follows.

> We oscillate between thinking ourself out through the selection of objects that promote inner experience and being thought out, so to speak, by the environment which plays upon the self. . . . In this respect, then, the objects of our world are potential forms of transformation [p. 4].

This poetic enhancement of the concept of the independent aspects of the object that are able to affect and transform us can be extended to art and to language. Objects in words, painting, and music, for instance, can transform us.

Aleatory object: Bollas (1992) says of the object that emerges "by chance" that we are intermediates, engaged in an interplay between our idiom and its subjective objects. Some self experience out of the thing's play on the subject as much as from the subject's use of the object, because as we move through space and time many things pop up by chance (as *aleatory objects*) and sponsor a unit of experience in us that has . . . been contained within the real (p. 21, italics added).

Analytic object: Bion (1962b, 1963, 1965, 1967b, 1970) conceived of the "analytic object" as the analysand's presentation of the maximum unconscious anxiety during the analytic session. It is the "object" on which the analyst must be focused. Bion believed that it represents O, the "thing-in-itself," the "beta (nonmentalized) elements of experience awaiting a "transformation in K" (knowledge) by the analyst's reverie and use of "alpha function," "translating" the analysand's beta elements into knowledge about mental pain (the analytic object). A paradox is implicit in the notion of the analytic object, however. I argue in chapter 10 that what Bion called the analytic object is really the analytic subject revealing its symptomotology. I believe that, if we undo the Cartesian division between subject and object in analysis, then what is presented to the analyst from the analysand's unconscious can be considered to be the analysand's pained subjectivity itself.

Background presence (object) of primary identification: I developed this object concept to help me understand some of the clinical differences between those analysands who underwent cataclysmic regressions versus those who were able to "regress in the service of the ego." It is similar to Winnicott's (1960b) "holding environment." Fundamentally, it

10. My own designation for this subjective object is *existential coach*.

represents "backing" for one's journey through life and "backup" support when one is discouraged (see chapter 4).

Object of destiny: Bion often spoke of the relationship between Freud's psychic apparatus in terms of verb tenses. The ego is the organ of the past; the id is the organ of the forever present; and the superego and ego ideal are the organs for the future. I therefore conceived of a teleological object that is guardian, monitor, and shepherd to our future (see chapter 1).

Selfobjects: Kohut's (1977) definition of selfobjects (mirroring, twinning, and idealizable) revealed a new category of object function in infancy, childhood, and adulthood. These are background objects; they as individuals are less important than the functions they provide. Unlike the objects and part-objects of Freud, Klein, Fairbairn, and Jacobson, they seem to be derived from Winnicott's (1960b) "holding environment" objects.

Dead objects: Analysands commonly provide dreams and associations in which "dead objects" or "dead selves" appear. These may result from unconscious infantile attacks against the objects or object unions (primal scene) or may be due to the infant's having "fallen through the cracks" as a result of serious and continuing neglect (Grotstein, 1995b, c, in preparation-b). In general, unconscious "clinical death" occurs when patients believe they have made a "Faustian bargain" (a "pact with the devil")—that is when they have "died a little" in order to be safe.

"Tricky" object: I alluded to this object earlier in this chapter. It can sometimes be experienced as a double agent, that is, as disingenuously loyal to differing conflictual entities within the self and also as a troublemaking superego insofar as it may often induce the subject to perform an act that justifies the latter's being reproved by the former. Psychoanalysis can be thought of as an example. We encourage analysands to retrieve the awareness of their infantile longings only to remind them of the superego injunctions that they must inescapably encounter.

The magus object: I named this object (see chapter 1) after John Fowles's *The Magus*, referring to the singular of "magi," magician-priests in Zoroastrianism. The particular use I impute to them is their power as a superego-type internal object to ensorcell their subjects to play out scenarios seemingly belonging to them, the magi, but which they compel the subjects to enact, for their own good. What I seek to emphasize here is an unusual angle on the origin of the sense of agency as scenarios or activities that are felt originally to be imposed on one by a higher authority. Being given a mission begins to express this idea. The magus object is another way of designating the Ineffable Subject of the

Unconscious, the Dreamer Who Dreams the Dream, and so on. It is the Ineffable Director who occupies the position that Ogden (1994b, 1997) accords to the psychoanalytic third subject. This "thirdness" acts in such a way as to control the thinking of both analysand and analyst and behaves very much like a ouija board, an activity without a known source.

One also sees this phenomenon clinically in patients who suffer from ideas or delusions of reference. These ideas are formed by the splitting off and projective reidentification of despised aspects of the subject and the scenarios of a person's daily life, which he or she wishes to disown.

Wasted and *wasting objects:* Often in clinical practice one runs into patients who believe that they have wasted their opportunities and objects, and, furthermore, they feel compelled to go on doing so. The origin of their need to waste the goodness of their objects and the opportunities these objects afford them often devolves into envy of the goodness of the object but may have other causes as well. In the very act of wasting, these patients have unconsciously projectively reidentified a wasting aspect of themselves into their image of the object, which, when internalized, becomes a *wasting* superego-object that further enforces wasting activities by the patients.

Alien object: Britton (1998) gives this name to a type of internal object that combines a seemingly realistic portrait of an actually injurious external object with an overlay of attributions projectively reidentified within it and that originate in the subject (patient). Fairbairn (1944) prefigured this object concept with his notion of the "rejecting object" (RO).

Toilet-breast object: This term applies to that aspect of the part-object function of the mother that absorbs and detoxifies her infant's distress. First used by Klein (1932) and then by Meltzer (1967), it gradually became absorbed into Bion's (1959, 1962b) concept of the container. The original conception of the "toilet-breast" function is close to that of the macrophage, a white blood cell that seeks out and absorbs poisonous intruders.

Jung's (1934) *archetypal terrible mother*[11] can be thought of as a conflation by the infant of its omnipotent needy instinctual feelings *and* its raw experience of "O" (Bion's term for the thing-in-itself, the noumena) projected into its image of mother.

Sacred and *profane objects:* Clinically, certain patients, out of envy or voyeurism, seek to desecrate their analysts in one way or another. Those aspects of the analyst that a patient may have idealized may

---

11. I cannot do justice in this chapter to the wealth of Jung's archetypal images.

later be desecrated out of rage. Klein (1928) revealed a universal unconscious infantile phantasy that inaugurates the archaic Oedipus complex in which the infant voyeuristically and sadistically seeks to enter mother's insides and explore her sacred internal contents (including father's penis, the blessed "unborn" babies, and her profane or sacred feces). Analytically we see this phenomenon in countless ways, often in an analysand's valorization or contempt of trinkets in our offices.

Perverse, cruel, subjugating, sadistic, manipulating, sabotaging, mocking, flaunting, shaming, fostering, aesthetic, prey–predatory, scavengering objects, and combinations of them are formed through the projective identification of primitive negative aspects of the infantile personality into the object, followed by introjective identification. Each of these negative objects has a passive complementary counterpart; that is, the sadistic object relates to a masochistic object, a "wasting" object relates to a "wasted" object, and so forth.

Scar-tissue object: I have coined this term, which I also think of as the "scar-tissue mother," from my analytic experiences with patients whom I characterize as "Orphans of the Real"; these are people who have suffered from what appeared to be infantile or childhood catastrophes because of traumata or neglect of varying degrees and types. Once, while treating one of these patients, I spontaneously thought of traumatic transsections of the spinal cord. One of the reasons for the permanency of the paralysis and anaesthesia that occur below the lesion is alleged to be that, once severed, the two disparate sections of the spinal cord cannot reunite. Experimental surgical research has found that one of the factors that underlies this permanency of damage is that bleeding takes place at the site of the wound, which is followed by the formation of scar tissue. It is the scar tissue that ultimately prevents the rehealing of the severed cord because the scar tissue is thick enough to prevent the severed nerve fibers from reuniting. If the scar tissue is removed, then a chance for reunion can theoretically occur.

This idea immediately offered a valuable (to me) metaphor for chronic resistances in patients. I thought of Fairbairn's (1944) involuting endopsychic structures ("involuting," insofar as they pull the escaping subject back into the endopsyche); Steiner's (1993) psychic retreats, which have much in common with Fairbairn's concept; and Hedges's (1998) concept of the "never-again" signal in patients who have been traumatized early. Put succinctly, the "scar-tissue" object is the default object, one the traumatized infant child creates and turns to for solace in its travail. It functions by numbing the victim and allowing him to escape from the reality of his distress. Over time, it becomes a harsh superego-tyrant who warns the victim against involving in an intimate alliance, such as psychoanalysis. In Hedges's (1998) terms, it warns, "Never again. . ."

THE CONTAINER AS OBJECT OF EXPRESSION AND REPRESSION

An object of sorts is also implied in Bion's (1962b) concept of the container and the contained. Bion seemed to think of the container as a maternal grid,[12] one that first suspends and then "translates" the infant's emotional, protomental, or nonmental messages in order to "inform" the infant (through appropriate, attuned interventions) of its needs. I believe, in addition, that the container is an object—insofar as it is a function—that, when internalized, can be considered to be the container for the infant's repressed. The infant can project what it cannot yet tolerate to know or realize into the internalized container for the future "return of the repressed." Thus, the container is the earliest model for repression insofar as its function allows for the delay or postponement, in the infant, of the awareness or recognition of the seriousness of the emotional facts he has encountered but could not process.

PATHOLOGICAL ORGANIZATIONS (PSYCHIC RETREATS) AS ENDOPSYCHIC STRUCTURES

Meltzer (1973), Rosenfeld (1987), and Steiner (1993) have conceived of groupings of pathological objects as "internal Mafias," "narcissistic organizations," and "pathological organizations" or "psychic retreats" respectively. Their idea is that a grouping of destructive internal objects formed a coalition against the analysand, often causing a negative therapeutic reaction as these internal objects gang up on the analysand when there is progress in the analysis and in life. I think that this "gang" or "Mafia" may originate when an analysand has come from a dysfunctional family. In actuality or in phantasy, the analysand may have dissociated from the family and formed a "little oedipal family" that often becomes a real gang. The analysand has lost respect for the "law of the father" and is substituting as new head of the real or imagined "little

12. It is important to bear in mind that father also functions as a container either independently of mother or in complementary collaboration as a background function to protect the nursing couple.

family." A fixation from an earlier stage of infant development may also contribute to the development of this "gang" organization.

Klein (1928) described the infant's envy of mother's insides, especially of the so-called internal babies, the ones who are blessed by being able to remain inside mother and have not had to become separated. Phantasied voyeuristic and sadistic attacks against these "internal babies" may result in the belief that the patient has successfully invaded mother, stolen the babies, and compromised or converted them to his subjugating will. They thereafter become installed as a "gang" or "Mafia" superego. This unconscious phantasy is reminiscent of Freud's (1913) concept of the primal horde of brothers who overthrew and slew the primal father in mythical times.

OBJECTS AS PSYCHIC PRESENCES

In contrast to psychoanalysts of the various Freudian schools, Jung and his followers have been very interested in what I refer to as the *denizens* or preferably the *presences*, that occupy—or we may say haunt—the Unconscious. These can be called objects, but when we examine clinical material closely, especially dreams, it is apparent that this term is impersonal, inapproximate, and attenuated. The idea of the *archetypes* of the collective unconscious is closer to the patient's inner subjective experience, and I emphasize the Kleinian and Bionian equivalent, *inherent preconceptions* and *unconscious phantasies* of *phantoms/monsters/chimerae* produced by *projective identification*. In other words, the origin of the experience of an object may be either through inherent anticipation as a preconception (archetype, e.g., breast-mother) or through projective identification, which thereby creates subjective objects.

Ogden (1994b), as I have already mentioned, has elegantly applied the concept of dialectical intersubjectivity to the transference–countertransference situation and has shown how a third area of encounter emerges that represents an amalgam of each participant in the encounter. This concept allows us to see that, in virtually every relationship, the participants become "haunted," as it were, by a newly constituted "demon." That mysterious third entity, the subjectivity of the relationship itself, ultimately defines, organizes, directs, controls, manipulates, and subjugates each of the participants. The participants, in turn, find themselves behaving according to a script or choreography that they do not know they are following, and they may be bewildered by how they are mysteriously behaving, frequently projecting blame on the other participant.

A case in point is that of a 33-year-old single female analysand who complained of long-standing troubling relationships with men. At the time of the following dream she had begun to date a man whom she liked. The dream was as follows: She and her boyfriend went out for a drive and then parked to become intimate. As they were kissing each other, they were suddenly accosted by a thief with a gun. The thief struck the analysand on the head and rendered her unconscious. When she revived (within the dream), he was still there. He then pointed his finger at her boyfriend to indicate that it was the boyfriend who had struck her.

Her associations led to her fear of her belligerent and physically intimidating older brother when she was a child. I was able to interpret that she had projected her internalized brother imago into her boyfriend and sided with a brutish aspect of herself, which she projected into the thief. She always looked for a man who would be strong enough to counter her internalized brother, but when she found one, she thereupon, paradoxically, projected the brother into him and then "got even" by rejecting him—but at her expense, the expense of a good future relationship.

Winnicott, with his appreciation of dialectics and paradox, seemed to fathom the importance of the imaginary nature of the object. His concept of the *subjective object* conveys the oxymoron status implicit in the concept of the object's nature (Winnicott, 1969). This subjective object is imaginatively created by the infant (and adults) in the presence of the real object (person). Winnicott, following Klein's (1946, 1955) concept of projective identification, saw all of daily life as imbued with transference.

THE INTERNAL WORLD AS A THIRD AREA OF EXPERIENCE

I use the term *third form* for a concept that has been hidden in the psychoanalytic understanding of the term *object*. Whether located externally or internally, the object is always a montage, a palimpsest of subjective (because subjectified) images. The external object is known to us through the apperceptive distortion of our senses. On internalization, it becomes further mythified. The external (real) object, actually a subject presented as an object, is first of all ineffable and unknowable in its Otherness (Bion's O) insofar as it is an *individual and* is indivisible. We can only know *about* it. What we perceive is compounded, complicated, and altered by the subjectivity of our "transferences," those from past object cathexes and those from projective identifications in the present, all emerging from our subjective states, or, to put the matter with greater clinical precision, from our "subject in variegated states of mind" (see chapter 5). The knowable object is reconstructed for us by the unconscious activities of our object usage (a subjective object) and by the cooperation/collusion of the real object itself—acting as a subject in its own right—in terms of the dialectical interaction of thirdness described by Jung (1953, 1958), Ferguson (1982), Schwartz-Salant (1989), and Ogden (1994b, 1997). The "knowable object" is a living, interactive constructivist mannequin that always cloaks and dissembles the ineffable "*Object-who-is-Subject*" (Kant, 1787; Hoffman, 1992, 1994; Ogden, 1994b, 1997; Wilkinson, 1998; see also chapter 10).

Bloom (1996) states the following in regard to Avicenna, the great Persian philosopher of Islam in the 11th century:

> Avicenna . . . argued for a Hermetic angelology that posited a *middle reality* between ordinary perceptions and the realm of the divine. This middle world of angelic perception is equated with the human world of the awakened imagination, the dwelling place of sages and poets, and of all of us in certain exalted or enlightened moments when we see, feel, and think lucidly. Those moments, according to the Sufis, introduce us into what they call the world of Hurqalya, the angelic world, Hurqalya is called both a city and world, and sometimes is also called "the Celestial Earth," since it is our earth reimagined [pp. 147–148, italics added].

Blooms's "angels" can be translated into internal objects and object representations. The third form is an invisible world. We do not know we inhabit it because of our faith in the verdict of our senses; all the while we fail to realize that are senses themselves are heavily tinted with Kantian and Freudian filters of transference. In other words, the world we believe we live in is a consensually mythified one and becomes personally mythified upon internalization.

The concept of *third form* comes from the Kleinian notion of the "internal object" and its phantasmal creation via splitting and projective identification. According to Kleinian theory, the infant, trying to preserve the state of mind that Freud (1911b) called "the purified pleasure ego," splits off the bad feelings and urges that discomfit it, disidentifies from them in unconscious phantasy, and reidentifies them in the (image of the) "object," which thereupon is transformed in the infant's mind—as a *third form*. In virtually every act of projective identification, the qualities of omnipotent intentionality, agency (will), subjectivity, and personification are attributed to the object's new contents. When this image is then re-introjected, it becomes an "internal (subjective) object" in at least three ways: (1) concordantly, (2) complementarily (Racker, 1968), and (3) oppositionally (Grotstein, 1994, 1995a). The projecting subject's reidentification with the projection causes the emergence of a state of *misrecognition* or internal *alienation* and a vulnerability to identity diffusion and fragmentation. The projecting subject also experiences the sense of déjà vu and is haunted by the strangely familiar but unknowable aspects of its former self.

The clinical phenomenon of heightened neediness (greed) illustrates concordant projective and introjective identifications. In this situation, the infant may split off its painfully needy feelings and project them into the object, the concordant transformation of which would be the phantasied creation of an omnipotently demanding and suffocating object. This concordantly transformed object is then internalized and introjectively identified as an omnipotently demanding and suffocating superego. Additionally, insofar as the infant believes that it has damaged the breast by its greedy projective attacks, it creates the image of a complementary damaged or mutilated object (a "scooped-out breast"), which is internalized and introjectively identified with as a damaged, mutilated, impoverished, and impotent ego. The infant may then inaugurate a manic defense (triumph, contempt, and control over the object of need and over the dependent infant) and oppose the authority of the concordant superego object and the submissively dependent complementary ego/object.

The consequences of the creation of this image are far reaching. For instance, the scooped-out breast image, when internalized and introjectively identified with, may become the forerunner of the infant's image of the female vagina, to which the projected and then introjected image of its imagined teeth may be added to create a frightening ensemble of images for later hauntings—in both female and male analysands. The two images, concordant and complementary, are like "Siamese twins," paradoxically connected and disconnected at the same time. The damag*ed* image, according to Freud (1917), is lodged in the ego, which identifies with it. The concordant damag*ing* image, on the other hand, is identified with the ego ideal, later the superego, in a "gradient in the ego" (Freud, 1923a). Thus, the damaged and damaging images are linked, and each is compounded with respective aspects of the ego.

The damag*ing* (ego ideal/superego) objects maintain a hypnotic dominance over the damag*ed* objects in the ego, which use *depressive defenses*[13]

13. In chapter 10, I discuss the importance for considering the concept of the depressive defense in clinical depressive illness as a necessary counterpart to Klein's (1940) concept of the manic defense in pathological narcissism.

to counter this dominance with a passive–aggressive depressive (masochistic) counterdefense. The internalized image, to say nothing of its external counterpart, has undergone a significant transformation —a compounding and montaging exaggeration or caricaturing and an uncanny, preternatural alienation. From these transformations third forms emerge in the internal world as dissociated alter egos or second subjective selves within the personality.

Klein (1929b) hinted at but did not explicate another aspect of internal mental life, that of *personification* or *animation*, which, I suggest, is a component of *subjectification* of the object. For instance, clinically patients, insofar as they are identified with an infantile aspect of their personality, believe that they, through extractive projective identification (Bollas, 1989), have marauded father's image and have taken his penis for themselves and identified with it, a phantasy that Klein (1940) termed the manic defense. The part-object penis is then animated and imbued with life, subjectivity, and *will* (agency, purpose, intent, conation). It becomes a willful demon, positive or negative in its intent. In addition, the projective attribution of omnipotence is the unconscious phantasy of the personal ownership of infinity (Matte-Blanco, 1975, 1988). The highest mediator of infinity, of course, is God, but the lesser archangels, angels, fairies, and spirits are included, albeit conditionally (Bloom, 1996).[14]

All internal objects (*subjective demons*) are multifariously constructed. The term monster encompasses the gallimaufry of cannibalized parts that contribute to the grotesque, misshapen, bizarre otherness that characterizes these demons. I have often encountered the notion of monstrousness in patients who phantasied, for instance, that a lost child-self had been imprisoned, through projective/introjective "kidnaping," in a sealed internal object, where it grew distortedly. Images of dwarfs, elves, and pixies may be variants of this idea of the monster.

"ROGUE SUBJECTIVE OBJECTS" AS MISRECOGNIZED SUBJECTS

Another aspect of the fate of the self in this alienating thirdness is the concept of misrecognition described by Lacan (1936) as a feature of the mirror phase. I apply the concept of misrecognition to the fate of the split-off aspect of the self that undergoes an alienating projective exile into the object and then returns to the projecting subject as a misrecognized and

14. For further reading on mythical creatures, see Bulfinch (1935), Briggs (1976), Caldwell (1989), and Calasso (1993).

misrecognizing stranger. Thus, the object aspect of the internalized object acts as a barrier to keep the two "brothers" or "sisters" apart.

FATE VERSUS DESTINY[15]

Whereas Freud and Klein spoke from the orthodox analytic perspective of psychic determinism, which predicates a concept of inherently "guilty man" ("original sin"), Fairbairn spoke from the empirical perspective of primal innocence" ("tragic man"). He believed that the infant and child, in their pragmatic propensity toward adaptation, selectively internalized and introjectively identified with only those aspects of the needed mother—and father—that they believed endangered their welfare. As a result, Fairbairn's endopsychic structures consist of part-objects and whole objects that were initially rejected by the infant and then, upon internalization, were transformed (by dissociative splitting and projective identification, presumably) into rejecting objects and exciting objects. It is only when we undo the artificial division between the exciting and the rejecting objects that another, more diabolical structure begins to appear, that of the *rejecting and yet paradoxically simultaneously tantalizing presence of the devil himself!* Fairbairn, to his credit, spoke often of demoniacal possession and likened endopsychic structure to the "religion of the crypt."

A more fundamental contribution to the formation of the internal world is the platonic notion of Ideal Forms. These can be understood as the universal collective archetypes elaborated by Jung (1934) and the inherent preconceptions ("memoirs of the future") conceived by Bion (1970, 1975, 1977b, 1979). In all probability, the phantoms, ghosts, monsters, and chimerae that occupy and haunt our internal world are part of our inherent template of possibilities *and* at the same time are created anew from the raw clay of our autochthonous creative projective identifications (including animation and personification).

Dodds (1951) integrated his study of madness in ancient Greece with the anthropological studies of Sir James G. Frazer (1910) and discussed the progression of Greek religious cosmology from the most primitive times of the *Iliad* through the later, more sophisticated era of the more humanlike Olympian deities. For archaic Greeks, extreme affects came from outside, that is, from divine temptation (Dodds, 1951, pp. 2–3). He refers to "the Erynes, the vengeful spirits who walk in dark-

15. Bollas (1989) also discusses the dialectic of fate and destiny but from another angle.

ness . . . for Zeus the counselor took away his understanding" (p. 4) and from Ate, the demon of irrationality (p. 5). The agencies include Zeus, Moira (Fate-ful portion), and the Erynes (which Klein, 1963, associated with the internal objects of the paranoid/schizoid position and which transform into the Eumenides in the depressive position).

Daemon is considered to be a god (p. 12). Thumos is a primitive breath-soul or life-soul and is the organ of feeling; it is not a part of the self but an independent inner voice (p. 16). "When he acts in a manner contrary to the system of conscious dispositions which he is said to 'know,' his action is not properly his own, but has been dictated to him" (p. 17). The daemon Phthonous produces jealousy; Hubris, primary evil; Koros, complacency. The Titans, who represented the unbound powers of infinity in nature (which can be associated with the proto-affects of borderline and psychotic patients), preceded and were overthrown by the Olympians, who represented the conquest of infinity through symbolic containment and reduction of infinity and chaos. The unconscious, earthly impulses that escaped Olympian mediation were represented in the return of the orgiastic Dionysian rites and in the sexual earthiness and depravity that characterized the Olympian deities.[16]

The ancient Greeks were surrounded by nature and its denizens, the tame as well as the wild and threatening animals, to say nothing of thunder, lightening, earthquakes, tornadoes, floods, volcanoes. Thus, lions, eagles, vultures, and other predatory animals were part of everyday experience. These animals later became powerful signifiers in the traditions and rituals of cultures far removed from their threatening presence. For instance, the lion, which played an everyday role in village life in ancient Egypt and Israel, became a predominant feature of European heraldry and a totemic symbol for Scotland, England, and many other countries. Perhaps the presence of these symbols represents the migrations of peoples and their totemic religious practices from areas where there was familiarity with them, so that their beastly nature came to symbolize aspects of our own and found its way into our internal demons. For instance, in the legend of Oedipus we encounter the chimera of the sphinx, an omnipotent and omniscient monster that consists of the head of a woman, the body of a lion, the wings of a bird, and the tail of a serpent.

From the Kleinian point of view, the various creature constituents of the sphinx's nature constitute projective identifications of fearsome and intimidating beastly attributes from the infantile self. The mother, who is female, is physically a large and intimidating superperson relative to the littleness of her infant. The lion represents the fierceness and

16. Sexual intercourse once constituted a religious fertility rite.

predatory nature that the infant projects into her from its own beastly nature. The bird represents the power of flight with which the infant imbues her. The serpent represents her projected treacherous nature, treacherous in the Biblical sense as the mother, Eve, who, after giving birth to "God" and creating an Eden atmosphere for Him, deserts Him to have intercourse with God's father, Adam (see chapter 2).

The sphinx (whose root word is sphincter and which in Greek means, "she who squeezes") is therefore a "subjective object," one that poses a riddle to our sense of identity. The answer to the famous riddle of the sphinx ("What walks on four legs, then two legs, and then three legs?) is man, that is, the self. Once we know who we are, we also know who we are not, and we also know who the other is and is not. Our ability to define ourselves as we really are constitutes the death knell of the sphinx as subjective object (Winnicott, 1969) because in knowing ourselves we reown the projective identifications we sent into a diaspora of misrecognition with the object, misattributing them to others. Our repatriation of these projective identifications from their diaspora in mythified others reconstitutes ourselves on an expanded level of consciousness and attenuates our need to lose ourselves in states of misrecognition in others. Thus, the sphinx, by being a chimerical subjective object, constitutes a condensed narrative signifier that, when analytically expanded, reveals itself to be a compressed hieroglyphic narrative. The sphinx is archetypal *and* idiosyncratically personal. It is always there in the collective unconscious *and* is constructed anew by splitting and projective identification.

Another chimerical monster in Greek legend is the Minotaur (see chapter 7), the shameful offspring of Pasiphaë and Zeus who disguised himself as the great white bull of the sea. The bull was a sacred scapegoat animal in ancient Crete and other Mediterranean countries during the ancient era of matriarchal hegemony. The totemic animal sacrifices that characterized the sacred practices of matriarchal religions followed an earlier phase in which male—and sometimes female—youths were ritualistically sacrificed (Graves, 1958; Girard, 1972, 1978, 1986, 1987; Gimbutas, 1974; Bergmann, 1992). In clinical terms, the signifier of the scapegoat and child sacrifice constitutes perhaps the most profound aspect of the Oedipus complex, religion, and psychopathology. There is always an abject self within us that seems to be unconsciously chosen to be sacrificed, scapegoated, self-abused, and often projected into others—we believe that, once we attribute malevolent agency to it for all the bad things that happen to us, we can hope to change our fortunes. The first form of justice, after all, involves locating, blaming, and punishing the criminal to eradicate the "pollution" in the community, both social and internal. The justice of understanding must await the mercy of the depressive position.[17] The acrobatic games and sacrificial rituals involving the bull probably represented the female power to intimidate the male phallus in the form of the bull.

The Minotaur is a subjective object, a chimera like the sphinx and also like its relative, the centaur. Centaurs galloped across the plains of the pre-Hellenic imagination and were even counted among the wise men. Kyros, the centaur, was a physician who practiced with Aesculapius. The amalgam of half-human, half-beast exists in a binary opposition with the half-human, half-divine heroes who sprang from unions between gods and humans, for example, Achilles and Cadmus. Descent from a god constituted the certification of omnipotence, whereas descent from beasts conveyed both animal wisdom, in the sense of knowledge about the natural world ("all the unpublished virtues of this earth"), and animalistic excess.

The theme of the labyrinth and the Minotaur is reflected in Klein's (1928) conception of the archaic Oedipus complex, which she conjectured occurred as early as the oral stage of development and was characterized by an unconscious infantile phantasy of father's penis and internal babies dwelling inside mother's body (see chapter 7). Therefore the Minotaur is a signifier of the paternal phallus as (1) a conquered prisoner incarcerated within the maternal "stockade" in a continuing state of sadomasochistic intercourse; (2) a subordinate but intimidating sentinel that patrols, guards, and protects mother's insides from invasive intruders; (3) a subjective object, like the sphinx, which is created by illusion and challenges the identity of its would-be invader and killer; and (4) a condensation of the infant's idea of parental intercourse and the shame that it feels about it insofar as it reveals the beastly nature of their union. The primal scene, sadomasochism, and the inherent preconception of the "covenant" between prey and predator are condensed in this theme.

Minos and Pasiphaë are later editions of the matriarchal deity/combined couple (Klein's, 1928, combined parent) in which the wife's untamed (Dionysian) sexuality could be satisfied only by the divine "bull from the sea," Zeus. Paglia (1990) has described the sense of intimidation that men share as an instinctive response to the "sexual persona" of the female genitalia. The insideness of the female genital has always been associated with infinite depths in which the male penis can become overwhelmed and lost, never to return. The phantasy of vagina dentata testifies additionally to the projective identification of the infant's teeth into the image of the vagina. The aura of female intimidation and the

---

17. See chapters 8 and 9 for a fuller explication of human sacrifice as the hidden organizer of the Oedipus complex.

primitive, beastly, insatiable nature that mankind has projectively attributed to the female sex organ and the sexual persona have origins in prehistory and in the days of the matriarchal cultures that dominated Europe, particularly around the Mediterranean rim. The female genital was both deified and contemned and thought of as mysterious and treacherous. Thus it was a "labyrinth" guarded by special sentinels, sometimes the snake (which later became the dragon) or by the Minotaur, which became a signifier of Pasiphaë's beastly passion as well as a symbol of her abjectly shameful excessiveness in a culture that was transforming into patriarchal restraint.

THE "CHANGELING"

One of the most touching legends from ancient folklore is that of the "changeling," which is the myth of fairy theft of newborn babies and substitution by one of their own (Briggs, 1976). The concept of the changeling can be applied clinically to those situations where there seems to have been a difficulty in bonding and attachment, situations in which the infant and mother could not develop an intimate closeness. The result often was one in which the infant felt that he or she did not belong to that mother or family, was an outsider as compared with the other siblings. In these situations, one frequently finds that the analysand either recalls feeling detached from the family or believes that he "divorced" the family at an early age without anyone really knowing it. Some of these analysands develop compensatory "family romances" (Freud, 1909) in which they seek to belong, in phantasy or actuality, to other families. The clinical case presentation in this chapter is a good example of the changeling phantasy.

THE "BLESSED OBJECTS"

A class of subjective objects exists that deserves mention, the fortunate or blessed ones. These objects may actually exist in real life, at least as estimated by our own individual envy or admiration, but I am here referring to a class of putatively blessed ones that exist in our imagination. Klein (1928, 1932) described a universal phantasy that takes place in the infant's mental life during the hegemony of the archaic Oedipus complex. In this stage the epistemophilic and sadistic part-instincts operate together and at a maximum. One of the features of the phantasmagoria of this stage is the infant's unconscious phantasy of invading mother's body and sadistically appropriating her "internal" or "unborn babies," those projectively created phantoms that are believed by the infant to be so special to mother and so blessed by her that they escape the penalty of birth and separation and are permitted to remain inside her. These "unborns" may become resurrected in later life to accommodate one's belief that fortunate or blessed individuals do indeed exist. Legislation has been enacted in England to abolish the hereditary privilege of the peers in the House of Lords. These hereditary peers, as well as the members of various monarchies, exemplify the reification of this universal need to believe that people do exist who are born to privilege and who therefore, in retrospect, were blessed.

"RELIGIOUS OBJECTS"

The major religious themes of the human soul and in human history can be characterized as pagan, moral, and spiritual; as dominated by the paranoid/schizoid, depressive, and transcendent positions (Grotstein, 1996); as reflecting a gender-deity hegemony from matriarchal through patriarchal to divine parental couple to the desexualized godhead; and as the parental religions (individually and collectively) or the child-centered religions. Associated with matriarchy, the religion of fertility, were the ecstatic religious rites of Dionysus and Pan and the goddess' defenders, the snake-dragon or the unicorn and others. In the history of mankind, there has always been a cultural and religious dialectic between female and male domination, and the predominance of the later is a manic defense against the natural fertility and generativity of the former. This dialectic is reflected in the conflict between the ecstatic and the stoic religions.

The human mind, like ancient Troy, includes a layering of archetypal spiritual-religious levels or landscapes that are constrained to a succession of hegemonies beginning with the autochthonous, continuing through first the female-dominated and then the male-dominated parthenogenic conception of intercourse, on its way to an ultimate equality between the values of each member of the parental couple in their mutually sanctifying union.

The first religion is the religion by and for the self, portrayed in *Genesis* and in the Tower of Babel myth and culminating in the crucifixion of the "Man who thought He was God." The religion of the "Man who thought He was God" may be related to Freud's (1914b) portrayal of the fate of primary narcissism. As the infant becomes increasingly aware of its neediness, it forfeits its grandiosity and becomes an ordinary human mortal, who is forced to leave the Garden of Eden. Another aspect of the infant, however, maintains this grandiosity or omnipotence but in effect (as I read Freud) must forfeit its earthly humanness to become the ego ideal, forever situated in "a gradient in the ego." I believe that this is the Christ archetype (Jung, 1934; Edinger, 1989), one who shares suffering with its earthly counterpart and who has become part of the human/divine quaternary with the superego in the Gnostic sense of the presence of an internal divinity.

Klein's (1928) concept of the "internal babies," the blessed ones who are privileged never to have to leave the womb, may owe its provenance to this mysterious, inchoate grandiose self. From another view, that of Lacan (1966), this primordial self may be seen as the object, *le petit a*, that once constituted the primordial couple-as-one, the inchoate subject before separation. Thus, the loss of the grandiose self is equated with the loss of the object-as-subjective-self that once was oneself and is no longer.

The matriarchal divinity presupposes ecstatic, orgiastic rites, not so much for our sensual enjoyment, but to engender fertility. Freud tactfully but sentiently reminded us that the libidinal instinct in effect tricks us into desiring sex in order to procreate, in contrast to the life-preservative instincts of the ego.[18] The ecstatic, orgiastic, procreative religion constitutes what I believe to be a compulsive religious ritual. We are not only *im*pelled but also *com*pelled (religiously) to have sex in order to satisfy our own individual longings as well as the longings of the Earth Mother archetype. The third religion, the patriarchal, introduces the "law of the father," "No," the ban on incest. The tragedy in the story of Oedipus and his forebears in the Labdacid Dynasty of Thebes is understandable in terms of four factors: (1) fate and its will; (2) the ineluctability of human sacrifice; (3) the matriarchally holy compulsion to procreate; and (4) the imposition of the law of the father, the last of which has become ritualized as the incest taboo secularly and the stoic practice of spirituality.

THE DEVIL

In discussing the origins of the devil, Thomas (1971) stated:

> Demons had no corporeal existence, but it was notorious that they could borrow or counterfeit human shape. . . . The horns,

18. Lacan's pithy way of picturing this jest of Nature is the following: "A chicken is an egg's way of making another egg" (cited in Skelton, 1995b).

> tail and brimstone of the medieval stage, and the grotesque creature of church sculpture and woodcarving, helped to form the popular conception of Satan which has remained iconographically familiar until the present day [p. 470].

Paradoxically, however, "The Devil also played a prominent part in the execution of divine judgments. He was 'God's hangman,' as James I called him" (p. 472).

> But Satan was not only an agent of divine retribution. He was also a tempter. Once the possibility of his personal appearance in this world had been accepted, it was but a shortcut to the notion that there were individuals who entered into a semi-feudal contract with him, mortgaging their souls in return for a temporary access of supernatural knowledge or power. Such Faustian legends were in common circulation during the Sixteenth and Seventeenth Centuries [p. 473].

The devil's medieval portrait as a demon with horns, tail, and cloven feet seems to be a transformation of the Dionysian goat-god, Pan, who symbolized both libidinal excess and its opposite, panic, and the ram-goat, the scapegoat and Pascal lamb of the Jews, upon whom they ritualistically projected their sins and then sent it into the wilderness. The ancestry of Satan, who once sat at the right hand of God as an archangel, lies in the projective identification of human envy. God, who is absolute and therefore unable to countenance error (i.e., negative transference), must be split into a good God and a bad one. Thus, when the human being envies God, that envy is split off and projected into a correspondingly split-off aspect of God, who then falls from grace as a diabolically envious superego within us. Hell is a spiritual-religious domain ruled by this fallen god-angel, who once reigned supreme when the goat-god Pan sat at the right hand of Dionysus.

We know from scripture that, when Abraham swore allegiance to the ineffable and inscrutable One God, Yahweh (Adonai), he was asked to prove his devotion by sacrificing his son Isaac. When Abraham showed his willingness to do this, God recanted and established a covenant with mankind that a pars pro toto circumcision, in addition to the sacrifice of a ram, would suffice as the test of devotion. Thus, the sacrifice of the innocent infant underwent a substitutive transformation into the sacrifice of the innocent goat or sheep. Insofar as the innocent sheep or goat can *contain* and thereby *transform* the parishioners' projective identifications, the sheep becomes the Pascal Lamb, Christ, whose resurrection represents a spiritual transcendence and therefore forgiveness of and salvation for human suffering.

As the lamb is transformed by the projective suffering, however, it becomes the devil, Christ's alter ego. Thus, human innocence is an imprisoned hostage within the substance of the god of the abject, the devil himself. In his very abjectness the devil paradoxically symbolizes the most holy aspect of ourselves, the innocent self that we sold into bondage and left in the embrace of the dark demon, whom we also created to be the hermetic seal for the nuclear waste we projected into it, a waste that goes back to Sodom and Gomorrah.

I suggest (chapters 2, 8, 9) that the almost divine authority that we invest in the superego and the ego ideal may be understood as having two major roots. Klein (1935) first stated that the omnipotence we attribute to the superego was due to the projective identification of the infant's own sense of omnipotence into the maternal (and paternal) image. That sense of impotence is then introjected and secondarily identified with, now in the infant's superego, to which it is afterwards in a state of hypnotic thralldom and subjugation. I add to Klein's explanation that human sacrifice is the most sacred part of the oedipal theme and that it has continued in its descendant myth of the crucifixion of Christ. Freud (1913) hypothesized that the mythical father in prehistoric times became totemized as a god after being sacrificed. Klein and her followers explicated the sacrifice of the mother in terms of the infant's attacks against the breast. Others have shown that the infant and child are subjected to abuse that can be understood as an atavistic religious ritual of "sacrifice of the innocents as scapegoats" (Girard, 1972, 1978, 1986, 1987; Bergmann, 1992; Grotstein, 1998a).[19]

WITCHCRAFT

Witchcraft is a survival from pagan times, undoubtedly an atavistic residue of the matriarchal religions and maternal earth rites. Witches were also connected in the medieval church to the Manichaean and Cathar heresies, both considered devil worshiping. Malevolent magic stood side by side with beneficent magic in the medieval concept of witchcraft. A new element was added to it with the rise of the belief in the devil in the late Middle Ages, when it began to be believed that a

19. A fuller discussion on the concept of the devil is beyond the scope of this present work. For more in-depth studies see Russell, 1977; Padel, 1992, 1995; Black and Hyatt, 1993; Pagels, 1995; and Bloom, 1996, amongst many.

witch owed her powers to having made a deliberate pact with the devil. The devil's aim was always to capture men's souls, and he was ever-ready to exploit any situation to do so (Thomas, 1971, p. 590). Often an accusation of witchcraft occurred because a nonconformist and malcontent would be isolated, alienated, and ostracized in tightly controlled village life.

Jong (1981), examining the origins of witchcraft, states, "The witch is one who uses magic to bend things according to her desires" (p. 14). This definition seems to imply that the idea of witches and witchcraft fundamentally involves the projective identification of infantile omnipotence into a maternal figure. Thomas (1971) distinguishes between "witchcraft" and "sorcery":

> Witchcraft is an innate quality, an involuntary personal trait, deriving from a physiological peculiarity which can be discovered by autopsy. The witch exercises his malevolent power by occult means, and needs no words, rite, spell, or potion. His is a purely psychic act. Sorcery, on the other hand, is the deliberate employment of maleficent magic; it involves the use of a spell or technical aide and it can be performed by anyone who knows the correct formula. Witchcraft, on this definition, is thus an impossible crime and not empirically observable, whereas sorcery really is practiced in many primitive societies [p. 463].

ALTERNATIVE LEGACIES OF MOURNING AND MELANCHOLIA IN THE FORMATION OF THE SUPEREGO

The superego is a universal pre-Enlightenment demon that exists in the unconscious of all individuals and is significantly present in the minds of our patients, especially those suffering from psychoses or primitive mental disorders. The Kleinian superego *is* the projected aspects of the infant modified by their sojourn in the object; that is, it is the id transformed and stored in an object, whose image it modifies by its presence. Klein's (1935, 1940) conception of the origin of the superego differs from Freud's (1923a). For Freud, the superego arises as the inheritor of the Oedipus complex in the late phallic phase. For Klein, the superego originates inchoately with the infant's projections of parts of itself (i.e., affects, impulses, needs, omnipotence, intentionality, agency, etc.) into its image of the object, which, upon subsequent introjection, becomes an archaic superego object. In other words, the Kleinian superego comprises split-off and projected aspects of the infant deceptively clothed in the object's garb.

The emergence of this superego is manifest in psychoanalysis and psychotherapy and in love. Our patients choose certain love objects frequently because the loved ones are embodiments of the patients' projected superego. The superego is, after all, the object that knows one better than anyone. Choosing a superego proxy gives one the illusion of a chance for appeal for redemption and reprieve. Further, by virtue of the omnipotence that the infantile self grants the superego, anyone who seems able to portray that power becomes a manic attraction for a fellow narcissist.

When we as analysts observe the presence of an archaic superego and its harmful effect on the patient, we generally call attention to the patient's entranced fealty to that inner—or projected—demon. From another perspective, however, paradoxically this superego demon can be seen as a friend in disguise who caricatures the projectively foresworn abject aspects of the self for the patient to recognize and reaccept. Freud (1917) proposed that the melancholic, owing to his narcissistic immaturity, cannot allow for the fact of the object's departure and confines the lost object internally in two separate aspects of the ego, the ego ideal (superego) and the ego proper.

This posture is tantamount to a failure to allow mourning for the object, and the departed object becomes a haunting, undead, yet unalive *ghost*. One aspect of the self is identified with this ghost, which shares unaliveness and undeadness with the object to which it is "Siamese-twinned." The person who is capable of mourning, by contrast, can release control of the relationship and allow the object to pass on and become a *spirit*, who graces, blesses, and substantiates the psyche in which it is now ensconced. The person who is able to mourn can allow for the departure or disappearance of the cherished other, can contemplate the other's goodness in its absence, favorably balance that goodness against past grievances with this other, and then ultimately experience a sense of well-being that seems to affirm that the departed loved one remains internally *in spirit*.

CONCLUDING REMARKS

I should like to conclude this chapter by correlating the concept of internal objects (subjective objects) with the concept of images. Internal objects are concretely perceived sensory images (from the sensorimotor stage), which can be perceived and apprehended by the "sense organ responsive to internal qualities" (Freud, 1900). They become denizens and characters of the paranoid-schizoid position. In the depressive position, however, the infant is able to release its sensory control or mandate over the *image* of the object and allow it its freedom but, having released it, is able thereafter to *evoke* its image at will. This evoked image is also situated in the internal world but on a higher and more mature level ("on a gradient in the ego"). This object—now a whole object—has externally become a *subject* in its own right and a separate person vis-à-vis the infant.

The infant's experience and awareness of this whole object's autonomous and independent personhood has been described by Klein (1935) as the attainment of the depressive position, by Trevarthen (1979, 1980) as the dawn of intersubjectivity, and by Fonagy (1991, 1995; Fonagy et al., 1991) as the beginning of mindedness (self-reflection). From Bion's (1965, 1970, 1992) standpoint, one may consider symbolic (whole) objects as constitutive of K (knowledge) *about* the object, awaiting yet a further stage, a transformation from K to O, from *knowledge* to *wisdom*, to "becoming" the object, not in the sense of identification but in the sense of a resonance with an elusive, mysterious essence of the Other. I refer to this phenomenon as the transient attainment of the *transcendent position* (chapter 10). One can find allusions to it in Freud (1917) when he discusses how the successful mourner, rather than identifying with the lost object, as the melancholic patient does in order to deny the object's loss, *becomes* the object in a way that is suggestive of sublimation.

Thus, it is my belief—and perhaps Freud's and Bion's as well—that human beings relate to each other only through their phantasmal (paranoid/schizoid) or "realistic" (depressive position) *images* of the object, not to the subject (who the whole object has now become) in its own right—its Otherness. In its Otherness, the object qua subject is elusive and unknowable It is O. Thus, human relationships, when considered from this perspective, can be likened to the "dance of images" rather than the thing-in-itself, O. In a forthcoming work, which is a revision of my earlier work on "projective identification" (Grotstein, 1981a), I assert that one can never project into another person; one can only project into one's *image* (phantasmal or symbolic) of that person. When the other person *seems* to respond to the projection, I now term that interactive phenomenon projective- and introjective-*trans*identification.

The subject relates to external objects, not only through projective- and then introjective-identifications; it also relates to them in terms of what Bion (1962b) referred to as L (love), H (hate), and K (knowledge) linkages in both positive and negative valences. L and H have their counterparts in Jacobson's (1964) concept of libidinization versus delibidinization and aggressivization versus deaggressivization, all under the rubric of neutralization and deneutralization. The counterpart to the K link would be what Hartmann (1939) thought of as a "change of function" from the id drives to drive representations in the ego's representational world.

Further, I posit that a link, or maybe even a continuity, exists between the concepts of an external object, an internal object, and Bion's "container/contained." Let us take the extreme: In the instance in which the infant splits off and projects its unwanted and dreaded feelings (unwanted and dreaded feeling self) as translocated identifications into the external object, that object ipso facto becomes a container for these projective reidentifications (whether effectual, ineffectual, or in-between these extremes is unimportant at the moment). The external object, now compounded with the translocated aspects of the subject, becomes internalized by the infant as a container inside. If the projections from the subject are believed by the subject to have transformed the object and thereby to have become the predominant component of the new amalgam, then a persecutory archaic superego (internal) object results, along with its counterpart in the ego, the object, which has been putatively overwhelmed, deformed, and mutilated by the projected subject.

Insofar as the external object is believed to have transformed the painful, unwanted aspects of itself and not to have succumbed to these projective attacks, the compounded object is internalized as a helpful, benign, and trustworthy internal object and thus as an effective, permanent internal container. With this internal container in place, one can see the operation of the mechanisms of expression and of repression, expression insofar as the container object vouchsafes the reasonableness of the infant's messages, and repression insofar as the object, in its own inscrutable wisdom, knows how much of the infant's projections should be absorbed by it and stored for a return of the repressed in the future (see my reference to "dosage of sorrow" in chapter 1).

In the meanwhile, the container object may, by displacement, become the substitute object for symptomatology. The container object may become split or divided, one portion remaining within the subject's internal world and the other externalized as a displacement for a symptom substitute. For instance, a patient who heard from his physician that he might have a malignant tumor began developing obsessive and compulsive phobic symptoms. While maintaining confidence in his physician (and his analyst), he nevertheless began feeling that the outside world was no longer safe. He avoided, as best as he could, touching doorknobs, washed his hands after shaking hands with others, returned often to his residence to see if he had locked the doors, and so on. In other words, while maintaining confidence in his physician and the latter's ability to combat his malignancy successfully, the patient projected a portion of his container object plus the representation of the malignancy into the outside world and took omnipotent measures to avoid it.

The outside world became the displacement for the scene of the dread within. Furthermore, the firm establishment of a container object within the infant's internal world valorizes it as an object that internally delays, sustains, transforms, translates, and, in general, facilitates the expressiveness and creativeness of the infant. Moreover, it serves as a gate that screens, detoxifies, and postpones potentially dangerous awarenesses on the part of the infant until a later time—all in the service of maintaining the infant's sense of innocence and safety. One aspect of the latter task can be thought of as under the rubric of damage control. Fairbairn (1943b, 1944) dealt with this idea when he suggested that repression develops to help protect the infant from his awareness of having already become divided or split in his ego. This would be an instance in which the ego that has attained symbolic or self-reflective capacity benignly represses its antecedent presymbolic, prereflective, bicameral, cyclopean self.

Finally, innumerable intrapsychic relationships occur between different internal objects and between them and aspects of the self. Freud (1917) first referred to these internal relationships in his discussion about the narcissist's defense against object loss. In this case, the narcissist, unable to countenance separation or loss, [projectively][20] identifies with the object, then internalizes the object, [then splits it into two objects],[21] following which he then [introjectively][22] identifies with each thus divided object, one in a gradient in the ego, and another within the ego proper, according to Freud. The object that becomes identified within a gradient in the ego becomes an ego ideal, Freud initially stated; but it is clear that, once he formulated the structural theory (Freud, 1923a), he really meant superego. The relationship between them is as follows: the superego object, in identification with an ideal ego self, employs a maximum of sadism toward the ego in its identification with the other object.

The long and short of the relationships that transpire between differing internal subjective (rogue) objects and the self is that these relationships generally fall into the categories of hypnotic, sadistic thralldom (superego object → object in ego or self identified with that object), and its victims generally counter complementarily with a corresponding masochistic, obedient passive-aggressive response. Once analysis

20. Text within brackets constitutes my own interpretation.

21. See Footnote 21.

22. See Footnotes 21 and 22.

resolves the persecutory nature of these unfair gradient relationships, respect and dialogue take their place. Bakhtin (1981), in his concept of the "dialogic imagination," especially as he surveys the dialogues between the characters in Dostoevsky's novels, seems to have approximated the picture of the internal world that I am presenting.

The concept of object, both external and internal, is in need of reevaluation in view of the concept of subjectivity. The idea of the object was an empirical product of Enlightenment positivism and belied the nameless dread it was counterposed to mediate, a dread that we today can see is and always was ineffable—chaos, infinity, the thing-in-itself, the Real. The external object is always a cosubjective other that may transiently and continuously be *used* as an object of need, but always in the shadow of its ineffable humanness and uniqueness. The object we perceive (*ap*perceive) thus becomes a subjective object to our senses. Upon internalization, it becomes further modified by internal introjective and then projective identifications and thus becomes transformed into demons (monsters, chimerae). When later reprojected anew into images of other external objects, they become "rogue subjective objects" and represent continuing deteriorative process of alienation and misrecognition.

Chapter 7

THE MYTH OF THE LABYRINTH

KLEIN'S ARCHAIC OEDIPUS COMPLEX AND ITS POSSIBLE RELATIONSHIP TO THE MYTH OF THE LABYRINTH

An aged patient who was contemplating his own death said, "You know, when a person begins to die, they say that they suddenly see themselves at the last moment as they really are and always were—underneath the disguises and garb of their character and posturing. It's like Paul's 'First Letter to the Corinthians,' 'Now through a glass darkly, then face to face.' Until then we are trapped in our labyrinth of deceit, but we don't realize it until that last moment." What he said haunted and inspired me, offering me a rare glimpse of my own Otherness to myself (Ricoeur, 1992) and reminding me of an aspect of myself that had not yet been liberated from encryptment in my own personal "labyrinth of deceit." The impact of his ontological pronouncement led me to realize the importance of his chance association to the labyrinth.

Another analytic patient, a 47-year-old surgeon, entered analysis because of depression and despair over his unfortunate personal life; his fourth marriage was ending in divorce. He always chose the same kind of wife, he believed, one that was aggressive, "castrating," and demanding. He had felt belittled and suffocated in each of the relationships. Moreover, he felt intimidated by the colleagues with whom he shared a group practice. It became apparent in the analysis that he was passive, diffident, and self-effacing. He believed that in his childhood, although he had been closer to his mother than to his passive and ineffectual minister-father, this closeness was conditional on her having control over him. She apparently had suffered a severe postpartum depression when the patient was born and had been so depressed during the subsequent years that the elders of the family church frequently came to their home to pray for her because they believed that she was dying.

The patient was not sure but sometimes thought that "they came there to pray for her in order to exorcize her of her bad demons." In the course of the fourth year of the analysis, the patient's mother fell ill with a fatal illness. A few days before her death he accompanied her to the cemetery to help her choose her final resting place. The event was filled with emotion for each of them. The day before she died, the patient had a lengthy dream of a peculiar labyrinth. The dream led me to connect Klein's (1928) concepts of "internal babies" and the paternal phallus, universal unconscious phantasies of the content of the mother's body, with the ancient Greek legend of the labyrinth and the Minotaur.

A search of the psychoanalytic literature on the subject revealed no references to the labyrinth or the Minotaur (except for Jungian contributions). However, Klein's work on the subject of the archaic Oedipus complex, the epistemophilic and sadistic part-instincts, personification, and projective identification (Klein, 1926, 1927, 1928, 1929a, 1946, 1955) seemed to include themes that were highly suggestive of the labyrinth myth. To put it briefly, Klein, in attempting to extend Freud's concept of the Oedipus complex to developmental stages that antedated the phallic phase of childhood, discovered its presence and activity in the second oral stage. Further, she found clinical evidence from child analyses that infants expressed early oedipal feelings in the form of epistemophilic and sadistic impulses whose trajectory was the inside of mother's body. Furthermore, infants unconsciously phantasied that mother's body contained the paternal penis, "unborn children," and feces.

Similar themes also emerged in Winnicott's works, particularly in his contributions on "the spontaneous gesture," the subjective object, object usage, and play (Winnicott, 1963a, 1968b, 1969, 1971b). Klein (1926) stated, for instance:

> As we know, children form relations with the outside world by directing to objects from which pleasure is obtained the libido that was originally attached exclusively to the child's own ego. . . . It is in this way, however, that children arrive at their relations with reality [p. 140].
>
> Besides this archaic mode of representation [unconscious phantasy] children employ another primitive mechanism. . . . They substitute actions (which were the precursors of thoughts) for words: with children *acting* plays a prominent part [p. 147].

The patient's dream and the analysis of it suggested a possible further relationship between Klein's (1928) idea of the early Oedipus complex and its locale, in the infant's unconscious phantasy, inside mother's womb. It is my thesis that the infant undergoes a series of heroic challenges (rites of passage) as part of its developmental agenda. These challenges can be thought of as *tasks*, similar to Hagman's (1995) concept of the task of mourning. They involve the activation of the tropism of mastery, with an epigenesis from passivity to activity with a sense of competence.

The labyrinth myth also suggests two other themes: (1) the transformative function of sexual intercourse, that is, as a series of developmental phantasy-stages in which the male needs to have the courage to enter the female labyrinth and challenge all the "demonic" internal objects that he feels are lying in waiting for him—and, for the woman, to be identified with her male forebears that lie within her labyrinth but at the same time to encourage her lover to overcome them[1]; and (2) the analytic process itself as a guided journey into the labyrinth of the unconscious. I shall discuss the sexual theme later when I elaborate the theme of the Minotaur.

Theseus's journey into the confounding maze, guided by Ariadne's thread, seems to represent the analytic exploration of the unconscious. The Minotaur within the labyrinth perhaps represents a composite image of internal objects that, in turn, symbolize the domain of the demonic as well as the experience of being imprisoned, as it were, by psychical conflict. The labyrinth and the Minotaur may be seen as an allegory that expresses the archaic Oedipus complex defined by Klein (1928) and an allegory for a hitherto unnoticed developmental line, that of the ontogenesis of courage and competence—exploration, adventure, risk taking, rescue phantasies, and thinking (in the sense of daring to have thoughts).

The labyrinth also suggests those personality types which seem to be characterized by a perverse, depressive, and schizoid withdrawal, possibly encompassing the character-armored (Reich, 1928) patients described by Fairbairn (1944) as trapped within their endopsychic structures, by Rosenfeld (1987) as imprisoned in "pathological organizations," and by Steiner (1993) as living in "psychic retreats." It is only a short

1. This chapter deals with some psychoanalytic aspects of a universal myth or legend. I realize that the contributions of infant development research, of self psychology, and of intersubjectivity are legitimately disposed to emphasize the overarching importance of the self–object attuning environment that constitutes a sine qua non for the development of courage and competence. I too hold to that perspective, but that is not immediately relevant to my theme.

step from the idea of a "labyrinthine personality type" to analogize to a more general entrapment suggested in the theme of Michelangelo's "Prisoners," those unborns who have never been released from the marble of their fixity.

COURAGE AS A DEVELOPMENTAL TASK

Somewhere between the absolute psychic determinism of Freud's and Klein's concepts of infant development and Winnicott's concept of play one may postulate either a stage (in the classical sense) or a position (in the Kleinian sense) of activities and phantasies that constitute "rehearsals for adulthood."[2] This hypothesis was adumbrated by Erikson's (1959) concept of the life cycle and has been explored empirically in studies of bonding and attachment in infant development, especially regarding the relationship of secure attachment in the home environment to performance, competence, and executive capacity in infant play (Belsky, Gardugue, and Harnci, 1984) and relationship to the "strange situation" (Ainsworth and Wittig, 1969; Main, 1973; Ainsworth, Bell, and Stayton, 1974; Cassidy and Berlin, 1994).

The development of ontological courage is such a developmental task that occurs in the dialectic of "to be or not to be"—that is, whether or not to accept one's life as a life to live and to claim one's position in one's family and culture and what follows that decision: to become, to create, to explore, to do, to challenge, to undertake risks, to rescue, to initiate, to think. These tasks are related to the infant's struggles with epistemophilic, sadistic (Klein, 1928), and creative (Winnicott, 1971c) propensities and are worked out in a series of dialectical struggles between the exercise of the infant's vigorous, enthusiastic, exploratory, self-expressive, and assertive activities and the opposition to those activities by fears of persecutory retaliation and primitive guilt (Klein, 1928, 1945; Segal, 1989).

When Klein correlated the ascendancy of the epistemophilic part-instinct with that of sadism at the time of weaning from the breast, she hinted—and all but stated—that a challenge takes place between the infant (actually toddler) and the internalized (in mother) "penis-father" (subjective or mythical object) in anticipation of the later conflict with the real father. In other words, weaning (physical or psychological or both) is a marker for the onset of the toddler's sadistic attempts to recap-

---

2. That infancy and childhood were "rehearsals for adulthood, the thing-in-itself," was one of Bion's (personal communication) favorite expressions.

ture the lost mother by an epistemophilic assault into her interior, where the infant now, in phantasy, encounters father's penis (swallowed by mother's Gargantuan "greed"), the "unborn children" (those whom mother loves so much that they do not have to suffer real birth, let alone weaning), and mother's feces. One must remember that one of the later accompaniments of weaning is toilet training. The toddler entertains unconscious phantasies that, when mother forces him to "surrender the feces," she (mother) hoards them as *her* valuable treasure. Thus, they are valorized positively as valuable and contemptibly as poisonous and destructive—by virtue of the toddler's projective identifications into them.

What seems to distinguish the earlier from the later oedipal encounter is that the infant must challenge and win the battle with a *mythic, phantasmal "father-beast"* (the metaphoric Minotaur/subjective object) in the earlier phase in order to be able subsequently to surrender authentically to the law of the real father (and mother). The dialectical struggle in the earlier phase is that between *challenge* and *nemesis* (surrender, default). Klein (1927) stated:

> The analysis of very young children has shown me that even a three-year-old child has left behind him the most important part of the development of his Oedipus complex. Consequently he is already far removed, through repression and feelings of guilt, from the objects whom he originally desired. His relations to them have undergone distortion and transformation so that the present love-objects are now *imagos* of the original objects [p. 165].

And later:

> The early connection between the epistemophilic impulse and sadism is very important for the whole mental development. This instinct, activated by the rise of the Oedipus tendencies, at first mainly concerns itself with the mother's body, which is assumed to be the scene of all sexual processes and developments [Klein, 1928, p. 204].

There seems to be a connection between universal ontological anxiety and the metaphors inherent in the ancient Greek myth of the labyrinth and its characteristics of encryptment, puzzlement, lostness, alienation, and a sense of failure. The Minotaur haunting the labyrinth recalls Klein's (1928) notion of the infant's unconscious phantasy of a "combined parent," specifically an incompletely differentiated maternal object (incompletely differentiated from the father as well as from the infant because of projective identification) that is believed to contain, entrap, and control the paternal penis located in her awesome interior. In other words, mother plus father's penis is equated variously with "combined parent" or "phallic woman."

Additional considerations include heroic rescue phantasies and the importance of the symbolism of the Minotaur. Specifically, I conjecture that the infant has the ontological task of confronting and triumphing over the metaphoric Minotaur/subjective object as a developmental task in the paranoid-schizoid position. That is, the infant must locate, confront, challenge, and triumph over the terror of the Minotaur/demon. The origin of the image can be attributed to the infant's epistemophilic and sadistic projective identifications into mother's body; that is, the Minotaur is a chimerical internal subjective object created by the infant who, having created it and having become terrified by it, must heroically rescue itself and the good parent from this mythical demon—in preparation for and in anticipation of authentic oedipal surrender to the "Law of the Father" (Lacan, 1966) in the climax of the Oedipus complex in the depressive position.

The labyrinth and the Minotaur, I suggest, allegorically represent the epic of infantile sexual and assertive development on their way to consummation in genital sexuality. The labyrinth represents the scene of this violence–love union, the successful outcome of which offers the legacy of competence and courage in regard to sex, thinking (epistemophilic), subjectivity, and being. I assume here that the assertive-instinctual drive ensemble, whether considered from the classical perspective of aggression or from the Kleinian perspective of the death instinct, is always object dedicated, as is its counterpart, the life instinct. Thus, I believe there is a teleological principle that organizes the relationship between the assertive ensemble and its subjective—and later real—objects.

THE DREAM OF A LABYRINTH

The following lengthy dream illustrates the operation of the imagery of the labyrinth and the Minotaur. The patient seems to be exploring his mother's womb in unconscious phantasy just before her anticipated death. The dream constitutes, among its many meanings, a last pilgrimage to his "first home," his mother's womb. It also deals with a revival of the patient's archaic oedipal relationship with the combined parental couple and the heroic confrontations with the metaphoric Minotaur.

I was in a large cavern, like a cave. On the right side there was a path that went down along the side where there was water coming from a stream. I was near one end of the room looking in the opposite direction, and I do not know what was at my back, but I looked toward one end and saw light at the end of a tunnel. I noticed that there were many trout in the water. I thought, "This would be a really great place to fish; look at all these trout. If I could just get some bait and fish for them, I could catch a lot of them." I was frustrated at not having some bait. On the left side of the room up against the wall, close to the ceiling, was what appeared to be an aquarium, or glassed-in area. This had a light over it so that it was very well lit. In the water was a ferocious eel or dragonlike creature, probably about six inches in diameter and perhaps six feet long, with sharp teeth. As I was standing in the water and looking down into it for the trout, I remembered thinking that I was glad that the creature was confined up there behind the glass. The floor of the bottom of the cave underneath the water was very irregular and rugged with many very irregular grooves in the floor. The trout were lying in these grooves with their tails hidden back in holes and the front half of their bodies lying in these grooves. There were many of them, and they were all laying eggs.

Suddenly the dragon or eel-like creature jumped out of the aquarium and landed in the water where I was standing. Until this time I could see easily into the water and could see the trout, but after this the water was murky green in color and opaque, and I could not see whether the creature was coming toward me or not. I could see down toward the mouth of the tunnel through the water, and I could see the creature swimming. Initially I was frightened that it might attack me and injure me by biting me. In fact I was afraid that it might bite off my penis. Then I thought suddenly that this type of creature does not eat people, so I must be safe. I was somewhat reassured by this thought, though still a bit apprehensive that I might be attacked. I wondered if I should try to escape or try to kill it in order to protect myself and the trout eggs.

I then remember making my way toward the mouth of the tunnel, and I believe I no longer thought about my fear of the creature in the water. I was on dry land, walking down the pathway toward the opening of the tunnel or the cave. There was a large dome of rock about four or five feet in diameter projecting about three feet from the surface. It was more or less rounded but with an irregular surface. On the side toward the path, facing toward the opening of the cave, was a hole in the rock about six inches in diameter. The rock seemed to be filled with water. Inside the rock was another large fish, with a rounded head, about three or four feet long. Again I thought, "If only I had some bait and a line so that I could catch this fish!" A few moments later I noticed this fish had turned to the side and was nibbling on some orange, frondlike structures that were projecting from the floor and wall The fronds were about two or three inches long. There were three of them, and they looked like the gills of a fish that had been detached from one end but were still connected at the other end.

As I said, many of the trout were lying in the grooves of the eroded surface of this cave with their tails back in holes and the front half of their bodies out. They were lying out of the water and seemed not to need any air. The large fish inside of rock seemed to be out of the water—but inside the rock. However, when I looked inside the rock and saw it nibbling on the frondlike structures, it was in the water. All the trout were laying eggs, and the large fish in the rock was also laying eggs.

Next I was outside the cave where there was a large canyon. First there was some level ground, and then the canyon fell off into a deep crevice, several hundred or a thousand feet deep. I was standing on a pathway and a number of people were around looking off into the canyon, though none right in the area where I was. I was facing the canyon on a pathway that was going down from the level ground down into the canyon. Standing on this pathway facing the canyon, I felt the dirt under my feet start to give way. I was terrified that I was going to fall into the canyon, and at the same time terrified that if I moved my feet any more at all that the ground would give way even worse, and then for sure I would go into the canyon. Any struggle would make a fall into the canyon certain.

I don't remember what happened, but a little later I was trying to walk down a pathway into the canyon from the plateau above. The pathway slanted to the left down along the wall of the canyon, and I had only gone a few feet, to the point where the plateau was. The path had descended from the plateau only about three or four feet. I was facing the plateau rather than the canyon, and when I felt that the ground was giving way under my feet, I clung to the edge of the ground above the canyon. Several people were sitting around looking off into the canyon. The one that was closest to me was a thin man who looked like a typical Texas cowboy. It was obvious to him that I was struggling and terrified, but he just looked at me with curiosity and casual interest without making any effort to save me. I asked him what his name was, and he said, "Texas," with a slow southern accent. I asked him to help me, but he only replied with the punchline of a bad joke that I cannot remember. It was the kind of joke that, when you hear it, it's so unclever that you wince. The cowboy just sat there on the ground, with his feet out in front of him and his hands on the ground, looking at me with casual interest.

There was a woman sitting ten or fifteen feet to his left; she appeared to be middle-aged, with curly but not very stylish hair, and wearing a polyester two-piece pants suit in an aqua or green color. She stood up and said, "Well, I'll help him." The woman was mildly obese, with a rather round face. She was not particularly stylish; the pantsuit looked as though it was from a bargain basement. The woman was not anyone that I knew, but the round face, the hairstyle, and the mild obesity are not unlike my mother. She came over to me, reached out her right hand and took mine. With her support I was able to clamber back up onto the flat ground.

Then it seemed that 15 or 20 feet further away from the edge there was a walkway about eight feet wide made of asphalt. A lot of people were there, walking up and down this walkway as though they were viewing the canyon with interest, as though the area was a tourist attraction. Even farther away from the canyon, behind this walkway, there was a high bank or a mountain, and the cave that I had been in opened out from this mountain onto a flat area slightly above the inclined walkway. The walkway gradually descended parallel to the canyon, and the ground sloped off from the walkway toward the canyon, but the abrupt falloff of the canyon was out perhaps 300 or 400 feet so there was a plateau slightly below the level of the walkway below the canyon drop-off. On this plateau there was a broad sidewalk with steps going to the plateau and on this plateau was a large, round building like a railroad house.

At this point I saw my second oldest daughter, who is now 10 but in the dream was about three years old, the same age as my third daughter is currently. I began looking for Frank Sinatra, because I knew that my daughter was with him. As I walked down the sidewalk and steps toward this round building, there were many people standing in line. The line filled the entire width of the sidewalk, which was about six or eight feet, and went around the outer portion of the building. There were two more parts to the building; an outer portion was walled off or separate from the inner portion. There was a fence, like a chain-link fence. separating the outer part of the building from the inner portion.

I do not know what was in the center portion of the building. In the outer portion, many people were milling around, moving in a slow line. It seemed like they were going to eat. There was a separate portion of the building off to the left side, and I headed off this way, looking for Frank Sinatra and my daughter. The first large room that I came to was a cafeteria. There was no line that I had to wait in to get into the cafeteria. I looked around a bit and went along to a rectangular hallway or room just beyond the cafeteria. I entered another room where there was a restaurant. Opposite the entrance into this restaurant was a glass display cabinet and cash register. I do not remember what was in the cabinet. There was a man I assumed was a maître d' whom I think I recognized, but I cannot remember who it was. He was in a black tuxedo with ruffles on his shirt and was carrying some booster chairs into the restaurant. At the first table to the right, almost sitting in the entryway area of the restaurant, was an old college and medical school classmate of mine of whom I was very fond. He was in the class ahead of me, but we were very good friends. We sang in a quartet together one summer. He was a German, with dark brownish-red hair. After he finished medical school, he married a nurse, and I was an usher at his wedding. He was sitting with his wife and two children, both girls. One was a girl; I remember noticing that she had copious amounts of frizzy, red hair. I think that I said hello to him, but I do not remember anything else about the dream.

ASSOCIATIONS TO THE DREAM

The obvious adaptive context for the dream was his mother's imminent death and the associated loss of his "first home." Some of the patient's associations to the dream were as follows:[3]

I do not know the significance of Frank Sinatra, but to me he represents awesome power. I once knew a woman who worked as a receptionist for him for a time, and she was awestruck with his power. She considered him a benevolent dictator, one with generosity and a great sensitivity for his children. For instance, any time one of his children called him on the telephone he was never too busy to talk with them. Because of this I do not believe that I feared for my daughter's safety. The woman I knew also mentioned Sinatra's generosity toward a man who had rescued Sinatra when he nearly drowned. Sinatra gave the man a job and took care of him financially for the rest of his life. He was also a hero to me as a child and also one who hung out with the Mafia.

The idea "Mafia" then conjured up a series of associations to the patient's difficulties with his colleagues, both at the hospital where he operated and in his office practice, of whom he was envious. He felt bullied, controlled, and demeaned by them. They corresponded to an internal Mafia or gang that organized his internal psychic retreat (Fairbairn, 1944; Rosenfeld, 1987; Steiner, 1993).

---

3. Because of space limitations I am able only to list a small sample of the patient's associations to this dream. In fact, it took over a year to do justice to this dream and its manifold associations.

The patient associated the water in the cavern to the bag of waters of the womb. Once he had identified the cave as a womb, he was at ease with that metaphor. The light at the end of the tunnel suggested the end of the birth canal and the patient "knew that he was being born" in the dream. The anxiety that phantasy counterposed was his fear of being buried alive with his mother, from whom he felt incompletely differentiated in life.

The eel or dragonlike creature he discovered in the water frightened him when it was not in the aquarium. He noted that it resembled a penis. It perhaps represented an archetypal image of the Minotaur, that is, his own unconscious version of his father's penis (condensed with mine and primitive aspects of himself—particularly his "sadistic-voyeuristic penis") inside his mother's womb along with the internal babies (the trout-laying eggs). The patient was apparently in touch with an unconscious phantasy of his father's penis inside mother's uterus fertilizing the eggs for his own birth.

In the next segment of the dream, the clear water became murky, and the eel threatened to bite off his penis. Analysis of this portion of the dream awakened his awareness of oedipal rivalry and led to a regressive intrusion into the mother's womb, where he encountered his father's penis containing his (the patient's) teeth projected onto it and now threatening to castrate the patient in retaliation for his trying to devour the father inside the womb. This juxtaposition of a genital oedipal theme with postnatal elements (biting) and intrauterine phantasies constitutes the mythic or phantasied reconstruction of his origins.

The primary-process mechanisms of condensation and displacement allowed a colorful and imaginative reconstruction as a montage of many different levels of archaic mental life, including the fetal, as Bion (1975, 1977a, 1979) described. Later, the patient encountered a dome-shaped mound with a fish nibbling in a stream inside it. His associations ran to a fetus and a placenta and phantasies of what it would be like to eat while in the womb.

Finally, he emerged from the cave and encountered a large canyon that was precarious and dangerous (perhaps an external labyrinthine structure). The people around the crevice were his family and the elders of the church who might have been around when he was born. He also associated the crevice to his mother's depression when he was 12 and recalled that she had suffered from a recurrence at this time. Here he seemed to be in touch with an unconscious phantasy that his inordinate need (greed) created a painful "cave" in his mother that manifested itself as her depression. The father's penis inside the womb was a protective Minotaur that tried to stop him from doing any more damage to his mate, the patient's mother.

The Texas cowboy seemed to be a cross between me as the dispassionate analyst and an indifferent father who had been dispossessed from the womb by the patient's conception. I called the patient's attention to the possibility that "cowboy" conflates the image of the "cow" as mother and himself as a "cowed boy" who was undifferentiated from her. The father was now hostile to the newborn baby and was not about to help him in his postnatal attempt to survive. These phantasies resulted from projective identifications secondary to jealous feelings toward father and guilt for making mother depressed. The bad joke the man told related to his belief that I was like his father, a "dirty old man," if I introduced him to sexual knowledge, particularly the knowledge of parental intercourse. His mother appeared and helped him reach stable ground again.

Insofar as the father/eel in the dream was terrifying and omnipotent, its image also contained projective identifications from the patient's infantile self. The patient's desire to fish in the lake was tantamount to poaching on the father's "game preserve"—mother. Insofar as the eel also represented omnipotent "monster" aspects of the patient that had been projected into the internalized father, it also constituted a threatening hybrid or chimera that had to be "destroyed" to defuse its terror. This "object use" or destruction constitutes his being able to confront it with the help of the real object (in this case, the analyst). Later, in the depressive position, being able to deconstruct its compounded imagery into its elemental components (projective identifications from the infantile aspects of the analysand) amounts to the "destruction" of the putative danger of the chimera by reowning the projections, that is, destroying its omnipotent mythicalness by reowning the projections that created it.

The descent down the canyon to a lower plateau was associated to "man's fall from grace" and the descent from omnipotence to infantile helplessness. At this point, the patient rediscovered the roundhouse, a symbol for the breast but also a labyrinth in its own right. The roundhouse appears to be a place where food was served, but there seemed to be a long line of people waiting, including his second-oldest daughter. Associations led to rivalry with his two older siblings and to his hatred of being kept waiting. At this point the primary presenting complaint of the analysis, his dilatoriness, underwent a resolution. He suddenly realized that he was keeping his whole future waiting as he believed his mother had kept him waiting for entrance into her roundhouse. He was on time for all future appointments with me. He realized that, by keeping others waiting for him, he had been indulging in a phantasy of projective identification in which he unconsciously invaded his mother, possessed the goodness of her "roundhouse," and then kept others waiting for the bountiful goodness of his presence, which he had to offer them but for which they must wait.

The whole scheme of dependency conflicts suddenly unraveled. The fence separating the outer portion from the inner portion of the roundhouse was associated to the nipple of the breast. He thought of his excitement over women's nipples and how he longed for contact with them. The inner portion of the nipple was a mystery—another labyrinth! The excitement women could give him was mysterious and elevated them to a particular level of idealization. He often revealed phantasies in which he seemed to believe that the female nipple was conflated with the paternal penis as if the latter were the woman's trophy.[4]

In the next section of the dream he went off to look for his daughter and Frank Sinatra. The cafeteria here was not quite so crowded. Associations led to his disappointment with the breasts of the mother at the roundhouse; by keeping him waiting for his turn along with his father and siblings, she created enormous envy in him of her and her breasts, as well as jealousy of the father and siblings, who also depended on her. Consequently, he forsook her for the father, who was felt to be a "better mommy than mommy," a belief reflected in the transference. The little daughter stood symbolically for his female dependent self, who needed daddy's penis to suck on as earlier he had needed to suck on his mother's breast.

His associations to Frank Sinatra went further than to a father-figure. He recalled Sinatra's generosity to ordinary people who had helped him. Further associations concerned Sinatra's nefarious aspects, especially his contacts with the Mafia. At this point, the patient began talking about masturbation and "things dirty." I linked these associations with his phantasies of infantile and childhood masturbation, including anal masturbation as well as to his envy of his siblings, both real and analytic, and also his colleagues, to whom I alluded earlier. The Frank Sinatra imago was another version of the Minotaur, whose imaginative creation his masturbation evoked as a retaliatory threat.

The friend from medical school represented a lost ego ideal that had reemerged. This particular friend was well known for his piety in medical school. After he graduated from medical school and married, he "sinned" by having an affair, but he subsequently repented and was now living an exemplary life.

Without consciously realizing that he was doing so, the patient continued to associate to the dream throughout his long mourning for his mother and beyond. The idea of the combined parent came to represent a condensation and syncretization of many images and

---

4. One of the developmental tasks of the infant is to separate the image of the paternal phallus from the maternal breast which derives from its earlier formation as the "combined (joined) couple."

phantasies. In a subsequent dream, his mother was portrayed as a depressed, guilt-producing martyr who seemed to be interchangeable both with his voraciously sexual maternal aunt, who was also felt to be "phallic," and with her husband, a rough and ready, intimidating uncle. The patient felt cowed by his sisters and bullied by his uncle and by peers. He came to realize that he had long been terrified by primitive guilt feelings, with associated persecutory anxiety about his phantasied role in causing his mother's postpartum (and continuing) depression. His mother and other members of the family often reminded him of her difficult pregnancy with him, of her troubled labor in delivery, and of her long postpartum depression.

At the same time, he felt intimidated by the "eel/father" who he felt was out to avenge the damage that the patient believed that he had done to mother. The eel-penis also came to represent his own sadistically intrusive, acquisitive, voyeuristic self. It resembled some of the surgical instruments he used in his profession and had appeared in previous dreams in which associations revealed that he often became voyeuristically excited while performing some of his surgical procedures—excited that, being a doctor, he was permitted to get an "inside peek" into people.

Another analysand presented the following dream: "I was falling asleep and had a dream. I saw rows of buildings packed together at 45-degree angles—brick, dusty pinkish-brownish pastel—like concrete blocks, rows of them. Mother was at a washboard scrubbing clothes."

This analysand frequently dreamed of being trapped in tunnels, caves, and fortresses. I cite this dream only to demonstrate its labyrinthine characteristics, which also include the idea of rows of concrete blocks. Ultimately, her associations to these blocks led to her memory of her mother's pregnancy with her younger brother (when she was four) and how she considered this to be a "block" to her happiness then. The rows of blocks organized at 45-degree angles is also reminiscent of a similar idea in the first patient's dream, that is, the lining up of the "internal babies."

THE LABYRINTH AND THE MINOTAUR AS AN ARCHAIC OEDIPAL MYTH AND AN EARLY STAGE OF NORMAL DEVELOPMENT

Analytical psychology has welcomed an array of collective myths into its discipline, while classical psychoanalysis has been dominated by the oedipal myth alone.[5] Freud took that myth from only one of the plays in the Sophoclean trilogy, and he emphasized the themes of incest and parricide, a conjunction that came to be known as the Oedipus complex. The oedipal legend that Freud singled out, however, was a *patriarchally*—and therefore a *phallically*—dominated one. Klein (1928) postulated in her concept of the archaic (early) Oedipus complex, first of all, that it was orally and then anally and urethrally dominated and that the infant experiences unconscious phantasies of wishing to explore mother's insides and sadistically to appropriate her internal content. In this phantasy, the infant imagines that mother's insides contain the paternal penis, internal babies, and valuable feces.

Klein seems to have been unaware, however, that these unconscious phantasies resonated with another ancient Greek myth, that of the labyrinth. The mythic labyrinth, consequently, may represent the matriarchal or feminine ("dominatrix") Kleinian counterpart to the patriarchal or masculine (orthodox/classical) oedipal myth. The Minotaur may symbolically represent the archaic internalized father phantasmally constituted as part of a combined parent imago or also as phallic mother, as well as assertive aspects that the toddler projects into the internal penis and that he is now destined to reclaim (Klein, 1928, 1945). Together, the labyrinth and the Minotaur signify the persecutory demons of the infant's creation that, in the course of development, must be sought, explored, *confronted*, challenged, defeated, and defused, and reclaimed—so that they can be known and realized as symbolic thoughts.

THE ORIGIN OF MYTH OF THE LABYRINTH

The elements of the labyrinth symbol are highly condensed in the classical Greek myth. Europa had been carried to Crete by a bull that was the animal metamorphosis of Zeus himself.[6] Minos was the product of that union. Then Pasiphaë, Minos's wife and Queen of Crete, was seduced by a white bull[7] that emerged from the sea. This union produced the Minotaur, and the shamed and fearful Pasiphaë hastened to

5. Exceptions include Klein's (1963) psychoanalytic essay on Aeschylus' *Oresteia* and Hamilton's (1993) comparison of the myths of Narcissus and Oedipus, to say nothing of Freud's (1914b) own brief reference to the Narcissus myth.

6. It is characteristic in the myths of the birth of heroes, as Rank (1910), Campbell (1949), Caldwell (1989), and others have pointed out, for one parent to be divine and the other mortal. The god aspect of one of the parents was frequently disguised in his or her animal totem form.

7. Bulls featured prominently in the religious rituals of matriarchally ori-

have the bull/child hidden in a labyrinthine enclosure constructed by the peerless architect, Daedalus. The Minotaur lived in the farthest reach of this prison and could not leave because of its mysterious mazelike construction. Meanwhile, since he had hegemony over the mainland poleis, every eight years Minos exacted from Athens a sacrificial tribute of eight male and eight female youths to be fed to the Minotaur every eight[8] years.

On the occasion of one of these cannibalistic *fest*ivals, Theseus, son of the tyrant of Athens, undertook the heroic task of ending the sacrifices by killing the Minotaur. He accompanied the designated victims on their voyage to Knossos, where he caught the gaze of Ariadne, the beautiful daughter of Minos and Pasiphaë and half-sister of the Minotaur. Falling in love with Theseus, Ariadne chose to save him by allowing him secret entry into the labyrinth. She gave him a thread woven by Daedalus that would guide him back to the entry after he slew the Minotaur. Holding the thread in one hand, he entered the chamber, located and killed the Minotaur,[9] and triumphantly emerged. When he reembarked for Athens with the spared youths, however, he abandoned Ariadne, and she committed suicide.[10] Theseus's heroic task was not only to locate the Minotaur in the maze, but also to slay this primitive rival for the mother during the hegemony of the matriarchal Oedipus complex.

Another reading of the relationship between the roles of Theseus and Ariadne bears mention. Ariadne can be understood as projectively identified with her shadow side, her animus, that is, with her half-brother, the half-man, half-beast Minotaur. She seeks Theseus as the analyst/hero to rescue her from her demonic, beastly nature—a castration, if you will. Thus, not only is she the heroine/analyst for Theseus, but he is her hero/analyst as well. Moreover, if she is integrated with her split-off, hidden animus self, Ariadne constitutes the combined parent

---

ented Cretan and pre-Hellenic culture, as the snake did in other matriarchal cultures in Asia Minor and elsewhere.

8. The number eight seems to have been important in the ancient world. As a multiple of the number four, it suggests Jung's (1953) concept of the quaternary.

9. Theseus's ability to locate the Minotaur in the labyrinthine maze is a testimony to his status as hero who, like Oedipus with the sphinx, could solve riddles.

10. Theseus's father, the tyrant of Athens, also committed suicide. On seeing that the ship returning Theseus from Crete had hoisted black sails rather than white, he threw himself off a cliff to his death—not knowing that Theseus had forgotten his prearranged agreement with his father to hoist white sails if he returned triumphantly.

that Klein posited. She therefore acts as a holographic representation and descendant of the larger combined figure of the personified labyrinth and Minotaur.[11] From this perspective, Ariadne's inner beastly nature constitutes a fractal hologram of the entirety of the myth.

I should comment on the mysterious nature of the creation of the labyrinth. It was designed and constructed by Daedelus to keep the Minotaur hidden in solitary confinement—to hide the royal family's shameful secret. It seems to have been an open prison, but only a clever hero could divine its secrets without himself getting lost. I suggest, therefore, that the labyrinth represents the *Unconscious*. The passageway of the labyrinth flows from the inside to the outside with the "discontinuous continuity" of the Moebius strip, like the repression barrier itself. My patient's dream and its labyrinth-like symbolism that so clearly represented mother's body led me to think that the labyrinth image, with its mysterious, puzzling, and preternatural aura, may constitute an archetypal signifier for *mother's body as a claustrum*.

Another element in the mystery of the construction of the labyrinth, however, lies in the nature of psychic space. As we evolve from fetus to adult, we metamorphose from an ontological existence in spacelessness and timelessness to one that is defined in space and time. On those occasions when our body seems to fall asleep before our mind, we are startled—presumably because we are "dropping" from the third dimension of space–time into the null dimension of no space and no time. The journey into the labyrinth may become uncanny when one moves from the third dimensionality of the outside world into its zero dimensionality.

From another perspective, the labyrinth, like the sphinx and other puzzle sources, exists today in such challenging activities as crossword and jigsaw puzzles and even the analytic process itself. The labyrinth may also find its analogue in the ancient Greek practice of consulting oracles. The Oracle at Delphi, like similar oracles, was originally dedicated to the earth-mother deity Gaia, who was later militantly replaced by the patriarchal deity Apollo, who thereafter presided over the oracle through a priestess-intermediary. She was called the "pythoness" because of her mythical affiliation to the sacred snake, which was a totemic residue from the days of Gaia. The Jew's phylacteries, which clearly resemble snakes, probably speak to their matriarchal, idol-worshiping heritage. The combination of the oracle, which was a tunnel in the ground, and the pythoness at the other end provides a variant of the combined object and the labyrinth.

11. I am indebted to Deborah Lynn for this perspective on the roles of Theseus, Ariadne, and the Minotaur.

THE MINOTAUR

In the labyrinth, the infant confronts the Minotaur, which represents the projective creation of sadistic and voyeuristic attributes, before which the infant cowers. The Minotaur is a chimera made of animal and human parts, like such other mythological monsters as the sphinx, manticore, and centaur. All internal subjective objects are chimeric phantasies, hybrid and therefore monstrous. The Minotaur is the demon who must be located, confronted, and killed and who thereupon becomes sacred because it has been sacrificed (Bergmann, 1992). The quest to kill the Minotaur (minotaurmachy), like the medieval quest to slay the dragon, its descendant, constitutes the mythic challenge of the hero in many cultures. If not confronted and properly "killed" (defused), these demons become our Nemesis—object superegos, which negate us and judge our cowardice. Satan represents such an object.[12]

The theme of beast sacrifice also occurs in Euripides' play, "The Bacchae," in which a ram or goat is chased up a tree and then killed. The beast then becomes reincarnated as a prince or Dionysus, the god. This sacrifice seems to follow the ancient superstition, "Out with the old, in with the new!" Derivatively, killing the beast within us as is equated with transformation.

The patient's heroic developmental task is to face the diabolical chimera and to challenge it by extracting and recalling what belongs to him and what belongs to his mother, father, and sibling relationships. These are the first steps toward the heroic motto that Freud borrowed from *Oedipus*,—"Know thyself!" The heroic task that occurs in the claustrum of the mythic labyrinth is to confront, deconstruct, decode ("kill"), reclaim, and thereby transform the Minotaur signifier.

My thinking about this task has been shaped by Bion's (1963) ideas of inherent preconceptions, tropisms, alpha function, maternal reverie, and the container–contained; by Bowlby's (1969) notion of the constitutionality and inheritability of "prey–predator anxiety"; by Schore's (1991, 1994) formulation of the neurobiological aspects of exploratory and display activity in the practicing subphase of separation and individuation; and by Lacan's (1966) concept of the mirror-experience, in which the ego finds a misrecognized image of itself in the mirror and thereby becomes alienated from itself.

Our fears of our own destructive feelings lead to confusion between the *persecutor* and the true *enemy* that threatens us and our loved ones.

---

12. In Goethe's *Faust*, Mephistopheles declares, "I am the angel who only negates!"

The Minotaur is our persecutor; that is, we have created it through projective identification; it is ourselves. The true enemy lies beyond the paranoid-schizoid and depressive positions; it is in the Real, Ananke (Necessity), Bion's (1965, 1970) O. more Bion's (1970) concept of *inherent preconceptions*, conflated with Bowlby's (1969) idea of the universal fear of the predator inherent in all animal species, suggests an inherent fear of the predator, which I believe anticipates stranger anxiety (Spitz, 1959). An unsuccessful attachment experience confuses this inherently feared object with our loved ones. That is, an infant who feels prematurely separate may misperceive (through projective identification) the mother's breast as the predator/enemy.

The heroic task devolves into an *epistemophilic* one, a *defensive* one, and an *assertive* one. One's rendezvous with the metaphoric labyrinth and the Minotaur (objects of challenge or nemesis) requires differentiating between the *infantile neurosis* and the *infantile/childhood traumatic state* (infantile catastrophe), differentiating between the enemy (Ananke) and the persecutor, and knowing and accepting who one is in the shadow of the mirrored (by circumstance) moira (fate) handed to each of us.

The infant/toddler has to learn to surmount the anxieties of separation, strange situations, and prey–predator relationships (being either the hunter or the hunted), and exploration or play (taking risks). These tasks involve mediating the balance between the surges of developmental boldness during the practicing subphase and the phase-specific development of shame as a way of controlling that boldness during the rapprochement subphase (Schore, 1991). Either courage or cowardice (shame, xenophobia, self-consciousness) is fated to develop at this time.

Girard (1972, 1978, 1986) postulates that human culture is founded on our need to mediate the inevitable violence that occurs when individuals (in families or cultures) become interdependent. This closeness and interdependency evoke a tropism that he terms *mimesis*. Persons tend to merge with—to become *like*—other persons they *like*. Violence allows for group solidarity by the *selection of a scapegoat to bear the violence because it is Other*. Upon being sacrificed, the scapegoat victim is sanctified.

From another perspective, Kristeva (1980) describes the experience of *abjection* as the opprobrium that the infant feels about his needy, therefore abjectly discardable, self, which then becomes projectively translocated into mother as her shameful, abject neediness for father's penis. The Minotaur was Pasiphaë's "abject," representing her shame and disgust over her intercourse with the "bull from the sea" and her shame that her own bestial side had become manifest.

A clinical vignette illustrates the idea that the Minotaur can metaphorically become a bisexual symbol that represents the sexual act itself as a vehicle for transformation. A 31-year-old single female patient had difficulty finding someone to love and ultimately to marry. Her father had abandoned her and her mother while she was still in utero, and, following her birth, her mother had left her with the maternal grandmother to raise.

The patient's anger about this double abandonment took years of analytic work to process. She had developed a hardened and critical personality. She was intolerant of stupidity in others and contemptuous of weak, dependent persons, particularly men. She became excited as a spectator at brutal sports and became an aficionado of prizefighting. She said that she had "found herself" in Paglia's (1990) *Sexual Personae,* which assigned qualities of preternatural horror and indomitableness to women. Once she told me, "If only you knew what was inside me! See if you can find it! You won't be sorry! Conquer me—or I'll kill you!"

One of her principal transference relationships to me was that I was weak and passive and therefore contemptible. Any attempt on my part to analyze her sadomasochistic phantasies was met with ridicule. Once, in a plaintive moment, she confided that she was terrified of ever being dependent on anyone and that she believed her humiliating vulnerability and dependency feelings doomed her to being impenetrable. She believed that she had to remain indomitable but yet hoped that someone would break her down, humiliate her, and force her to submit. She was a beast in her lair who could not be reasoned with, only conquered.

When this revelation emerged, she realized that she had invariably goaded her lovers to attack her in order to get through to her. She had contempt for them if they had loving feelings for her because she then would fall into a state of despair about not having been reached inside. I became aware that her provocative behavior was also her way of caricaturing her internal objects (the father and mother who had deserted her at her birth). The "hero" who conquers her liberates her from her imprisoning internal objects by separating her from them and punishing them. Her outrageousness was a call for help. Her true lover/analyst must be perceptive enough to know that the outrageous she is a chimera, a hybrid, a combination of many—herself, her mother, and her father.

I gradually realized that she contemptuously called her suitors and me "stupid," not "impotent" or "weak." This insight reminded me of the ancient Greek legend of Atalanta and Hippomenes and similar legends in which a man must risk himself totally in order to "feminize" a beast/woman. Hippomenes "conquered" Atalanta through cleverness (dropping golden apples to distract her) and thus won the race and her hand. Clever trickery and a subtle understanding of her nature allowed him to win. There are parallels with Oedipus and the sphinx and Jason and the Medusa. The conquest became an epistemophilic triumph rather than a violent one. It was transformative when I told the patient that she wanted me not to be deterred or threatened by her provocative posturing or to be driven into counterpunitive assaults against her to "break her"; rather, she needed me to decode her defensive armor by knowing and naming the anxieties that had forged them and the other people who were embedded in her behavior.

DEVELOPMENTAL ISSUES

The Greek myth of the labyrinth and its chimerical inhabitant, the Minotaur, represents a previously unrecognized developmental line, in my opinion (A. Freud, 1963), that of the ontological capacity to be courageous, competent, to *be*, to *face*, and to *do*! Every infant faces the task of accepting its lot, its moira ("portion" delivered by Fate)—that is, of accepting its self as a self, its mother as its mother. The infant must first indulge innocently in the "spontaneous gesture" (Winnicott, 1960a, p. 145) and then learn to *embody* itself and accept its *karma*. Winnicott (1968a, b, 1971b, c) stated that, before the infant can *discover* the object, the object must be *presented* for the infant to *create*. The infant must create the object in order to achieve a sense of *agency* and *responsibility* as an "I." This process is essential before the infant can encounter and then recognize another world of objects that it did *not* create (see chapter 2).

The experiences the infant undergoes are like a mythic journey in which obstacles seem to be placed in its path and must be overcome, as if some deity were continuously testing the infant's mettle and heroism. The suffering that can be tolerated without succumbing or surrendering are the test of the infant's endurance and constitute a certification of a "trial by ordeal." The infant's ability to confront obstacles as impersonal tasks to be dealt with attests to its courage, equanimity, and maturity, as well as its objectivity. From these rites of passage the infant achieves the status of hero (or heroine), and the successive objects that it confronts and transcends constitute the *Objects of Challenge*.

The infant becomes defined in its confrontational interaction with the nemesis (persecutory) object. Put another way, the nemesis or primitive superego object, the metaphoric Minotaur, is a challenge to the subject insofar as it seems to "colonize" the subject under its hegemony; it tends to impose its "name" and opinion onto the subject for the latter mimetically to submit to. Because the nemesis object casts a hypnotic spell onto the subject (because of the latter's projective identification into it [Mason, 1994]), the subject collusively believes that it has lost its will and is under the dominion of this alien within the self.

This has much in common with the Ogden's (1994a, 1997) concept of "the intersubjective subjugating third subject." The subject's tendency to submit to the alien "hypnotist" is furthered by the paranoid-schizoid *Weltanschauung*, a closed system characterized by quantitative absolutes rather than by qualitative variations and dominated by the condition of infinity. The subject's tendency to submit to the will, name, and verdict of the alien Other is overdetermined as well by an impulse to submit altruistically as a martyr for the benefit of the group and for the ultimate good of "the order of things" (Schreber, 1903; Freud, 1911a). I believe that the "altruistic surrender" (A. Freud, 1936) into being the martyr/victim/scapegoat for "the order of things" is part of a larger theme that includes the formation of covenants.

Stranger anxiety (Spitz, 1959, Emde and Buchsbaum, 1980, Emde et al., 1976), awareness of prey–predator anxiety (Bowlby, 1969), and Mahler's (1968) practicing subphase overlap at the end of the first year and the beginning of the second. In his work integrating neurodevelopment research with developmental psychology, Schore (1991, 1994) attributes importance to the phase-specific "adrenergic"[13] assertiveness that characterizes the practicing subphase. Premature foreclosure of this assertiveness can occur in the "cholinergically" dominated rapprochement subphase and lead presumably to a permanent aberration of the superego so that the infant is dominated by shame, diffidence, self-consciousness, the feeling of being a "loser," an "anti hero," a masochist. This is also the time when Winnicott (1960a) believed that the infant has evolved from holding and now is in the transitional stage of "playing."

I postulate that these themes overlap and are interconnected. For instance, the infant may experience *predator anxiety* when, fearing that it has transformed the breast into a *prey*, it finds itself aggressively attacking the breast. Alternately, Klein's (1940) concept of *persecutory anxiety* may be another way of stating that the infant fears becoming a *prey* to mother's *predator*. The teleological purpose of these phase-specific developmental tasks seems to be to allow the infant bite-sized confrontations with the Real (O) so that the infant can hone the adaptive (Hartmann, 1939) instrumentality of courage (to be the hunter/warrior hero) and transform the dread of O into the demonic phantasies of the Imaginary and later into symbolic representations in the Register of the Symbolic (Lacan, 1966).

---

13. "Adrenergic" refers to adrenaline and noradrenaline, the neurotransmitters that are believed to predominate in the developing central nervous system of the toddler in the practicing subphase of separation-individuation. Cholinergic refers to acetylcholine, the neurotransmitter that serves to offset the former during the subsequent subphase of rapprochement.

Thus, mother and father are not inherently enemies unless they allow themselves to become so, but mother's breast and father's penis are metaphoric "sparring partners," and the infant's use of them as objects allows it to differentiate the mythic world of persecutors from the real (not the "Real") world of actual parents. Stranger anxiety, whose constitutional template may be an inherent preconception of the enemy (Bion, 1962b, 1963; Bowlby, 1969), allows the infant/toddler adaptively to anticipate and deal with real predators. I believe that all these processes constitute the "labyrinth-Minotaur" archetypal developmental scenario.

TRAUMA AND COWARDICE

Trauma is the premature encounter with the impact of objects that we lacked the capacity to "create" (see chapter 2). Failure in the tests in life's rites of passage leads the infant subjectively to come to believe that it is a *coward*. Much mental illness can be thought of as the experience of being trapped within our character limitations in a prison surrounded on only three sides.[14] We are trapped within an object located within the self; the object is the labyrinth. One is out of contact—discontinuous with—oneself within oneself and therefore is misrecognized by the self, yet is hauntingly in contact, as if by déjà vu. This internalized prison becomes an inner labyrinth, ruled by an omnipotently harassing, taunting, and denigrating superego subjective object, which I term the *Nemesis object*, the shadow side of the ego ideal. Its counterpart in benign, non-traumatic play is the *Challenge object*, and the locale of this play is that intermediate area that Klein (1935) called "mother's insides," Meltzer (1992) the "claustrum," and Winnicott (1967) "potential space." In chapter 5 I assigned this scene to the topographic System Pcs.

The labyrinth is the unconscious counterpart to the potential space/claustrum and can be mediated by the "transformational object" (Bollas, 1987) of Challenge or by the "demon of Nemesis," depending respectively on whether we have hope or have forfeited our authenticity to the demon of Nemesis in a Faustian bargain (Blomfield, 1985). The outcome of this "trial-by-ordeal" depends largely on how much omnipotent authority the infant has invested in its cruel internal subjective objects.

---

14. In 1941 Eric Fromm's *Escape From Freedom* was first published. The dust jacket design of the original publication pictured a man in prison despondently yet desperately rattling the bars of the door to his cell—which was surrounded on only three sides.

The strength of the infant's persecutors is determined by the degree of this felt destructiveness toward its objects (in the paranoid-schizoid position) and how strongly the infant believes that it must sacrifice itself and surrender to the cruel internal objects in order to pacify them.

While the infant *believes* that it is innocuously destroying the subjective object (Winnicott, 1969, 1971)[15] that is superimposed as an invisible effigy over the actual object, the infant must believe deep down that it is thus, of necessity, hurting or harming the object. Only the survival of the actual object can save the infant from inexorable guilt. Thus, the actual object—and the subject's image of it—constitute the composite chimerical object of Challenge. The infant who is unprepared for such high adventure remains a divided self. In extreme circumstances, one aspect is relegated to the diabolical dungeon known as the labyrinth. The normal unconscious counterpart is the labyrinth of Challenge.

The hero, a mythic term that corresponds to Bion's (1970) concept of the messiah, mystic, and "man of achievement," dares to know himself as he is in the Mirror of the Real without the disguises of the Imaginary or the Symbolic. The hero must know himself in Bion's O, as did Oedipus when he answered the riddle of the sphinx. To do so, the infant must accept and "run" with the gift of life and transcend its "baggage" of felt curses and handicaps. Psychoanalytically, this means that the infant must accept its own life scenario in its entirety. Ultimately, those who would be heroes must separate out those aspects of their phantasmal internal world that belong to themselves from those that had to be endured from their objects. Thus they must distinguish among *persecutors, true enemies* (whether they be parents or strangers), and *safe loved* and *loving ones*.

To claim its own life, the infant must handle three potentially abusive situations: (1) the chaos of infinity (Matte-Blanco, 1975, 1988), inherent beta elements, dread of O (Bion, 1962b, 1963, 1965, 1970), and the instinctual drive urges and affects; (2) the traumatic impingements and mal- or misattunements (and counterprojective identifications) on the part of the parents and family; and (3) the natural predator-enemies of the family, clan, or culture (e.g., the situation in the Holocaust or Bosnia). The infant must do battle with the phantom chimerae of its own creation, the results of the inchoate "digestion" and processing of painful

15. The subjective object is Winnicott's way of designating the illusion of the object that the infant spontaneously creates, (either consciously or unconsciously). Although he fails to say so specifically, he clearly implies that this is accomplished through projective identification. The subjective object therefore corresponds to Klein's concept of an internal object, whether actually experienced as internalized or as externalized (via reprojective identification).

experiences. The infant must autochthonize (be the phantasied creator of) these traumas before it can begin (in the depressive position of separation-individuation/object-constancy) to distinguish *persecutors* (always the self) from *enemies* (always the object and never the self).

The infantile neurosis (Freud, 1918) is the archaic organizing state of "pathology" created by the infant in trying to mediate between narcissistic urges and the desire to adjust to the family. The next step is the battle of sorting out the self from the object, and both of those from the phantasmatic exaggerations of them. The infant must become the hero in its own saga, do battle with demons and overcome them—with the knowledge that emerges from courage. But our infant-who-would-be-hero needs the help of loving objects in this saga. In the myth it was Ariadne and her thread; in real life it is our loved and loving ones.

OBJECT USAGE AND THE EMERGENCE OF THE SELF

Winnicott's infant, like the God of Scripture, must have the power of life and death over its objects. It must first create them and then destroy them in order to be the author of its own life scenario and find the real external object by destroying the "eggshell" of protective subjective objects interposed between itself and the ineffable Other. For Winnicott the destruction of the subjective object is tantamount to destroying the self-made *myth* or *phantasy* of the object. In this precocious deconstruction, the infant discovers the realness and ineffable Otherness of the object as subject and at the same time discovers itself as an individuated subject in its own right, shorn of earlier subjective myths of omnipotent creativity.

This idea of the need to destroy the object—without hate—ultimately devolves to an ontological point that Winnicott failed to make clear, in my opinion. I may repeat my earlier citation of St. Paul, he stated in his "First Letter to the Corinthians," "Now through a glass darkly, then face to face. . . ." I take this to mean that human beings naturally and unconsciously "know" the other through the intermediary of the images they create of the other within their own minds. Ultimately, the realness of the other, that is, the Otherness, can never be known; one can only experience a resonance with it in O (Bion, 1970). In the journey toward O we must relentlessly destroy (deconstruct) the images we needed to apprehend the other.

The dissociation between the innocent play world of Winnicott and the fateful one of Klein may have a curious parallel neurobiologically in the delayed myelination of the corpus callosum in the infant. The corpus callosum, the bridge linking the two cerebral hemispheres, does not begin to myelinate until the infant is about four months of age (about the time of development of the depressive position or "hatching"), and myelination is not completed until early adulthood (LeCours, 1975; LeMire et al., 1975). Conceivably, then, the infant may normally be sufficiently neuronally unintegrated (primary dissociation) that it can theoretically maintain two separated modes of being. This natural dissociation may effectively blunt the *significance* of what would otherwise be affectively traumatic states.

The *destruction* of the subjective object must be distinguished from *hate* or *murder*, its dialectical opposite. Clinically, it is important for patients to emerge from the timidity and diffidence of their neuroses and be able to confront and kill the Minotaur, but they must never murder. Murder is the acting out of the failure to kill one's Nemesis demon. Its connection with sadism, is important. In regard to this sadism Steiner (1993) states:

> This means that the mourner must expose himself to the reality of the fact that he is unable to protect his objects from his own sadism that arises as a consequence of separation and loss. *So, the painful paradox is that the mourner must kill what he loves in order, ultimately, to be able to restore it at a symbolic level within the ego* [p. 53].

Once confronted with the Real—and surrendering to it—the victim of neurosis, trauma, or "cowardice" becomes an ontological prisoner of the labyrinth and is hounded by his personal identifying demon, the Minotaur. This object of Nemesis forever afterward taunts the victim for cowardice and will continue to taunt until the victim courageously undertakes the task of minotaurmachy, accepting the challenge of slaying the Minotaur. The Minotaur, like the sphinx, taunts those whom it can intimidate and, paradoxically, encourages the victim to slay it, by understanding that it is mythical.

A 30-year-old married patient suffered from impotence and demonstrated enormous passive-aggressiveness in the transference and toward his wife and children. His impotence and transference resistance were understood as his way of repeating with me his reaction to his own parents, who he felt had not been sufficiently attuned to him and to his unusual sensitivity. He had "divorced" them as a child and became cowardly and "internal." Masturbation was his main form of sexual release. It finally emerged that he was identified with a Minotaur-like demon that would attempt to seduce me and others to come to his rescue (since he was trapped within his inner labyrinth). When I (or others) tried, he would become critical and used manic defenses of triumph, contempt, and control. He represented both Ariadne (who would lure me into the labyrinth) and the Minotaur, who would attack me. He was able to improve once this unconscious phantasy was explicated.

THE INNER JOURNEY AND THE HOMING INSTINCT

Being "trapped in the labyrinth" is a potential danger for all of us, but it also seems to define a class of patients—"orphans of the Real" (Grotstein, 1995b, 1999a)—characterized by their lack of vitality or aliveness, preoccupation with safety over pleasure and adventure, withdrawal and alienation, preoccupation with inner reality, and a marked sense of "self-consciousness," which, in turn, is characterized by a sense of disembodiment and depersonalization, if not outright derealization. These patients seem to have undergone a spiritual death, often unobserved and unmourned. The self-abandonment may have been the consequence of trauma; the hapless patients felt overwhelmed by the trauma, personified it, identified with the aggressor (concordantly, complementarily, or oppositionally), felt penetrated and "broken" as a self, became lost in the object and lost to themselves as they "disappeared" into misrecognition (Lacan, 1966; Ogden, 1989b).

A 42-year-old single patient who typifies this syndrome recently reported the following dream:

> I was entering UCLA campus in order to go to the library. I decided to enter by way of the botanical gardens and suddenly felt a moment of fear when I had lost my way for a moment. I thought that getting into UCLA constituted an immediate challenge for me—how to get through the garden to the labyrinth, the forbidden space and how to exit without incurring injury. When I finally entered UCLA, I became aware that I was in the hospital building, not the upper campus proper. When I experienced the typical hospital odor, I was instantly reminded of my castration anxiety when I was a small child in a dentist's office.

This patient's history was suggestive of the Asperger syndrome. He belongs to Alcoholics Anonymous but has never drunk alcohol. He has never had sex; he professed to be, if anything, homosexual, but had never committed himself in that regard. A developing but sexually unconsummated relationship with an attractive young actress precipitated a dream in which this woman provoked him into throwing her onto the bed. He began to have sex and hated her for provoking what he felt was his demonic side, of which he was terrified. He realized, however, that this aspect of himself was associated with his sexuality. In his associations, he spoke of his

> fear of my labyrinthine, demonic, aggressive, lying, mendacious self, the monster within me who deceives, cheats, steals, and imitates others. My childhood was so awful. My mother and father hated each other, and both hated me. I could never be a self around them. I eventually learned that I didn't have to be myself if I could be someone else. It was the only path through the maze. Perseus—with the three one-eyed women—pretended to be someone else, as did Jacob and Ulysses. Becoming another person, putting on someone else's identity was the way to survive. If I had continued to be me, I'd have suicided, so I suicided partially so as to go on living. I guess I'm terrified of sex because it means entering the labyrinth and owning my demonic self.

This patient's dream demonstrated another feature of the mythic, voyeuristic journey into mother's claustrum, that of the tropism to return to one's "first home." We may term this the "homing instinct," and it may be a part-instinct within the epistemophilic instinct.

Meltzer and Harris's (1988) concept of the "apprehension of beauty" is relevant to the theme of the labyrinth in terms of the epigenesis of the epistemophilic instinct. The infant first apprehends mother's beautiful surfaces and seeks epistemophilically to penetrate her and enter her "labyrinth" in order to apprehend her *ineffable personalness*. Getting to "know" her insides constitutes the infant's "sexual" encounter with her humanness. Pornography is a fixation to the mother's attractive surfaces and belies the appreciation of her inner beauty.

Meltzer (1992) synthesized Klein's (1946, 1955) conceptualization of projective identification and Bion's (1962b) modifications of the "container–contained" and differentiated between Klein's original formulations of projective identification into a claustrum and Bion's expressive communication into a mother-as-container. In addition, Meltzer elaborated the "compartments of the maternal *claustrum*," designating the "breast/mind," the "genital," and the "rectum" and detailing the infant's unconscious phantasies of imaginatively inhabiting each of these "geographic" areas of mother's claustrum. This concept of the claustrum as a phantasmal image seems to approximate the mythic labyrinth, in the sense of the maternal (or paternal) rectum or cloacum as well as womb.

Through projective identification the infant equates the external world with the mother's insides as the locale for its exploratory zeal

(Klein, 1928, 1946, 1955). Winnicott (1967) located the area of cultural experience in potential space, an area intermediate between infant and mother. From the dialectical relationship between infant and mother and between patient and analyst, Ogden (1994a) constructed the "third area of experience," which Klein first associated with mother's internality. Jung (1969a), Ferguson (1982), and Schwartz-Salant (1989) also referred to this third area. I locate this third area of potential cultural experience in the System Pcs., as I have already stated, and call it "the transformational anteroom of the preconscious."

Here illusory images of the subjective objects that are phantasied by the infant/toddler are absorbed into the alchemical amalgam of their chimerical hybrid nature. These images, in turn, are projectively compared with the perceptual images of the external individuals involved, and "the moment of truth" occurs. The infant/toddler, in a courageous, exploratory zeal, must climb over, under, and "inside" each parent so as to "explore them all up" and "all over" and then epistemophilically absorb every detail of their physical and psychical essence—and even detect the mystery of their Otherness (their ineffable Subjectivity)—while the barriers of anxiety, shame, and guilt begin slowly to wane.

Infants then become retrospectively aware of the damage putatively or actually done to the object and may experience persecutory anxiety from the most primitive sources or even castration anxiety. Ultimately, they feel contrition, guilt, respect, and ultimately reconciliation (not compliance) with the "law of the nurturing mother" (of separateness), "the law of the father," and the "law of the parental couple," which ultimately devolves into the Law of the Covenant, which guarantees safety to each member of the family from the wanton destructiveness of the other.

The labyrinth myth thus anticipates the onset of the depressive position and constitutes a developmental milestone in its arrival. The heroic task of accepting one's life, destiny, and moira occurs in the metaphoric labyrinth and constitutes the normal narcissistic complement to the reconciliation with Otherness in the depressive position.

I am suggesting that, in order to enter the depressive position, the infant is obliged to conquer the fear of internal persecutory objects (of its own creation) by first heroically facing them and daring to *know* (conquer) them and then withdrawing projective identifications from their mythic architecture, whereby they finally become their real selves. This process constitutes *paranoid-schizoid-mastering validation of the self, the use of assertiveness, the courage to know and to face one's demons*. This task involves the integration of the epistemophilic, libidinal, and aggressive instinctual tropisms.

CONCLUDING REMARKS

The myth of the labyrinth symbolically and allegorically unites concepts of Freud and Jung and those of object relations theory, particularly those of Klein and Winnicott but also of Bion, Lacan, and Anna Freud. Jung's concepts of transcendence, of the personal and collective unconscious, of archetypes, and of alchemy are linked to Klein's conceptions of splitting, projective identification, and the combined parental imago and to Winnicott's concepts of object usage and the subjective object.

Those themes unite in the concept that the labyrinth may constitute an archetypal myth from the collective unconscious that designates the universal need of all infants and people generally (mythically represented by Theseus) to return to their mythic home (the womb/claustrum) in an epistemophilic/sadistic foray in order to encounter the phantom-beast that they have projected into it. They then must challenge it and win over it, thus obtaining their "spurs of combat" and its legacy, the courage to *know* and to *realize*.

The outcome determines whether the phantom object, the metaphoric Minotaur, becomes one's Nemesis Object or one's Challenge Object. In this heroic quest, one is encouraged and guided by one's magus object (Ariadne). The magus may appear with either a positive, shepherding function or a more disingenuous one, so that the hapless "hero" may feel goaded or lured into danger.

The major tasks of analysis—and of life—as seen from the concept of the myth of the labyrinth, are to confront the Object of Challenge or Nemesis in order to separate out and retrieve those projections that belong to oneself from those that are alien to the self from the beginning. One must be able to own and resolve one's infantile neurosis/psychosis and distinguish it from infantile catastrophe or trauma—and resolve that as well. Ultimately, the myth of the labyrinth signifies psychoanalysis and its relentless quest for uniting with unconscious truth.

Chapter 8

WHY OEDIPUS AND NOT CHRIST?

Part 1

A PSYCHOANALYTIC INQUIRY INTO INNOCENCE, HUMAN SACRIFICE, SPIRITUALITY, AND THE SACRED

Many readers may feel that in this chapter and the following one I have become an advocate for religious worship, and others may feel that this work is a blasphemy against the Jewish faith because I use the figure of Christ as an archetype[1] as well as a descendant of Oedipus[2], Isaac, Joseph, Moses, and other martyrs or would-be martyrs, as well as messiahs or would-be messiahs. (A messiah can be defined, according to Bion [1965, 1970] as anyone who comes up with the "messiah thought".) I employ Christ's history and myth only for psychoanalytic purposes, that is, for the highly useful models they offer for the clarification of unconscious invariants, as is exemplified in the story of the crucifixion and the Pietà, which constitute graphic exemplifications of the exorcistic nature of the transference–countertransference phenomenon, the relationship between the paranoid-schizoid positions, and the ultimate nature of Bion's container–contained model. Psychoanalysts who are of

1. By archetype I mean, following Plato as well as Jung, the idea of an inherent preconception, as Bion (1962b, 1963, 1965, 1970) suggested. In other words, it is as if the real Jesus Christ stepped into an archetypal role that was older than he, one older than man himself, one that belongs to the eternal Ideal Forms.

2. The story of Oedipus is, likewise, archetypal, as Velikovsky (1960) suggested from his explorations of its prefiguration in the story of Akhnaton.

the Jewish faith may consider my line of approach to be insensitive to Judaism because of the history of the persecution of Jews by Christians in the name of Christ. I therefore wish to make clear that I am respectfully Jewish, became Bar Mitzvah, am a grandson of a distinguished rabbi, and am a direct descendant of Rabbi Eliyahu ben Shelomo, Kalman, the Vilna Ga'on. Further, I see spiritual Christianity not only as an outgrowth of Judaism but also as a *continuation of Judaism in a different guise*. It is more than mere speculation that, were it not for the radical intercession of St. Paul, the Jewish foundations of Christianity would be more respected by Christians. Furthermore, Christ knew no Christians and refused to share his ministry with gentiles. His was a Jewish story from start to finish. Eisenmann (1997) suggests that Christ was one of many messiah-martyrs of the first century and was considered "the son of man."

There is an interesting sideline to the myth of Christ's birth. We are aware that, at his birth in Nazareth, he was visited by the three Magi. Magi were religious priests in the Zoroastrian faith. Pagels (1979) and Bloom (1996) suggest that the Zoroastrian, Gnostic, and Neoplatonic influences on first-century and later Judaism were of the greatest importance. The common denominator they represented was the mystical notion of the immanent God, the God within, separate from the all-pervasive Godhead. Judaism itself had no way of encompassing this idea because of the doctrine of the *Shma*, that God is one! It was only in the Kabbala that room was made for this immanence. This and the following chapter—in fact, the whole book—is about the immanence of a preternatural presence within us, the Dreamer Who Dreams the Dream, the Dreamer Who Understands the Dream, the Infinite Geometer Who Wields the Calipers of Fearful Symmetry, the Ineffable Subject of the Unconscious, the id, the ego ideal. "Christ" is merely a convenient historical mytheme-signifier that lends itself to the continuation and amplification of the Oedipus saga, with the additional benefit of tapping into the mystical and spiritual (nonlinear, chaotic, complex) aspects of our ineffable internal world.

I believe that Freud (1914b) himself hinted at the Christ- or martyr-archetype without mentioning the name when he discussed the formation of the ego ideal as a "gradient in the ego" and as enfranchised with the grandiosity that the ego itself had to forfeit.

Christ is known among Christians as the Pascal Lamb, reminiscent of the ancient Jewish custom of choosing a "scapegoat" or ram to sacrifice. One particular aspect of this custom is of note: the members of the congregation, in effect, projected (attributed) their sins to the goat or lamb, which was then taken into the wilderness and allowed to be preyed upon by predators. Psychoanalytically, one can posit that insofar as Christ, the Pascal Lamb, can transform and therefore transcend the projective identifications, he becomes sacred. Insofar as he may be transformed by the projections, however, and therefore fail to transcend them, he has become the devil, who thereupon demands redemption by his relentless "return of the repressed."

What I am attempting to do is to lift the Christ history and myth out of its religious context and use its story psychoanalytically as a palimpsest representing the tradition of martyrs or would-be martyrs (and messiahs), in line with Oedipus, Isaac, and Moses. I hasten to assure my readers that this work, when it does deal with spirituality, is meant only to highlight those aspects of spirituality, religion, and the life, myth, or legend of Christ, as well as of Oedipus, that lend themselves exclusively to psychoanalytic exploration, especially those suggesting the theme of human sacrifice, the sacred template that underlies the transference–countertransference situation and the nature of the unspoken covenants that are unconsciously created between two or more individuals.

I also put forward the idea that the ancient religious ritual of human sacrifice continues in modified form in the psychoanalytic experience of transference and countertransference. In this regard I consider, following Meltzer (1978), that transference ultimately constitutes the transfer of mental pain from one person to another. Thus, from this perspective, bridges can be erected between the psychoanalytic phenomena of transference and countertransference, on one hand, and the religious phenomena of crucifixion, human sacrifice, and "exorcism" on the other. I subsume all these components in what I term the "Pietà covenant" and the "Pietà transference–countertransference" phenomenon.

The major theme of this chapter and the following is one that has long been considered heresy in religious beliefs—the theme of an inner divinity that is immanent within man. I think of this inner divinity (The Dreamer Who Dreams the Dream and the Dreamer Who Understands the Dream) as a preternatural presence, sometimes called the Demiurge (by Plato and the Gnostics) or God (as opposed to the Godhead) by the mystics. I associate it with the unconscious[3] but prefer to name it the Ineffable (Numinous and Immanent) Subject of the Unconscious, the mysterious counterpart of and partner to the Phenomenal Subject of Consciousness, the one of which we are more cognizant (see chapter 5).

In this and in the next chapter I approach the concept of man's inner "divinity" from two perspectives. One is the inherent, immanent (residing

3. Bollas (1992) and Eigen (1998) write similarly about the mystic nature of the unconscious.

within), preternatural unconscious (the Ineffable Subject), and the other is the result of the experience of human sacrifice, symbolically and actually. Our sacrificing of our objects turns them into sacred images that haunt, persecute, and dominate our internal world—until they become analytically repatriated as benevolent superegos in the depressive position. Klein (1963), describing this spiritual epigenesis, traced the transformation of the archaic, persecutory Furies to their more benevolent descendants, the Eumenides.

As for the Godhead itself, I believe that it is the consummate and absolute Subject and can never become the object of understanding or scrutiny. Thus, God, especially as Godhead, is utterly ineffable and inscrutable. To attempt to study Him constitutes epistemic incest, as I suggested in chapter 5. Yet that proscription does not preclude psychoanalytic speculation. Put another way, it is not God whom I wish to study, only man's use of the deity.

CLINICAL EXAMPLE

In the course of analyzing a physician in his 30s who suffered from a lifelong depression presumably due, among other factors, to severe child abuse, I found myself experiencing a unique countersubjective response[4] with some of the patient's more graphic memories, which I understood as his unconscious communication to me of painful, abusive experiences from his childhood. This chronically depressed, early middle-aged Canadian Jewish physician had been in analysis with me for seven years at the time of this incident and had been in a state of prolonged and weary resistance for some time. Returning from a vacation to Paris, where he had visited the Cathedral de le Sacre Coeur, he reported that he had had a "religious experience" there. He gazed upon the statue of Christ, who, with His bleeding wounds, seemed to reach mercifully and forgivingly to the patient. The patient then exclaimed, "I don't need psychoanalysis! I need God in order to regain my innocence!"

This patient had no way of knowing that, during this session and even presciently during previous sessions with him, I had been countersubjectively visualizing the image of Michelangelo's "Pietà" and, equally mysteriously to me, had been silently reciting to myself,

4. The countertransference aspect of this intersubjective experience consisted of (1) my *trial* or partial *counter*introjective identification (Fliess, 1942; Money-Kyrle, 1956) with the patient's projective identifications, and (2) my subsequent projective *counter*identification (Grinberg, 1962, 1979a, b) to that with which I had partially introjectively counteridentified.

"washed in the blood of the Lamb!" (*Revelations* 7:14). Having made that inner connection, I began to experience feeling tentative identifications alternately with Mary and with Christ while the patient seemed to make protesting assaults against life in general, against his wife in his home life, and against me in the transference.

Some aspects of this patient's case material evoked psychoanalytic issues that seemed to fit into a pattern of clinical and theoretical themes that have not been significantly addressed in the psychoanalytic literature, including issues of religion, spirituality, demonism, crucifixion, the Pietà; such concepts as the covenant, blessings, curses; and such themes as innocence, human sacrifice, original sin, the Faustian bargain, and exorcism. In addition, other considerations arose having to do with redefining and expanding the psychoanalytic concepts of transference, countertransference, and the infantile and transference, as well as countertransference, neurosis.

THE PIETÀ COVENANT IN THE TREATMENT OF ABUSED INNOCENCE: "SAY YOU'RE SORRY!"[5]

Specifically, I developed the notion of a "Pietà covenant," which involves both a hitherto unmentioned aspect of projective identification on the part of the analysand and its interpersonal counterpart, the analyst's introjective and projective *counter*identification as a specific category of the transference–countertransference situation and a specific example as well of Bion's concept of the container–contained. The "Pietà covenant" is the implied (unconscious, unstated) agreement between infant and mother in which the infant agrees to do its best to survive and thrive if mother agrees to indemnify the infant against unnecessary pain, sorrow, or danger.

The projective identification aspect involves a series of expectations by the analysand that the analyst should (vicariously) experience the sorrow and guilt for all the pain the analysand has suffered, past and present, and should take responsibility for removing the pain and its source. The analyst, who, though innocent of the charge of childhood

5. A perplexingly mute child patient presented at the Grand Rounds of a prestigious psychiatric hospital suddenly began to speak after Dr. Lawrence Kubic, using remarkable intuition, spontaneously told her, "I'm sorry! I'm very sorry!" Immediately following this "confession," the patient broke her silence and exclaimed, "Say you're sorry!" to each member of the audience (Kubie and Israel, 1955).

abuse, may understandably concur with the patient's charges for another reason—that, by initiating and releasing the analytic juggernaut, the analyst may experience guilt for the pain that he is causing the patient. When I speak of the Pietà covenant or the transference–countertransference situation, I am speaking of a particular aspect of Bion's container–contained and the psychoanalytic third subjectivity (Ogden, 1994a, 1997), in which the analyst is expected to be penitent and responsible for the pain that the analysand experiences and has experienced from infancy and childhood. The analyst's guilt is a proxy guilt. He is to feel (as container) the repentance and failure of responsibility, as proxy, for the parents who failed to redeem themselves to their child (the analysand) long ago—under the "subjugating" influence of the analysand.

The analysand's pain, which can be equated with crucifixion, is transferred through projective "exorcism" into the analyst as proxy, scapegoat, and container, and the latter must be felt to suffer it long enough and effectively enough so that the analysand can believe that he has witnessed the transfer of his victimization and the demand for parental reparations to the analyst and, thereby, reclaim his own redemption. In regard to this new perspective, I am trying to create bridges between Klein's (1946, 1955) original conception of the phenomenon of projective identification, Bion's (1962a) and others' intersubjective extension of it (as container–contained), Winnicott's (1969, 1971) conceptions of the subjective object and object usage, and Hopkins's (1989) integration of the concepts of the crucifixion and object usage. Freud (1912) stated that one cannot cure a psychoneurosis per se; one can only cure an infantile neurosis that has been *transferred* into a transference neurosis. This belief of Freud's suggests to me object usage, the subjective object, and container–contained in the service of "exorcistic" transference. In other words, transference is not just the displacement of past object cathexes or the projective identifications of painful aspects of the analysand into the image of the analyst. Transference is indistinguishable at one point with countertransference—and fundamentally depends on the shared experience of a transference—"over to" and a countertransference in which what has been transferred "over to" has been accepted.

I hope to demonstrate the existence in mental life of a psychological dialectic between the sacred and the demonic (profane), innocence and original sin, the covenant and the Faustian bargain, blessing and curse, Christ and the devil as archetypes, and the miracle of psychological transformation and transcendence versus magic (omnipotence). In my psychoanalytic orientation to religion I have been guided especially by the works of Rizzuto (1974, 1976, 1991), Meissner (1984), Jones (1991), Spero (1992), Symington (1994), Leavy (1988), and de Mello Franco (1998), as well as by many others.

THE CASE PRESENTATION

I now shall go into greater detail in regard to the patient I alluded to earlier. When, after many years into the analysis, the patient began to recount his father's abuse and his mother's silent, passive collusion with it, I felt that he unconsciously wanted me to feel the pain and humiliation he had felt, to experience guilt, responsibility, and contrition for its having happened—that is, guilt as father for having abused him, responsibility as mother for having passively permitted it, and as himself in suffering it. The "father guilt" had to do with my inducing traumatic flashbacks by conducting the analysis in the first place, while the feeling of guilt-as-mother was associated to my "collusive passivity" in allowing the regressive reactivation of painful scenarios to unfold without offering relief.[6]

Earlier, the patient had made substantial progress in the analysis, but then he fell into a prolonged period of a negative therapeutic reaction in which progress often seemed to come to a standstill or would be slow and begrudging. It was several years before he began to allude to his history of being abused by his father and then only reluctantly at first, angrily later, and always with consummate shame. It also took a long time for me to grasp the significance of his belief that he had unconsciously signed a "Faustian bargain with the devil" (his words) in order to be safe from anxiety and terror. I came to realize that his concrete belief that he had signed that pact underlay his belief that he was cursed and doomed and had come from a cursed family. This belief created the seeming intransigence of his resistance in the latter phase of the analysis.

The Patient's Background

The patient's father left his pregnant wife for overseas duty with the Canadian army in the European theater during World War II and served in many combat operations. He also took part in the liberation of many concentration camps. Though he never complained of any symptoms himself, he was, by his own admission, depressed, distant, highly irritable, inflammable, and overdependent on his wife; he could not

6. Elswhere (Grotstein, 1981a) I have discussed the concept of the "magus," the mythical Zoroastrian sorcerer, made famous by John Fowles's (1965), as an internal object that appears in clinical practice. Its putative role is to enforce the patient's experiencing of repressed or split-off painful memories, thoughts, and feelings, all of which the patient would not allow to surface spontaneously. Obviously, the "magus object" is constructed from the split-off and projectively reidentified intentionality of the patient in the analyst. In psychotic states, the magus object is the putative source of ideas and delusions of reference.

concentrate for any length of time and had lost the ambition he had had before the war. These sounded like symptoms of "combat fatigue," as it was then known, but it was not diagnosed on his discharge from the service. He returned from the war to find a two-year-old son he had never before seen and with whom he never subsequently bonded, seemingly wanting his wife all to himself. The patient recalls many episodes of lectures, threats, and violence from his father when he "got on his nerves." The specifics of the father's violence took years of analysis to uncover. Originally he described his father as depressed and as a "loser" of whom he was ashamed.

His mother was described as phobic, distracted, and absent-minded, a poor homemaker (dinners were never on time), and an inconsistent attendant to his needs. She frequently forgot to pick him up after school and never protected him from his father's assaults. From our analysis of his feelings about his parents' families, we were able to decipher some of his phantasies about his family romance. We began to unveil his unconscious entanglement with both parents' unresolved infantile neuroses (the intergenerational and transgenerational neuroses) that had been projected into him; he had defensively introjectively identified with these projective identifications especially in his belief that he had become their scapegoat/victim as well as their hero/messiah.

Although his father had come from a poor, small-town Jewish family in one of the Canadian prairie provinces, his mother was related to a powerful, well-known east-coast Canadian family. The patient spent considerable time with his widowed maternal grandmother, and she frequently soothed him lovingly after some of his father's abusive episodes. She raised him as a "little prince," and he identified highly with the young protagonist of Antoine De Saint-Exupéry's (1943) story with that title. He seemed to have lived apart from his family much of the time, whereas his siblings, three younger brothers, who had also been abused by the father, were not so closely associated with the grandmother. They formed a subfamily of their own, setting up a "little oedipal" sibling family, the forerunner of the adolescent rebellion against the parental family and a tendency that is prominent in the formation of cults and gangs (Grotstein, 1997).

Synopsis of the Analysis

We spent considerable time analyzing his having adopted a fictive personality (Klein, 1955; Martin, 1988; Grotstein, 1995b, c).[7] In his associa-

---

7. I have dealt with the background of unattached or detached children in these contributions as "orphans of the Real."

tion with his grandmother the patient could pretend that he actually belonged to a "noble family" back on the east coast and was not related to his family of origin. This phantasy constituted a variation of the "family romance" (Freud, 1909) and occupied much of the analytic discourse. He revealed that as a teenager he had been deeply affected by Emily Brontë's *Wuthering Heights* and had secretly identified with Heathcliffe, feeling cursed because he did in fact come from an inferior family of which he was ashamed and which he wished to disown. He felt profoundly envious of the East-coast family that seemed to have ignored him (allegedly because of their contempt for his parents).

The patient's ultimate phantasy was to be reborn into a world where he was a prince or a scion of a wealthy and powerful family that would give him a sense of being *blessed*. One of the interesting aspects of this phantasied curse, which was to defend against the humiliation of the abuse by his father, was that, the more success he achieved in his professional life, the more bitterly depressed he became because he had to achieve this success on his own rather than having been handed it as a legacy or birthright! His lack of gratitude for progress in his analysis followed the same pattern: If he made progress (and he had made considerable progress in many areas), it meant only that he had been badly off and cursed to begin with. He evinced the character structure that Steiner (1993, 1996) refers to as psychic retreats due to grievances, resentment, and desire for revenge. My interpretations to him about envy, both his envy of the past that might have been, were it not for the abuse and emotional impoverishment he had suffered, and the sabotaging envy of his superego toward his emerging successful self, seemed to produce significant beneficial effects but failed to put his underlying depression to rest.

In his mid-40s he married a woman with whom he had had an on-and-off relationship for over 20 years. He phantasized her as the Cathy to his Heathcliffe, but on the darker side. Anger, petulance, envy, and hatred often characterized their relationship. It did not seem to help him very much in the analysis to learn that she unconsciously represented both the unmotherly and unsoothing aspects of his mother and a projective identification of his own bitter, cynical, depressed self. After marriage their relationship worsened, and he blamed me for its unhappy outcome as well as for other disappointing aspects of his life.

After three years of unhappy marriage, he and his wife traveled to Paris when suddenly an impulse to reexamine his spiritual emptiness came over him. One day he visited the Cathedral de le Sacre Coeur and was gripped for the first time in his life with the sense of "needing God to be redeemed," the scene I described earlier. His religious experience climaxed when he stood underneath the statue of Christ, whose wounds stood out, side by side with His outreaching, forgiving hands.

The power of the scene never left the patient, and his analysis henceforth was significantly altered, following his agonizing statement, "I don't need analysis! I need God in order to regain my innocence!" He then uttered something that penetrated me profoundly, "Why was I born? How could those selfish, ungrown-up people dare to have children?" I immediately thought of Kubie and Israel's (1955) poignant paper, "Say You're Sorry!" The tone and way in which he spoke caused me briefly to feel countertransferentially responsible—as if I represented both his parents—as well as his analytic guide who was responsible for his analytic rebaptism into memory.

It was at this moment, representative as it was of countless other similar moments, that I formulated the idea of potential parental and analytic guilt for bearing children when we cannot guarantee them "safe passage" through the straits of the "Real" (in the Lacanian sense) and cannot protect them reasonably from demons, both theirs and ours. This theme poses the generic question that forms the basis of this chapter: "If you knew that I was going to suffer, why did you give birth to me?"

LOSS OF INNOCENCE

One of the main issues in this patient's analysis was his continuous lamentation over the *loss of his innocence*. He meant by this that he had been victimized and abused by a cruel father, neglected and inconsistently treated by a perennially absent-minded, distracted, and selfishly neglectful but also seductive mother, cursed by their being the poor relatives of a rich and famous family, disillusioned by overidealized mentors and models in his later years, and "cursed" with a long run of bad luck in his own personal and professional life. "Bad luck" was his epithet for any professional setback, a designation authored by his depressive fatalism. Actually, he had become quite successful professionally but could not appreciate this success. Ultimately he was able to say that he believed that he had been abused by God and by Fate! In addition to these issues, however, he had long ago talked about a *dead child within*, who he despaired would never see life again. The specter of the dead child reemerged after the incident at le Sacre Coeur. *At other times he would speak of this child as wounded and bleeding.*[8]

8. Later in this chapter I suggest that the "bleeding child" is the truer nature of the Ineffable Subject of the Unconscious in its role as the ego ideal and that its provenance as ego ideal obligatorily lies in its covenant of suffering—for the ego—as the "Christ archetype" (Jung, 1934). I also argue that the "dead child"

Temperamentally, the patient was dour, moody, brooding, and withdrawn. He used his equally temperamental wife as the scapegoat for his projections. Bitterness—and the quiet joy of experiencing it—constituted the main part of his loneliness and schizoid isolation. He was both Scrooge (demeaning and ungiving) and Don Quixote at times to my Sancho Panza in the transference, the latter when he was deeply immersed in creative writing outside of his professional field. His inner life and his object relations were characterized by extreme scrupulousness to the point of obsessionality, moral self-righteousness, and restraint. Behind this was a sadomasochistic disposition in which he enjoyed triumphing over rivals and subordinates and yet found himself frequently persecuted or victimized by his wife and others. His Heathcliffe aspect was chronically bitter over the loss of his innocence, represented by Cathy and his *Wuthering Heights* "entitlement" and innocence. He demanded their return from me because I was responsible, in the transference, for their loss!

The oedipal aspects of the relationship between mother, "Cathy," and innocence and their transgression in his unconscious longings were dealt with. I was equated in the transference with the father, whose return from the war created a sudden breach in the patient's hitherto uninterrupted access to mother. Associations to this breach frequently emerged after a weekend or vacation break. I was also equated with his dilatory codependent mother, who collusively ignored the beatings. At other times, when his envy surfaced, I was equated with the remote, aristocratic family in eastern Canada. We also analyzed his experience of me as the breast-mother whom he had all to himself and who caused him to experience intense envy and rivalry upon separation and loss of princely omnipotence.

Throughout the whole course of the analysis the patient emphasized his feeling of being cursed, ill-fated, and doomed. Further, he frequently characterized himself as being demonic in the sense of believing that he was internally haunted and often dominated by a demonic force that caused him to be relatively friendless, to be rude to his employees and colleagues, and generally to be a curmudgeon.

As a consequence in part to my response to this and other of the patient's experiences, some aspects of my longstanding countersubjective responses (i.e., "trial" countertransference feelings, my introjective counteridentification plus my projective counteridentification) became

is universally ensconced in abused and traumatized patients and is transformed into the "undead child," the one who relentlessly haunts them for their having made a Faustian bargain with an internal dark force in order to survive. I also propose a similar origin for the superego.

clearer to me. These were my reactions to his hatred, vilification, and demeaning of me, both as a persecutory parent who "abused" him by causing him to feel emotional pain and as an ineffective parent who was helpless and inadequate to help or protect him from the "unfairness of life." When detailed memories of the abuse began to emerge more fully, the patient reviled me and became incensed when I offered interpretations that he felt were either naively empathic about his abusive experiences or seemed to place the responsibility for his problems on him, especially when I interpreted transference projections of his sadomasochistic need to punish me the way his father had abused him. He exclaimed on those occasions that I did not understand, that I was stupid and on the wrong path.

I took from this response that once he knew that I was available[9] to him and that I acknowledged his feelings about having been abused, I became a veritable poultice for the anguishing abscess of his hitherto sealed traumata. The following themes emerged: (1) Inasmuch as I was conducting the analysis, I was responsible for the regressive retrieval of painful memories that equated me with the original father who had committed the abuse. As such I was close to being the devil, the treacherous one who first seduces his prey into sin and then tantalizes and torments him.[10] I functioned in phantasy as the magus archetype, the one who stimulates the relentless unfolding of the inexorable unconscious scenario belonging to the regression. (2) I became partially identified both with Mary (the patient's complementary projective *and* my trial introjective and counterprojective identifications), who was nominally guilty for having conceived and then forsaken her child to martyrdom, *and* with Jesus, the innocent sacrificial lamb (patient's concordant projective and my counterprojective identifications), who must suffer the sins of others for their redemption and salvation (as the patient must have unconsciously felt in the case of his father).

---

9. My availability constituted not only the mutual acceptance of the therapeutic alliance (Greenson, 1965) but also what Ogden (1994a) calls the beginning of the intersubjective third subjectivity, and what I would call the covenant. Bion (1962a, 1970) conveyed this situation within the embrace of the container and the contained and reverie.

10. The patient presented a dream that included the presence of treacherous snakes. I was then able to appreciate one of the possible meanings of the snake in the Garden of Eden myth in *Genesis*. The treachery of the snake, in alignment with the theme of this chapter, is the treachery of God's (the infant's) parents, Adam and Eve, in giving birth to Him without warning Him of the pain of life into which He had not asked to be born, especially when mother (Eve) treacherously deserts Him for her primal scene rendezvous with father (Adam).

THE PIETÀ TRANSFERENCE–COUNTERTRANSFERENCE PHENOMENON

A range of countertransference feelings emerged in connection with my patient's account of his parents' abuse. In addition to the stark experience of feeling like each of the guilty parents (complementary, passive mother and active father), I also felt like the *martyr*, (in Greek, "witness to the truth"), the innocent and uninvolved one who must be dragged into the dramatic scenario in order to become the existentially involved notary public of a crime of unfairness and brutality. At times I found myself resisting his projections, at which time I assumed an oppositional projective counteridentification (resenting his attacks against me). Alternatively, I would find myself involved in the rescue phantasy of being his hero and messiah, who would save him from his holocaust by taking him away from his tragic, time-warped state of the past and bring him into the freedom of the present.

The most fundamental transference images he projected into me were that of the *apologist* or "public defender" for a now-discredited and morally bankrupt humanity that had sanctioned his "soul murder" and the *scapegoat*, or even *pariah*. The last image is that of an innocent victim who is transformed into the mutually agreed-upon guilty and responsible one (through mimesis or folie à deux) whose "crucifixional" suffering would allow a "*transference*" of pain from the patient to the therapist.

Meltzer (1978) innovatively reread Freud's concept of transference, modified by Klein's (1946, 1955) concept of projective identification, as the *transfer of mental pain from one person to another*, a phenomenon that inheres in the crucifixion-Pietà-confessional-exorcism signification. I became convinced that transference and countertransference are paradoxically separate, *intra*subjective partners that are, at the same time, inextricably conjoined in an *inter*subjective[11] union. Together they ultimately constitute an act of "exorcism" mediated by the profound mythic constraints that appear to issue from the archetypal imagery of the crucifixion and the Pietà.

Thus, as the patient's infantile neurosis transforms into the transference neurosis, the analyst's counterresponse is a corresponding countertransference (countersubjective) neurosis, sometimes (normally) trial

---

11. I am aware of Meissner's (personal communication) understandable objection to the concept of "intersubjective." He believes, and I think rightly so, that subjectivity is private and unknowable. Intimate communications are, to him, "interpersonal."

or tentative, and at other times, pathologically total. The former involves the analyst's *partial* or *trial introjective identification* with the projective identifications from the patient's transference neurosis; *partial* or *trial projective counteridentification* as the analyst's intuitive response to these introjective identifications; and the emergence of the analyst's own infantile neurosis proper, which may be either *trial (partial)* or *total*. When the response is *total* rather than partial so that the therapist is in a state of mimesis or folie à deux[12] (Mason, 1994), a pathological countertransference is in operation. Finally, all these enumerated responses can be understood as being mediated by the subjugating third subject (Ogden, 1994a, 1997), the subject-in-common between the analytic pair.

Once I formulated this transference–countertransference "constant conjunction" (dialectical binary opposition), I realized that this concept had been *im*plicit but not *ex*plicit in Bion's (1962a, b) idea of the container and the contained in the analytic situation. The analyst's "reverie" and "alpha function" (dream-work alpha [Bion, 1962a, 1963, 1992]) that it sponsors constitute the *intuition* (sense organ responsive to internal reality [Freud, 1900, p. 615]) *and* the trial countertransference ensemble of countersubjective responsivity to the patient's interactive subjectivity.

Thus, Bion's concept of the container–contained can be understood as the interaction of two subjectivities, that is, two infantile neuroses (that of the analysand and that of the analyst), in addition to the understanding, forbearance, wisdom, and intuition of the analyst-as-container. Earlier, I posited that when the analyst, who is able to be in a state of reverie (O, the transcendent position), can experience the complementary counteridentification (Racker, 1968) from the analysand, that constitutes what I now call the Pietà transference–countertransference covenant. Bion (1992) left little doubt about his view of the analyst's personal involvement in the psychoanalytic situation of reverie:

> [W]hile listening to the patient the analyst should dwell on those aspects of the patient's communication which come nearest to arousing feelings corresponding to persecution and depression. In my experience this gives as good a check on the soundness of one's interpretive validity as anything I know. On the whole I am more satisfied with my work if I feel that I have been through these emotional experiences than I do if the session has been more agreeable. I am fortified in this belief by the convic-

12. Mimesis and folie à deux are different ways of expressing mutual projective identification and predicate the conscious or unconscious complicity of the victim of the projective identifications in accepting them as being valid.

> tion that has been borne on me by the analysis of psychotic or borderline patients. *I do not think such a patient will ever accept an interpretation, however correct, unless he feels that the analyst has passed through this emotional crisis as a part of the act of giving the interpretation* [p. 291, italics added].

In addition, Ogden's (1994a, 1997) concept of the three psychoanalytic subjects explains how the subjective aspects of the analysand and the analyst become projectively reidentified and condensed in the third subject, the relationship itself that exists between them.

The patient projected the active (abuser) father identification into me. This projective identification took the form of his hating analysis and hating me for subjecting him to a process in which he was forced to experience painful memories. The patient also revealed how he had concordantly identified with his father's abusiveness by tormenting his younger brothers and by his longstanding unwillingness to have children, whom he was certain he would mistreat. His concordant identification with his father became commingled with the identity of the martyred (Christ) self in tormenting me and holding me responsible for his suffering since I was the analyst who withheld help from him.

It was important for me, consequently, to distinguish between my willingness to accept and absorb the patient's wounded feelings as my psychoanalytic task as container (Piéta). By undergoing this sacrifice on my part, I am Christ-like in the depressive position as I "accept the demons" from the patient, whose agony represents Christ in the paranoid-schizoid position. The Christ-like position of the analyst who "exorcizes" the patient conflates with the image of the "Madonna of Sorrows" in the Piéta. It is a paradox that the analyst, like Christ, must be innocent in order to accept the proxy guilt of sorrow for all that happened to the patient. In summary, the analyst, like the martyr (Christ) archetype, must absorb the patient's experience of pain out of dedication to the analytic Covenant, which is a form of "analytic love" but not out of guilt or a sense of mimetically arrogated (projected) responsibility.

One can consider that an analysand who employs martyrdom defensively is using the *depressive defense* against experiencing authentic pain and is at the same time indirectly causing the object to experience pain. The depressive defense can be considered to be the depressive analogue of the manic defense. In other words, the clinical phenomenon of *entitlement* may be the disingenuous use of martyrdom.

"EXORCISM" AND THE QUESTION OF THE DEPRESSIVE POSITION OF THE PARENT

Klein's (1935, 1946) concept of the death instinct involves the infant's acceptance of guilt for putative damage to the maternal and paternal objects, along with the desire to repair that damage in order to restore the objects. Her entire point of view depends on the one-person perspective, in regard to both infant development and psychoanalysis. Here I am dealing with the other side of the depressive position, that of the putative or actual guilt of parents in their dealings with the child and the child's need for redemption through the parental apology. Thus, the depressive position must be considered to be a mutual undertaking by child and parent as well as by analysand and analyst. The analyst, from this point of view, must be on the alert for projective transidentifications in which he is to experience (through trial introjective counteridentification) proxy guilt projected into him—that is, vicariously to stand in for the mother or father and feel both the pain felt by the suffering patient *and* the pain of parental guilt for having been the cause of the pain. It is as if the traumatized patient needs the analyst to become the scapegoat/stand-in (like Christ)[13] to know his suffering and to experience the sorrow for it. In other words, the analysand holds the analyst responsible, as the infant/child holds mother or father responsible for all that happens, beginning with the universal cry, "I didn't ask to be born!" and including frustrations, unfairnesses, illnesses, catastrophes.

I have treated patients who, at some point in their analyses, held their parents responsible for their exile from a hostile mother country. If the parents had not been of a certain faith or had been strong enough, the catastrophe would not have occurred, presumably. In the course of psychoanalytic transference regression, analysts are almost universally held responsible by the infantile portion of the personality for all that

---

13. I am aware of the confusion the reader must experience when I speak of the analysand as feeling crucified by traumatic experience and then place Christ in the role of the analyst/scapegoat who accepts the blame and responsibility for the analysand's pain. I shall explain this paradox as I proceed, but in the meanwhile I can say the following: Christ's is the voice of the innocent victim *and* the redeemer of guilt by accepting the projections of the victim. Mary of the Pietà is the mother of sorrow and guilt who *should* have felt guilty for agreeing to bear a child who was destined for martyrdom. Thus, the second function of the Christ (martyr) archetype is, as Fairbairn's (1944) concept of endopsychic structures prefigures, for Christ to experience the *proxy responsibility*—as martyr—that Mary refuses to acknowledge—except in my own vision of the Pietà at the Vatican.

happens to the analysand. Someone must pay the price, they feel. When the parent—or analyst—says he is sorry, the child is more able to enter his own depressive position. Further, when the parent/analyst keeps the faith, so to speak, the child can pardon him and become reconciled to *the parent's/analyst's* loss of omnipotence. In other words, the depressive position allows the infant/child to pardon its objects commensurately with its own self-pardoning for the putative damage *it* inflicted on the parents.

This sense of responsibility for one's psychic reality (in the light of owning one's psychic determinism) begins autochthonously (self-referentially, see chapter 2) within the infantile portion of the personality and is then split off and projectively reidentified in either or both parents in the paranoid-schizoid position. It is as if the newborn infant were saying that it cannot yet face the price of owning its sense of agency as a self; it cannot face unmentalized experiences (Bion, 1962b), O (Bion, 1965, 1970), Ananke (Necessity [Ricoeur, 1965]), or the Real (Lacan, 1966). One frequently finds this type of primitive transference expectation in borderlines and other patients suffering from primitive mental disorders. The countertransference response is frequently one in which the analyst or the therapist feels guilty, troubled, responsible, helpless, or incapable. These responses are undoubtedly built into the attachment-bonding repertory (Bowlby, 1969) and are universal. I am merely codifying them as understandable and expectable countertransference responses.

By introducing the concept with the appellation "Pietà," I mean to suggest the presence of a *covenant* between child and parent and between analysand and analyst in which moral obligations for mutual respect, protection, and responsibility are in place. It is the issue of felt responsibility that I should like to address. The covenant means that the infant/child and the analysand need to invest in one who is felt to be willing to suffer their pain (via trial or partial identification, i.e., empathy) until they are able to tolerate it themselves. This is the understood aspect of the function of Bion's container and is an extension of Winnicott's concept of object usage. The parent must feel responsible—as Mary should have—for bringing a child into the world and knowing that it was destined to suffer.

Earlier I referred to the feelings I experienced when I visualized the Pietà in the Vatican in Rome. I first was impressed by the look of profound sorrow on the face of the Madonna Dolorosa. I then imagined that I saw remorse. I am sure that this second thought was my personal attribution, but I started to wonder about the relationship between Mary and Christ in the first place. Why would Mary agree to give birth to a child who was destined for martyrdom? Mary, like all mothers and fathers, *must* feel remorse as well as joy for bringing innocent, "unconsulted" children into the world when the parents know ahead of time that they are, in effect, dooming these innocent ones to the "veil of tears." This thought became the starting point for my concept of the Pietà covenant. Parenthetically, it seems credible to link the Christ story as the second stage of the historical-mythic need for a messiah/hero to be born to a pairing couple (Mary and Joseph) to save the group, according to Bion (1961, 1970). It is as if mankind were forever "auditioning" a messiah/hero to solve its problems (the basis for idealization).

Parallel with this sense of moral responsibility on the part of the parents is that of the analyst with the analysand. First, the analyst is responsible in part for the pain that the analysand experiences in the analysis, particularly during regressions. Second, when the patient *is* in a state of regression, and especially when there has been a history of trauma or abuse, the analyst becomes transferentially transformed into the object felt to be responsible for all that happened to the analysand in the past. In other words, the analyst, who is innocent in regard to the analysand's past traumata, is held to be responsible now because, in his state of innocence, concern, and caring, the analyst is felt to be able to heal the analysand's wound vicariously through *absorption*, which facilitate the "*exorcism*" of the pain. Thus, innocence constitutes a veritable poultice for drawing the abscess of pain to the surface. Innocence in general seems to attract sadism.

The analyst must be initially innocent in the transaction and place himself in the position of asking the analysand to transfer past frustrating experiences with objects into him, the analyst, actually into an invisible image, the subjective object—that is to use the analyst as an *effigy*, as Christ in the symbolism of the Eucharist (i.e., "eating the flesh" and "drinking the blood" of Christ). In the Pietà covenant, the quintessence of object usage, the used/abused analyst, who is (initially) innocent—like Christ and other scapegoats[14], agrees to experience and to bear the pain of the analysand. In this role, the analyst occupies a position intermediary between Klein's (1946, 1955) original concept of unconscious intrapsychic projective identification and Bion's (1962a, b) container–contained, with its current offshoots, which we may call interpersonal or intersubjective projective identification, and which I now term projective *trans*identification. The first is strictly intrasubjective in

14. As we shall see in chapter 9, the scapegoat represents the group's attempt to find a synecdochic ritualization in which one scapegoat collectively represents all other sinful demons. Christ, who collectively absorbed the sins of everyone, represents this synecdochic ritualization. Do we not see this phenomenon in the "gathering of the transference" in psychoanalysis?

nature in terms of a one-person psychology. The second addresses the mutually interactive field of subjectivities as analysis really operates, as viewed from outside.

Furthermore, the concept of object usage allows us to ponder the deeper meaning of transference. Transference is not merely the displacement of past object cathexes. It is an actual internal psychic happening—of intended action by the subject on the image of the object—or the reverse, which image the subject is unable to differentiate from the actuality of the real object.

My own conception of the Pietà covenant can be integrated with Ogden's (1994a, 1997) ideas about the three psychoanalytic subjects, particularly, the intersubjective "subjugating third subject." I conceive of the subjugating third and the potential space in which it is located (which I believe to be System Preconscious) as the locale of the exorcism, a religious object usage, as it were. I conceive of the subjugating third as involving a transference–countertransference neurosis in each of the following: (1) the "crucified" analysand/subject, the one who suffers as victim (whether from the analyst's own superego or from trauma-induced internal objects); (2) the analyst/subject, who is held responsible for the analysand's suffering and must likewise suffer as the "Pietà"–parent/analyst, who is paradoxically as innocent as the child was originally and is now responsible for absorbing and exorcizing the analysand's pain while knowing how the innocent analysand-as-child felt when initially traumatized; and (3) the "Grand Inquisitor," who mentally persecutes and pillories the analyst's subjectivity in order to make the analyst experience the guilt and traumata.

All the while, mysteriously, the "ventriloquist" and "choreographer" of this sacred analytic passion play are secretly hidden in the preconscious of each of the performers, but most especially within the subjectivity of the analysand, whose use of intrusive and controlling magic omnipotent denial (Klein, 1946) becomes the prime subjugating subject, which ensorcells the analyst's subjectivity to participate in this passion play.

SOME THEMES EMERGING FROM THIS CASE

In a number of ways, the experience with the patient I have described resembled experiences with several other patients in my own practice and experiences described by many of my supervisees and colleagues. Consequently, many seemingly inextricably associated ideas began to cohere syndromically. What began as a conventional analysis of a depressed patient devolved into the analysis of a doubly abused patient—"abused" by his own psyche in the traditionally classical sense ("instinctual drive abuse") and abused by his caretaking objects.

Associated ideas that emerged include: (1) the role of religion, myth, spirituality, and demonism in psychoanalysis; (2) the concepts of innocence, original sin, blessing, birthright, entitlement, and curse; (3) the role of human sacrifice generally and of infant sacrifice particularly in our secular as well as in our religio-spiritual-demonic lives—and its role in child abuse (Burkert, 1983, 1996; Grotstein, 1998b); (4) the concept of the covenant[15] between infant/child and parent(s) (as well as patient and analyst), and between human beings and God, for mutual protection; (5) the importance of "soul murder" and the "Faustian bargain" as a consequence of the experience of trauma or abuse; (6) the possibility of extending Klein's (1946, 1955) conception of projective identification, Bion's (1962a, b, 1963) concept of the container and contained, and Winnicott's (1969, 1971) concept of object usage and the subjective object—as well as Money-Kyrle's (1956) concept of the therapist's introjective identification and Grinberg's (1962, 1979a, b) conception of projective counteridentification—to deepen our understanding of transference as well as the transformation of the infantile neurosis into the transference–countertransference neurosis, which, in turn, can be represented in the constellating myths of the crucifixion, and of the primal-horde sacrifice of father (Freud, 1913) and in the imagery of the Pietà; (7) an extension and revision of the psychoanalytic concept of the Oedipus complex[16] in many dimensions, especially to include the importance of the ritual of human sacrifice; (8) a new perspective on the concept of the death instinct; and (9) an understanding of patients that I designate "orphans of the Real," those patients who from infancy or childhood onward have suffered from the extremes of hypersensitivity, self-consciousness, neglect, poor attunement, abuse, torture, or molestation and who consequently mentally "die." These include Krystal's (1988) alexithymic patients, Hedges's (1994) "organizing children," and Herman's (1992) "complex post-traumatic stress disorders."

My patient's Oedipus complex turned out to be truly "complex." I was able to posit the existence of a "subcomplex" characterized by a renunciation of the oedipal authority of "the law of the father" (Lacan, 1966) in favor for the "law of the siblings," which I term the "little oedi-

15. I employ the ancient religious term covenant because of the its elegant inclusiveness and descriptiveness. The reader is referred to Hillers (1969) and Elazar (1994) for in-depth reviews of the covenant as a Biblical concept.

16. For an interesting review of the omnipresence of the Oedipus complex in all cultures, see Johnson and Price-Williams (1996).

pal family."[17] The latter is reminiscent of Freud's (1913) concept of the "primal horde." In addition, I saw considerable evidence for the existence of the transgenerational and intergenerational neurosis, following Bowen (1978), Bergmann (1992), Cramer (1982a, b, 1986), Apprey (1987a, b), Apprey and Stein (1991), and Rosenfeld (1987). A prototypical example would be the "Laius complex" (Balmary, 1979; Ross, 1982), which we can understand as the unresolved infantile neurosis of Oedipus' father that was fated to become projected into Oedipus.

REPRESSION OF THE CHRIST SIGNIFIER IN ORTHODOX/CLASSICAL, AND KLEINIAN THEORY

I began to wonder why the myth and history of Christ had rarely found its way into the mainstream of orthodox/classical and Kleinian psychoanalytic thinking, given that he was perhaps the most important historical and mythical individual in Western civilization and certainly the source of a generative myth whose historic and current importance cannot be exaggerated. It is conceivable that the Christ signifier was too closely connected with Freud's antisemitic experiences in Vienna and was too closely associated with magical *healing* and thus to hypnosis, which Freud foreswore. To my knowledge, the one exception in the classical analytic literature is Hopkins's (1989) attempt to link Christ's crucifixion with Winnicott's (1969, 1971) concept of object usage and transference.

Jung (1934) and his followers, on the other hand, *have* dealt with Christ analytically to a great extent. It is ironic that Freud, arguably one of the most famous atheists of all time, can be considered to be one of the true "messiahs" of our cultural age and one who, though "crucified," was culturally resurrected as a veritable god of Western thought.

I believe that another contribution to Christ's absence from psychoanalysis deserves discussion. The intense illumination of the Enlightenment, along with the rise of humanism and individuality, seems to have bleached out the preternatural numinousness of the spiritual and demonic worlds, associated as they were with the belief in esoteria, magic, miracles, monsters, ghosts, and the like. These legacies of ancient beliefs achieved an apogee of importance and reverence in medieval times only to become eclipsed with the rise of modern man and his putatively sacrilegious values. Lamentably aware of this trend, Nietzsche (1895) pronounced the "death of God." The Grand Inquisitor

17. See chapter 9 for further elaboration.

of Dostoevsky's (1880) *Brothers Karamazov* said virtually the same thing to Christ in a passage in that work. At the time of Freud's formative years, the God of medieval times was all but dead, replaced by a newer edition of pagan deities, German Romanticism, with its worship of preternatural, surrealistic Mother Nature, and another, newer deity, logical positivism, a "religion" that would all but eschew Christ's "miracles" and his role as messiah or healer.

A BRIEF NOTE ON THE CHRISTIAN ACCEPTANCE AND JEWISH REJECTION OF CHRIST

Recent insight into the history of the first century AD suggests that, if there really was such a man as Jesus, his history was strictly Jewish (Pfleiderer, 1905; Endo, 1973; Pelikan, 1985; Fredriksen, 1988; Meier, 1990; Crossan, 1991; Saldarini, 1994; Watson, 1995a, b; and Heschel, 1998).[18] The story of Christ's passage into Christian religious belief, however, seems to have rendered his life a more complex legendary phenomenon. St. Paul may have virtually "kidnaped" Jesus from his Jewish roots. If we consider that Christians have immemorially accused the Jews of being "Christ-killers," we might posit that the mechanism of projective identification (out of guilt) may underlie the accusation (Schonfield, 1997). In other words, the Christian accusation may have scapegoated the Jews for the Christians' own sense of guilt for "kidnapping" Jesus the Jew from the Jews, so that the Jews have themselves become yet another version of the projected, martyred Christ.

That the Jews may seem to have colluded with that projective identification is yet another story. The history of Christ's rejection by the Jews is known to us mostly through the Synoptic Gospels and belongs, consequently, to a tendentious rewriting (i.e., propagandizing) of history. One subtext in that alleged rejection must have been Christ's claim to be not only the Son of Man but also the Son of God, which was heresy to the Jews, whose religious beliefs centered on God being One. Again, this chapter is not a monograph on religion, but I would cautiously and tentatively suggest that Freud discovered and explored a phenomenon

18. Heschel (1998), states: "Geiger, writing as a Jew about Jesus, reversed the position of the observer, from Christians writing about Judaism to a Jew writing about Christianity. . . . The Jewish scholar [Geiger] in narrating the Jesus story, becomes the hero, capturing the power of the story and attempting the same destabilization of Christianity that Christians have attempted of Judaism" (p. 242).

that his loyalty to deterministic science may have prevented him from realizing—the near-"divinity," if not actual divinity, of the unconscious. From one point of view, I trust that one can agree that theology is a reification of mythical cosmology (see chapter 2).

RECONCILIATION

In retrospect, we can now conjecture that the human ensemble of worship—religion, mystery, and spirituality—stands, alongside literature, myth, and aesthetics, as the lost family from which psychoanalysis was spawned. I want to compare and contrast Oedipus, the analytic riddle-solver, and Christ, the healer through transcendence, and assess the contributions of each to psychoanalysis. Dodds (1951, 1965, 1968) reminds us that Oedipus, after being rescued by the shepherd and taken to Corinth, where he was adopted by the royal couple there, grew up as if that were his real home. When Oedipus consulted an oracle at age 18, it was foretold that he would commit incest and parricide, just as the oracle a generation earlier had foretold about him to his real father, Laius. Horrified at the thought of committing this doubly vile deed on his beloved parents, Oedipus fled Corinth out of love for them, only to meet his fate on the crossroads to Thebes. The tragedy of Oedipus, according to Dodds, is that he sought to *evade his fate*, only to encounter it in his flight. One is mindful here of John O'Hara's (1934) *Appointment in Samarra*. Freud (1916, 1923b) and Deutsch (1933) refer to this character pattern as examples of the "fate neurosis" or the "neurosis of destiny." Bollas (1989) approaches the phenomenon from the perspective of the differentiation between being haplessly "fated" and being enthusiastically "destined."

From a rereading of the oedipal saga from this perspective, the Christ theme might devolve as follows. Oedipus, the psychoanalytic Everyman, represents the infant who is destined to "use the object" with erotic and sadistic vigorousness and enthusiasm, acts that are destined ultimately (in the depressive position) to bring him into contact with deeds to which he had to blind himself in order to undergo these life-honing rituals of normal development. The infant, like Oedipus, finds itself on the horns of a dilemma: it *must* use and imaginatively destroy its subjective object (Winnicott, 1969) and thereby place the objects and its own innocence in jeopardy. Yet, if the infant does not undergo this fateful ritual of inexorable development and avoids its fate, it defaults into ontological shame for being untrue to its destiny. The infant then becomes self-branded as a coward (see chapter 7).

In some uncanny and numinous way, Christian theology seems to have gone to the heart of this matter by instituting the rite of the confessional, in which sinners can be properly "shriven" (in anticipation of psychoanalytic "exorcism"), and the ceremony of the Eucharist, in which the sinful participant (from object usage and misusage) experiences absolution (the transfer of his sinfulness to the image of Christ) by actually drinking his symbolic (believed by some to be actual) blood and eating his symbolic flesh. By ritualistically recommitting the destructive act on Christ, the synecdochic sacrifice for all mankind, the sinner is absolved and restored to innocence. This process entails the sacrifice of an innocent one whose very innocence acts as a sacred poultice to draw and absorb the emotional abscesses of the pained one. It represents the quintessence of the "exorcism" of transference, the transference of mental  pain from one who cannot bear it to another, who in love and innocence can. Keep in mind, however, that Catholic worshipers are religiously constrained and obligated to eat and drink (destroy) Christ over and over again. Not to do so itself constitutes a sin!

It is as if the infant, like the analysand, plaintively asks, "I cannot bear my pain! Will you?" The rider to this plea, which is as old as man, is, "Will you also, though innocent, be willing to feel guilty for my having suffered this pain?" Thereby, the archetype of the ancient sacrificial  scapegoat emerges as the provenance of psychoanalytic transference. Accordingly, since our innocence is jeopardized when we relate to our needed objects, we must allow ourselves to risk feelings of guilt toward them and jeopardize our innocence by living our lives to the fullest, as long as we pay authentic homage to them with contrition, always with an aim toward redemption. And we must never lose sight of the fundamental truth of object relations, that our very lives are predicated on the sacrifice of others for us, beginning with the placenta, whose death initiates our birth. One must kill the subjective object, without fully realizing that it is *not* the real object, and experience the guilt for this passionate epistemic murder.

THREE STAGES IN THE DEVELOPMENT OF PSYCHOANALYTIC "EXORCISM"

The experience of crucifixion, like martyrdom, inheres in the patient's agony in the paranoid-schizoid position and is projected into the analyst. The analyst must bear the patient's crucifixion-like experience as his own in the depressive position in order to allow for its transformation (Bion, 1965) into the depressive position—in preparation for a similar subsequent transformation in the patient. My experience of my patient's pain was as my trial counteridentification with his "abusive" internal objects and my partial guilt for feeling this identification. There are at least three stages to the Christ/martyr motif.

The first phase is the persecutory experience of the paranoid-schizoid position in which the patient *protested the unfairness of the pain that had been inflicted upon him* ("My God, my God, why hast thou forsaken me? [*Matthew*, 27:46]). In this posture, he was the *innocent* and suffering martyr, and I became identified either with Mary of the Pietà or even God the Father, who is felt to have needlessly caused him to suffer pain. My partial countertransference response to my patient was to feel this guilt "experimentally" and to feel a sense of responsibility for his pain, linked with his real objects of the past and his internal objects.

The second phase was the *exorcism* of his pain into me, in phantasy, associated with my willingness to accept this as a trial experience. My accepting (containing) his pain was made possible by my alpha function (Bion, 1962a, 1963) or "dream-work alpha" (Bion, 1992), which predicates that I, the therapist, having already attained the depressive position, am prepared to be "my brother's keeper" with empathic concern and without retaliation.

In the third phase the patient responded to my processing his exorcistic projections by accepting the return of his now transformed pain as his own authentic experience ("I don't hate my father so much now because I know that he suffered too, and I don't like the vengeful aspects of myself"). This shift in his attitude toward his father represented the onset of the capability for *mercy* and *forgiveness*, attributes that I believe are achieved in the depressive position.

THE EPIGENESIS OF SUFFERING

Implicit in the foregoing scheme of intra- and intersubjective suffering is a conception of the epigenesis of the experience of suffering itself. In the paranoid-schizoid position, the infant (or patient) feels that suffering has been purposely inflicted by sadistic persecutors because of the effect of projective identification into his objects in regard to the infant's own sadistic impulses. As the infant, who is a separate whole subject, approaches the threshold of the depressive position and faces the whole-object mother (now a separate whole subject in her own right), the infant more nearly completely realizes that it exists in a state of dependency; it may then begin the process of converting the experience of suffering from the passive to the active phase in which the infant becomes a *martyr*, like Christ.[19]

This phenomenon of martyrdom as a counterphobic defense constitutes the manic (or "depressive") defense aspect of clinical depressive illness, since the sufferers believe unconsciously that they are controlling and triumphing over the objects, that is, that they are magically controlling the object by holding it to an implied covenant, half of which is already fulfilled by the martyr's suffering. When the infant actually achieves the depressive position, it (like the loving martyr archetype) is able to suffer the pain of others and thus to relieve them with *agape* (nonerotic love or sympathy) as part of the altruistic instinct (Lumsden and Wilson, 1981, 1983).

Taking an ascetic and celibate posture in abandoning sensual desire, like the priest, the analyst undergoes many sorts of volitional suffering in the course of doing analysis. In the depressive position, suffering may be redemptive in the felt or actual damage done to others, or it may be realistic in the vicissitudes of the "cosmic lottery" if the traumatic stimuli causing the suffering are not personally causally connected with the self. In other words, a person in the depressive position is able to experience the difference between *persecutors* and *enemies*. The concept of sacrifice is also intimately interwoven with the phenomenon of suffering; one may suffer persecutorily and must therefore resign to being sacrificed for the purposes of others (see, e.g., Schreber, 1903), or one may sacrifice oneself as a martyr in order to control others, or one may undergo voluntary sacrifice in the state of *agape*. The ultimate resolution of my patient's traumatic infantile neurosis consequently involved the integration of the realness of the trauma and of the felt complicity of his parents with it; his own narcissistic personality structure; his unresolved infantile neurosis; and the developmental progression of his ability to *suffer* his pain knowingly rather than *endure* it without realizing its meaning. With these changes, he emerged from the "psychic retreat" (Steiner, 1993) characterized by resentment and vengeance (Steiner, 1996) to that of resolution through mercy and forgiveness.

OBJECT USAGE AND HUMAN SACRIFICE

My thinking, prompted by this patient, led me to extend Winnicott's (1969a) concept of object usage, a subject that Hopkins (1989) has already

19. The experience of Christ-like martyrdom is characteristic of the course of illness in many manic–depressive and schizophrenic patients (Grotstein, 1990a, b, c).

explored by linking Winnicott's object usage with the crucifixion. This concept is characterized by paradox, as is much of Winnicott's work. The infant first "knows" its mother in a state of a primary confusion between the real (external) experience of her and the "subjective object" that it creates in its imagination. This image is "transferentially" interposed between them in potential space as a montage—thus the confusion. The infant (actually toddler) must destroy this subjective object—that is, must destroy the *mythology* of it—while at the same time perceiving the real external mother as surviving the attack without retaliation.

Oedipus' solution of the riddle of the sphynx and her subsequent self-destruction because he revealed his knowledge of her mythic (unreal) existence can be understood as an example of the developmental workings of object usage. We discover the truth of the real object by continuously destroying our myths about it and are thereby enabled to abandon a relationship with the object based on identification with one based on separateness, individuation, and acknowledged dependency.

Object usage is implicated in Bion's (1962a, b) concept of the container and the contained; in reality the container must sustain the infant's "digestive" acts of murdering it with a lethal cargo of projected terror. Ogden (1994a) has written of the dialectical interface between mother and infant, or between analyst and patient, in which both partners are engaged in a mutually confronting, interfacing, defining, and destructive modification of one another. From this intersubjective perspective, the container–contained metaphor implies also that each is the container *and* the contained for the other. I believe that the concept of the subjective object is Winnicott's unique way of addressing Klein's (1946, 1955) ideas of unconscious phantasy generally and projective identification specifically. Winnicott added the notion of the transitional *effigy* object, the basis for analytic transference (and countertransference).

It also seems to me that the destruction of the subjective object represents the challenge that all infants, toddlers, and children must confront: the need to accept their predatory zeal in apposing the full panoply of their successive autoerotic and instinctual demands onto the image of the object in that intermediate zone of paradoxical reality–unreality (potential space) where, they believe, at any given moment their neediness (libidinal, aggressive, assertive, epistemophilic) *has*—and, they hope has *not*—destroyed their needed and beloved object. In other words, object usage is the mythic unconscious scenario of infant development. Phantasies of object *mis*usage constitute its pathology. Infant misusage by parents constitutes its trauma.

Object misusage phantasies also represents the infant's unconscious drive to break through successive postnatal barriers to its emergence into separateness (breaking its metaphoric eggshell to be born and successively reborn). In this mythic scenario, the subjective object is subjected to *sacrifice*; but, from an ontological perspective, one could say that the destruction of the subjective aspect of the object is necessary in order to interrupt one's *habituation* to it, that is, taking it for granted. I think this is what Winnicott really had in mind. Through projective and then introjective identification, the introjected sacrificial object becomes persecutory toward the infant's ego, which then becomes vulnerable to being sacrificed to this new "deity" in its superego.

My elaboration of Winnicott's idea of object usage involves not only the infant/toddler's innocent, playful destructiveness but also the concept of the infant's "revenge" on the real mother (and father) for the pain of its helplessness, which the infant feels was caused by the parent. Object usage thus constitutes the infant's phantasmal epigenesis from being a passively helpless victim to becoming an active, self-determining predator, and his first prey is mother's breast. Winnicott's concept of object usage concerned the infant's spontaneous creation of a subjective object (invisible, transitional effigy image) that it could not differentiate from the real object, a concept that beautifully and economically depicts the psychoanalytic transference situation. Winnicott seems to have emphasized that the playful infant here is innocently ("pre-ruth") destructive in its attitude toward the subjective object. Klein would disagree. She believed that the infant is clearly demonstrating its felt aggressiveness toward the object, an aggressiveness that prefigured the development of first persecutory and then depressive anxieties. Where they would seem to agree is in the realm of displacement: both Klein (1960) and Winnicott (1971b) believed that a sufficient amount of displacement from the overtly serious implications of its own destructiveness was necessary for the child to be able to tolerate the act of playing.

Another aspect of object usage and the teleological advocacy of the object's continuous destruction is apposite to our theme. When Oedipus effectively destroyed the sphinx in the act of knowing himself (and, by innuendo, knowing who she was not), he thereby pronounced his separation from mother-as-a-subjective object. Christ, similarly, battled the adhesions of decay in a ritualized society that did not realize that its rituals had regressively become transformed into idols. He set himself against *formalism* by curing on the Sabbath (*Matthew*, 12:10) and against legalism (*Matthew*, 15:7-21; *Luke*, 6:1-5), and he said that salvation was a matter of having compassion for one another (*Matthew*, 25:32-46; *Luke*, 10:25-37).[20]

20. I am indebted to Dawn George for these biblical sources.

We take our objects and concepts for granted and allow them to atrophy into mythic ritualized structures. From this point of view, the destruction of the subjective object is the ever-continuing task of one's necessary emotional and epistemic "house cleaning."

RELIGION AND HUMAN SACRIFICE

Human sacrifice[21] in general and infant sacrifice in particular have been characteristic of virtually all religions since the beginning of time. Today we witness their more tepid derivatives in the form of the Eucharist, fasts, circumcision, and the like. In the remote, archaic times of the matriarchal religions, sacrifices were common, for example, the annual sacrifice of the "Wicker Man" amongst the pre-historic Celts[22] (Devereux, 1953, 1966; Graves, 1955, 1958; Gimbutas, 1974; Bergmann, 1992). The unconscious motive behind the relationship between cultural matriarchy and sacrifice was probably the absolute dependence of agricultures on the caprices of Mother Nature. Another factor originates in individual psychology. Klein unfolded the primitive terrors of the infant and revealed how the infant worsens the image of the mother in monstrous proportions through splitting, projective identification, and positive and negative idealization[23] (Klein, 1946, 1955). In so doing, she bequeathed to us the concept of infantile "transferences" to mother, which accounted for mother's savage transformations and metamorphoses in the infant's imagination.

The composite mythic image of the mother that emerged from archetypal preconceptions, the willful and treacherous caprices of Mother Nature, and the mythic transformations of the personal mother resulted in the creation of such chimerical creatures as the sphynx and the Medusa and such myths as Medea. The sacrifice of human infants was a natural "curative" remedy for ancient man. A notable transition occurs in the "quest of the hero" at the transition from matriarchal to

---

21. Note Toni Morrison's (1998) book *Beloved*, in which a loving mother sacrificed her children—out of love—rather than seeing them endure slavery.

22. The ancient Scottish Picts chose their kings along the lines of matrilineal succession, as did the ancient Thebans in the time of Oedipus. In matrilineal succession, the mother's brother has claim to the rights. Thus, for instance, in Oedipus' Thebes, after Oedipus exiled himself, the role of tyrant was acquired by Creon, Jocasta's brother, rather than by the eldest son of Oedipus.

23. It may be that the instinct to worship—and the need to find a god or devil to satisfy it—belongs to the mechanism of idealization in both its negative and its positive sense.

patriarchal cultures (Neumann, 1954; Campbell, 1955; Gimbutas, 1974). Emblematically, Theseus, the hero from Athens, ended the hegemony of the matriarch-dominated Cretan civilization and its requirement of the sacrifice of Athenian youths when he entered the labyrinth and slew the Minotaur. The hero's role is to rescue or even murder his mother-dependent, mother-bound infant self and rescue his father (the Minotaur) in *his* entrapment in the metaphorical labyrinth of matriarchal/vaginal hegemony.

Behind all this terror of the mother, Klein argued, lies the infant's horror at dependence on her, his envy of her bountifulness, and the greed with which the infant appropriates the larder of her goodness and the phantasmal consequences, its destructive transformations of her image due to its need to devalue the object in order to emerge as an adequate infant in its own right. Persecutory images of mother develop in the infant's mind as a result of object usage *and* misusage.

In the depressive position, infants can accept retrospective responsibility for their phantasies—and the actualities—of object usage and misusage. Until then, the infant cannot tolerate its guilt feelings, splits them off, and projectively reidentifies them in the part-object breast/mother, who then becomes installed as an external—then internal—persecutor. When the internal, cruel maternal superego persecutor is reprojected into objects in the world at large, we find the monsters of ancient religions intact.

Andresen (1984), having studied the phenomenon of religious sacrifice in depth from the psychoanalytic perspective, emphasizes the relationship between sacrifice and the desire of the victim to preserve the object out of love rather than from unconscious hate. He identifies the "sacrifice complex":

> The nodal points of the sacrifice complex are these: (1) the offerer's concern for the state of the deity or beloved; (2) the offerer's interpretation of his strivings and the events of his life as determiners of the fate of the deity or the beloved; (3) the offerer's intention to have the deity or beloved profit from an offering which in some fashion depletes the state of the offerer [p. 543].

THE "RELIGIOUS" ASPECTS OF CHILD ABUSE: SCAPEGOATS, MESSIAHS, AND PARIAHS

I believe that one of the fundamental dynamics of child abuse and of abuse generally involves parental envy of the child's innocence because of the parents' belief that they have lost their own sense of innocence. They seek to regain it by purloining that of their child, as they believe was done to them when they were children. More generally, I believe that all parents, families, and cultures are in danger of projectively arrogating and reidentifying their own unresolved infantile neuroses (trans and intergenerational) into their offspring either as *heroes* and *messiahs* or as *scapegoats* and *pariahs*.[24] The universality of scapegoating (Girard, 1986) accompanies the religious and cultural (and institutional) practice of ritualizing human sacrifice, including infant and child sacrifice (Bergmann, 1992). From the religiomythic perspective, scapegoating superstitiously achieves the cure of "pollution" by pacifying angry pagan gods; or, from the more empirical sociohistoric perspective, it regulates populations and effects group survival by sacrificing unwanted children and the infirm.

Girard (1972, 1978, 1986, and personal communication), speaking from a sociomythic point of view, believes that the function of the scapegoat developed as a way of mediating clan feuds in archaic times. Warring parties would exhaust themselves and exsanguinate in repeated retaliations and counterretaliations, but the appointment of a scapegoat allowed for an armistice between the warring parties and for a discharge of their accumulated hatred into the object, who would not and could not retaliate. The concept of mimesis designates the mutual identifications with one another, including the scapegoat. According to the principle of mimesis, the warring parties collude with each other that the scapegoat is to be held responsible for the mutual troubles of the group. Furthermore, *the scapegoat himself agrees to this imputation of responsibility.* Girard (1986) believes that, according to each of the synoptic Gospels, Christ was appointed as the scapegoat by the Jewish Sanhedrin but refused to accept that role. Instead, according to Girard, Christ agreed to be their synecdochic ("one for the many") sacrifice, the one who dies for the sake of the others—out of love—and who forgives them ("Father, forgive them; they know not what they do" [*Luke*, 23:34]).

The sacrifice of Oedipus on Mount Cithaeron and the crucifixion of Christ mythically apply here. I have already hinted at this phenomenon in the case material when I suggested that I, the analyst, initially had to be considered innocent in order to be able to help the patient exorcize his own sense of badness into me as the ultimate crucifixional countertransference neurosis. The phenomenon of transference can be under-

24. See Apprey (1987a, b), Apprey and Stein (1991), and Cramer (1986) for similar views. They were able to conclude from the findings of their respective researches that the mothers' unconscious phantasies, when projected into their infants, had a powerful influence on their infants' future personality development.

stood, as Meltzer (1978) has redefined it, as the transfer of mental pain from one person to another. I add that the Other who receives the transference must be initially innocent and yet paradoxically able to be a "stand-in" scapegoat that *seems* to warrant sacrifice. This phenomenon typifies the passion of the crucifixion and of psychoanalytic (exorcistic) transferences. The sacrificed victim's innocence acts as a sacred poultice that draws the original sufferer's "abscess" to the surface, an occurrence congruent with psychoanalytic therapy.

Following Winnicott's (1969, 1971) idea of object usage, Hopkins (1989) theorized that the myth of Christ's crucifixion is closely paralleled by the countertransference situation, in which the patient "uses" the analytic object in potential space in the analytic treatment. I am in accord with Hopkins's hypothesis and would extend it as follows: The patient, in the act of suffering the infantile neurosis and its transformation into the transference neurosis, can be understood as suffering as the crucified Christ in the paranoid-schizoid position; that is, the patient protests about why he is suffering ("My God, my God, Why hast thou forsaken me?" [*Matthew*, 27:46]). This pathetic plea represents the infant's protest to the parent and constitutes a demand for an explanation of the infant's suffering, and an angry rebuke as well, as an attempt at a projective induction of the painful feeling into the parent.

Teething provides a universal example of object usage. The infant's gums begin to hurt as the budding teeth press through the gums. To obtain relief, the infant must counter it by biting down on a firm but resilient object, one that stands as an *effigy* for the human one. *Transference in all its permutations constitutes the phantasied translocation of feelings and internal objects to an imaginary (because invisible) effigy-image of the real object (which to the projecting subject is indistinguishable from the real object) that is used or even misused!* Transference, in and outside analysis, always constitutes a form of exorcism—a translocation of demons, benign or malevolent, into an intermediary effigy.

From the standpoint of Christian theology as revealed in the *Act of the Apostles*, it is the *paraclete*, the advocate who succeeds Christ following his ascension into heaven, who mediates between God and mankind and whose medieval descendant became the guardian angel. Whether the parent or analyst contains—or colludes with—this experience depends on whether the introjective counteridentification is a partial or total one! The analyst who receives the transferred pain in the act of therapeutic exorcism suffers the pain as a *trial* introjective identification, that is, as an act of therapeutic containment and, like the infant's mother, applies reverie, patience, and "dream-work alpha" to process and to translate the pain into its ultimate meaning for the infant/patient. Insofar as the analyst is able to transcend the pain (not suffer it as personal), he, like Christ in the crucifixion ("Father, forgive them; they know not what they do" *Luke*, 23:34), can dispel the painfulness of the transferred feeling and convert it into meaning. In so doing, the analyst suffers the patient's pain in the depressive position and thereby allows the patient to resuffer the pain once again but on a more tolerable level—as the patient's own pain—in *the patient's own* depressive position.

When the infant/patient finally suffers his own reclaimed pain, he is also aware that this very pain—and the act of having it suffered by another—involved his triple use of the object. The first use of the object was the experience of being pained not only by an inchoate instinctual impulse or affect, but also by a hate-transformed image of the object that was felt to have tormented the infant/patient by causing the experience of hunger, for example, without instantly relieving it (Klein, 1940). Thus the first usage of the (part-)object is for satisfaction and attunement. The second use is for "blaming one's pain" into the object because the object seems to wish the infant to suffer. The third use is that of heroic mastery of the subjective object. The second use of the object is characterized by projective identification of the pained-self-confused-with-object into the containing mother/therapist in the act of exorcism. Winnicott (1969, 1971) suggested that the subjective object (the object image that is subjectively imagined via projective identification) must be destroyed so that the infant can finally recognize the external (real) counterpart to the subjective object.[25] Further, the real object beyond it must survive this destruction of its imaginary double in potential space. I believe that, in the process of this act of destruction, the infant/patient by way of this subjective medium, transfers its own feeling of being virtually destroyed to the external object.

The subjective medium is the *transference effigy*, that is, an invisible image of the object interposed between the analytic subject and the analyst, one that the subject cannot distinguish from the analyst without the analyst's interpretative intervention. The analyst, on the other hand, though able to distinguish between the image and his own self, is nevertheless caught up in the quandary of feeling both connected to (identified with) and disconnected from (not identified with) the effigy object. Ultimately the successfully destroyed internal object ("bad breast-mother-part-subjective object" as well as the "good breast-mother-part-

25. "For now we see through a glass, darkly; but then face to face: now I know in part; but then shall I know even as also I am known. And now abideth faith, hope, charity, these three; but the greatest of these is charity" (*1. Corinthians*, 13:12-13). Thus, the infant (actually, the "once-and-forever-infant of the abiding unconscious") achieves the depressive position with the resolution of object usage *by accepting its inelucatbility*, as in the Eucharist.

subjective object") becomes the scapegoat/victim and is sacred as a *sacrifice* when it is successfully transformed by the analyst/mother, or doubly persecutory when not transformed. "These are they which came out of great tribulation, and have washed their robes, and made them white in the blood of the Lamb" (*Revelations*, 7:14).

CONCLUDING REMARKS

I believe that the numinous experience of human sacrifice subtends infant/child development and secular life generally and that it constitutes the deepest aspect of the Oedipus complex and the preoedipal situation. The experience of sacrifice normally characterizes the infant's inchoate experience of life.[26] The infant "transfers" this pain to the "container"—"subjective object"—mother, who then normally sacrifices herself to bear it before returning it in a benevolently altered form as does the analyst. As she experiences this transferred pain, she also experiences (via trial introjective identification) the pain of "being destroyed," that is, being sacrificed by the infant.

A similar process occurs between patient and analyst. The infantile neurosis occupies a dual track between its autochthonous origin in phantasy and its traumatic origin in the projectively reidentified, unresolved infantile neuroses of the parents and of previous generations (*inter*- and *trans*generational neuroses). As these origins enter the analytic text, this complex becomes the transference–countertransference neurosis, to which I append the prefix Pietà to designate its religio-spiritual-numinous dimension.

The ultimate dialectic that occurs in analysis as well as in life generally is that between good and evil, which is played out as innocence versus original sin. The concept of the covenant bridges the gap between biblical and modern quotidian existence as the conflict between the patient's accepting his own life, with all its existential "baggage," versus needing to blame-it-into the mother/analyst in the act of exorcism. On the other hand, the infant must be able to hold mother—and father—accountable for suffering the pains of a life that the infant did not agree to live. Thus, the parent is both innocent and guilty and consequently accountable in the covenant with the infant/child. Similarly, the inno-

26. Many patients have dreamed of or even believe that they can distantly remember their experience of that "splendour in the grass" (in the womb) with their first playmate, the placenta, whose "death" (sacrificial?) is required to initiate the act of birth.

cent analyst must tentatively accept (within the transference–countertransference covenant) the alleged guilt for the transferred guilt felt to belong to the parents and the guilt for inducing the relentless analytic regression that is responsible for the "flashbacks" of one's existence.

Finally, I have posited the existence of the "position of innocence" and the "redemptive position," each of which must be understood in the context of an interpersonal relationship in which a covenant exists. The "position of innocence" is the guardian of the soul.

Chapter 9

WHY OEDIPUS AND NOT CHRIST?

Part II

THE NUMINOUS AND SPIRITUAL DIMENSION AS A METAPSYCHOLOGICAL PERSPECTIVE

In chapter 8, I presented case material that had struck me as rich in religious, spiritual, and demonic dimensions of psychoanalysis. Following Bion (1965, 1970, 1992; personal communication), I distinguish between religion, spirituality, the moral or religious "instinctual drive," and numinousness. Religion, generally speaking, refers to the administrative organization (middle management, as it were) for the distribution of the tenets of spirituality and the mediation of one's relationship to God through rituals and observances. Spirituality comes closer to representing one's relationship to the deity. Numinousness refers to the sense of awe and wonder and the inward journey (into the self) associated with the mystical and meditative contact with the ineffable. Numinousness is associated with the Gnostic belief that God is within us as a component of our very subjectivity (Mead, 1900; Pfleiderer, 1905; Pagels, 1979; Mack, 1993; Sells, 1994; Webb and Sells, 1995).

That a religious theme may qualify as a metapsychological perspective has already been hinted at by Bion (1970, 1992; personal communication), Rizzuto (1974, 1976, 1991), Meissner (1984), Symington (1994), de Mello Franco (1998), and others. I feel that these elements of mental life have been "bleached out" by the dazzling illumination of the Enlightenment and by its sterile descendent, deterministic logical positivism. Ultimately the fate of man's soul (in terms of the psychoanalytic argot, one's internalized values) rests on the dialectic between the sense of innocence and guilt.

The themes that emerged from my patient's material included (1) the importance of *innocence* and of its dialectical counterpart, *original sin*, the psychoanalytic version of which is the psychic identification with (ownership of) and putative use of one's instinctual drive endowment (the presumed guilt for object usage); (2) the importance of *blessing, curse*, and *mercy* (or forgiveness, especially toward wayward parents as the patient's wounds heal in treatment); (3) the need for an *autochthonous* (spontaneous, self-originating or self-creating) theory of causality; and (4) a *cosmogonic explanation*, a world view by which to mediate and organize the chaos of "cosmic roulette" and life's vicissitudes. Primitive as well as modern—and post-modern—man seems to be driven to contemplate a numinous, overarching, preternatural "architect" (the Demiurge) of consummate meaning for the universe to offset the chaos from which and into which man is born. Bion (1992, personal communication) posited that man possesses a *moral instinct* and consequently has a need to pray—and to create or to find a God to justify his inherent need to pray.

It seems to me that the problems that the Jews had with Christ's alleged claim to divinity sprang not only from his alleged violation of the sacred concept of God's unity but also from their rejection of the Gnostic-Zoroastrian, and later mystical, tradition that a god resided within human beings as well as in heaven. The Christian concept of the Holy Ghost[1] and its relationship within the Trinity seems to approximate what Meister Eckhart and other mystics thought of as the distinction between God and the Godhead, the former residing within the human individual and the other beyond the human (Fox, 1980, 1981a, b; Sells, 1994). Paradoxically, this God, who is the "object of prayer," must never be found (as object) because He is the Subject[2] (beyond, because before, contemplation) in order to satisfy that inherent craving.

Sacrifice and the Covenant

Even though I am concerned primarily with *psychoanalytic* perspectives on man's spiritual needs, it is tempting to contemplate that the legend

1. Dr. Mariam Cohen (personal communication) suggests that the mystical Jewish concept of the *Shekinah* (in the *Kabbalah*) may parallel the Christian concept of the Holy Ghost. The *Shekinah* is the feminine aspect of God's presence in the world.

2. "Tell them that I am that I am" (*Exodus* 3:14).

of Christ in the Christian faith serves as God's "alter ego,"[3] who is presented to mankind for "object usage," that is continuous crucifixion through the transubstantiating ritual of the Eucharist (the "eating" of Christ's "flesh" and the "drinking" of His "blood")—all as God's "apology" and contrition in answer to Christ's human plea to God, "My God, my God, why hast thou forsaken me?" (*Matthew*, 27:46). In other words, God, the consummate superego as well as the divine, peremptory abuser of mankind, Himself needs to make amends to mankind by first begetting and then sacrificing His only begotten son—over and over again—in the Eucharist. But if God is the Subject, may not Christ also be a subject—and also mankind?

It seems suggestive that theology, religious mythology, and human psychological development run parallel courses. I am proposing that, theologically and psychologically, mankind needs to sacrifice to his God(s) and that God correspondingly needs to sacrifice to his worshipers; and that the common denominator, the act of sacrifice, constitutes a sacred covenant that binds man to God and God to man thereafter. The sacrifice is thus *sacralized* and becomes a new deity or a new version of the deity, represented by the *covenant*, which becomes the "subjugating third" (Ogden, 1994a, 1997) for God and his worshipers and for the worshipers amongst themselves. In the analytic situation the covenant entails the mutual sacrifices that the analysand and analyst must agree to undergo in order for the analysis to take place.

THE "PSYCHOANALYTIC THIRD SUBJECT" AND THE "SUBJUGATING THIRD"

The concept of an intermediary is important in religious history and tradition. Although Moses served as an intermediary for the Jews, that role seems to have passed into disuse with them, whereas with the Christians it has always played a very important role. The role of the intermediary can be compared with Winnicott's (1951, 1967) concepts of the transitional phenomenon and transitional space where cultural experience occurs. We must also remember that the analyst is the intermediary between the analysand and his unconscious. Ogden's (1994a, 1997) concept of the *psychoanalytic third subject* may pertain here as well, particularly in its active role as the *subjugating third subject* to the figure of Christ. Christ may be the "third subject" intermediary insofar as he represents the union of God, the Divine Subject, and man, the earthly subject. The

3. The devil surely is yet another alter ego to God.

analogy to the psychoanalytic situation in terms of the distribution of the subjectivities is striking, as just alluded to, especially if we analogize the analyst to the intermediary, the analysand to the human worshiper, and the analysand's unconscious to God.

Thus Christ[4] would serve as the third mutually created subject—a martyred "being"—and the conflation of God's guilt toward mankind *and* man's guilt toward God. He also serves as the "subjugating third-as-*agent*" (Grotstein, 1998b, and chapter 8) to mediate (and control) man's and God's guilt unto perpetuity. If this formulation is credible, then religion in general and Christianity in particular have an intersubjective, interactive, dialectical dimension that has not been hitherto revealed. The covenant, the real religious intermediary or "third," may be what the Christians call the Holy Ghost.

We must never lose sight of the two aspects of God, the one that we are driven to create and the one whose existence—if at all—is utterly ineffable. What does it mean that the God whom we can consider as Object is created by man himself in terms of the third subject? To me it means that man unconsciously bears within him a "ventriloquist-puppeteer" who speaks and choreographs both God and man in the passions of the sacred. As Voltaire observed, "God created man in His own image, and man repaid Him in kind."

We have to consider two aspects of God in the context of the intersubjective third. The first aspect has to do with the dialectic of man's beseeching God and God's counterintentional designs toward man. That "controlling–controlled" paradigm fits in with Ogden's concept of the subjugating third, Mason's (1994) folie à deux (mutual hypnosis or projective identification), Girard's (1972) concept of mimesis, and the concepts of "thirdness" in the transference put forth by Jung (1934)—especially as "mysterium coniunctionis" (Jung, 1966)—Tresan (1966), and Schwartz-Salant (1989, 1995, 1998). To be in a state of what Bion (1970) termed reverie, which connotes a "transformation" or "evolution in O," one must be without memory, desire (intentionality), understanding, knowledge, or preconception. At that serene moment, the subject (which may also be God) just *is*—as a cosmic and ineffable being.

4. I use the signifier Christ as a universal mythical entity that is equated with Oedipus, Isaac, Moses, and other martyrs or would-be martyrs. The covenant constitutes a "sacred third" that binds God as well as man to mutual protection and respect. I also see the story of the allegedly real Christ to be a pivotal moment in Jewish history, one that was somehow rewritten and removed from what I have come to believe were its proper Jewish roots (Fredriksen, 1988; Watson, 1995a, b).

THE "POSITION OF INNOCENCE": "ORIGINAL SIN," BLESSING, AND SHAME

Patients who have been the victims of trauma or abuse believe that their humanness has been violated. They therefore come to believe that they have lost their *innocence*, a phenomenon associated with "soul murder" (Schreber, 1903; Freud, 1911a; Shengold, 1989). The poignancy of my patient's lament made me realize that I had all too often heard this complaint from other patients who had suffered from tragic backgrounds, and I sought to explore what was meant by the experience of innocence as well as its loss and its dialectical counterpart, sin. The concept of innocence has legal/moral/ethical dimensions and importance in the history of all religions and cultures. Blake (1789–1794) in his *Songs of Innocence and Experience* gave a poetic, spiritual, and cultural dimension to the concept and postulated an epigenesis to one's experience of it. The infant is born into primal innocence and then, as a growing child, enters into the Forest of Experience ("Error"), where his capacity to maintain his innocence is put to the test. If one's innocence is successfully maintained, one transcendently moves on to "Higher Innocence."

This analysand's story and those of many others led me to rethink Klein's (1935, 1946) concept of the paranoid-schizoid and depressive positions.[5] Ogden (1989a) has added his own "autistic contiguous position," Steiner (1993) his concept of "psychic retreats," and I the "transcendent position" (Grotstein, 1997). Now I should like to add two more, the "position of innocence" and the "redemptive position." The concept of a position of innocence embraces the unspoken but highly implied conceptualizations of infantile mental life that are inherent in the works of Ferenczi, Suttie, Fairbairn, Winnicott, Bowlby, and Kohut. I would introduce the idea of innocence as a developmental line (A. Freud, 1963) *and* as a position that interacts dialectically with both the paranoid-schizoid and the depressive positions. In fact, the paranoid-schizoid position can be understood as a position in which the infant protests the jeopardy to or loss of innocence to its objects. Finally, the concept of innocence and the position that corresponds to it become situated in the developing personality as that aspect of its subjectivity that we have since ancient times referred to as the *soul.*

Innocence has been neglected as a developmental line in psychoanalytic theory, largely perhaps because of the traditional emphasis that

5. I have already briefly discussed my proposed alterations of the concept of the depressive position in the previous chapter and in chapter 10. My point of view is that the depressive position should be considered from the standpoints of both the infant *and* the parent.

psychoanalysts impute to the "original sin" motif associated with the psychoanalytic canon of psychic determinism. It may have been implied in the concept of primary narcissism (Freud, 1914a) and in Abraham's (1924) preambivalent stage of the oral phase. Orthodox, classical, and Kleinian schools adhere to a putatively "hedonic-demonic" emphasis on the original sin concept of psychic determinism and the drives. When Abraham spoke of the preambivalent stage of libidinal development in the first oral stage, he was clearly alluding to a notion of innocence, as was Fairbairn (1952) when he spoke of the preambivalent object. I suggest that each human being experiences a sense of potential loss of innocence (as "sin") upon the acceptance of one's sense of *agency*.

Winnicott was the most outspoken advocate of the concept of normal developmental innocence in regard to his idea of a stage of "pre-concern" or normal ruthlessness. Winnicott's (1963a) "being infant," his concept of "pre-ruth" (Winnicott, 1954), and his idea of object usage (Winnicott, 1969, 1971) irrefragably stake the claim for infantile and childhood innocence. This may very well have been his most serious disagreement with Melanie Klein, who subscribed to the classical analytic theory of the infant's innate responsibility for its psychic life. Winnicott saw the infant as an innocent hostage with a mother who was not always "good enough." Winnicott's idea of the being infant can be related to innocence, whereas the breast-seeking infant initiates the journey into inescapable guilt over object usage. Kohut (1971, 1977, 1984) and his followers, as well as most of the various relational and intersubjective schools, also allude to innocence but without specifying it. They depart from the primacy of the drives and imply that the newborn infant is free of inchoate demonic taint; according to them, the infant's instinctual drive repertoire is inherently guiltless except insofar as it is excessively mobilized as the result of environmental failure.

Innocence has many dimensions in the infant's mental life and in the life of the family and culture into which the child is born. Parents seem to attribute innocence to their infants but often paradoxically envy and attack that very innocence in acts of child abuse. The infant feels its innocence side-by-side with its unconscious sense of autochthonous (self-caused) belief that all that happens is its responsibility. Innocence signifies the child's sense of being blessed and protected by its objects and thus anticipating safety in its life and wanderings. It suggests guilessness of anticipation of experience.

Loss of innocence occurs not in only the encounter with the infant's putatively destructive unconscious phantasies or conscious thoughts and behavior but also in the collapse of its faith and trust in its objects when they either *critically* disappoint, neglect, or abuse the infant or when random circumstances traumatically cause the infant to believe that the world is unsafe. These infants then become "orphans of the Real" (Grotstein, 1995b,c). Innocence, therefore, has two major dimensions: the infant's own innocence and that of the parents and the culture. In traumatic situations the infant/child, like my analysand, may come to believe that "the world has lost *its* innocence."

From the vertex of innocence and its dialectical counterpart, original sin, one can conceive of a dual track (see chapter 4) in which the child must struggle to maintain a sense of innocence about itself and about the world it lives in while at the same time succumbing to the tide of instinctual demands. The impact of needs threatens to compromise the infant's self by traumatically overwhelming the threshold of tolerance, thus dissociating the infant from itself and leading to ontological guilt and the Faustian bargain phenomenon. The infant must own its life karma, so to speak; to discard it is felt to be an ontological offense.

The paradoxical problem is that the infant, like its descendant, the adult or the analytic patient, is constrained to accept its oedipal, guilt-inducing legacy. At the same time, it must experience the guilt that inheres in its acceptance and its awareness of that legacy—hence the treachery of the snake in the Garden of Eden myth. To attempt to escape from one's fate is to follow in the tragic footsteps of Oedipus, who tried to evade his own oedipal fate by exiling himself from Corinth only to find it awaiting him in Thebes.

In the practical, clinical sense, the phenomenon of innocence can ultimately be thought of as the absence of pettiness toward one's objects and oneself. Innocence must be differentiated from naiveté, where feelings of pettiness lurk under the surface. True innocence conveys a forgiving, merciful attitude toward oneself and others.

While I agree with Abraham, Fairbairn, and Winnicott about the probability of inchoate developmental innocence that they seem to imply, I also believe that this innocence must occur in a dialectical relationship with unconscious phantasies that are suffused with the persecutory consequences of future, as well as current destructiveness due to damage done to the object (Klein, 1940), or object usage (Winnicott, 1969, 1971). Innocence, when it is present, always exists in a dialectical relationship with assumed or actual guilt toward objects and the sense of responsibility for the object's welfare; innocence and guilt are like conjoined twins, paradoxically separate and inextricably connected at the same time. How the infant confronts its persecutory terrors in the paranoid-schizoid position—that is, how it maintains its authentic connectedness to the objects and to itself without detaching from them or betraying either—allows for the development of a sense of "higher innocence" in the depressive position in the challenge presented in Blake's (1789–1794) "Forest of Experience."

The experience of innocence is associated with the parental assignment of a "blessing" to the infant. This blessing is a birthright that gives the infant a feeling of benign, omnipotent protection, a sense of safety in a world ruled by God, the guarantor of justice and fairness. When the experience of trauma is critically intense, that is, when the protective shield (Freud, 1920) is perforated, the sense of innocence, protection, and fairness is felt to be abrogated. Abject defenselessness intervenes to introduce a more troubling kind of healing process, a renunciation of goodness, love, and attachment. In its place, cynical despair rises, followed often by militant martyrdom, perverseness, schizoid detachment and endopsychic fortresses (Fairbairn, 1944); malignant narcissism (Rosenfeld, 1987); or psychic retreats (Steiner, 1993). The disillusioned child victims become, by default, "orphans of the Real" by default (Grotstein, 1995b,c). In the internal world of these "orphans," there is almost invariably a loss of the sense of self, a loss of identity and an identification with the aggressor (A. Freud, 1936). A submission, a transfer of the victim's ego with its sense of agency (power of attorney, so to speak) to the victimizer (actual or phantasied), takes place.

Pathological compliance, associated with humiliation, rather than adjustment with pride occurs. It is well known that trauma victims frequently feel shame and humiliation, as do sufferers from envy (Malin, 1990). Less obvious, except to Fairbairn (1943b), is that victimized patients frequently feel *guilt* as well. Fairbairn explained this on the basis of their unconscious assessment of the bad objects within them and the idea that their internal presence predicates a curse on the victim. In other words, those who did not contain bad objects would not have been victimized if they had been protected by good internal objects. They would be their objects' "protégés."

How parents handle their child's trauma is decisive. Trauma from instinct and affect abuse is reflected in the fate of the infant's projective and subsequent introjective identifications in relationship to the parents' mediating and attuning container capacity. When the needed parent is the abuser, the infant is especially at risk and must psychically mediate the parent's projective counteridentifications (the parent as negative container of the infant's "object usage") at its own expense by assuming the role of scapegoat, hero, messiah, or pariah. Whatever the actual cause, failure to dispel the impact of the trauma places the infant at risk for feeling cursed, as was the case with my patient.

I am also suggesting that the Oedipus complex can be thought of as having an inextricably linked complement; that is, the infantile neurosis of the infant paradoxically exists both separately and inextricably bound to that of each of his parents. The mysterious third subject, the intermediary, is who the infant is supposed to be, from the infant's and the parents' perspectives. Thus, the infant, because of developmentally progressive object-usage phantasies, experiences guilt toward the maternal, then paternal, then combined parental superego. Each of the parents, as well as the parents together as a parental group, also experiences guilt toward the child, who was given them in "trusteeship." The Oedipus complex is a complex of guilt and sacrifice involving each member and subgroup of the oedipal family intersubjectively.

At issue is how best to conceive of and treat patients who have been seriously victimized. I have formulated three basic dimensions to psychopathology: (1) conflict (due to "instinct abuse"); (2) privation/deprivation (failures of necessary, requisite attunement); and (3) trauma/impingement (including Herman's, 1992, "complex" posttraumatic stress disorders). Herman persuasively argues for a special consideration in psychoanalytic theory and practice to account for and treat these victims. Suffice it to say that these victims believe that they have lost faith, hope, and innocence and are irredeemable.

THE INTER- AND TRANSGENERATIONAL NEUROSIS

Child abuse implicates the psychology of the abusive family and culture. Innate counterparts in group processes appear to correspond to the innate releasing mechanisms (Lorenz, cited in Emde, 1983) in individuals that predicate the continuity of behavioral practices down generational lines. Bowen (1960), Jucovy (1983, 1985) Rosenfeld (1987), Apprey (1987a, b; Apprey and Stein, 1991), and Cramer (1982a, b, 1986; Cramer and Stern, 1988) have all dealt with the apparent transmission of psychopathology from one generation to the other. Dodds (1951) pointed out that in ancient Greece the "pollution" that characterized a particular cultural generation had to be "cleansed" through *transgenerational transfer to an innocent person in a distant generation for expiation*. Oedipus was such an example, in Dodds's opinion.

One aspect of this transmission leads to the concept of the "Pietà covenant" as a covenant of "thirdness." The analyst brings not only analytic training and wisdom to the therapeutic situation but also countertransference responses (his "analytic instrument") as well, as we now recognize. The analyst and the analysand each projects his individual subjectivities into a third "collective," intermediate subjectivity (Jung, 1966;[6] Bion, 1962a, 1963, 1965, 1970; Tresan, 1966; Schwartz-Salant, 1989,

6. In particular see Jung's (1963) "mysterium coniunctioni," which can be translated as the mysterious (third) connection between analysand and analyst.

1995, 1998; Ogden, 1994a, 1997), which becomes the analysand's "innocent infant's subjectivity" plus the "innocent analyst's subjectivity." The contributing subjects seek to protect *and*, unconsciously, abuse or be abused or controlled by this third subject. This idea can be extended to include the analyst's *innocence* in the patient's life (beyond any communicative or countertransference errors that may complicate but not contradict that innocence).

The Pietà covenant is so asymmetrically constructed that the "exorcism" of the analysand's "demons" ("toxic" internal [subjective] objects) transpires in the potential (transitional or intermediary) space (Winnicott, 1951) between the analysand and analyst, where the unsaturated (free from memory, desire, understanding, or preconception) but felt image of the analyst is invisibly positioned. The "cure" is the transfer of mental pain from the analysand to the analyst. The analysand's stance in analysis is generally one in which he is dominated by persecutory anxiety (paranoid-schizoid position). The analyst must be in the depressive position—or really in the "transcendent position" (a state of reverie in O), a stance that corresponds to Klein's (1940) description of the status of the infant in its own depressive position, first tragic, then mournfully pining, as reparations are instituted.

Redemption and the Depressive Position

The analyst's state of transcendent reverie (O) as container permits him to experience a trial or partial introjective and projective counteridentifications with the analysand's projective identifications so that the analyst feels (partially, on a trial basis) not only the analysand's feelings of pain (concordant counteridentification) but also the feelings of guilt apposite to the experience of the depressive position in the parent(s); that is, the feelings of guilt, responsibility, and contrition (complementary counteridentification) that the analysand originally wished the parent had experienced. In other words, the analyst must first allow himself to be transcendently in O so that he can be in a position to experience his own depressive position as summoned by the analytic exorcism-from analysand to analyst.

This process finally allows the analysand to experience feelings of *redemption* from the shame and helplessness of his pain. I believe that, redemption constitutes an essential part of the concept of the depressive position, and I assign it the status of a position in its own right to emphasize its importance.

THE ORIGIN OF THE SUPEREGO

Freud (1923b) understood the origin of the authority of the superego as lying in the introjection of the values of the parents and even of the grandparents. Klein (1940) linked the omnipotence of the superego with the infant's projective identifications of its own omnipotence into the object, which is subsequently internalized and introjectively identified with. Actually Freud (1914a) had thought of this factor when he posited that the ego ideal develops as a gradient in the ego and carries with it the grandiosity of the infant at birth, whereas the ego proper forfeits its claim to such grandiosity when it begins to experience frustration in life. I believe that a reasonably faithful reinterpretation of Freud's view on the origin of the ego ideal could legitimately read as follows: The ego ideal, in its future role as "High Priest" in a gradient in the ego, forfeits its sensuality in order to attain the authority of the ideal. The ego, on its part, must forfeit its omnipotence and idealness in order to acquire the vitality and aliveness of sensual life. Sacrifice is implicit in each of these role assignments. The ego ideal then becomes the ego's *paraclete* (advocate) and constitutes what Jung (1934) termed the Christ archetype, and what I call the martyr archetype.

A hostile, cruel, or perverse ego ideal is a secondary construct that results from its misperception by the ego when the ego's uncontainable anxieties are projected onto the ego ideal. The patient discussed in chapter 8 revealed something about the nature of the inner experience of the ego ideal when he dreamed first of a dead child and later of a bleeding one. Associations revealed that, whenever he believed he was not living up to his ideals, his inner ideal would bleed in painful silence, as if rebuking him.

The sacrifice involved in the formation of the superego follows similar lines. Freud (1913) was aware of the rite of sacrifice when he discussed the concept of the primal horde and the brothers' sacrificial murder of the father, who then became deified (sacred) as the totem of the horde. Klein (1940) likewise dealt with the infant's developing awareness at the threshold of the depressive position when it realizes in retrospect that it has inescapably damaged and destroyed its objects (primarily the mother) in order to survive and thrive. She later elaborated this theme from the religious vertex (the transformation of the persecutory Furies or Erynes into the depressive Eumenides) (Klein, 1963a).

Winnicott's (1969, 1971) concept of object usage and of its corollary, the destruction of the subjective object, in addition to his concept of potential space (Winnicott, 1951), supply the missing links in this puzzle. As in the rite of the Eucharist, the infant (and patient) *must* destroy the beloved object in order to survive and *must* continuously repeat this destruction of the object in order to renew its vows of gratitude and allegiance to the object for its selfless sacrifice. One must repeat the sacred cannibalistic ritual and the violent act of the destruction of the object at one's own hand in order to maintain the hard-won return of innocence—but only at the expense of realizing the cost of one's developmental or analytic salvation to the object (in the shadow of one's "original sin").

The ego ideal (the Christ[7] within, from the Christian perspective) will continue to reflect our closeness to the ideal values it represents by its continuing reminder to us of its silent suffering.[8] Thus, an internal "holy family" is formed consisting of the compulsively and relentlessly martyred father, mother, and child, the ultimate "trinity" of oedipal martyrdom.

OBJECT USAGE, HUMAN SACRIFICE, AND THE DEPRESSIVE POSITION

In a seminal paper on this subject from a Kleinian perspective, Likierman (1995) finds two distinct phases in Klein's conception of the depressive position.[9] The first is the "tragic phase," in which the infant feels hopeless because the (putative, phantasied) damage done to the object is utterly irreparable. In the second phase, the infant experiences the need to *try* to repair or restore the object even though it is felt to be too late. During this phase, pining for the lost object begins. A feeling of redemption follows from the sincerity of the attempt.

In his concept of play, Winnicott (1967) emphasized the existence of a potential space, which constitutes a sanctuary against guilt or persecutory retaliation when the infant or toddler conducts object-usage destructiveness (pre-ruth) against subjective objects qua toys. Klein

---

7. I wish once again to remind the reader that I am using the name Christ as a mythical symbol and metaphor to explicate a psychoanalytic theme. I do not want to espouse Christianity or critique religion per se.

8. Other motives certainly exist for the destruction of the object. One in particular would be the need to destroy the illusory intermediate iconic image of the object that interposes itself between us and our authentic confrontation with the ineffability of the object as subject—so as to be able to bear its presence directly—without possessing it. We must remember that a symbolic object representation is *not* the object within. *It is an absence that is reserved in memory of it.*

9. Other critiques of Klein's changing conception of the depressive position have been dealt with by Meltzer (1978), Eigen (1993, 1995), Grotstein (1997), and Maizels (1996). These are discussed in greater depth in chapter 10.

(1960) similarly believed that, when children play, they need sufficient displacement to take place in order to feel safe in their destructive playing. Yet she, unlike Winnicott, always felt that retaliatory anxiety was ever-present.

Infants, from the earlier Kleinian point of view, consequently need to go through the tragedy, then the contrition of object damage and loss before achieving redemption through reparation. If we put Klein and Winnicott together, we see that the infant/toddler is normally an obligatory explorer and adventurer who must examine, play with, and destroy images and toys (object usage) to find out what they are made of and who must destroy self-created images of the object to leave primary identification for separateness from the object so as to be able now to know the object in its Otherness (see chapter 7). Object usage may therefore be considered to be "safe play" on one hand and, paradoxically, "fated play," on the other, fated referring to its felt consequences in the depressive position.

THE "HOLY FAMILY" OF THE SUPEREGO

Object usage also, according to Hopkins (1989), can be associated with the crucifixion of Christ. In the Eucharist, Christians must symbolically eat his flesh and drink his blood, that is, "cannibalize" him in order to be redeemed. In this ritual sacrifice he becomes sacralized (holy). We then recall Freud's (1913) theory of the primal horde and the sacrifice of the father, and Abraham's (1924) and Klein's (1923) notions of cannibalistic ideation in regard to the infant's phantasied relationship to its mother. In the depressive position, the child "Christ" sacrifices itself for the putatively damaged parent. Thus, we have three family sacrifices: the father, the mother, and the child. Their sacrifices result in their becoming sacralized as an internal holy family.

I believe that this internal "holy family," along with its covenant of grace to the ego, constitutes a "holy quaternary" (Jung, 1934) insofar as the Holy Ghost is concerned. My psychoanalytic translation of the Holy Ghost is that it is the intermediate internal connectedness between us and the internal "trinity," a connectedness that evolves from one's developmental experiences in the purgatory of the paranoid-schizoid position and the initial phase of the depressive position. There is a negative or shadow side to this trinity that becomes the diabolical ensemble of Hell and the internal "mafia-like gangs" described by Fairbairn (1944), Rosenfeld (1987), and Steiner (1993). The victims of this unholy internal family enter into the psychic retreats described by Steiner and demonstrate the revenge and resentment that he describes as a part of a pathological oedipal relationship.

THE OEDIPUS COMPLEX REDEFINED

Freud (1950, Letter 69, Sept. 21, 1897) thought of the Oedipus complex as a universal, mythic way station, an internal rite of passage, for the child (no longer an infant) in the late phallic phase of development. The child develops sexual feelings for one parent and murderously rivalrous feelings for the other. Klein (1928, 1945) retroextended the Oedipus complex to the late oral phase of infancy and placed it within the hegemony of the depressive position. Later she added another concept, that of *envy*, designating an earlier stage of rivalry in the two-person relationship between the infant and the breast. Envy is the progenitor of jealousy in the three-person relationship in later oedipal rivalry.

The classical concept of the Oedipus complex is one of a developmental hegemony that takes precedence over the preoedipal (pregenital) organizations; that is, fixations in the oral and anal phases are seen as regressive elaborations of the Oedipus complex, which orbitally constellates these regressive elaborations around it (Fenichel, 1945). Freud's concept of the Oedipus complex is described in terms of the libidinal desire implicit to libido theory and *infantile sexuality*, and Klein's conception is based on her basic assumption of *infantile dependency* as well as inherent destructiveness.

In elaborating the oral origins of the Oedipus complex, Klein uncovered the mother-dominated aspects of this complex; some of its associative dimensions extend to such atavistic and totemic derivatives as the myths of the sphynx, hydra, Gorgon Medusa, and so on. Another is an aspect of the matriarchal complex uncovered by Malinowski (1927) in the Trobriand Islands and elaborated by Spero (1982); where there is a matriarchal heritage and laws of matrilineal succession, the mother's brother, not her husband, becomes the dominant male (as did Creon at Thebes in the Oedipus myth). Klein's (1928) conception of the combined parent, really of the infant's phantasy that father's penis is trapped inside the mother's body and consequently fused with it (as the phallic female, for example), is reminiscent of this matriarchal/matrilineal era. Klein, in other words, uncovered the earliest roots of the archaic Oedipus complex in which the mother is conceived of by the infant as a virtual dominatrix of the family, enclosing father's penis and the imaginary siblings within her body. According to Klein, the infant constructs this image of the dominatrix mother during the emergence of its epistemophilic and sadistic instincts. Its conception of mother and father as an inseparably combined couple is due to the projective identification onto their relationship of its own difficulty in allowing for its own separation from mother. One of the tasks of the infant at this stage is to separate itself from mother and to separate the breast-mother from the phallus-bearing father, as I discussed in chapter 7.[10]

The Greek legend of the labyrinth in which the Minotaur (who ritualistically devours appropriated human sacrifices) is trapped is congruent with this earlier phase of the Oedipus complex. Finally, Lacan (1966) saw the Oedipus complex as representing the infant's descent into the laws of the symbolic order of language defined in the name of the father as the signifier of "no."

The Oedipus complex is multifarious in depth and duration and is certainly more complex than has hitherto been thought. I hypothesize that there is a matriarchal oedipal phase that is superseded by a patriarchal phase. At the same time the neuroses/psychoses of the infant *and* each—and both—of the parents form a dual-track ("Siamese-twinship") arrangement, that is, separate from each other while inextricably bound to one another. When we analyze the infantile neurosis in a patient, consequently, we are arbitrarily isolating the patient's own neurosis. At the same time, we realize that the person's infantile neurosis actually belongs to a conglomeration with those of his mother, father, siblings, grandparents, uncles, aunts, and culture at large. These would constitute the *intergenerational* and *transgenerational neuroses*.

I also hypothesize the existence of a "little oedipal family or "gang" of siblings (later, peers) that rivals the parents' family authority.[11] Further, I conceive of the Oedipus complex as a "neurosis of destiny," which constitutes a dialectical journey between Fate, "original sin" (one's animal nature), and innocence and is fundamentally conducted in the *shadow of human sacrifice* (of father, mother, and infant).

---

10. It is highly suggestive that in the traditional Christian version of the Christ story one can see traces of the matriarchal Oedipus complex. Mary, for instance, looms far more important in the story than does Joseph, the father.

11. Abelin (1980) postulated the existence of a the "Madonna Complex," by which he meant a triangulation that took place before the oedipal triangulation, during the rapprochement subphase of separation-individuation. He posited that triangulation occurs between the siblings and mother and may be the foundation for the establishment of later peer relationships.

ACKNOWLEDGING MAN'S SPIRITUAL LIFE IN PSYCHOANALYTIC THINKING

This chapter sprang from a spiritual outcry from a patient who came to believe that he was God-deprived. In the course of my analytic work with him and with other patients like him, I had to rethink the roles of God, Christ, the Messiah, and other aspects of religion and spirituality in psychoanalytic thinking. A psychoanalyst constantly deals with issues that could easily be thought of as religious. When the infantile neurosis emerges in the transference, the analyst must address the *gap* between sessions in which the patient feels potentially unprotected and who must develop a sense of *faith* and *trust* in the analyst and a belief that the analyst-as-phantasied parent is intact and will return.

Does this need for faith not parallel David's Psalm 23? Is not one principal aspect of the narcissistic personality disorder the narcissist's protest over the loss of a felt entitlement and *blessing*? Are not the protests of traumatized, abused, or molested children and their adult-survivor counterparts a plaintive plea to regain their lost *innocence*? Is not the mechanism of *idealization* but a way to find an object that is worthy of being worshiped? Is not the ego ideal deeply reminiscent of our putatively *sanctified self* and the superego of our *sanctified objects*? Do we not need an object to worship—and to personify as well as to mystify—in order to mediate the infinities and chaos of our unconscious mental life as well as of external reality and to represent *coherence, balance, harmony, and serenity* in the form of a unified cosmogonic explanations?

The immanent preternatural presence within us constitutes what has been called the demiurge and the ineffable one beyond humanness, *God* (Fox, 1980, 1981a,b; Sells, 1994). C. S. Lewis (1943) stated that we require a god in order to justify our need to worship (see also Bion, 1992). Is not the need for the patient in analysis to surrender, in effect, his self-control over to the analysis but a parallel to Alcoholics Anonymous's concept of surrendering to a higher power? More to the point, do we not as analysts conceive of the unconscious as a Godlike connection, one that is oracular and sacred?

On the other hand, we must not forget that religion originated as a mythic or phantasmal cosmology, that is, a linear way of trying to organize the nonlinear data of random or chaotic existence. We are all aware that, once religion becomes institutionalized and becomes the tool of "middle management," we begin to observe its more disingenuous side—its primitive, corrupt, perverse, and violent propensities, as attested to by Frazer (1910, 1922), Freud (1913, 1927, 1930, 1939), Lévi-Strauss (1958, 1970), Girard (1972, 1978, 1986, 1987), DeMause (1974,

1990), Montgomery (1976), Taylor (1978), Sagan (1979), Brown (1991), Bergmann (1992), Williams (1992), and others.

The infant is born with a libidinal frenzy to survive and a potential array of aggressive armament to be, metaphorically, a "hunter," "warrior," and competitor in the primeval jungle of experience. These darker, shadow instincts must be regulated and mediated for the sake of the survival of the individual, the family, and the group. Talion law[12] was the provenance of a primeval covenant that helped to curb violence. Another covenant was the development of the rituals of human sacrifice and the scapegoat to placate feared animistic deities.

The need to develop a sense of cosmic coherence in dangerous environs in addition to an inherent tropism to worship must have caused primitive tribes to develop an obsessive-compulsive-like religion of mutual accountability between them and their deities, which were multiple, tangible, and peremptory. This religion was one in which a covenant would be required as a "legal" agreement between the gods and mankind for protection and divine intercession in return for worship and dedicated sacrifices for appeasement.

Man's unconscious mental life is dominated by savage pagan gods, which can be thought of as divided into blessing-giving and curse-giving, according to Klein's (1946) concept of the splitting of the maternal breast into a good and bad breast. The "pagan deities" constitute what Klein (1940) termed the primitive superegos of the paranoid-schizoid position. In the depressive position, these primitive pagan deities become repatriated and transmogrified into a unified whole-object God, one who is ineffable, inscrutable, and intangible. Thus, the gods undergo an epigenesis into "God," in the ego ideal and superego but also in regard to the ineffable subject of the unconscious (see chapter 5) and the Godhead, the god that is utterly beyond contemplation.

De Mello Franco (1998) states:

> [P]sychoanalysis should not seek solely to reduce religious beliefs to their roots in unconscious fantasies but should lead to a reorganization of the analysand's image of God and the assignment of new meaning to it. . . . The author contends that if psychoanalysis dismisses religion as illusion, it is running the risk of becoming an established religion [p. 113].

The author discusses what he believes to be a universal epigenesis of religious belief that begins as "man-as-God" to "man-with-God," the

12. Klein (1946, 1955) was the first to decode the concept of talion law with her ideas of splitting and projective identification.

former being associated with infantile omnipotence and the paranoid-schizoid position and the latter with reconciliation with feelings of humility in the depressive position.

Toward the Concept of a "Transcendent Position"

Elsewhere (Grotstein, 1993a) and in chapters 3 and 10, I suggest that we need a concept of a "transcendent position," one that reconciles and harmonizes the oppositional-dialectical relationship that Bion (1962a, 1963) proposed exists between Klein's (1940) paranoid-schizoid and depressive positions. I contemplated this addition because I was dissatisfied with some ambiguities in the Kleinian conception of the depressive position. The depressive position deals with the infant's transition from part-object to whole-object relationships and with reownership of its projected protests against putative frustration by the part-objects. Mourning for the loss of the part-object relationship and for the sense of omnipotence that goes with it allows for a newer relationship based on love for, sparing and repair of, and respect and appreciation for the real mother—and father. Along with those developments, the infant also experiences an increased awareness of its separateness from the object and the object's separateness from it.

Klein's (1940) concept of the depressive position may be overinclusive insofar as she does not adequately distinguish between the presence of clinical depressive illness and the transcendence of this depressive illness in mourning and reparations. In her discussion of the depressive position, Klein (1935) discussed the manic defenses, which seek to help the infantile portion of the personality triumph over, contemn, and control the object of dependency *and* the dependent aspect of the infant. She neglected, I feel, to discuss the *depressive defenses*, the internalized counterpart of the manic defenses, the chief manifestation of which is *martyrdom*, in which the infant suffers in order to control the object. The depressive defense may help us understand the pathological misuse of martyrdom generally and of an identification specifically with Christ among some psychotic patients.

The depressive position can be redefined in terms of the *covenant* that is binding not only on the infant/child but equally on mother and father as coparticipants in the oedipal saga in respect for the integrity of each other and in moral responsibility to protect one another from harm from the predator and from the self. The task of the infant in the depressive position is to enter into this covenant with its object (now also a subject in its own right), which protects each and establishes the awareness of the infant's dependency on its parents and their responsibility to respect and meet these dependency needs. It is also a time when the infant begins to introject more and project less. Its task is to "clean up its act" and to own a sense of responsibility for caring not only for the object but for itself—with the object's help.

Once the infant has begun to take care of itself and to accept responsibilities to care for its object relationships (which never end), and when mourning is, relatively speaking, felt to be completed, there is a propensity to transcend to yet another level of experience, one beyond the lurking pettiness of the paranoid-schizoid position and the lugubriousness of the depressive position, with its seemingly eternal depressive dialectic with the anxieties and "beta elements" of the paranoid-schizoid position. This new level is the transcendent position, in which one may experience a transformation in O, the domain of *numinous* experience, as distinguished from *phenomenal* experience (K) (Bion, 1965; see also chapter 10).

These distinctions follow from Kant's (1787) concept of primary and secondary qualities, according to Bion. I would also add Lacan's (1966) concept of the Registers of the Imaginary, the Symbolic, and the Real. The Register of the Imaginary is associated with sensory image formations and their subsequent significations as well as unconscious phantasies, which are formed ultimately from sensory imagery. The Register of the Symbolic deals with the transformation of sensory imagery into linguistic symbols (Bion's K). However, the Real exists before and beyond the capacities of these first two registers. The Real is Kant's "thing-in-itself," Bion's Absolute Truth, Ultimate Reality, an experience beyond imaging, imagining, and symbolizing (Bion's O). Although most of us shudder and shrink away from the dread of the Real (O), the power to encompass and countenance it qualifies one as having undergone a transformation in O, which corresponds to a numinous, spiritual experience.

An epigenetic progression of transformations of one's religio-spiritual-mystical sense seems to parallel the oedipal progression that I have described. The first stage is characterized, as Freud (1913) observed, by animism, that is, projective identification of hopes, fears, expectations, omniscience, and omnipotent intentionality to a preternatural but personified set of sensorily tangible idol-deities; the tangibility to the senses betrays their provenance in the infant–mother relationship.

The Old Testament, particularly *Genesis*, is a palimpsest in which a patriarchal He seems to have superinscribed atop His predecessor the matriarchal deities of the Jews. Their totemic descendant survives in the form of phylacteries, whose visible appearance leaves little doubt of their being "snake idols," a residue of the rituals that characterized ancient Semitic rites and which were sacred to the mother earth deities. The portrait of the Hebrew God of *Genesis* seems to be strikingly close to that of an impetuous, intolerant, demanding, self-centered infant or child—certainly a willful and capricious narcissist.

In chapter 2, I posited that *Genesis* portrays the birth not of Adam or Eve but of their child, the God-Infant Himself, who believes that He created everything He opened up His eyes to, including Himself, the world around Him, and even His parents, Adam and Eve (Grotstein, 1981a; see also chapters 1 and 6). The snake of primal treachery informs God that it was His parents' intercourse that created Him, not the other way around, upon which realization God undergoes a metamorphosis in which He is forced to become a normal human infant, who leaves Eden for reality (*East of Eden*).

As Freud (1914a) poignantly and presciently indicated, however, a portion of the God-Infant's omnipotence is left behind and is thereafter attributed to the ego ideal (the "god" within us). Yet, probably because of a spiritual manic defense on the part of His worshipers, the God who persists in the Old Testament remains a childish and churlish one. His demand for sacrifice reveals His infantilism and His (Kleinian) divisiveness. When He prefers Abel's sacrifice of the lamb to Cain's offer of the fruit of the field, God appears as a cruel, capricious, and unfair, cannibalistic superego who plays favorites with mankind, like the child splitting the parental couple, as He tried to do earlier in Eden.

Consequently, the infant is held to be sacred and, ambiguously, vulnerable as scapegoat and sacrifice. The "rage in Heaven" between the gods has to do with "turf" clashes for hegemony between the matriarchal, patriarchal, and child deities (e.g., Kronos versus Zeus, Zeus versus Prometheus). Even in these examples a paradox is inescapable: the son who must submit to the healthy father must also depose a tyrannical father in order to reestablish the "law of the father." Kronos ate his children (child abuse), and Zeus had to kill his father to end that abuse. The heroes in many of the Greek legends had to defeat divine significations of contemporaneous deities in order to free the captive, victimized, sacrificial children, for example, in the legend of Theseus, the Minotaur, and the labyrinth.

With the injunction against graven images and idols and with the concept of the ultrasensual God of mystery, whose name was too holy to utter and whose essence was inscrutably and ineffably beyond contemplation as an Object, the Hebrews gave to the world the legacy of faith in the unknowable and uncontemplatable Subject. They created a truly cosmic deity, but one nevertheless who carried with Him the indelible stamp of His lowly origin in the infantile paranoid-schizoid position.

It is interesting how spiritual and theological themes, as well as philosophical themes, seem to parallel psychological attempts to comprehend epistemology—how we come to understand what we know and how we were able to learn it. Epistemology for the ancient Hebrews was God-given, "In the beginning was the Word . . ." (*John*, 1:1). The ancient Greeks sought the word of Apollo through oracles (interpreted by "pythonesses," descendants from matriarchal religions), and the Hebrews highly regarded prophecies, which were believed to have had a divine origin.

The concept of God seems, consequently, to follow an epigenesis that parallels infant developmental stages. The most primitive concept of the deity is that of many tangible, sensuous idols, matriarchal and sensory in nature, sacred transitional objects, as it were. These deities seemed to desire appeasement by human sacrifice (Graves, 1955, 1958; Graves and Patai, 1963). The most primitive Titans, which were nature deities, were superseded by more less grandiose and more human deities, the Olympians (Caldwell, 1989). Finally, the concept of the unseen One God, the deity that was ultrasensual developed among the Hebrews and became the most important theological heritage of Western man. Reading the Bible one can observe an epigenesis of the relationship of God to man that can be understood in part by a transformation from the paranoid-schizoid position through the depressive position to the transcendent position.

God did not achieve the true grace of the depressive position, however, until He offered Christ, His only begotten son for sacrifice—out of His guilt for mankind's suffering![13] Once upon a time Abraham was prepared to offer his own son for sacrifice to God. Now we see the reverse. One of the common denominators of virtually all religions is the requirement of human sacrifice—or token sacrifice, as in the case of circumcision among the Jews. It may very well be—and I have never seen this idea spoken or written about before—that God Himself had to achieve the depressive position, acknowledge *His* contrition toward mankind, and offer His own son for sacrifice in order to achieve reparations. Thus, a new covenant between man and God was formed.

After Christ accepted the role of the synecdochic, cosmic martyr for all men for all time, not only was mankind saved, but God was also saved, cleansed, and free to be unfetteredly divine as the *Godhead*, as well as the *Immanent God* who functions as *God*, (Fox, 1980, 1981a; Sells, 1994), or maybe even the *Demiurge*, the One who in effect gets His hands dirty with earthly affairs. Put another way, the sacrifice of Christ allowed for the ultimate purification and sanctification of God, who then assumes Bion's (1965) O-ness in the transcendent position. This cosmic sense of

13. I hasten to inform the reader that this concept is mine and does not belong to Christian theology, which in fact it contradicts.

at-one-ment, attained by the inner journey into oneself, is reminiscent of the rites of the Gnostics (Pagels, 1979).

From a more practical standpoint, what I am suggesting is that we have an inherent need to relate to the domain of holiness within ourselves and that in this pursuit of the sacred each of us recapitulates his own pilgrimage from the pettiness, selfishness, unfairness, and cruelty of the paranoid-schizoid position, through the sorrow, mercy, pity, mourning, and repentance of the depressive position—and with it the suspension of "ego." Then may we enter the transcendent position of mystical at-one-ment with O.

There seem to be two domains of holiness, just as there are two Gods (the Godhead and the Immanent "God"), a notion inherent in the Gnostic Gospels (Pagels, 1979) and in the Manichaean conception. One is that which we *can* contemplate and which is in the domain of our experiences, the one that matures as we mature. The other is truly numinous, ineffable, and inscrutable. *In psychoanalytic experience we can never meet the Godhead, but we can feel its shadow by our intuition of its presence as the Unconscious, which, as I have stated earlier, is as close to God and Godliness as we are ever likely to reach.*

"FATHER, FORGIVE THEM; THEY KNOW NOT WHAT THEY ARE DOING"

Girard (1986) wrote of this quotation from Luke:

> The sentence that defines the unconscious persecutor lies at the heart of the Passion story in the Gospel of Luke: "Father, forgive them; they know not what they do" (*Luke* 23:34). If we are to restore this sentence to its true savor we must recognize its almost technical role in the revelation of the scapegoat mechanism. It says something precise about the men gathered together by their scapegoat. *They do not know what they are doing*. That is why they must be pardoned. *In this passage we are given the first definition of the unconscious in human history, that from which all the others originate and develop in weaker form* [pp. 110–111; final italics added].

Thus, by being willing to be sacrificed—out of love, mercy, and forgiveness—Christ[14] becomes the Sacrificial Lamb for all time before and after, having exposed the dark mythology of persecutory mimesis and

14. I ask the reader once again to remember that I think of Christ as myth-

scapegoatism. In so doing, he rendered the persecutory "cure" through sacrificial scapegoating obsolete and null and void for all time. It is as if he were saying that, by participating symbolically in his suffering (the Eucharist), one not only becomes one with him—and with God—but also has permission to be the hunter and predator for one's legitimate needs—as long as he is your prey and you him preditor![15]

This is the guiding metaphor and template for my concept of the "Pietà covenant" and the exorcistic sacrifices it entails. When this concept is integrated with Ogden's (1994a) concept of the three psychoanalytic subjectivities, our conception of what transference and countertransference really entail is profoundly deepened. We can perhaps conceive that the covenant binding man to God (what Christians call the Holy Ghost) comprises a "subjugating thirdness" whose omnipotent power of subjugating His worshipers arises from the projective identification of their ego ideals "unto Him" (Freud, 1921; Bion, 1961; Anzieu, 1984). The God we create is a composite subjective object and should be distinguished from the concept of the deity who, as the consummate and ineffable Subject, is unthinkable for humans, ultimately the "Strange Attractor" that "knows" and coheres our chaos.

PSYCHOANALYSIS AND THE SOUL

Finally, I should like to touch on a theme that psychoanalytic language and thought seem to have avoided. The true religion of psychoanalysis since Freud seems to have been an orthodox atheistic (ontic, "scientific") modernistic positivism and determinism. Traditional religions and the human wisdom they have accumulated about man have been marginalized. The concept of the soul has long occupied a prominent role in the history of religion, culture, spirituality, and older psychologies. Bettelheim (1983) told us that Freud used the word soul when he spoke of the psychic apparatus. To me the concept of the soul belongs in the psychoanalytic lexicon as the moral perspective of the subject. In other words, from a holographic perspective, the soul describes the moral dimension of the individual vis-à-vis identification with the superego and ego ideal, and as I have redefined them in this chapter.[16]

---

ically continuous with Isaac, Moses, and Oedipus, that is, a universal archetype (in the platonic sense) of martyrs.

15. Again, I use "Christ" as a psychoanalytic signifier. Furthermore, I wish also to remind the reader that Christ knew no "Christians." His was a Jewish life and story from beginning to end.

16. The Reverend Sebastian Moore's (1985) *Let This Mind Be in You: The*

CONCLUDING REMARKS

The human beings known as Oedipus and Jesus Christ have had a profound effect on human history and on our psychological and spiritual lives. Circumventing a psychohistorical approach to each of their lives, I cite instead the works of Meg Harris Williams (1994) on Oedipus the man and Chessick (1995) on Christ the man. These works focus on each of them as representative, collective archetypes that have left us mythic legacies that underlie our epistemological, spiritual, and psychological foundations.

Oedipus, as archetypal scapegoat, *innocently* suffered "the sins of his fathers" and, failing in his ability to "contain" their projected guilt, became secondarily *guilty* himself. He was guilty for avoiding his proper "oedipal fate" by leaving Corinth for Thebes, where his fate awaited him. He also was guilty of having introjectively identified with "the sins of his fathers" by passing on the taint of his ill-fated house to his own children, two of whom slew each other in his name (Aegisthus and Polyneices), and a third, Antigone, died out of loyalty to the dead Polyneices.

The legacy that Oedipus left us is not only the complex that Freud uncovered. It is also that of the curious analytic "detective" who challenged the Establishment barrier (repression) to attempt to find the truth—as his truth—and then blinded himself. Thus, Oedipus is the forerunner of those two trends in psychoanalysis, the seeker of the truth and the antianalyst who seeks to blind himself to the truth (Steiner, 1985). Together they constitute the dialectical conflict of the analysand and the analyst.

The ontological authenticity of Oedipus has been dealt with by Williams (1994). Using the vertices of Bion's (1970) concept of catastrophic change and Keats's notion of negative capability, she states:

> The first-written play, *Antigone*, concludes with the curse of revenge which falls when the mind-city fails to integrate conflicting emotions. The hero of *Oedipus Tyrannus*, however, overcomes the mindless pessimism which would deflect him from self-knowledge, by means of a necessary weaning process founded on memories from infancy. Finally, *Oedipus at Colonus* shows how mental beauty or poetry metamorphoses from the appearance of ugliness and makes ideas transmissible [p. 232].

Quest for Identity Through Oedipus to Christ just came to my attention as this work was going to press. I therefore regret that I shall not be able to reap its rich harvest at this time.

Christ appears to be the prototype for all sacrifices and for the miracle of the transformation of the soul (mind) under the condition of absolution, mercy, forgiveness, and grace. He represents the outcry of the innocently "crucified" infant who did not ask to be born into the "veil of tears" ("Oh Father, why hast thou forsaken me?"). He further represents the immortal stance of the analyst-as-shriver and as exorcist of the pain of the other ("Forgive them, Father, they know not what they do").

The miracle of transformation is the phenomenon of psychic change that occurs in analysis, a happening that we take so much for granted that we ignore its miraculous aspect. At the same time, we are able to see that the myth of Oedipus prefigured the story of Christ and was, like his theme, ultimately a spiritual one.

Chapter 10

BION'S TRANSFORMATIONS IN O

The Concept of the "Transcendent Position"

> *"The rising world of waters dark and deep*
> *Won from the void and formless infinite."*
> —John Milton: *Paradise Lost, Book III.*

Perhaps what unites all of us who read (and who have listened to) Bion is a conviction that he was on to something about psychoanalysis that was just beyond and yet, paradoxically, just within, our ken, something that thrust psychoanalysis into unparalleled perspectives and unheard of dimensions. He had become a navigator of "the deep and formless infinite" who charted waters even unknown to Freud. The landscape Bion charted is O, where psychoanalysis—and the individual—have always dwelled without realizing it. What we have hitherto understood as the unconscious now has an even more imponderable and numinous home. Bion's concept of O brings the epistemological and ontological dimensions to psychoanalysis in a most innovative manner. Much of this chapter is about O, its significance, both theoretically and clinically, and the transcendent position that I believe one must attain to be at peace (at one) with it.

To take Bion seriously is not the same as taking him literally. He advised us to ignore him and attend instead to how we resonate, or fail to resonate, with his ideas. I say these things to prepare the reader for a treatise on what *I* believe to be the apotheosis of his contributions. In my analysis with him I learned over and over again that he was far more interested in *my response* to his interpretations than in whether I *understood* them or got them right. This chapter follows in that tradition. In pursuing that trajectory, I shall show how Bion anticipated my views about the numinous and ineffable nature both of the subject and of the objects of the unconscious, each of whose origins he assigns to Kant's transcendental a priori concepts. In addition, I shall discuss his innovative views about what I call a "cosmic unconscious" and proffer my own idea of a "transcendent position" to account for the state of serenity that accompanies one who finally, after traversing the nightmares of the paranoid-schizoid position and the black holes and mournful inner cathedrals of the depressive position, is able to become reconciled to the experience of pure, unadulterated Being and Happening.

Notwithstanding the seeming reconditeness of Bion's episteme, it all boils down to his utmost belief in the centrality of emotions as the nucleus of our "heart of darkness" and of our very being. "Reason," he states, "is emotion's slave and exists to rationalize emotional experience" (Bion, 1970, p. 1). Our task is first to emotionalize O and then to bear what we have done with equanimity. The ultimate importance of feelings lies in their constituting our personal intersection and confrontation with impersonal O.

DEFINITIONS[1] OF O

O is an empty sign used by Bion (1965, 1970), the penumbra of whose associations allows it to represent a variety of experiences that have never before been addressed in psychoanalytic thinking. O can be understood to be a parallel reality without categories.[2] This means that it is beyond the capacity of imagination, phantasy, or symbolization to apprehend. Bion (1970) stated: "It [O] can "become" but cannot be known. It is darkness and formlessness, but enters K when it has evolved to a point where it can be known" (p. 89). First of all, O is "Absolute" in many perspectives because of its infinite nature. It connotes Absolute Happening, Circumstance, Inevitability, or Reality-as-it-ultimately-is before human beings transform it. It can be equated with Sodom and Gomorrah, the boiling magma of a volcano, absolute pandemonium, or unimaginable beauty all mixed together. Classical analysis knew it as "unbound cathexes," as in the psychoses, "actual neuroses,"[3] and in obsessive–compulsive disorders. To give a hint of my thesis, I now believe that

1. I am aware that to define O is an oxymoron. I mean only to suggest knowable analogues for something that is and will always be utterly unknowable and thus undefinable,

2. I am indebted to Edmund Cohen for this Kantian version of O.

3. Panic disorder.

what Freud termed the psychoneuroses ultimately constitute effective and plausible substitutions or screens for the experience of O.

Other associations to O include Absolute Truth (good and evil), Ultimate Reality, infinity, beta elements,[4] things-in-themselves, noumena, Plato's Eternal or Ideal Forms, the Godhead, the analytic object, real life, wisdom and realization (as distinguished from knowledge), experience, all change, especially "catastrophic," the domain of the ineffable and inscrutable, the grid,[5] the crossroads of Thebes in the Oedipus saga, the vertex-center of cartesian coordinates in the polar-coordinated space of the grid, "what the analysand is talking about," the ultimate concept of the object and of the incarnated self as godhead, the messianic idea, and so on. O is the quintessence of *Being* in the context of inevitable Happening. It also suggests the ancient Christian mystical notion of "the cloud of Unknowing."

In short, O is Bion's way of talking about the whole panoply of emotional experiences both prior to and following its reception by the subject. Furthermore, O *evolves*; it is always changing. Bion often cited Heraclitus' adage that one cannot enter the same river twice. Hercalitus' river relentlessly moves on. Spontaneous transformation becomes automatic and ineluctable. The problem for the individual in the river of experience is to accept the transformations by personal transformations of these impersonal transformations of O. Thus, to me. the important transformation is from impersonal O to personal (emotional) O. This transformation usually occurs indirectly through traditional detours L, H, and K until sufficient maturity allows a transcendence beyond the depressive position to the transcendent position, where one has reentered "the unknown remembered gate." Whereas many Bion scholars have attached importance to his concept of *transformations* between O and K, I should like to emphasize his ideas about *evolutions* of O in infant and mother as well as in analysand and analyst.

Bion also stated that not only can O not be known, grasped, apprehended (by the senses), or understood, one can only "become" it (in the Platonic sense of always becoming but never achieving). This "becoming" is not to be confused with identifying. It is more like an intimate resonance with it—or with the other's experience of it. It is

4. Bion's (1962b, 1963) term for (as yet) unmentalized emotional experiences. Their normal fate is to be transformed into mentalized "alpha elements" suitable for "mental digestion" (thinking).

5. Bion's (1963, 1977b) concept of the grid can be understood as a model for the disciplined way in which the analyst, having caught hold of an insight about his analysand's material, then begins to test it, categorize it, evaluate it, and finally comment on it.

the quintessence of sublimated countertransference phenomena as well as what Winnicott (1956) termed "primary maternal preoccupation." "The psychoanalyst must *be* O." Bion (1970) went on to say, "Every object known or knowable to man, including himself, must be an *evolution* of O. It is O when it has evolved sufficiently to be met by K capacities in the psychoanalyst" (p. 27). Bion counterposed the capacity of the genius or messiah to his ability to appreciate the Absolute (Emotional) Truth and Ultimate Reality of O, which he also conflated with "God." I believe that Bion reveals here implications of Gnosticism and mysticism, that is, that there is an immanent "God" within us that, to me, constitutes the Thinker of "the thoughts without a thinker" (O as imminent "thoughts" qua the analytic object, i.e., dreams, free associations, symptoms) to be intercepted and transduced by the phenomenal subject of psychoanalysis with the collaboration of the analyst's reverie, containment, and translating function.

ANALOGUES OF O

Before I enter into a discussion of what I believe to be the ultimate significance of O for psychoanalysis, I should like to link it with some proposed analogues, which would include Lacan's (1966) concept of the Register of the Real,[6] Ricoeur's (1970) idea, borrowed from the ancient Greeks, of Ananke (Necessity), Peirce's (1931) "brute reality," and Kauffman's (1993, 1995) and Palombo's (1999) concepts of chaos, complexity, and self-organization. To these I would add Heidegger's (1927) concept of *Dasein* or Being, especially in conjunction with "aletheia" (unconcealment). I would also add some of the rich harvest of Matte-Blanco's (1975, 1981, 1988) mathematical reinterpretation of the unconscious; that is, such concepts as infinite sets and categories, bi-logic, symmetry, infinite symmetry.

These analogues of O reveal the profundity of Bion's explorations into ontology, epistemology, spirituality, mysticism, logic, mathematics, aesthetics, and philosophy and show how he radically altered the nature of the psychoanalytic quest as well as of our conception of the unconscious. What ultimately seems to emerge from his explanation of O is the concept of a "cosmic unconscious," one that is both internal and all-

6. Lacan (1966) distinguished between the Registers of the Imaginary, Symbolic, and the Real. The Register of the Symbolic is what we ordinarily mean by "reality." The Real connotes that which cannot be imagined or symbolized. It just *is*.

pervasive. From his work, we would now say that the task for the infant and for the analysand is to be able to confront the indifference of O, own one's experience of it (allow O to intersect with one's feelings), and thereby render one's experience of it *personal* (subjective, emotional).

To these I should like to add yet another idea, that of "Circumstance," a conception that predicates happenings that occur independently of human will, happenings that are indifferent to our welfare, happenings that are seemingly random but, when they occur to us in harmful ways, cause us to feel personally persecuted by an "unfair" fate. This prime impersonalness and indifference of O reminds one of Freud's concept of *das Es* (the id), which he borrowed from Nietzsche and Groddeck and whose "it"-ness parallels the cosmic impersonalness of Bion's conception of O.

NOTES ON TRANSFORMATIONS

Bion's (1965, 1970) concept of transformations depends on the activity of container–contained, the mother's or analyst's use of reverie and dream-work alpha, L, H, and K[7] linkages, and the dialectical relationship between the paranoid-schizoid and depressive positions—and, I would add, the transient attainment of the transcendent position. Bion stated that the analyst must abandon memory, desire, understanding, preconception, and sensuous data generally (and ego, in the Eastern sense) in order for his psyche to be empty or unsaturated ($\varphi\xi$)[8] so as to be able to be ready for the detection of the pattern, the selected fact (Poincaré, 1952) (or "strange attractor") that gives coherence to the O of the analysand's unconscious experience of the "analytic object." This transformation is expressed by Bion thus: $Ta\alpha \rightarrow Ta\beta$ so as to be able to induce $Tp\alpha \rightarrow Tp\beta$ (where "a" is the analyst and "p" is the patient, and "α" is the beginning state, and "β" is the end state of transformation).

Bion tells us that our intuitive deciphering instrument begins with our ability to be patient during the long moments of uncertainty while we faithfully await the arrival of the selected fact (Poincaré, 1952). The selected fact emerges from within us as a *resonance* of ineffably selected elements from our vast internal repertoire of experiences with objects that are able to achieve a correspondence with the "strange attractors" that organize the infant's (analysand's) O. These "strange attractors"

7. Love, Hate, and Knowledge.

8. ($\varphi\xi$) is Bion's (1970) way of designating the unsaturated psyche, after one has divested oneself of memory, desire, understanding, and preconception.

constitute the hidden order of personalized O, the code that gives O personal coherence.

The mother's alpha function, in her state of reverie, is able to "create," while she "discovers" (through epiphany) the "selected fact" (Poincaré, 1952) that she intuits in the randomness of her infant's pleas for affective attunement. She intuits through a resonance or (symmetrical) matching of affect experiences with those of her infant, much as Stanislavski (1933) recommended in method acting. In mother's being able to experience the selected fact—that is, the code that unlocks the hidden order that cryptically organizes the putative randomness—she is able, through that epiphanic experience, to resonate with the hidden order (the "strange attractor") that is implicit within her infant's unknown, his random protoaffects, his O.

Bion's injunction to abandon memory and desire can be equated with achieving Matte-Blanco's state of bi-logic dominance. Forfeiting for the moment the use of bivalent logic, the latter, because of its domination by the principle of negation, becomes a formidable opponent to the expression of whimsical, imaginative fancy and intuition.

Transformations from O to L and H (P-S), from L and H to K (depressive position) seem parallel to Hartmann's (1939) concept of adaptation, drive neutralization (e.g., delibidinization and deaggressivization), and change of function whereby instinctual drives are converted from peremptory unbound cathexes to neutralized members in the "parliament" of stable self- and object representations. The transformation from K (knowledge) to O (wisdom) may parallel the classical conception of sublimation.

The analyst must undergo "becoming O" to allow a transformation within himself of his counterexperience of the analysand's *alien* and *alienating* analytic object, O, so as to divine the pattern that orders and organizes it ("selected fact" or "strange attractor") and bind its infinity, chaos, and complexity with a name that gives it coherence as a constant conjunction. Bion referred to this as a transformation from O to K (T O→K). I believe that this formulation can be misleading.

It is my impression that the transformation that normally takes place (in the analyst) is one from (the experience of the analysand's) *alien* or *alienating* O to *accepted* O through the medium of *indexical* K. In other words, by virtue of the analysand's perception that his analyst (and, once upon a time, his mother) could *bear* O and be patient enough to wait and sort it out and be able to "translate" versions of it, the analysand, like his infant forebear, is able to accept his O as his own experience.

Thus, I see K as the catalyst, the midwife, as it were, to a transformation in the analysand's experience of O. *O remains O, however*. K is merely our way of binding not O per se, but our *experience* of O for tolerability. The O that we transform is thus a different (version of) O, an emotionally and personally bound one. It is almost as if K were our epistemological and ontological "transitional object" in the face of O, which we can bear only by making psychic icons of it, but really our "translation" of O is indexical, not iconic; our "translations" can only indicate or hint about the immediate intersection with us that O imposes. O always remains ineffable and inscrutable. It is as if O were saying, "Believe what you want about me. I am still O and you shall never know me."

However, I still believe that the essential transformation that takes place is between impersonal O and personal (emotional) O.

The name of a concept constantly conjoins its unknowable noumenal essence, the "thing-in-itself" with a phenomenal counterpart for normal symbolical linguistic employment. When we think or speak, we do so in terms of what Bion called "psychical mathematics," that is, the equivalents of abstractions of the original concept denoted by the symbols. Words may either be *iconic* (word) representations of the thing-in-itself, implying a direct correspondence to the experience being represented, or *indexical*, indicating a penumbra of associated meanings to the experience (Peirce, 1931). I understand Bion's use of transformations from O to K to imply that K is indexical and not generally iconic, the latter of which may connote more of a concrete transformation of O (e.g., the pagan gods of primitive religions or even the God of many current religions). Here I can only refer the reader to Jaynes's (1976) thesis that a primitive stage of nonconsciousness exists in the human being (he says in primitive man, but, by innuendo, also in the infant) who has a "bicameral mind" (for convenience, a two-hemisphere brain-mind dominated by the right hemisphere) in which Godlike voices in one domain exert omnipotent authority and control over another, subservient personality in the other domain.

EVOLUTIONS IN O: "O IS A DARK SPOT THAT MUST BE ILLUMINATED BY BLINDNESS"

Bion frequently appended the term evolutions to O experiences. Earlier I referred to his allusion to Heraclitus' adage that one could not enter the same river twice. I believe that the model of the river or the stream inheres in Bion's concept of "evolutions in O" in the following way: O is never static; it is always evolving. Thus, acceptance of its constantly evolving nature predicates the experience of "catastrophic change" (Bion, 1970). Bion suggested that O is constantly evolving in the analyst as well as in the analysand. In the analytic situation of container–contained (♀♂) the analyst's evolving O intersects with the analysand's evolving O. When this intersection becomes incarnate as an epiphany in the form of the "selected fact" (in the analyst), then the analyst is able to transmit his epiphany to the analysand, who, if agreeably prepared, accepts his analyst's version (transformation) of his O (unconscious experience as "analytic object") and experiences relief.[9] Eigen (1998) says," O represents the realness of anything. . . . O is inaccessible, unknowable, yet nothing is more accessible, since O is everywhere and everything We cannot know O, but what else can one know? (p. 81).

This sense of relief stems from the fact that his alien and alienating experience of emotional pain (O, the analytic object) has been converted (transduced downward) from ineffability and unbearable infinity, chaos, and complexity to tangible, finite terms that are acceptable (e.g., "good breast" and "bad breast"). In the meanwhile, his alien and alienating O (now transformed by alpha function) reenters the stream of O's continuing, cyclical evolution within one's emotional purview; that is, O continues to evolve but with progressively less intimidation to us. I conceive of this evolution of O as being continuous and continuing, and cyclical, connoting both the "the cycle of eternal return" posited by Nietzsche (1866) and the helical cycle of Giambattista Vico (1744). As Omar Khayyam advised in one of his Quatrains, "Pray ye not to the heavens for the heavens roll on as impotent as you and I." Put another way, because of the analyst's transformations of the analysand's psychic pain, the analysand is enabled to undergo a *metamorphosis* in which his alien and alienating experience of O is transformed into *personally* accepted O, as his own feelings belonging to his own being-in-the-world. In my analysis with Bion, he would never repeat an interpretation. He would say, "It cannot be repeated because it has already evolved while we are here talking. We must await its later transformation, downstream, so to speak."

---

9. I am grateful to Professor Ross Skelton (personal communication, 1999) for reminding me of Borges's (1989) haunting story, "The Aleph," in which he movingly captures both the essence of Bion's O and Matte-Blanco's concept of infinity and total symmetry in the first letter of the Hebrew alphabet and a point in space that contains all points.

THE UNCONSCIOUS FROM THE VERTEX[10] OF O: TOWARD THE CONCEPT OF A "COSMIC UNCONSCIOUS"

If we take Bion's concept of O to its full significance, we come upon a radical revision of the psychoanalytic concept of the unconscious. We must recall that, whereas Freud originally assigned unacceptable memories of childhood trauma to the unconscious, he thereupon discovered the importance that unconscious phantasies hold for infantile sexuality and for the libidinal drive, culminating in the Oedipus complex, which thereafter became the canon for then orthodox and later classical Freudian dogma. It was a psychology in which the vicissitudes of libido became the hidden order. Later, he was to append the death instinct, but his followers demurred in favor of plain aggression. It was Melanie Klein who was to make the death instinct the centerpiece for her unique version of infantile mental life. Thus, the ultimate content of the repressed for orthodox/classical or Kleinian analysis became the drives, variously considered.

Though Bion did not say so per se, his metatheory, with O as its centerpiece, suggests otherwise. Bion seems to imply that the unrepressed unconscious (that aspect of it which is under primal repression) contains the Platonic and Kantian "hardware" (Ideal Forms, inherent preconceptions, noumena, things-in-themselves, etc.). His conception of the dynamic unconscious is similar to Freud's. The inherent preconceptions are equated with O, the things-in-themselves, and noumena and constitute "thoughts without a thinker," which include the most inchoate notions of an as yet unrealized object,[11, 12] the breast, for instance. The inherent "hardware" also includes the "incarnation of the Godhead," by which I infer that he is suggesting the immanence of a numinous ("numen" [Greek] "god of the place") presence within us. He does not discuss this numinous entity in any detail, however.

---

10. Vertex is Bion's mathematical way of designating points of view or dimensions.

11. Segal's (1957) concept of symbolic equations refers to the primary process proliferation of possible meanings in the concrete mind of the psychotic. It is my impression that her concept fits in with my idea of the inchoate "incarnation" of the object emerging precociously from its a priori foundation as a preconception and prematurely meeting up with its realization.

12. I am indebted to Edmund Cohen (1999) for his illuminating distinction between Kant's concept of "Gegenstand" and "Object," the latter designating a phenomenal object of the senses and the former a noumenal, ineffable status of an object, really a subject.

I believe that Bion was implying that the immanent, "incarnate Godhead" *is* "the thinker of "the (alleged) thoughts without a thinker." Thus, to Bion the inchoate (ineffable subject) and the inchoate object are, in the first instance, numinous. My addendum to this notion is that what Bion called "Godhead" or "incarnation of the Godhead" is a preternatural entity that I term the "ineffable subject of the unconscious" (see chapter 5). A further addendum would be that the primordial, preternatural object, which Bion equated with the concept of inherent preconceptions and "things-in-themselves" constitute O in the first instance—and that these are the prime content of the infant's "fear of dying," which it must project into mother-as-container for her to alleviate. Thus, we have two preternatural presences (Godhead and object-as-thing-in-itself) occupying the unrepressed unconscious.

So far I have been discussing O as the primordially "subjective" and "objective" component of the unrepressed unconscious (that which remains under primal repression). O is also in the dynamic unconscious in the form of incompletely processed internalized container (subjective) objects into which O was formerly projected but without adequate containment by the real object. That to me is what an internalized object really is. I agree with Fairbairn (1941) that good objects do not need to be internalized. They, unlike bad subjective objects, can be mourned and thus allowed their freedom. An internalized object, in other words, represents unfinished business with processing O.

We must also take the work of Matte-Blanco (1975, 1981, 1988) into consideration (see chapter 3). In his mathematical treatises on the unconscious he was able to fathom that (a) the unconscious consists of categories rather than persons; (b) these categories (which include objects and affects) are infinite in nature, and (c) the unconscious is dominated by "bi-logic" (differing proportions of symmetrical and asymmetrical logic under the control of the principle of symmetry). His concepts helped to elaborate Bion's notion of the absoluteness and infinite nature of O, as well as the more subtle preternatural quality of psychic presences in the internal world. These "other-worldly' qualities owe their unique nature to the imaginative use of the scales of the bi-logic register, where the Infinite Geometer, or the demiurge, fashions them according to arbitrary choices of symmetry and asymmetry. O, then, would correspond to the coexistence of infinite symmetry (absolute indivisibility) and infinite *a*symmetry (absolute divisibility).

Bion divided the unconscious into what we may call, after Kant (1787), the transcendental, that is, the inborn apparatuses for "formatting" or apprehending phenomena in reality, and the phenomenal, experience with objects, the intersection with or impact from we must prepare ourselves for through primary and secondary categories; that is, to what preconception does the actual object correspond as a potential realization so as to form a conception, and then a concept?

In the transcendental category, under O, he included primary qualities, noumena, things-in-themselves, a priori categories (space, time, and causality), and others. To these Bion added Plato's archetypal Ideal Forms and inherent preconceptions. It is the other ingredients he adds to the mixture that cause us pause. These include Absolute Truth, Ultimate Reality, Emotional Truth, incarnation as the "Godhead," and so on. I shall focus on the first two now and return to the third later.

These ideas constitute a radical change for the concept of the unconscious. Instead of the drives being the ultimate signified horror of the repressed, we now see them in a more subordinate role as mediators, signifiers, and modifiers of something even more profound and more all-embracing—Absolute Truth, Ultimate Reality (not symbolic reality), which initially are inpersonal, indifferent, and obtrusive. To "learn from experience" we must come to grips with their presence and acknowledge our intersection with them by accepting our personal, subjective contact with them and accept their verdict. Existentially, they are our *Appointment in Samara*. Bion often stated that man's psyche needs truth as much as his body needs food. Thus, the search for truth, emotional truth, becomes the prime driving force of every human being, yet the fear of its consequences and realizations becomes his resistance. In other words, "evolving O" is identical with the relentless surge of Truth and Reality.

I have used the previous chapters of this book to develop the theme of psychic presences from different perspectives. Bion's contributions pave the way for our being able to conceptualize a primordial, transcendental, preternatural concept of a subject and an object, each awaiting its rendevous with realizations in life, not unlike Wordsworth's immortal infants awaiting earthly assignment in his "Intimations of Immortality."

WHERE IS THE UNCONSCIOUS—IN LIGHT OF O?

At this juncture I should like to explore the question of the location of the unconscious since Bion did not seem to confine the presence of O to an internal world. In this regard, Lacan (1966), many of whose radical views parallel those of Bion, proffered the idea that the unconscious is the Other and is structured like a language; that, in fact, it emerges from culture and language, that is, that it is a socially and linguistically collective unconscious and is all around us outside our awareness. One gets a hint of this same externality of the unconscious from Klein inadvertently from her depiction of the iterative and cyclical nature of projective identification—to the point that everyone eventually, to one degree or another, lives in a world inhabited by objects into whom they have projected aspects of themselves; thus, their unconscious surrounds them at any given moment.

But Bion implied something more. He postulated, as I have stated, that O comprises the a priori categories of the unrepressed unconscious (primal repression). It is *my* counterpostulation that this O is "potential O"—as noumenon or thing-in-itself or inherent preconception. Potential O becomes activated as "active O" when the inherent preconceptions too actively and thus chaotically seek their realizations in external reality *in advance of the infant's—and mother's—ability to harness them into orderly containment*. Thus, whereas the unrepressed unconscious may be internal, the dynamic one may be all too external as well as internal—thus cosmic.

An analysand reported the following dream.

Mother was living in two-story penthouse. She abruptly left because she could not handle the baby. A crazy girl then appeared who tried to attack the baby. Meanwhile, after mother left, she tried to hire a taxi to return to the penthouse but had no money so she walked home. Mother couldn't sleep when she returned. She knew that I had been in danger and realized that somebody had been trying to break into the penthouse. A nice guy then appeared who was trying to help us. We did a show for him.

I report this dream to demonstrate the analysand's experience of supposedly being mothered by an immature woman who was afraid of not being able to handle her baby and so fled. The analysand was stimulated to dream these thoughts because of my vacation break. Thus, I, the analyst, was both the mother and the "nice guy" who helped. The "crazy girl" who broke in was a primitive and omnipotent aspect of the analysand who took control in the object's absence. Of importance here is her estimation of her mother's (analyst's) capacity to bear her daughter's experience of dread (O) and her own experience of dread as well.

Bion, in discussing container and contained, states that the mother contains her infant's fear of dying. I understand this to mean that the infant fears dying because of the spontaneous activation of its death instinct, which is automatically brought into operation by its initial confrontation of experiences with O. One of the effects of maternal containment of the infant's anxiety is: if O is O.K. with mother, then it can have faith that it will ultimately be O.K. with itself. In the meantime, the infant must trust that mother will repress those aspects of O for which it does not yet feel ready to accept back from mother at this time. The return of O must await the infant's maturation and development, at which time it becomes experienced as the "return of the repressed" (Freud, 1915). The mother—and the father—should have achieved the depressive position in regard to their experiencing a sense of responsibility and penitence for initiating the conception and birth of an unaware and unconsulted individual. Their penitence and sorrow constitutes their side of a covenant with their newborn. Their ratification of the covenant, paves the way for the newborn child's willingness to accept responsibility for his own life experiences.

Extremes of persecutory anxiety reveal the *failure* of P-S to mediate O. P-S, through its propensity for protest of unfairness, allows the subject to have his sense of agency stamped and notarized by his belief in the subjective personalness of his alleged victimization on the part of the alleged persecutor.

INTERNAL OBJECTS AND O

Another idea springs from these thoughts: what are traditionally called internal objects might now be understood to be "carriers of O" in various states of incomplete-to-complete containment. In other words, the inherent preconception is the inchoate "object" that represents O. The later internal object of the individual represents the combination of the perceived external object plus the O that the infant has projected into it as container. Klein's concept of reparations in the depressive position would, from this point of view, have new meaning; the task of reparation for the infant is to "deprogram" its objects by reaccepting the projected O from them.

Yet another aspect of the projective identification of O is that of the intergenerational and transgenerational neurosis (see chapter 8), which can now be understood, from the vertex of O, as the parents (and their parents and culture), who are unable to tolerate the O of their lives, unconsciously pass on to their own children (via projective identification) their own failure to contain O. They thereby create the default obligation for their children—and their children's children—to become their future messiahs (and, secretly, scapegoats) of omnipotent hope for the future. One of the most damaging effects of child abuse may be the child's perception that his abusive or corrupting parent is unable to face life (O); therefore the child cannot either. This recognition may set in operation what Fairbairn (1943b) called the "moral defense," in which the child selectively internalizes and identifies with the bad and feared aspects of the needed object in order to maintain the illusion of the parent's goodness and fitness to be a parent.

The impact of the bad object on the subject is such that it selectively mobilizes those horrifying premonitions of the former within the subject, which Bion (1963) termed "inherent preconceptions" and associated with Kant's noumena and "things-in-themselves." These comprise an inherent template of possibilities, an experience-anticipating repertoire, as it were, that helps the subject to format its receptive sensory screen in order to make sense of what otherwise would be utterly unrecognizable. Given the reality of a truly bad mother, consequently, the selective mobilization of these corresponding preconceptions would thereupon impart a negatively loaded validity to the subject's conviction of being implicitly bad vis-à-vis his inherent being.

"THOUGHTS WITHOUT A THINKER"

The concept of the incarnation as the "Godhead" requires more discussion. The unconscious is also characterized by infinity (infinite sets—Matte-Blanco, 1975, 1981, 1988), absolute indivisibility (total symmetry), and absolute divisibility (total asymmetry), thus eventuating in chaos or complexity. Furthermore, Bion, the polymath, informs us that every object in the unconscious implies its opposite or its negative. The human being is apparently predisposed unconsciously to personify the chaos with Godhead and devil, each negating the other while "containing" the chaos. Further, Bion's insistence on a Godhead within derives from the heretical mystic Christians, such as the Gnostics and such mystics as Meister Eckhart, as well as the Jewish mystic Isaac Luria.

To the whirling swarm of infinites and fearful symmetries and asymmetries coursing across the inner, boundless landscape Bion attached the term "thoughts without a thinker," particularizing them as beta (β) elements, which he considered as equivalent to, noumena, things-in-themselves, and so on. He considered them nonmental until they have undergone "alpha-bet(a)-ization" by alpha function. I disagree. If we juxtapose Bion's concept of one's incarnation with the Godhead, we can contemplate an internal "deity," one whom I have termed the "Ineffable Subject of the Unconscious," a numinous entity within us who organizes the unconscious. I now believe that the phenomena that Bion observed in the disturbed thinking processes of psychotics and borderlines, which he characterized as being dominated by "beta elements," should be reclassified as "beta" (prime) elements, the "prime" designating that the infant or psychotic "knows" them as premonitions but denies knowing them after the fact because of feeling unable to tolerate the significance their acceptance would generate.

I have characterized this numen as the Dreamer Who Dreams the Dream and the Dreamer Who Understands It. It is the one who decides what is to be the subject for the analytic session's "free" associations." It is the Thinker of the putative "thoughts without a thinker." It is also the infinite geometer who wields the arms of the mighty calipers of symmetry and asymmetry over the infinite landscape of the unconscious. It is also Plato's demiurge, the architect and creator of our internal world, who also is the dramaturge, who arranges the dialectical passion plays of our dreams and our analyses. It is also the mystic or genius, in Bion's (1970) lexicon, who carries the "messianic message," and who, therefore, corresponds to Bollas's (1979) "transformational object."

To clarify the problem, one must consider the matter of perspective. We must remember that O, that is, beta elements, do not ever change. They do not become transformed. They only evolve. It is the individual who must change in regard to his experience of the beta elements, O. They are thoughts all along. The human being must achieve the maturity and development to encompass their presence so as to accommodate to them and assimilate them.

Bion called attention to the fact that the Eden, Tower of Babel, and oedipal myths all point to the idea of the deity's injunction against the pursuit of knowledge—or even truth. The infant needs to be protected against too much—or too premature—realization of K because K may lead to O, thus precipitating an avalanche in which things-in-themselves (noumena) become realized prematurely as precocious conceptions, a catastrophic state in which they become "orphans of the Real." Here one might invoke the idea of the "overdosage of sorrow" (see chapter 1). We can now hypothesize that Klein's (1946) concept of the paranoid-schizoid position can be read as an imagistic gating system that mercifully, because selectively, permits indifferent O to become gradually personified, emotionalized, and subjectified.

CONTAINER–CONTAINED AND O

Bion (1962a) originally formulated the concept of the container and contained when he began to realize that his psychotic patients had suffered from too little opportunity for a maternal container for their infantile projections. In the course of working out how the mother functions as a container, he discovered the maternal state of reverie, which he found was achieved through the abandonment of the verdict of the senses, that is, memory, desire, understanding, preconceptions, or anything sensuously apprehended. In other words, the mother had to achieve a state of meditative surrender to her task as monitor over her infant's states of mind. The infant projects its raw, "unmentalized" protoaffects into mother-as-container for mother to accept, sustain, delay, and process so as to translate for appropriate action.

It generally is thought that in her container function she sorts out those signals that need effective responses from her. How she does this is so interesting that Bion virtually created a whole new psychoanalytic technology around it. As I understand it, the mother (and analyst), after attaining a meditative-like state of reverie (abandonment of memory, desire), employs her "sense organ that is sensitive to internal stimuli" using her alpha function in the form of intuition. In this ready-alert state of immersion, she becomes able to tune in to her own inner feelings and emotional scenarios that match up with or correspond to those she experiences—by way of an ineffable process of resonance—with her infant's projected protofeelings. This operation bears some resemblance to the "method acting" techniques of Stanislavski (1936).[13]

While this is true, I believe that her container function also includes mirroring and repression. The infant externalizes itself into mother for what Bion often referred to as a "second opinion." Mother's response constitutes a mirroring "second opinion" about who the infant is—to her—and thus to itself.

Further, Alpha function must transform beta elements from O into alpha elements in the form of images. Here we may link Lacan's (1966) concept of the Register of the Imaginary with Klein's (1946) concept of the paranoid-schizoid position and Bick's (1968, 1986) and Melzer's (1975) concept of adhesive identification, Anzieu's (1985) "skin ego," and Ogden's (1989) idea of the autistic-contiguous position, all concepts that address the archaic skin-perceptual organization of experience. Thus, transformations in L and H, governed as they are by superseding K (or –K) produce phantasies or perceptual narrative myths (Tomkins, 1978), which reside in archetypal or collective myths (inherent preconceptions).

The maternal container as an agency for repression has not been suggested. Before mother must decide how much of O the infant can process and how much has to be postponed–by her–in her. When the infant internalizes the mother-as-container, the process of repression

13. As I stated earlier, Bion (1962a, 1963) believed that initially the infant possesses no alpha function of its own and then internalizes and identifies with its experiences with its mother's use of her alpha function. I believe otherwise—that alpha function, like Chomsky's (1968) transformational generative syntax, constitutes a Kantian a priori given.

itself becomes internalized with her within the infant. The "return of the repressed" is then stimulated by circumstance within the context of the now internalized maternal protectiveness.

THE DEATH INSTINCT AND O

Klein (1933) believed that how the infant was able to handle his death instinct was the ultimate criterion for his mental health or psychopathology. It is now my impression that the ultimate feared signified is *alien* and *alienating* O and that the infant unconsciously summons the "light militia of the lower sky," its death instinct, as it were, in order to combat this infinite emotional turbulence, by obliterating either the perception of the experience or the mind that cannot bear the experience. Something similar may be said about omnipotence. In my analysis with Bion he frequently stressed that "one is *reduced* to feeling omnipotent because of one's feelings of helplessness and vulnerability." Thus, omnipotence, which is secondary, is summoned, along with the death instinct, by the beleaguered infant within us to control or even destroy our connections to reality in order for us to survive.

THE POSITION OF THE "POSITIONS"

Bion frequently referred to a dialectical relationship between the paranoid-schizoid and depressive positions as thus: P-S ↔D. He also suggested that the term paranoid-schizoid should be reserved for pathological states; he would employ the term patience for the normal stance of the person who encounters the beta elements of O and can be patient long enough for a pattern to emerge. He assigned "security" to the achievement of the depressive position upon the victory of patience. Thus, patience and security became his protocol, along with the abandonment of memory, desire, understanding, and preconception, for being a psychoanalyst—or mother. At other times, particularly in *Cogitations* (Bion, 1992), he also recommended that the analyst collect and make use of as many myths as he can get hold of because he believed that myths constitute binding, constant conjunctions. By myths he meant collective, as well as individual, myths and phantasies.

In other contributions I have reconsidered the evolution of the Kleinian concepts of the paranoid-schizoid and depressive positions (Grotstein, 1993a, 1996, see also chapters 8 and 9) and came to the following conclusions: (a) that the paranoid-schizoid position is not necessarily pathological but, rather, is a mediator or filter for O, as are the activities of the depressive position;[14] and (b) that the depressive position has never been sufficiently defined in terms of differentiating between an infantile depressive illness (melancholia) to be transcended and a state of successful mourning over departed objects that one is to achieve.

Bion spoke of L, H, and K linkages to objects but never suggested that they participate in transformations. It is my impression that the P-S position constitutes a mediating filter against the blinding glare of O's radiant darkness and terror and inchoately transforms the beta elements of O into KL and KH. In other words, the infant begins to "know about" O through the medium of conscious and unconscious phantasies, inherent affect scenarios (Tomkins, 1978), fairy stories, and various kinds of myths in order to bind his anxiety. When he is able to accept his separateness, he then is able to tolerate the depressive position.

To me, both positions shield[15] the infant from O. It has been generally understood since Klein that the infant attacks the breast in the paranoid-schizoid position and must repair the damage in the depressive position. I now believe that the infant must project its intolerable experiences with O into mother and then reown these projections in the depressive position as well as recognize the putative impact these projections may have had for her. Finally, the infant must, after achieving the depressive position, transcend it so as to achieve serenity in the transcendent position.

THE MUTUALITY OF THE DEPRESSIVE POSITIONS OF INFANT AND MOTHER

Bion often suggested that the analyst—and, by implication, the mother—must be in the depressive position in order to be able to attain the state of reverie and must use patience so as to access their alpha function and achieve intuition. Klein (1945) suggested that, to undertake the task of

14. Here I can only hint at my belief that the Kleinian concept of the depressive position is seriously in need of reconceptualization. Briefly, the depressive position is being asked to satisfy two incompatible tasks: (a) the registration of clinical infantile *depressive (melancholic) illness*, and (b) *mourning*. The manic and the depressive defenses constitute the former, and pining and reparation the latter.

15. Thus, from this point of view, the paranoid-schizoid positions constitute a veritable "ozone layer" or "Reitschutz" (shield—Freud, 1920) against the potential devastation of O.

reparations, the infant needs the help of its object. I take these two points as one theorem to help launch yet a new theorem, that of the *mutual depressive position*, by which I mean that, to enter the depressive position, the infant (or analysand) requires a mother (or analyst) who is securely ensconced within it. This is another way of stating that, whereas Klein dealt with the positions from the vertex of the infant's autochthonous (self-created) psychic reality alone (infantile neurosis), Fairbairn (1949) dealt with the positions strictly from the vertex of external reality as correctly perceived by the infant (infantile trauma). I suggest that the two points of view occupy a "dual-track" (Grotstein, 1978a).

I believe that this principle—about the necessity for the mutuality of the depressive positions in infant and mother—also applies to another, even more foundational experience in the infant. Bion repeatedly stated that, to be able to think (learn from experience), the infant must be able to tolerate frustration long enough to allow for the concept of an empty space (a "no-breast"), which then can facilitate the mating of a preconception of a breast with a realization of it to form a conception of it. He alluded to constitutional variations in infants as the background for this tolerance or intolerance of frustration. Today we realize, thanks to infant-development research, that this infantile capacity for tolerance of frustration is largely a function of successful maternal bonding and attunement. Once again, the mother must have achieved the depressive position if her infant hopes to do so.

One must also recognize the presence of yet another mutual enterprise, that of the mutuality of the alpha function in the infant with its mother's alpha function and, correspondingly, between analysand and analyst. Whereas Bion spoke only of the presence and activity of alpha function in the mother analyst, it is my belief that the infant is born with the rudiments of its own alpha function as an inherent category corresponding to Chomsky's (1957, 1968) concept of an inherent "deep structure." Thus, the infant/analysand, does not wantonly project into its mother/analyst; *it projects in a prearranged code whose wavelength is understandable to* the container/mother/analyst.

THE GRID

It is logical to assume that Bion's grid is not only a tool for the analyst to use after an analytic session. After one really examines the grid, it becomes apparent, at least to me, that the grid represents a universal Rosetta Stone, as it were, whereby the analyst *and* the analysand unconsciously process the "hieroglyphic" of new information, particularly emotional information and follow its developmental progression and evolution as thoughts *and* the uses to which these thought are destined. Put another way, the grid symbolically represents how we normally respond emotionally-epistemophilically, how we *unconsciously* process new ideas, correlate them with already established ones, and confront the "catastrophic change" that emerges on the frontier between the new and the old. Further, the grid represents not only how the analyst thinks (left brain) after receiving the "selected fact" (right brain), it also represents how the analysand unconsciously processes the insights from the analyst. In other words, the grid represents how we normally think without realizing it.

THE TRANSCENDENT POSITION

My conception of the transcendent position differs from that of the paranoid-schizoid and depressive positions insofar as it is even less time- or stage-bound than they are. Transcendent means having the ability to transcend our defensiveness, our pettiness, our guilt, our shame, our narcissism, our need for certainty, our strictures in order to achieve or to become "one with O," which I interpret as becoming one with our *aliveness* (Ogden, 1997) or with our very *being-ness* (our *Dasein*; Heidegger, 1927).

Caveats

Some caveats are in order before I proceed. First, I use the term transcendent or transcending as a way of approximating Bion's quintessential episteme; and while it may *seem* to have religious/spiritual/ "mystical" overtones, as well as a parallel usage in analytical psychology (Jung, 1939), my usage is confined to the psychoanalytic and epistemological vertices even when applied to mysticism itself. The concept of a transcendent position does not constitute a whimsical journey into lofty, ethereal abandon, nor does it necessarily validate religion, spirituality, or the belief in God, except as a need by humans whereby they attempt to close the maw of the ineffable with an all-encompassing name. It is not in the oeuvre of W. Somerset Maugham's Larry Darrell, the protagonist in *The Razor's Edge* who sought "enlightenment" atop the Himalayas. In other words, it is not a blissful, "autistic enclave." O is one's reality without pretense or distortion. This reality can be a symptom, the pain of viewing beautiful autumn leaves, gazing on the mystique of Mona Lisa de la Giocanda, contemplating the horror of Ypres (for Bion), trying to remember Hiroshima, Nagasaki, Auschwitz, or Viet Nam, or resting comfortably beside one's mate trying to contemplate the exquisiteness and ineffability of the moment.

Transcendence is the mute "Other" that lies "just beyond, within, and around" where we are. It is the core of our very Being-in-itself. The mystic or genius is that aspect of us which is potentially able to be at one (transcendent) with O—but only after we have "cleared" with P-S and D. *The mystic, according to Bion, is one who sees things as they really are—through the deception or camouflage of words and symbols.* It is fascinating how the word mysticism has acquired such prejudice. The generally feared connotation of "mysticism" has occurred through the projective identification of "mystique" onto it by those who, according to Bion, are afraid of truth and so mystify its clarity.

The quality of rationalism has always distinguished psychoanalysis from other empirically based phenomenological psychologies, but the rationalism that inheres in psychoanalysis had always been confined to its positivistic *Zeitgeist* in regard to the instinctual drives. The question that Bion confronted was *how do we format our minds to receive the events we confront in order to render (transduce) them into personal and then objective experiences?* Bion became dissatisfied, I believe, with the positivistic limitations of Freud's drive theory and even of Klein's extension of them as unconscious phantasies. He was aware that the rationalistic enterprise required transcendental (a priori) considerations beyond the drives that could account for the uniqueness of how we format our experiences, that is, prepare a suitable container that can anticipate its future contents. In considering these a priori categories, he borrowed the concept of the Ideal Forms from Plato and termed them "inherent preconceptions," which, along with the sensory apparatus (as "common sense"), container–contained, L, H, and K linkages, and intuition (with reverie), became the instruments of apprehending the "psychoanalytic object" and resonating with O (Ultimate Truth, Absolute Reality).

In his epistemological pilgrimage, Bion retraced the philosophical contributions of leading thinkers of the past, including Plato, Aristotle, Meister Eckhart, Hume, and Kant in particular. He also consulted mathematicians like Poincaré and Georg Cantor. The point of resorting to mathematics was to arrive at tools for understanding that were unsaturated with preconceived meanings. His endeavor was to find out what inheres within us that allows us to grasp, process, and internalize our experiences so that we can grow from them. Ultimately, he was to come upon *O* and *intuition*, the former being, in the Kantian sense, a *transcendent* entity and the latter a *transcendental* (a priori) entity which allows us to divine the beyond from the inherent, a priori "beyond" within us (Bion, 1965, 1970, 1992). These achievements are hard to overestimate. They constitute an epistemic and ontological metapsychological metatheory that elegantly extends and graces Klein's enterprise as well as that of Freud's. This metatheory, especially with the Truth[16] of emotional experience as its centerpiece and driving force, Faith as its all-hovering guardian and presence[17] and O as its origin and realization introduce not only epistemic and ontological theory into psychoanalysis but also teleology and especially transcendence.

CLINICAL EXAMPLES

Of the countless case examples I could employ to illustrate O in the clinical setting, let me give two brief ones:

R.W. is a 32-year-old married woman who has been in psychotherapy on and off since she was a child. She entered analysis with me because of obsessively intrusive thoughts about the welfare of her twin brother. Her parents divorced when she was two years old, whereupon she and her twin were sent to live with an aunt in a distant part of the country. Apparently her mother was emotionally unable to care for them, and her father showed little or no interest or concern. She has a haunting early memory of getting on a train and feeling absolute terror.

One Monday morning, early in the analysis after a vacation break, she burst into my office in a starkly terrified state of mind. She had not heard from her brother, she exclaimed, and dreaded that he had "gone off the wagon" and would die. I cannot summon all the associations in her mind and mine that led me to the following interpretation, but the "clinical facts" had been gathered for some time and had a coherence to them for me.

I interpreted: "My being gone for so long [on my vacation] left you alone with your inner voices without my protection. I think you might have felt that my leaving had become equated with mother's sending you away on the train because she couldn't bear *your* needy demands, let alone those of your brother. You felt you were a bad child because you were needy and demanding. More than that, you were so terrified that mother—and father too—could not bear not only you and your brother but life as well. They capitulated, and that scared you even more."

---

16. I believe that Ogden's (1997) new concept of "aliveness" is either congruent or closely associated with Bion's concept of Absolute Truth/Ultimate Reality as well as with Heidegger's (1927) beingness (*Dasein*).

17. By "presence" in this situation I have in mind my concept of the background presence of primary identification (Grotstein, 1978).

The analysand became silent and thoughtful for an extended moment and then replied: "I feel so relieved that you're not afraid of me, that you can have your own life and then can return to me ready to help me. It gives me confidence when I see that you are confident."

Another analysand, M.R., was brilliant poet and writer from a background in which he had felt terribly ignored by his parents, who disregarded his sensitivities, awkwardness, and eccentricity. As a child he was diagnosed as "autistic" (which I believe was a misdiagnosis). But he was facing a stressful situation in his professional life with great courage. He then had the following dream:

I was in a far-out laser theater or studio. There were other people there, and there were also special-effects personnel putting away their gear. And then the people began slowly to disappear, one by one—or I thought they did, but then they seemed to reappear differently. I then had a monologue with myself in the dream in which I said: "We are all props and are put away at the end of the play—or we put them away—until the illusion is needed again. Human beings are not supposed to know this. Only God does. Nothing is real. We are not real. We are taken out for the recurrence of the illusion and put away again afterwards. In the dream I felt that for a human being to realize this was rare or maybe even dangerous.

Associations

"This was not knowledge for a human to have. It's like life is a play in which we let the play generate the emotions of life. God was giving me a vision of this awareness. Maybe there are people who are dying to know this. Maybe that's a pun. Maybe people realize this only when they *are* dying. Death is the storage of this truth. Am I learning this because I'm about to die? Or am I getting this knowledge in order to keep sane and not go over the brink?

"The studio or theater with the lasers displays was more than a special-effects studio. It was the condition of life. People appear to us, recite their immediate agonies and griefs, and then the sun comes up, and the people are still there but the grief is gone. The need to be miserable is a service of self-enactment.

"One needs to do this to call attention to oneself. Otherwise, one needs to have compassion for oneself. In other words, there seems to be a need for reenactment and demonstration of one's senses or feelings. But *it* is always going on. We witness *it* only when our sorrows seem to need to be reenacted. The human condition is always going on. *It* causes us a pinprick when out attention wanders and goes somewhere else. The suffering, the hunger, the grief, the guy in Kosovo?—No, that's not *it*.

"The examples are everywhere and are constant. We believe that our sadness is important at our own peril. Kosovo, no matter how horrible, has no real significance—except as an example of the ongoing human condition. It is part of the saturated solution of circumstance and part of our compelling propensity for repetition and reactivation. We need compassion and recognition, yet to have tantrums about our pains, though real, is unnecessary. Responding to a crisis by entering or declaring a crisis is a disguise of *it*. None of the mobilization I set in motion yesterday in regard to my job was really necessary. I was in a state of unnecessary overkill. I need to acknowledge, in daily, minute-by-minute episodes, that I do not need to get hysterical and enter into crises. In the scheme of things I did not need to create a crisis. The whole thing did not need that response. One was only a prop for the reenactment of the evolving human condition. The insistence that everything is personal is not required."

I leave the discussion of this case at this point with the assurance to the reader that the analysand is, in my opinion, not psychotic. I believe he comes closer to being what Bion termed a mystic, who, in the epiphany of this dream and in his subsequent associations, hinted that he might contain the "messiah thought"—about O. In other words, he had, in my opinion, touched the transcendent position.

> World, world, I am scared
> and waver in awe before the wilderness
> of raw consciousness; and it is real
> this passion that we feel for forms.
> But the forms are never real.
> Are not really there. Are not.
>
> —William M. Bronck (1956)
> from *Light and Dark*.

REFERENCES

Abelin, E. L. (1980). Triangulation: The role of the father in the origin of core-gender identity during the rapprochement sub-phase. In: *Rapprochement*, ed. R. F. Lax, S. Bach & J. A. Burlend. New York: Aronson, pp. 151–169.

Abraham, K. (1924). The influence of oral erotism on character formation. In: *Selected Papers*. London: Hogarth Press, 1948, pp. 393–406.

Ainsworth, M. D., Bell, S. & Stayton, D. J. (1974). Infant-mother attachment and social development: Socialization as a product of reciprocal responsiveness to signals In: *The Integration of a Child into a Social World*, ed. M. D. M. Richard. Cambridge: Cambridge University Press, pp. 99–135.

Ainsworth, M. D. S. & Wittig, B. (1969). Attachment and exploratory behavior of one-year olds in a strange situation. In: *Determinants of Infant Behavior, Vol. 4*, ed. B. M. Foss. London: Methuen, pp. 111–136.

Andresen, J. J. (1984). The motif of sacrifice and the sacrifice complex. *Contemp. Psychoanal.*, 20:526–559.

Anzieu, D. (1984). *The Group and the Unconscious*, trans. B. Kilbourne. London: Routledge & Kegan Paul.

Apprey, M. (1987a). Projective identification and maternal misconception in disturbed mothers. *Brit. J. Psychother.*, 4(1):5–22.

Apprey, (1987b). "When one dies another lives": The invariant unconscious fantasy in response to a destructive maternal. *J. Melanie Klein Soc.*, 2:18–53.

Apprey, M. & Stein, H. F. (1991). *Intersubjectivity, Projective Identification, and Otherness*. Charlottesville: University Press of Virginia.

Bakhtin, M. (1981). *The Dialogic Imagination: Four Essays*, ed. M. Holguist (trans. C. Emerson). Austin: University of Texas Press.

Balmary, M. (1979). *Psychoanalyzing Psychoanalysis: Freud and the Hidden Fault of the Father*, trans. N. Lukacher. Baltimore, MD: Johns Hopkins University Press, 1982.

Baron-Cohen, S. (1995). *Mindblindness: Essays on Autism and Theory of Mind*. Cambridge, MA: MIT Press.

Baudelaire, C. (1857). *Les Fleur du Mal [The Flowers of Evil]*, trans. R. Howard. Boston, MA: Godine, 1982.

Beaconsfield, P., Birdwood, G. & Beaconsfield, R. (1980). The placenta. *Scient. Amer.*, 243(2):94–102.

Belsky, J., Garduque, L. & Harncir, E. (1984). Assessing performance, competence, and executive capacity in infant play: Relations to home environment and security of attachment. *Devel. Psychol.*, 20:406–417.

Benjamin, J. (1995). *Like Subjects, Love Objects: Essays on Recognition and Sexual Difference*. New Haven, CT: Yale University Press.

Bergmann, M. (1992). *In the Shadow of Moloch: The Sacrifice of Children and Its Impact on Western Religions*. New York: Columbia University Press.

Bettelheim, B. (1976). *The Uses of Enchantment*. New York: Knopf.
Bettelheim, B. (1983). *Freud and Man's Soul*. New York: Knopf.
Bick, E. (1968). The experience of the skin in early object relations. *Internat. J. Psycho-Anal.*, 49:484–486.
Bion, W. R. (1959). Attacks on linking. In: *Second Thoughts*. London: Heinemann, 1967, pp. 93–109.
Bion, W. R. (1961). *Experiences in Groups*. London: Tavistock.
Bion, W. R. (1962b). *Learning From Experience*. London: Heinemann.
Bion, W. R. (1962a). A theory of thinking. *Internat. J. Psycho- Anal.*, 43:306–310.
Bion, W. R. (1963). *Elements of Psycho-analysis*. London: Heinemann.
Bion, W. R. (1965). *Transformations: Change from Learning to Growth*. New York: Basic Books.
Bion, W. R. (1967). *Second Thoughts: Selected Papers on Psychoanalysis*. London: Heinemann.
Bion, W. R. (1970). *Attention and Interpretation*. London: Tavistock.
Bion, W. R. (1975). *A Memoir of the Future. Book I: The Dream*, ed. J. Salomão. Rio de Janeiro: Imago Editora.
Bion, W. R. (1977a). *Two Papers: The Grid and the Caesura*, ed. J. Salomâo. Rio de Janeiro: Imago Editora.
Bion, W. R. (1977b). *A Memoir of the Future. Book II: The Past Presented*. Rio de Janeiro: Imago Editora.
Bion, W. R. (1979). *A Memoir of the Future. Book III: The Dawn of Oblivion*. Perthshire, UK: Clunie Press.
Bion, W. R. (1982). *The Long Week-End 1897–1919: Part of a Life*, ed. F. Bion. Oxfordshire, UK: Perthshire Press.
Bion, W. R. (1992). *Cogitations*, ed. F. Bion. London: Karnac Books.
Black, S. J. & Hyatt, C. S. (1993). *Pacts with the Devil: A Chronicle of Sex, Blasphemy, and Liberation*. Phoenix, AZ: New Falcon.
Blake, W. (1789–1794). *Songs of Innocence and Experience*. Oxford: Oxford University Press, 1967.
Blomfield, O. H. D. (1985). Parasitism, projective identification and the Faustian bargain. *Internat. J. Psycho-Anal.*, 12:299–310.
Bloom, H. (1983). *Kabbalah and Criticism*. New York: Seabury Press.
Bloom, H. (1996). *Omens of Millennium: The Gnosis of Angels, Dreams, and Resurrection*. New York: Riverhead Books.
Bollas, C. (1979). The transformational object. *Internat. J. Psycho-Anal.*, 60:97–107.
Bollas, C. (1987). *The Shadow of the Object: Psychoanalysis of the Unthought Known*. London: Free Association Books.
Bollas, C. (1989). *Forces of Destiny: Psychoanalysis and Human Idiom*. London: Free Association Books.
Bollas, C. (1992). *Being a Character: Psychoanalysis and Self Experience*. New York: Hill & Wang.
Bomford, R. (1990). The attributes of God and the characteristics of the unconscious. *Internat. Rev. Psycho-Anal.*, 17:485–492.
Bomford, R. (1996). One, two, three, and God. Presented at the Ulmer Workshop: The Logic of the Unconscious: An Introduction to Matte-Blanco's Bi-Logic, March 22/23, Ulm, Germany.

Bomford, R. (1999). *The Symmetry of God*. London: Free Association Books.

Boothby, R. (1991). *Death and Desire: Psychoanalytic Theory in Lacan's Return to Freud*. New York: Routledge.

Borch-Jacobsen, M. (1982). *The Freudian Subject*, trans. C. Porter. Stanford, CA: Stanford University Press.

Borch-Jacobsen, M. (1996). *Remembering Anna O: A Century of Mystification*. London: Routledge.

Borges, J. L. (1989). The Aleph. In: *Jorge Luis Borges: Collected Fictions*, trans. A. Hurley. New York: Viking, 1998, pp. 274–286.

Boston, M. (1975). Recent research in developmental psychology. *J. Child Psychother.*, 4:15– 34.

Bowen, M. (1960). The family concept of schizophrenia. In: *The Idealogy of Schizophrenia*, ed. D. D. Jackson. New York: Basic Books.

Bowen, M. (1978). *Family Therapy in Clinical Practice*. New York: Aronson.

Bower, T. G. R. (1971). The object in the world of the infant. *Scient. Amer.*, Oct:30–38.

Bower, T. G. R. (1974). *Development in Infancy*. San Francisco: Freeman.

Bowlby, J. (1969). *Attachment and Loss, Vol. I: Attachment*. New York: Basic Books.

Breger, L. (1967). Function of dreams. *J. Abn. Psychol.*, 72:1–28.

Breger, L., Hunter, I. & Lane, R. W. (1971). *The Effect of Stress on Dreams*. New York: International Universities Press.

Brentano, F. (1874). *Psychology from an Empirical Standpoint*, trans. A. C. Rancurello, D. B. Terrell & L. L. McAllister. New York: Humanities Press, 1973.

Briggs, K. (1976). *An Encyclopedia of Fairies: Hobgoblins, Brownies, Bogies, and Other Supernatural Creatures*. New York: Pantheon Books.

Britton, R. (1998). *Belief and Imagination: Explorations in Psychoanalysis*. London: Routledge.

Britton, R. & Steiner, J. (1994). Interpretation: Selected fact or overvalued idea? *Internat. J. Psycho-Anal.*, 75:1069–1078.

Bronk, W. (1956). *Light and Dark*. Hoboken, NJ: Talisman House.

Brown, L. J. (1987). Borderline personality organization and the transition to the depressive position. In: *The Borderline Patient: Emerging Concepts in Diagnosis, Psychodynamics, and Treatment*, Vol. 1, ed. J. S. Grotstein, M. F. Solomon & J. A. Lang. Hillsdale, NJ: The Analytic Press, pp. 147–180.

Brown, S. (1991). *Late Corsican Child Sacrifice and the Sacrificial Monuments in the Mediterranean Context*. Sheffield, UK: JSOT Press.

Bucci, W. (1985). Dual coding: A cognitive model for psychoanalytic research. *J. Amer. Psychoanal. Assn.*, 33:571–608.

Bulfinch, T. (1935). *The Age of Fable or Beauties of Mythology*. New York: Tudor.

Burkert, W. (1983). *Homo Necans: The Anthropology of Ancient Greek Sacrificial Ritual and Myth*, trans. P. Bing. Berkeley: University of California Press.

Burkert, W. (1996). *Creation of the Sacred: Tracks of Biology in Early Religions*. Cambridge, MA: Harvard University Press.

Busch, F. (1996). *The Ego at the Center of Clinical Technique*. Northvale, NJ: Aronson.

Butterworth, G. E., Harris, P. L., Leslie, A. M. & Wellman, H. M., eds. (1991). *Perspectives on the Child's Theory of Mind*. Oxford: Oxford University Press.

Calasso, R. (1993). *The Marriage of Cadmus and Harmony*. New York: Vintage Books.

Caldwell, R. (1989). *The Origin of the Gods: A Psychoanalytic Study of Greek Theogonic Myth*. New York: Oxford University Press.

Campbell, J. (1949). *The Hero with a Thousand Faces*. Princeton, NJ: Princeton University Press.

Campbell, J., ed. (1955). *The Mysteries: Papers from the Eranos Yearbooks*. Bollinger Series XXX. Princeton, NJ: Princeton University Press.

Cantor, G. (1915). *Contributions to the Founding of the Theory of Transfinite Numbers*, trans. P. E. B. Jourdain. New York: Dover.

Carroll, L. (1872). *Through the Looking-Glass and What Alice Found There*. New York: Macmillan, 1971.

Cassam, Q. (1997). *Self and World*. Oxford: Clarendon Press.

Cassidy, J. & Berlin, L. J. (1994). The insecure/ambivalent pattern of attachment: theory and research. *Child Devel.*, 65:971–991.

Cath, S. H. (1982). Adolescence and addiction to alternative belief systems: Psychoanalytic and psychophysiological considerations. *Psychoanal. Inq.*, 2:619–676.

Chessick, R. (1995). Who does He think *He* is: Remarks on the psychology of Jesus. *Amer. J. Psychoanal.*, 55:29–40.

Chomsky, N. (1957). *Syntactic Structures*. The Hague: Mouton.

Chomsky, N. (1968). *Language and Mind*. New York: Harcourt, Brace & World.

Cohen, E. (1999). Clinical Kant: Reflections on some origins of Bion's transcendental constructs. Unpublished ms.

Coles, P. (1997). Vico in the consulting room [letter to the editor]. *Brit. Psychother.*, 14:233.

Cox, S. D. (1980). *The Stranger Within Thee: Concepts of the Self in Late-Eighteenth-Century Literature*. Pittsburgh, PA: University of Pittsburgh Press.

Cramer, B. (1982a). Interaction réelle, interaction fantasmatique: Réflexions au sujet des thèrapies et des observations de nourrissons, *Psychothèrapies*, 1:39–47.

Cramer, B. (1982b). La psychiatrie du bèbè: Une introduction. In: *La Dynamique du Nourrisson*, ed. M. Soulè. Paris: Editions Sociales Françaises, pp. 28–83.

Cramer, B. (1986). Assessment of parent–infant relationship. In: *Affective Development in Infancy*, eds. T. B. Brazelton & M. W. Yogman. Norwood, NJ: Ablex, pp. 27–38.

Cramer, B. & Stern, D. (1988). Evaluation of changes in mother-infant brief psychotherapy: A single case study. *Infant Ment. Health J.*, 9:20–45.

Crossan, J. D. (1991). *The Historical Jesus: The Life of a Mediterranean Jewish Peasant*. San Francisco: Harper.

Damasio, A. R. (1994). *Descartes' Error: Emotion, Reason, and the Human Brain*. New York: Grossett/Putnam.

de Bianchedi, E. T. (1993). Lies and falsities. *J. Melanie Klein & Object Rel.*, 11:30–46.

de Bianchedi, E. T. (1997). From objects to links: Discovering relatedness, *J. Melanie Klein & Object Rel.*, 15:227–234.

De Saint-Exupéry, A. (1943). *The Little Prince,* trans. K. Woods. New York: Harcourt Brace & World.

Dehing, J. (1993). The transcendent function: A critical re-evaluation. The transcendent function: Individual and collective aspects. *Proceedings of the Twelfth International Congress for Analytical Psychology.* Chicago, Einssiedeln, Switzerland: Daimon Verlag, pp. 15–30.

Deikman, A. J. (1971). Bimodal consciousness. *Arch. Gen. Psychiat.,* 25:481–489.

de Mattos, J. A. J. (1997). Transference and counter-transference as transience. Presented at the International Centennial Conference on the Work of W. R. Bion, Turin, Italy, July 16, 1997.

DeMause, L. (1974). The evolution of childhood. In: *The History of Childhood,* ed. L. DeMause. New York: Psychohistory Press, pp. 1–73.

DeMause, L. (1990). The history of child assault. *J. Psychohist.,* 18:1–29.

de Mello Franco, F. O. (1998). Religious experience in psychoanalysis: From man-as-God to man-with-God. *Internat. J. Psycho-Anal.,* 79:113–132.

Dennett, D. (1991) *Consciousness Explained.* Boston: Little, Brown.

de Saussure, F. (1966). *Course in General Linguistics,* trans. W. Baskin. New York: McGraw-Hill.

Descartes, R. (1644). *Philosophical Works, Vols. 1 & 2,* trans. E. S. Haldane & G. R. T. Ross. Cambridge, MA: Yale University Press, 1972.

Deutsch, H. (1933). *Psychoanalyses of the Neuroses.* London: Hogarth Press.

Devereux, G. (1953). Why Oedipus killed Laius. *Internat. J. Psycho-Anal.,* 34:132–141.

Devereux, G. (1966). The cannibalistic impulses of parents. *Psychoanalytic Forum,* 1:114–131.

Dilthey, W. (1883). *Introduction to the Human Sciences,* ed. R. A. Maldereel & F. Rodi. Princeton, NJ: Princeton University Press.

Dodds, E. R. (1951). *The Greeks and the Irrational.* Berkeley: University of California Press.

Dodds, E. R. (1965). *Pagan and Christian in an Age of Anxiety.* Cambridge: Cambridge University Press.

Dodds, E. R. (1968). On misunderstanding the *Oedipus Rex.* In: *Twentieth-Century Interpretations of Oedipus Rex,* ed. M. J. O'Brien. Englewood Cliffs, NJ: Prentice-Hall, pp. 17–29.

Dorpat, T. L. & Miller, M. L. (1994). Primary process meaning analysis. *Contemp. Psychoanal.,* 30:201–212.

Dostoyevsky, F. (1880). *The Brothers Karamazov,* trans. C. Garnett. New York: Modern Library, 1937.

Dunne, J. (1995). Intersubjectivity in psychoanalysis: A critical review. *Internat. J. Psycho-Anal.,* 76:723–738.

Edinger, E. F. (1989). *The Christian Archetype: A Jungian Commentary on the Life of Christ.* Toronto, CAN: Inner City Books.

Ehrenzweig, A. (1967). *The Hidden Order of Art: A Study in the Psychology of Artistic Imagination.* Berkeley: University of California Press.

Eigen, M. (1983). Dual union or undifferentiation? A critique of Marion Milner's review of the sense of psychic creativeness. *Internat. Rev. Psycho-Anal.,* 10:415–428.

Eigen, M. (1993). *The Electrified Tightrope*. Northvale, NJ: Aronson.

Eigen, M. (1995a). On Bion's nothing. *J. Melanie Klein & Object Rel.*, 13:31–36.

Eigen, M. (1997). Musings on O. *J. Melanie Klein & Object Rel.*, 13:46–64.

Eigen, M. (1998). *The Psychoanalytic Mystic*. Binghamton, NY: ESF.

Eisenmann, R. (1997). *James the Brother of Jesus: The Key to Unlocking the Secrets of Early Christianity and the Dead Sea Scrolls*. London: Penguin Books.

Elazar, D. J. (1994). *Covenant and Polity in Biblical Israel. Biblical Foundations and Jewish Expressions. The Covenant Tradition in Politics, Vol. 1*. New Brunswick, NJ: Transactions.

Eliot, T. S. (1943). Little Gidding, In: *T. S. Eliot: Four Quartets*. New York: Harvest/Harcourt Brace Jovanovich, 1971, pp. 49–59.

Emde, R. & Buchsbaum, H. K. (1980). Toward a psychoanalytic theory of affect. Part II. Emerging models of emotional development in infancy. In: *The Course of Life: Infancy and Early Childhood, Vol. 1*, ed. S. I. Greenspan & G. H. Pollock. Madison, CT: International Universities Press, pp. 85–112.

Emde, R. N., Gaensbauer, T. J. & Harmon, R. J. (1976). *Emotional Expression in Infancy*. New York: International Universities Press.

Emde, R., Kubicek, L. & Oppenheim, D. (1997). Imaginative reality observed during early language development. *Internat. J. Psycho-Anal.*, 78:115–134.

Emerson, C., ed. (1984). *Problems of Dostoevsky's Poetics: Mikhail Bakhtin*. Minneapolis: University of Minnesota Press.

Emery, E. (1997). Mnemosyne, death, memory, and mourning. *J. Melanie Klein & Object Rel.*, 15:397–416.

Endo, S. (1973). *A Life of Jesus*, trans. from Japanese by R. A. Schucert. Mahwah: Paulist Press.

Entralgo, P. L. (1970). *The Therapy of the Word in Classical Antiquity*, ed. & trans. L. J. Rather & J. M. Sharp. New Haven, CT: Yale University Press.

Erikson, E. H. (1959). *Identity and the Life Cycle*. New York: International Universities Press.

Evans, D. (1996). *An Introductory Dictionary of Lacanian Psychoanalysis*. London: Routledge.

Fairbairn, W. R. D. (1940). Schizoid factors in the personality. In: *Psychoanalytic Studies of the Personality*. London: Routledge & Kegan Paul, 1952, pp. 3–27.

Fairbairn, W. R. D. (1941). A revised psychopathology of the psychoses and psychoneuroses. In: *Psychoanalytic Studies of the Personality*. London: Routledge & Kegan Paul, 1952, pp. 28–58.

Fairbairn, W. R. D. (1943a). The war neuroses—their nature and significance. In: *Psychoanalytic Studies of the Personality*. London: Routledge & Kegan Paul, 1952, pp. 256–287.

Fairbairn, W. R. D. (1943b). The repression and the return of bad objects (with special reference to the "war neuroses"). In: *Psychoanalytic Studies of the Personality*. London: Routledge & Kegan Paul, 1952, pp. 59–81.

Fairbairn, W. R. D. (1944). Endopsychic structure considered in terms of object-relationships. In: *Psychoanalytic Studies of the Personality*. London: Routledge & Kegan Paul, 1952, pp. 82–136.

Fairbairn, W. R. D. (1946). Object-relationships and dynamic structure. In:

Psychoanalytic Studies of the Personality. London: Routledge & Kegan Paul, 1952, pp. 137–151.
Fairbairn, W. R. D. (1949). Steps in the development of an object-relations theory of the personality. In: *Psychoanalytic Studies of the Personality*. London: Routledge & Kegan Paul, 1952, pp. 152–161.
Fairbairn, W. R. D. (1951). A synopsis of the development of the author's views regarding the structure of the personality. In: *Psychoanalytic Studies of the Personality*. London: Routledge & Kegan Paul, 1952, pp. 162–182.
Fairbairn, W. R. D. (1952). *Psychoanalytic Studies of the Personality*. London: Routledge & Kegan Paul. [Published in U. S. as *An Object Relations Theory of the Personality*. New York: Basic Books, 1954.]
Federn, P. (1932). Ego feelings in dreams. *Psychoanal. Quart.*, 1:511–542.
Federn, P. (1952). *Ego Psychology and the Psychoses*. New York: Basic Books.
Feldman, M. (1989). The Oedipus complex: Manifestations in the inner world and the therapeutic situation: In: *The Oedipus Complex Today: Clinical Implications*, ed. R. Britton, M. Feldman & E. O'Shaughnessy. London: Karnac Books, pp. 103–128.
Fenichel, O. (1945). *The Psychoanalytic Theory of the Neuroses*. New York: Norton.
Ferenczi, S. (1932). Some clinical observations on cases of paranoia and paraphrenia. *Revue Française de Psychanalyse*, 5:97–105.
Ferguson, M. (1982). The transcendent function. In: *The Holographic Paradigm and other Paradoxes: The Leading Edge of Science*, ed. K. Wilber. Boulder, CO: Shambala Press, pp. 15–26.
Fink, B. (1995). *The Lacanian Subject: Between Language and Jouissance*. Princeton, NJ: Princeton University Press.
Fliess, R. (1942). The metapsychology of the analyst. *Psychoanal. Quart.*, 11:211–227.
Fonagy, P. (1991). Thinking about thinking: Some developmental and theoretical considerations in the psychotherapy of a borderline patient. *Internat. J. Psycho-Anal.*, 72:639–656.
Fonagy, P. (1995). Playing with reality: The development of psychic reality and its malfunction in borderline patients. *Internat. J. Psycho-Anal.*, 76:39–44.
Fonagy, P., Steele, M., Steele, H., Moran, G. S. & Higgitt, A. C. (1991). The capacity for understanding mental states: The reflective self in parent and child and its significance for security of attachment. *Infant Ment. Health J.*, 13:201–218.
Fosshage, J. L. (1997). The organizing functions of dream mentation. *Contemp. Psychoanal.*, 33:429–458.
Fowles, J. (1965). *The Magus*. Boston: Little, Brown.
Fox, M. (1980). *Breakthrough: Meister Eckhardt's Creation. Spirituality in New Translation*. New York: Image Books (Doubleday).
Fox, M. (1981a). Meister Eckhart on the fourfold path of a creation-centered spiritual journey. In: *Western Spirituality: Historical Roots, Ecumenical Routes*, ed. M. Fox. Santa Fe, NM: Bear, pp. 215–248.
Fox, M, ed. (1981b), *Western Spirituality: Historical Roots, Ecumenical Roots*. Santa Fe, NM: Bear.
Fraiberg, S. (1969). Libidinal object constancy and mental representation. *The*

Psychoanalytic Study of the Child, 24:9–47. New York: International Universities Press.

Frazer, J. G. (1910). *Totem and Exogamy, A Treatise on Certain Early Forms of Superstition and Society*, 4 vols. London: Macmillan.

Frazer, J. G. (1922). *The Golden Bough: A Study in Magic and Religion*. New York: Macmillan.

Fredriksen, P. (1988). *From Jesus to Christ: The Origins of the New Testament. Images of Jesus*. New Haven, CT: Yale University Press.

Freud, A. (1936). *The Ego and Mechanisms of Defense*. New York: International Universities Press.

Freud, A. (1963). The concept of developmental lines. *The Psychoanalytic Study of the Child*, 18:245–265. New York: International Universities Press.

Freud, S. (1895). Project for a scientific psychology. *Standard Edition*, 1:281–397. London: Hogarth Press, 1966.

Freud, S. (1900). The interpretation of dreams. *Standard Edition*, 5:339–630. London: Hogarth Press, 1953.

Freud, S. (1905a). Jokes and their relationship to the unconscious. *Standard Edition*, 8:3–23. London: Hogarth Press, 1953.

Freud, S. (1905b). Three essays on the theory of sexuality. *Standard Edition*, 7:125–245. London: Hogarth Press, 1953.

Freud, S. (1909). Family romances. *Standard Edition*, 9:235–244. London: Hogarth Press, 1959.

Freud, S. (1911a). Psycho-analytic notes on an autobiographical account of a case of paranoia (dementia paranoides). *Standard Edition*, 12:3–82. London: Hogarth Press, 1958.

Freud, S. (1911b). Formulations of the two principles of mental functioning. *Standard Edition*, 12:213–226. London: Hogarth Press, 1958.

Freud, S. (1912). Recommendations to physicians practicing psychoanalysis. *Standard Editions*, 12:109–120. London: Hogarth Press, 1958.

Freud, S. (1913). Totem and taboo. *Standard Edition*, 13:1–161. London: Hogarth Press, 1957.

Freud, S. (1914a). Remembering, repeating, and working-through. (Further recommendations on the technique of psycho-analysis, II). *Standard Edition*, 12:145–156. London: Hogarth Press, 1958.

Freud, S. (1914b). On narcissism: An introduction. *Standard Edition*, 14:67–104. London: Hogarth Press, 1957.

Freud, S. (1915a). Instincts and their vicissitudes. *Standard Edition*, 14:109–140. London: Hogarth Press, 1957.

Freud, S. (1915b). The unconscious. *Standard Edition*, 14:159–215. London: Hogarth Press, 1957.

Freud, S. (1916). Some character-types met in psycho-analytic work, *Standard Edition*, 14:309–336. London: Hogarth Press, 1957.

Freud, S. (1916–17). Introductory lectures on psycho-analysis. *Standard Edition*, 15 and 16. London: Hogarth Press, 1957.

Freud, S. (1917). Mourning and melancholy. *Standard Edition*, 14:237–260. London: Hogarth Press, 1957.

Freud, S. (1919). The "uncanny." *Standard Edition*, 17:217–252. London: Hogarth Press, 1955.

Freud, S. (1920). Beyond the pleasure principle. *Standard Edition*, 18:3–66. London: Hogarth Press, 1955.

Freud, S. (1921). Group psychology and the analysis of the ego. *Standard Edition*, 18:67–144. London: Hogarth Press, 1955.

Freud, S. (1922). Dreams and telepathy. *Standard Edition*, 18:195–220. London: Hogarth Press, 1955.

Freud, S. (1923a). The ego and the id. *Standard Edition*, 19:3–66. London: Hogarth Press, 1961.

Freud, S. (1923b). A seventeenth-century demonological neurosis. *Standard Edition*, 19:69–108. London: Hogarth Press, 1961.

Freud, S. (1927). The future of an illusion. *Standard Edition*, 21:3–58. London: Hogarth Press, 1961.

Freud, S. (1930). Civilization and its discontents. *Standard Edition*, 21:59–149. London: Hogarth Press, 1961.

Freud, S. (1939). Moses and monotheism: Three essays. *Standard Edition*, 23:3–140. London: Hogarth Press, 1964.

Freud, S. (1950). Extracts from the Fleiss papers. *Standard Edition*, 1:175–280. London: Hogarth Press, 1966.

Fromm, E. (1941). *Escape from Freedom*. New York: Farrar & Rinehart.

Gabbard, G. (1995). Countertransference: The emerging common ground. *Internat. J. Psycho-Anal.*, 76:475–486.

Gimbutas, M. (1974). *The Gods and Goddesses of Old Europe 7000–3500 BC: Myths, Legends and Cult Images*. Berkeley: University of California Press.

Girard, R. (1972). *Violence and the Sacred*, trans. P. Gregory. Baltimore, MD: Johns Hopkins University Press.

Girard, R. (1978). *Things Hidden Since the Foundation of the World*, trans. S. Bann & M. Metteer. Stanford, CA: Stanford University Press, 1987.

Girard, R. (1986). *The Scapegoat*, trans. Y. Freccero. Baltimore, MD: Johns Hopkins University Press.

Girard, R. (1987). *Job: The Victim of His People*. Stanford, CA: Stanford University Press.

Gleik, J. (1987). *Chaos: Making a New Science*. New York: Viking Press.

Graves, R. (1955). *The Greek Myths, Vols. I & II*. London: Penguin Books.

Graves, R. (1958). *The White Goddess*. New York: Vintage Books.

Graves, R. & Patai, R. (1963). *Hebrew Myths: The Book of Genesis*. New York: McGraw-Hill.

Gray, P. (1982). "Developmental lag" in the evolution of technique for psychoanalysis of a neurotic conflict. *J. Amer. Psychoanal. Assn.*, 30:621–656.

Green, A. (1992). Review of *Cogitations*, by Wilfred R. Bion. *Internat. J. Psycho-Anal.*, 73:585–589.

Green, J. (1947). *If I Were You . . .* , trans. J. H. F. McEwen. London: Eyre & Spottiswoode, 1950.

Greenson, R. R. (1965). The working alliance and the transference neurosis. *Psychoanal. Quart.*, 34:155–181.

Grinberg, L. (1962). On a specific aspect of counter-transference due to the patient's projective identification. *Internat. J. Psycho-Anal.*, 43:436–440.

Grinberg, L. (1979a). Projective counter identification. In: *Countertransference*, ed. L. Epstein & A. Feiner. New York: Aronson, pp. 169–191.

Grinberg, L. (1979b). Countertransference and projective counteridentification. *Contemp. Psychoanal.*, 15:226–247.

Groddeck, G. W. (1923). *The Book of the It*. New York: Mentor Books, 1961.

Grotstein, J. S. (1977a). The psychoanalytic concept of schizophrenia: I. The dilemma. *Internat. J. Psycho-Anal.*, 58:403–425.

Grotstein, J. S. (1977b). The psychoanalytic concept of schizophrenia II. Reconciliation. *Internat. J. Psycho- Anal.*, 58:427–452.

Grotstein, J. S. (1978). Inner space: Its dimensions and its coordinates. *Internat. J. Psycho-Anal.*, 59:55–61.

Grotstein, J. S. (1981a). *Splitting and Projective Identification*. New York: Aronson.

Grotstein, J. S. (1981b). Bion the man, the psychoanalyst, and the mystic: A perspective on his life and work. In: *Do I Dare Disturb the Universe? A Memorial to Wilfred R. Bion*, ed. J. S. Grotstein. Beverly Hills: Caesura Press, pp. 1–36.

Grotstein, J. S. (1986). The dual-track: A contribution toward a neurobehavioral model of cerebral processing. *Psychiatric Clinics North America*, 9:353–366.

Grotstein, J. S. (1990a). The "black hole" as the basic psychotic experience: Some newer psychoanalytic and neuroscience perspectives on psychosis. *J. Amer. Acad. Psychoanal.*, 18:29–46.

Grotstein, J. S. (1990b). Nothingness, meaninglessness, chaos and the "black hole": I. The importance of nothingness, meaninglessness, and chaos in psychoanalysis. *Contemp. Psychoanal.*, 26:257–290.

Grotstein, J. S. (1990c). Nothingness, meaninglessness, chaos, and the "black hole": II. The black hole. *Contemp. Psychoanal.*, 26:377–407.

Grotstein, J. S. (1993a). Towards the concept of the transcendent position: Reflections on some of "the unborns" in Bion's *Cogitations*. *J. Melanie Klein & Object Rel.*, 11(2):55–73.

Grotstein, J. S. (1993b). The world view (*Weltanschauung*) of primitive mental disorders: Boundary difficulties in borderline patients and their relationship to issues of entitlement. In: *Master Clinicians, Vol. II: On Treating the Regressed Patient in the Consultation Room and in the Residential Setting*, ed. L. B. Boyer & P. L. Giovacchini. Northvale, NJ: Aronson, pp. 107–142.

Grotstein, J. S. (1994a). I. Notes on Fairbairn's metapsychology. In: *Fairbairn and the Origins of Object Relations*, ed. J. Grotstein & D. Rinsley. New York: Guilford, pp. 112–148.

Grotstein, J. S. (1994b). II. Endopsychic structures and the cartography of the internal world: Six endopsychic characters in search of an author. In: *Fairbairn and the Origins of Object Relations*, ed. J. Grotstein & D. Rinsley. New York: Guilford, pp. 174–194.

Grotstein, J. S. (1994c). Projective identification reappraised: Projective identification, introjective identification, the transference/countertransference neurosis/psychosis, and their consummate expression in the crucifixion, the Pietà, and "therapeutic exorcism": Part I. Projective identification. *Contemp. Psychoanal.*, 30:708–746.

Grotstein, J. S. (1995a). Projective identification reappraised: Projective identification, introjective identification, the transference/countertransference neurosis/psychosis, and their consummate expression in the crucifixion, the Pietà, and "therapeutic exorcism": Part II. The countertransference complex. *Contemp. Psychoanal.*, 31:479–511.

Grotstein, J. S. (1995b). Orphans of the "Real": I. Some modern and post-modern perspectives on the neurobiological and psychosocial dimensions of psychosis and primitive mental disorders. *Bull. Menn. Clin.*, 59:287–311.

Grotstein, J. S. (1995c). Orphans of the "Real": II. The future of object relations theory in the treatment of psychoses and other primitive mental disorders. *Bull. Menn. Clin.*, 59:312–332.

Grotstein, J. S. (1995d). The infantile neurosis reassessed: The impact upon it of infant development research. In: *The Handbook of Infant, Child, and Adolescent Psychotherapy: A Guide to Diagnosis and Treatment*, ed. B. S. Mark & J. A. Incorvaia. Northvale, NJ: Aronson, pp. 43–80.

Grotstein, J. S. (1996). The subject in question: The hidden order of the ineffable in psychoanalysis. Presented at conference on "The Emergence of the Subject in Psychoanalysis," sponsored by the Extension Division of the Psychoanalytic Center of California, Los Angeles, June 15.

Grotstein, J. S. (1997). The sins of the fathers. . . human sacrifice and the inter- and trans-generational neurosis/psychosis. *Internat. J. Psycho-Anal.*, 2:11–25.

Grotstein, J. S. (1998a). A comparison of Fairbairn's endopsychic structure and Klein's internal world. In: *Fairbairn Then and Now*, ed. N. Skolnick & D. Scharff. Analytic Press, pp. 71–97.

Grotstein, J. S. (1998b). The numinous and immanent nature of the psychoanalytic subject. *J. Anal. Psychol.*, 43:41–68.

Grotstein, J. S. (1999a). Bion's "transformation in O and the concept of the transcendent position. In: *W. R. Bion: Between Past and Future*, ed. P. Bion, F. Borgogno & S. A. Merciai. London: Karnac Books.

Grotstein, J. S. (1999b). The significance of Bion's concepts of PS→D and transformations in "O": A reconsideration of the relationship between Klein's "positions." In: *Psychoanalytic Schemas and Models and Their Graphic Representations*, ed. K. Hall & O. Rathbone. London: Rebus Press.

Grotstein, J. (1999c). Projective identification reassessed: Commentary on papers by Stephen Seligman and by Robin C. Silverman and Alicia F. Lieberman. *Psychoanal. Dial.*, 9:187–204.

Grotstein, J. (1999d). The alter ego and déjà vu phenomena: Notes and reflections. In: *The Plural Self: Multiplicity in Everyday Life*, ed. J. Rowan & M. Cooper. Thousand Oaks, CA: Sage, pp. 28–50.

Grotstein, J. S. (in preparation-a). *Projective Identification and Projective Transidentification.*

Grotstein, J. S. (in preparation-b). The dual-track theorem and the "Siamese-twinship" paradigm for psychoanalytic concepts.

Hagman, G. (1995). Mourning: A review and consideration. *Internat. J. Psycho-Anal.*, 76:909–926.

Hamilton, E. & Huntington, C., eds. (1961). *The Collected Dialogues of Plato.* Princeton, NJ: Princeton University Press.

Hamilton, V. (1993). *Narcissus and Oedipus: The Children of Psychoanalysis*. London: Routledge & Kegan Paul.
Hamilton, V. (1996). *The Analyst's Preconscious*. Hillsdale, NJ: The Analytic Press.
Hartmann, H. (1939). *Ego Psychology and the Problem of Adaptation*, trans. D. Rapaport. New York: International Universities Press.
Hawking, S. (1988). *A Brief History of Time: From the Big Bang to Black Holes*. New York: Bantam Books.
Hartmann, H. (1954). *Essays on Ego Psychology*. New York: International Universities Press.
Hedges, L. (1994). *Working the Organizing Experience: Transforming Psychotic, Schizoid, and Autistic States*. Northvale, NJ: Aronson.
Hedges, L. (1998). Achieving optimal responsiveness with early developmental trauma. Presented at 21st Annual Conference on the Psychology of the Self, San Diego, CA, October 26.
Hegel, G. W. F. (1807). *Phenomenology of Spirit*, trans. A. B. Miller. London: Oxford University Press, 1977.
Heidegger, M. (1927). *Being and Time*, trans. J. Macquarrie & E. Robinson. San Francisco: HarperCollins, 1962.
Heidegger, M. (1954). *What Is Called Thinking?* trans. F. Wieck & G. Gray. New York: Harper & Row.
Herman, J. (1992). *Trauma and Recovery: The Aftermath of Violence—from Domestic Abuse to Political Terror*. New York: Basic Books.
Heschel, S. (1998). *Abraham Geiger and the Jewish Jesus*. Chicago: University of Chicago Press.
Hillers, D. R. (1969). *Covenant: The History of a Biblical Idea*. Baltimore, MD: Johns Hopkins University Press.
Hinshelwood, R. (1997). The elusive concept of "internal objects" (1934–1943): Its role in the formation of the Klein group. *Internat. J. Psycho-Anal.*, 78:877–898.
Hocart, A. M. (1954). *The Life-Giving Myth and Other Essays*. London: Methuen.
Hoffman, I. Z. (1992). Some practical implications of a social constructivist view of the psychoanalytic situation. *Psychoanal. Dial.*, 2:287–304.
Hoffman, I. Z. (1994). Dialectical thinking and therapeutic action in the psychoanalytic process. *Psychoanal. Quart.*, 63:187–218.
Hofstadter, D. R. (1979). *Gödel, Escher, Bach: An Eternal Golden Braid*. New York: Basic Books.
Hofstadter, D. R. & Dennett, D. C. (1981). *Fantasies and Reflections on Self and Soul*. New York: Basic Books.
Holland, J. H. (1999). *Emergence: From Chaos to Order*. Oxford: Oxford University Press.
Holquist, M., ed. (1981). *The Dialogic Imagination: Four Essays*, trans. C. Emerson & M. Holquist. Austin: University of Texas Press.
Hopkins, B. (1989). Jesus and object-use: A Winnicottian account of the resurrection myth. *Internat. Rev. Psycho-Anal.*, 16:93–100.
Hunt, S. (1976). *Ouija: The Most Dangerous Game*. New York: Harper & Row.
Husserl, E. (1931). *Ideas: An Introduction to Pure Phenomenology*. New York: Macmillan.

Husserl, E. (1962). *Phenomenological Psychology*, ed. W. Biemel (trans. W. Scanlon). The Hague: Nijhoff, 1977.

Isakower, O. (1938). A contribution to the pathopsychology of phenomena associated with falling asleep. *Internat. J. Psycho-Anal.*, 19:331–345.

Jacobson, E. (1964). *The Self and the Object World*. New York: International Universities Press.

Jacobson, E. (1971). *Selected Writings, Vols. 1–4*. The Hague: Mouton Press.

Jaynes, J. (1976). *The Origins of Consciousness in the Breakdown of the Bicameral Mind*. Boston: Houghton Mifflin.

Johnson, A. W. & Price-Williams, D. (1966). *The Family Complex in World Folk Literature*. Stanford, CA: Stanford University Press.

Jones, J. W. (1991). *Contemporary Psychoanalysis and Religion: Transference and Transcendence*. New Haven, CT: Yale University Press.

Jong, E. (1981). *Witches*. New York: H. A. Abrams.

Jucovy, M. E. (1983). The effects of the Holocaust on the second generation: Psychoanalytic studies. *Amer. J. Social Psychiat.*, 3:15–20.

Jucovy, M. E. (1985). Telling the Holocaust story: A link between generations. *Psychoanal. Inq.*, 5:31–49.

Jung, C. G. (1934). Archetypes and the collective unconscious, In: *The Collected Works of C. G. Jung*, trans. R. F. C. Hull. Bollingen Series XX, Vol. 9. Princeton, NJ: Princeton University Press.

Jung, C. G. (1939). Conscious, unconscious, and individuation. In: *The Essential Jung*, selected & introduced by A. Storr. Princeton, NJ: Princeton University Press, pp. 212–226.

Jung, C. G. (1953). Psychology and alchemy. In: *The Collected Works of C. G. Jung*, trans. R. F. C. Hull. Bollingen Series XX, Vol. 10. Princeton, NJ: Princeton University Press.

Jung, C. G. (1966). The psychology of transference. In: The *Collected Works of C. G. Jung*, trans R. F. C. Hull, Bollingen Series XX, Vol. 9. Princeton, NJ: Princeton University Press.

Jung, C. G. (1969). The psychology of the child archetype. In: *The Collected Works of C. G. Jung*, trans. R. F. C. Hull. Bollingen Series XX, Vol. 9. Princeton, NJ: Princeton University Press.

Kant, I. (1787). *Critique of Pure Reason*. New York: Dobbs-Merrill, 1956.

Kantrowitz, J. (1997). The role of the preconscious in psychoanalysis. Presented at midwinter meeting of American Psychoanalytic Association, New York City, December 18.

Kauffman, S. (1993). *The Origin of Order: Self-Organization and Selection in Evolution*. New York: Oxford University Press.

Kauffman, S. (1995). *At Home in the Universe: The Search for the Laws of Self-Organization and Complexity*. New York: Oxford University Press.

Kennedy, R. (1997). Aspects of consciousness: One voice or many. *Psychoanal. Dial.*, 6:73–96.

Kennedy, R. (1998). *The Illusive Human Subject: A Psychoanalytic Theory of Subject Relations*. London: Free Association Books.

Klein, M. (1921). The development of the child. In: *Contributions to Psycho-Analysis, 1921–1945*. London: Hogarth Press, 1950, pp. 13–64.

Klein, M. (1923). The role of the school in the libidinal development of the child. In: *The Writings of Melanie Klein. Vol. 1*, ed. R. E. Money-Kyrle. London: Hogarth Press, 1981, pp. 59– 76.

Klein, M. (1926). The psychological principles of infant analysis. In: *Contributions to Psycho-Analysis, 1921–1945*. London: Hogarth Press, 1950, pp. 140–151.

Klein, M. (1927). Symposium on child analysis. In: *Contributions to Psycho-Analysis, 1921–1945*. London: Hogarth Press, 1950, pp. 152–184.

Klein, M. (1928). Early stages of the oedipus conflict. In: *Contributions to Psycho-Analysis, 1921–1945*. London: Hogarth Press, 1950, pp. 202–214.

Klein, M. (1929a). Personification in the play of children. In: *Contributions to Psycho-Analysis, 1921–1945*. London: Hogarth Press, 1950, pp. 215–226.

Klein, M. (1929b). Infantile anxiety-situations reflected in a work of art and in the creative impulse. In: *Contributions to Psycho-Analysis, 1921–1945*. London: Hogarth Press, 1950, pp. 227–235.

Klein, M. (1930). The importance of symbol formation in the development of the ego. In: *Contributions to Psychoanalysis, 1921–1945*. London: Hogarth Press, 1950, pp. 215–226.

Klein, M. (1931). A contribution to the theory of intellectual inhibition. In: *Contributions to Psychoanalysis, 1921–1945*. London: Hogarth Press, 1950, pp. 254–266.

Klein, M. (1932). *The Psycho-Analysis of Children*. London: Hogarth Press.

Klein, M. (1933). The early development of conscience in the child. In: *Contributions to Psycho-Analysis*. London: Hogarth Press, 1948, pp. 267–277.

Klein, M. (1935). A contribution to the psychogenesis of manic-depressive states. In: *Contributions to Psycho-Analysis, 1921–1945*. London: Hogarth Press, 1950, pp. 282–310.

Klein, M. (1940). Mourning and its relation to manic-depressive states. In: *Contributions to Psychoanalysis, 1921–1945*. London: Hogarth Press, 1950, pp. 311–338.

Klein, M. (1945). The oedipus complex in the light of early anxieties. In: *Contributions to Psychoanalysis, 1921–1945*. London: Hogarth Press, 1950, pp. 339–390.

Klein, M. (1946). Notes on some schizoid mechanisms. In: *Developments of Psycho-Analysis*, ed. M. Klein, P. Heimann, S. Isaacs & J. Riviere. London: Hogarth Press, 1952, pp. 292–320.

Klein, M. (1952). On identification. In: *New Directions in Psycho-Analysis*, ed. M. Klein, P. Heimann, S. Isaacs & J. Riviere. London: Hogarth Press, pp. 309–345.

Klein, M.(1960). *Narrative of a Child Analysis*. New York: Basic Books.

Klein, M. (1963). Some reflections on "The Oresteia of Aeschylus." In: *Our Adult World and Other Essays*. London: William Heinemann, pp. 23–54.

Knorr, W. R. (1982). Infinity and continuity: The interaction of mathematics and philosophy in antiquity. In: *Infinity and Continuity in Ancient and Medieval Thought*, ed. N. Kreitzmann. Ithaca, NY: Cornell University Press, pp. 112–145.

Kohut, H. (1971). *The Analysis of the Self: A Systematic Approach to the Psycho-*

analytic Treatment of Narcissistic Personality Disorders. New York: International Universities Press.

Kohut, H. (1977). *The Restoration of the Self*. New York: International Universities Press.

Kohut, H. (1984). *How Does Analysis Cure?* ed. A. Goldberg with P. E. Stepansky. Chicago: University of Chicago Press.

Kojève, A. (1934–1935). *Introduction to the Reading of Hegel*, trans. J. Nichols, Jr. Ithaca, NY: Cornell University Press.

Kristeva, J. (1980). *Powers of Horror: An Essay on Abjection*, trans. L. Roudiez. New York: Columbia University Press, 1982.

Krystal, H. (1988). *Integration and Self-Healing: Affect, Trauma, Alexithymia*. Hillsdale, NJ: The Analytic Press.

Kubie, L. & Israel, H. (1955). Say you're sorry! *The Psychoanalytic Study of the Child*, 10:289–299. New York: International Universities Press.

Kuhn, T. (1962). *The Structure of Scientific Revolutions*. Chicago: University of Chicago Press

Lacan, J. (1936). The mirror stage as formative of the function of the I. In: *Écrits: A Selection*, trans. A. Sheridan. New York: Norton, pp. 1–7.

Lacan, J. (1954–1955). *The Seminars of Jacques Lacan. Book II: The Ego in Freud's Theory and in the Technique of Psychoanalysis, 1954–1955*, trans. S. Tomascelli. New York: Norton, 1988.

Lacan, J. (1956). The Freudian thing or the meaning of the return to Freud in psychoanalysis. In: *Écrits: A Selection*, trans. A. Sheridan. New York: Norton, 1977, pp. 114–145.

Lacan, J.(1966). *Écrits*, trans. A. Sheridan. New York: Norton, 1977.

Leavy, S. (1988). *In the Image of God*. Hillsdale, NJ: The Analytic Press, 1997.

LeCours, A. R. (1975). Myelogenetic correlates of the development of speech and language. In: *Foundations of Language Development: A Multi-Disciplinary Approach, Vol. 1*. New York: Academic Press, pp. 121–134.

LeMire, R. J., Loesser, J. D., Leech, R. W. & Alvord, E. C. (1975). *Normal and Abnormal Development of the Human Nervous System*. Hagerstown, MD: Harper & Row.

Lévi-Strauss, C. (1958). *Structural Anthropology*, trans. C. Jacobson & B. Grundfest. Harmondsworth, UK: Penguin, 1968.

Lewin, B. D. (1950). *The Psychoanalysis of Elation*. New York: Norton.

Lewis, C. S. (1943). *Mere Christianity*. New York: Macmillan.

Likierman, M. (1995). Loss of the object: Tragic motifs in Melanie Klein's concept of the depressive position. *Brit. J. Psychother.*, 12:147–159.

Lorenz, K. (1950). The comparative method for studying innate behavior patterns. Presented at Symposia for the Society of Experimental Biology.

Lowy, S. (1942). *Psychological and Biological Foundations of Dream Interpretation*. London: Kegan Paul Ltd.

Lumsden, C. J. & Wilson, E. O. (1981). *Genes, Mind, and Culture: The Co-Evolutionary Process*. Cambridge, MA: Harvard University Press.

Lumsden, C. J. & Wilson, E. O.(1983). *Promethean Fire: Reflections on the Origin of Mind*. Cambridge, MA: Harvard University Press.

Mack, B. L. (1993). *The Lost Gospel: The Book of Q and Christian Origins*. San Francisco: Harper San Francisco.

Mahler, M. S. (1968). *On Human Symbiosis and the Vicissitudes of Individuation*. New York: International Universities Press.

Mahler, M. S., Pine, F. & Bergman, A. (1975). *The Psychological Birth of the Human Infant*. New York: Basic Books.

Main, M. (1973). *Exploration, Play and Cognitive Functioning as Related to Child–Mother Attachment*. Baltimore, MD: Johns Hopkins University Press.

Maizels, N. (1996). Working-through, or beyond the depressive position? (Achievements and defenses of the spiritual position, and the heart's content). *J. Melanie Klein & Object Rel.*, 14:143–176.

Malin, B. (1990). Shame and envy: A re-examination. Presented to the Los Angeles Psychoanalytic Society, March 18.

Malinowski, B. (1927). *Sex and Repression in Savage Society*. New York: Meridian Books, 1955.

Martin, J. (1988). *Who Am I This Time? Uncovering the Fictive Personality*. New York: Norton.

Mason, A. (1994). A psychoanalysts looks at a hypnotist: A study of folie à deux. *Psychoanal. Quart.*, 63:641–679.

Matte-Blanco, I. (1975). *The Unconscious as Infinite Sets*. London: Duckworth Press.

Matte-Blanco, I. (1981). Reflecting with Bion. In: *Do I Dare Disturb the Universe: A Memorial to Wilfred R. Bion*, ed. J. S. Grotstein. Beverly Hills, CA: Caesura Press, pp. 489–528.

Matte-Blanco, I. (1988). *Thinking, Feeling, and Being: Clinical Reflections on the Fundamental Antinomy of Human Beings*. London: Tavistock & Routledge.

Maturana, H. R. & Varela, F. J. (1972). *Autopoiesis in Cognition: The Realization of the Living*. Dordretcht, Holland: D. Rydell.

McDougall, J. (1985). *Theaters of the Mind: Illusion and Truth on the Psychoanalytic Stage*. New York: Basic Books.

McDougall, J. (1989). *Theaters of the Body: A Psychoanalytic Approach to Psychosomatic Illness*. New York: Norton.

Mead, G. R. S. (1900). *Fragments of a Faith Forgotten*. New Hyde Park, NY: University Books, 1960.

Meares, M. (1984). Inner space: Its constriction in anxiety states and narcissistic personality. *Psychiat.*, 47:162–171.

Meier, J. P. (1990). *The Mission of Christ and His Church: Studies in Christology and Ecolesiology*. Wilmington, DE: Michael Glazier.

Meissner, W. W. (1984). *Psychoanalysis and Religious Experience*. New Haven, CT: Yale University Press.

Meissner, W. W. (1993). Self-as-agent in psychoanalysis. *Psychoanal. Contemp. Thought*, 16:459–495.

Meissner, W. W. (1996). The self-as-object in psychoanalysis. *Psychoanal. Contemp. Thought*, 19:425–459.

Meltzer, D. (1967). *The Psycho-Analytic Press*. London: Heinnemann.

Meltzer, D. W. (1978). *The Kleinian Development*. Perthshire, Scotland: Clunie Press.

Meltzer, D. W. (1992). *The Claustrum: An Investigation of Claustrophobic Phenomena*. Perthshire, Scotland: Clunie Press.

Meltzer, D. W. & Harris, M. (1988). *The Role of Aesthetic Conflict in Development, Art, and Violence*. Perthshire, Scotland: Clunie Press.

Mitchell, S. A. (1997). *Influence and Autonomy in Psychoanalysis*. Hillsdale, NJ: The Analytic Press.

Modell, A. H. (1993). *The Private Self*. Cambridge, MA: Harvard University Press.

Money-Kyrle, R. (1956). Normal counter-transference and some of its deviations. In: *The Collected Papers of Roger Money-Kyrle*, ed. D. Meltzer. Perthshire, Scotland: Clunie Press, 1978, pp. 330–342.

Montgomery, J. W., ed. (1976). *Demon Possession*. Minneapolis, MN: Bethany House.

Moore, S. (1985). *Let This Mind Be in You: The Quest for Identity through Oedipus to Christ*. London: Darton, Longman & Todd.

Moran, F. M. (1993). *Subject and Agency in Psychoanalysis: Which Is to Be the Master?* New York: New York University Press.

Mordant, I. (1990). Using attribute memories to resolve a contradiction in the work of Matte-Blanco. *Internat. Rev. Psycho-Anal.*, 17:475–480.

Morgan, C. (1998). Matte-Blanco, neuroscience, developmental perspectives. Presented to Los Angeles Society and Institute for Psychoanalytic Studies, February 23.

Morrison, T. (1998). *Beloved*. New York: Signet.

Morson, G. S. & Emerson, C. (1990). *Mikhail Bakhtin: Creation of a Prosaics*. Stanford, CA: Stanford University Press.

Muller, J. P. (1996). *Beyond the Psychoanalytic Dialogues: Developmental Semiotics in Freud, Peirce and Lacan*. New York: Routledge.

Murdoch, J. E. (1982). William of Ockham and the logic of infinity and continuity. In: *Infinity and Continuity in Ancient and Medieval Thought*, ed. N. Kreitzmann. Ithaca, NY: Cornell University Press, pp. 165–206.

Natterson, J. (1991). *Beyond Countertransference: The Therapist's Subjectivity in the Therapeutic Process*. Northvale, NJ: Aronson.

Neumann, E. (1954). *Art and the Creative Unconscious*. Princeton, NJ: Princeton University Press.

Nietzsche, F. (1883). *Thus Spake Zarathustra*, trans. W. Kaufman. London: Penguin Books, 1961.

Nietzsche, F. (1886). *Beyond Good and Evil*, trans. H. Zimmern. New York: Boni & Liveright, 1917.

Nietzsche, F. (1889). *The Twilight of the Idols*, trans. A. M. Ludovici. London: T. N. Foulis, 1915.

Nietzsche, F. (1895). *The Anti-Christ*, trans. R. J. Hollingdale. London: Penguin Books, 1990.

Ogden, T. (1986). *Matrix of the Mind: Object Relations and the Psychoanalytic Dialogue*. Northvale, NJ: Aronson.

Ogden, T. (1989a). On the concept of an autistic-contiguous position. *Internat. J. Psycho-Anal.*, 70:127–140.

Ogden, T. (1989b). *The Primitive Edge of Experience*. Northvale, NJ: Aronson.

Ogden, T. (1994a). The analytic third: Working with intersubjective clinical facts. *Internat. J. Psycho-Anal.*, 75:3–20.

Ogden, T. (1994b). *Subjects of Analysis*. Northvale, NJ: Aronson.

Ogden, T. (1997). *Reverie and Interpretation: Sensing Something Human*. Northvale, NJ: Aronson.

O'Hara, J. (1934). *Appointment in Samarra*. New York: Harcourt Brace.

Opie, I. & Opie, P. (1959). *The Lore and Language of School Children*. Oxford, UK: Clarendon Press at Oxford University.

Orange, D. M., Atwood, G. E. & Stolorow, R. D. (1997). *Working Intersubjectively: Contextualism in Psychoanalytic Practice*. Hillsdale, NJ: The Analytic Press.

O'Shaugnessy, E. (1989). The invisible Oedipus complex. In: *The Oedipus Complex Today: Clinical Implications*, ed. R. Britton, M. Feldman & E. O'Shaughnessy. London: Karnac Books, pp. 29–150.

Padel, R. (1992). *In and Out of the Mind: Greek Images of the Tragic Self*. Princeton, NJ: Princeton University Press.

Padel, R. (1995). *Whom Gods Destroy: Elements of Greek and Tragic Madness*. Princeton, NJ: Princeton University Press.

Pagels, E. (1979). *The Gnostic Gospels*. New York: Vintage Books.

Pagels, E. (1995). *The Origin of Satan*. New York: Random House.

Paglia, C. (1990). *Sexual Personae: Art and Decadence from Nefertiti to Emily Dickinson*. New Haven, CT: Yale University Press.

Palombo, S. R. (1978). *Dreaming and Memory: A New Information-Processing Model*. New York: Basic Books.

Palombo, S. R. (1999). *The Emergent Ego: Complexity and Coevolution in the Psychoanalytic Process*. Madison, CT: International Universities Press.

Peirce, C. S. (1931). *Collected Papers, Vols. I–VIII*, ed. C. Hartshorne & P. Weiss. Cambridge, MA: Harvard University Press.

Pelikan, J. (1985). *Jesus Through the Centuries: His Place in the History of Culture*. New York: Harper & Row.

Peltz, R. (1998). The dialectic of presence and absence: Impasses and the reteieval of meaning states. *Psychoanal. Dial.*, 8:385–411.

Pfleiderer, O. (1905). *The Early Christian Conception of Christ: Its Significance and Value in the History of Religion*. New York: J. P. Putnam's Sons.

Piaget, J. (1923a). *The Language and Thought of the Child*, trans. M. Gabain. New York: Meridian Books.

Piaget, J. (1923b). *The Moral Judgement of the Child*, trans. M. Gabain. New York: Free Press.

Piaget, J. (1924). *Judgement and Reasoning in the Child*, trans. M. Warden. Totowa, NJ: Littlefied, Adams.

Piaget, J. (1926). *The Child's Conception of the World*, trans. J. & A. Tomlinson. Totowa, NJ: Littlefied, Adams.

Pinker, S. (1994), *The Language Instinct*. New York: Norton.

Poincaré, H. (1952). *Science and Method*. New York: Dover.

Poe, E. A. (1845). The story of William Wilson. In: *The Collected Tales and Poems of Edgar Allan Poe*. New York: Modern Library, 1992.

Polti, G. (1917). *The Thirty-Six Dramatic Situations*, trans. L. Ray. Boston: The Writer, 1960.

Pribram, K. (1971). *Languages of the Brain: Experimental Paradoxes and Principles in Neuropsychology*. Englewood Cliffs, NJ: Prentice-Hall.

Racker, H. (1953). A contribution to the problem of countertransference. *Internat. J. Psycho-Anal.*, 34:313–324.

Racker, H. (1957). The meanings and uses of countertransference. *Psychoanal. Quart.*, 26:303–357.

Racker, H. (1968). *Transference and Countertransference*. London: Hogarth. Press.

Rangell, L. (1969). Choice conflict and the decision-making function of the ego. *Internat. J. Psycho-Anal.*, 50:599–602.

Rangell, L. (1971). The decision-making process. *The Psychoanalytic Study of the Child*, 26;425–452. New Haven, CT: Yale University Press.

Rangell, L. (1990). *The Human Core: The Intrapsychic Base of Behavior. Volume I. Action within the Structural View*. Madison, CT: International Universities Press.

Rank, O. (1910). *In Quest of the Hero: The Myth of the Birth of the Hero*. Princeton, NJ: Princeton University Press, 1990.

Reich, W. (1928). On character analysis. In: *The Psychoanalytic Reader*. ed. R. Fliess. New York: International Universities Press, 1948, pp. 129–147.

Renik, O. (1994). A wrong turn in the psychoanalytic theory of motivation. Presented to Los Angeles Society and Institute for Psychoanalytic Studies, September 17.

Rhode, E. (1998). *On Hallucination, Intuition, and the Becoming of "O."* Binghamton, NY: ESF.

Ricoeur, P. (1970). *Freud and Philosophy: An Essay on Interpretation*, trans. D. Savage. New Haven, CT: Yale University Press.

Ricoeur, P. (1992). *Oneself As Another*, trans. K. Balmey. Chicago: University of Chicago Press.

Rizzuto, A-M. (1974). Object relations and the formation of the image of God. *Brit. J. Med. Psychol.*, 47:83–99.

Rizzuto, A-M.(1976). Freud, God, the devil and the theory of object representation. *Internat. Rev. Psycho-Anal.*, 3:165–180.

Rizzuto, A-M. (1991). Religious development: A psychoanalytic point of view. In: *Religious Development in Childhood and Adolescence*, ed. F. K. Oser & W. G. Scarlett. San Francisco: Jossey-Bass.

Rosenfeld, R. (1987). *Impasse and Interpretation*. London: Tavistock.

Ross, J. M. (1982). Oedipus revisited: Laius and the "Laius complex." *The Psychoanalytic Study of the Child*, 37:169–200. New Haven, CT: Yale University Press.

Rotman, B. (1987). *Signifying Nothing: The Semiotics of Zero*. New York: St. Martin's Press.

Rucker, R. (1982). *Infinity and the Mind: The Science and Philosophy of the Infinite*. New York: Bantam Books.

Russell, J. B. (1977). *The Devil: Perceptions of Evil from Antiquity to Primitive Christianity*. Ithaca, NY: Cornell University Press.

Ryle, G. (1949). *The Concept of Mind*. London: Hutchinson's Universal Library.

Sagan, E. (1979). *The Lust to Annihilate: A Psychoanalytic Study of Violence in Ancient Greek Culture*. New York: Psychohistory Press.

Saldarini, A. J. (1994). *Matthew's Christian-Jewish Community*. Chicago: University of Chicago Press.

Sandler, J. (1960). The background of safety. *Internat. J. Psycho-Anal.*, 41:352–356.

Sass, L. A. (1994). *The Paradoxes of Delusion: Wittgenstein, Schreber, and the Schizophrenic Mind*. Ithaca, NY: Cornell University Press.

Schilder, P. (1933). The vestibular apparatus in neurosis and psychosis. *J. Nerv. Ment. Dis.*, 78:137–164.

Scholem, G. (1969). *The Kabbalah and Its Symbolism*, trans. R. Manheim. New York: Schocken.

Scholem, G. (1976). *On the Mystical Shape of the Godhead: Basic Concepts in the Kabbalah*, trans. J. Neugroschel. New York: Schocken Books, 1991.

Schonfield, H. (1997). *Proclaiming the Messiah*. London: Open Gate Press.

Schore, A. (1991). Early superego development: The emergence of shame and narcissistic affect regulation in the practicing period. *Psychoanal. Contemp. Thought*, 14:187–250.

Schore, A. (1994). *Affect Regulation and the Origin of the Self: The Neurobiology of Emotional Development*. Hillsdale, NJ: Lawrence Erlbaum Associates.

Schou, P. (1977). Potential subjectivity: The dimension of the future in the psychoanalytic situation. Presented at meeting of American Psychoanalytic Association, Dec. 17, New York City.

Schreber, D. P. (1903). *Memoirs of My Mental Illness*, ed. & trans. I. Macalpine & R. Hunter. London: William Dawson & Sons, 1955.

Schwalbe, M. L. (1991). The autogenesis of the self. *J. Theory Soc. Behav.*, 21:269–295.

Schwartz-Salant, N. (1988). Archetypal foundations of projective identification. *J. Analyt. Psychol.*, 33:39–64.

Schwartz-Salant, N. (1989). *The Borderline Personality: Vision and Healing*. Wilmette, IL: Chiron.

Schwartz-Salant, N. (1995). *Jung on Alchemy: Encountering Jung*. Princeton, NJ: Princeton University Press.

Schwartz-Salant, N. (1998). *The Mystery of Human Relationship: Alchemy and the Transformation of Self*. London: Routledge.

Scott, W. C. M. (1975). Remembering sleep and dreams. *Internat. Rev. Psycho-Anal.*, 2:253–354.

Segal, H. (1957). Notes on symbol formation. In: *The Work of Hanna Segal: A Kleinian Approach to Clinical Practice*. New York: Aronson, 1981, pp. 49–68.

Segal, H. (1989). Introduction. In: *The Oedipus Complex Today: Clinical Implications*, ed. R. Britton, M. Feldman & E. O'Shaughnessy. London: Karnac Books, pp. 1–10.

Sells, M. A. (1994). *Mystical Languages of Unsaying*. Chicago: University of Chicago Press.

Share, L. (1994). *If Someone Speaks, It Gets Lighter: Dreams and the Reconstruction of Infant Trauma*. Hillsdale, NJ: The Analytic Press.

Shengold, L. (1989). *Soul Murder: The Effects of Childhood Abuse and Deprivation*. New Haven, CT Yale University Press.

Skelton, R. (1990). Generalisation from Freud to MatteBlanco. *Internat. Rev. Psycho-Anal.*, 17:471–474.

Skelton, R. (1995a). Bion's use of modern logic. *Internat. J. Psycho-Anal.*, 76:389–397.

Skelton, R. (1995b). Is the unconscious structured like a language. *Internat. Forum Psychoanal.*, 4:168–178.

Spero, M. E. (1982). *Oedipus in the Trobriands*. Chicago: University of Chicago Press.

Spitz, R. (1959). *A Genetic Field Theory of Ego Formation: Its Implications for Pathology*. New York: International Universities Press.

Spitz, R. A. (1965). *The First Year of Life*. New York: International Universities Press.

Stanislavski, C. (1936). *An Actor Prepares*, trans. E. R. Hapgood. New York: Theatre Arts.

Steele, R. S. (1979). Psychoanalysis and hermeneutics. *Internat. Rev. Psycho-Anal.*, 6:389–411.

Steiner, J. (1993). *Psychic Retreats*. London: Routledge.

Steiner, J. (1996). Revenge and resentment in the "oedipal situation." *Internat. J. Psycho-Anal.*, 77:433–443.

Stern, D. (1985). *The Interpersonal World of the Infant*. New York: Basic Books.

Stern, D. (1989). The representation of relational patterns: Developmental considerations. In: *Relation Disturbances and Early Childhood: A Developmental Approach*, ed. A. J. Sameroff & R. N. Emde. New York: Basic Books, pp. 52–69.

Sylla, E. D. (1982). Infinite indivisibles and continuity in fourteenth-century theories of alteration. In: *Infinity and Continuity in Ancient and Medieval Thought*, ed. N. Kreitzmann. Ithaca, NY: Cornell University Press, pp. 231–254.

Symington, J. & Symington, N. (1996). *The Clinical Thinking of Wilfred Bion*. London: Routledge.

Symington, N. (1994). *Emotion and Spirit: Questioning the Claims of Psychoanalysis and Religion*. London: Cassell.

Tausk, V. (1919). On the origin of the "influencing machine" in schizophrenia, trans. D. Feigenbaum. In: *The Psychoanalytic Reader: An Anthology of Essential Papers with Critical Introductions*, ed. R. Fliess. New York: International Universities Press, 1948., pp. 52–85.

Taylor, G. (1978). Demoniacal possession and psychoanalytic theory. *Brit. J. Med. Psychol.*, 51:53–60.

Thom, R. (1975). *Structural Stability and Morphogenesis*. Reading, MS: Benjamin

Thomas, K. (1971). *Religion and the Decline of Magic*. New York: Scribner.

Tomkins, S. S. (1978). Script theory: Differential magnification of affects. *Nebraska Symposium on Motivation, Vol. I*. Lincoln: University of Nebraska Press, pp. 201–236.

Tresan, D. (1996). Jungian metapsychology and neurobiological theory. *J. Anal. Psych.*, 41:399–436.

Trevarthen, C. (1974). Conversations with a two-month old. *New Scientist*, 62:230–235.

Trevarthen, C. (1979). Communication and cooperation in early infancy: A description of primary intersubjectivity. In: *Before Speech: The Beginning of*

Interpersonal Communication, ed. M. Bellowa. Cambridge, UK: Cambridge University Press, pp. 321–347.

Trevarthen, C. (1980). The foundations of intersubjectivity: Development of interpersonal and cooperative understanding in infants. In: *The Social Foundations of Language and Thought: Essays in Honor of J. S. Bruner*, ed. D. Olson. New York: Norton, pp. 316–342.

Trevarthen, C. (1983). Development of the cerebral mechanisms of language. In: *Neuropsychology of Language, Reading, and Spelling*, ed. U. Kirk. New York: Academic Press, pp. 45–80.

Trevarthen, C. (1987). Sharing making sense: Intersubjectivity and the making of an infant's meaning. In: *Language Topics: Essays in Honor of Michael Halliday, Vol. 1*, ed. R. Steele & T. Threadgold. Amsterdam: John Benjamins, pp. 177–199.

Trevarthen, C. (1988). Universal cooperative motives: How infants begin to know language and skills of culture. In: *Ethnographic Perspectives on Cognitive Development*, ed. G. Jahoda & I. Lewis. London: Croon Helm, pp. 37–90.

Trevarthen, C. (1991). The other in the infant mind. Paper and videotape presented at "The Psychic Life of the Infant: Origins of Human Identity," a conference sponsored by the University of Massachusetts at Amherst, June 29.

Trevarthen, C. & Hubley, P. (1978). Secondary intersubjectivity: Confidence, confiding, and acts of meaning in the first year. In: *Action, Gesture and Symbol: The Emergence of Language*, ed. A. Lock. London: Academic Press, pp. 183–229.

Tucker, W. & Tucker, K. (1988). *The Dark Matter: Contemporary Science's Quest for the Mass Hidden in Our Universe*. New York: William Morrow.

Velikovsky, I. (1960). *Oedipus and Akhnaton: Myth and History: The Tragic Events in the Life of the Royal House of the Hundred Gated Thebes*. New York: Doubleday.

Verene, D. P. (1997). Freud's consulting room archeology and Vico's principles of humanity: A communication. *Brit. J. Psychother.*, 13:499–505.

Vico, G. B. (1744). *The New Science of Giambattista Vico*, trans. T. G. Bergin & M. H. Fisch. Ithaca, NY: Cornell University Press, 1948.

von Kleist, H. (1810). On the marionette theater, trans. I. Parry. In: *Essays on Dolls*, ed. I. Parry. London: Penguin, 1994, pp. 1–14.

Waldrop, M. M. (1992). *Complexity: The Emerging Science on the Edge of Order and Chaos*. New York: Simon & Schuster.

Watson, A. (1995a). *The Trial of Jesus*. Athens: University of Georgia Press.

Watson, A. (1995b). *Jesus and the Jews: The Pharisaic Tradition in John*. Athens: University of Georgia Press.

Webb, R. E. & Sells, M. A. (1995). Lacan and Bion: Psychoanalysis and the mystical language of "unsaying." *Theory and Psychol.*, 5:195–215.

Westen, D. (1997). Towards a clinically and empirically sound theory of motivation. *Internat. J. Psycho-Anal.*, 78:521–548.

Wilde, O. (1890). The picture of Dorian Gray. In: *Complete Works of Oscar Wilde. Vol. II*, ed. R. Ross. New York: Bigelow, Brown, 1905, pp. 1–272.

Wilkinson, H. (1998). Phenomenological causality and why we avoid examining the nature of causality in psychotherapy: A dialogue. *Internat. J. Psychother.*, 3:147–164.

Williams, J. G. (1992). *The Bible, Violence, and the Sacred*. San Francisco: Harper San Francisco.

Williams, M. H. (1985). The tiger and "O": A reading of Bion's *Memoir of the Future. Free Assoc.*, 1:33–56.

Williams, M. H. (1994). A man of achievement—Sophocles' Oedipus. *Brit. J. Psychother.*, 11:232–241.

Winnicott, D. W. (1948). Reparation in respect of mother's organized defences against depression. In: *Collected Papers: Through Paediatrics to Psycho-Analysis*. New York: Basic Books, 1958, pp. 91–96.

Winnicott, D. W. (1950). Aggression in relation to emotional development. In: *Collected Papers: Through Paediatrics to Psycho-Analysis*. New York: Basic Books, 1958, pp. 204–218.

Winnicott, D. W. (1951). Transitional objects and transitional phenomena. In: *Collected Papers: Through Paediatrics to Psycho-Analysis*. New York: Basic Books, 1958, pp. 229–242.

Winnicott, D. W. (1956). Primary maternal preoccupation. In: *Collected Papers: Through Paediatrics to Psycho-Analysis*. New York: Basic Books, 1958, pp. 300–305.

Winnicott, D. W. (1958). The capacity to be alone. In: *The Maturational Processes and the Facilitating Environment: Studies in the Theory of Emotional Development*. New York: International Universities Press, 1965, pp. 29–36.

Winnicott, D. W. (1960a). Ego distortion in terms of true and false self. In: *The Maturational Processes and the Facilitating Environment. Studies in the Theory of Emotional Development*. New York: International Universities Press, 1965, pp. 140–152.

Winnicott, D. W. (1960b). The theory of the parent-infant relationship. In: *The Maturational Processes and the Facilitating Environment: Studies in the Theory of Emotional Development*. New York: International Universities Press, 1965, pp. 37–55.

Winnicott, D. W. (1963a). The development of the capacity for concern. In: *The Maturational Processes and the Facilitating Environment: Studies in the Theory of Emotional Development*. New York: International Universities Press, 1965, pp. 73–82.

Winnicott, D. W. (1963b). Communicating and not communicating leading to a study of certain opposites. In: *The Maturational Processes and the Facilitating Environment: Studies in the Theory of Emotional Development*. New York: International Universities Press, 1965, pp. 37–55.

Winnicott, D. W. (1967). The location of cultural experience. In: *Playing and Reality*. London: Tavistock, pp. 95–103.

Winnicott, D. W. (1968a). Playing: Its theoretical status in the clinical situation. *Internat. J. Psycho-Anal.*, 49:591–599.

Winnicott, D. W. (1968b). Playing: A theoretical statement. In: *Playing and Reality*. London: Tavistock, pp. 38–52.

Winnicott, D. W. (1969). The use of an object and relating through identification. In: *Playing and Reality*. London: Tavistock, 1971, pp. 86–94.

Winnicott, D. W. (1971a). *Playing and Reality*. London: Tavistock.

Winnicott, D. W. (1971b). Playing: Creative activity and the search for the self. In: *Playing and Reality*. London: Tavistock, pp. 53–64.

Winnicott, D. W. (1971c). Creativity and its origins. In: *Playing and Reality*. London: Tavistock, 1971, pp. 65–85.

Wisdom, J. O. (1963). Comparison and development of the psychoanalytical theories of melancholia. *Internat. J. Psycho-Anal.*, 43:113–132.

Wittgenstein, L. (1921) *Tractatus Logico-Philosophicus*. London.

Wittgenstein, L. (1933–1935). *The Blue and Brown Books*. New York: Harper & Row, 1958.

Wordsworth, W. (1798). Intimations of immortality. In: *William Wordsworth: The Poems, Vol. 1*. London: Penguin Books.

Zohar, D. (1990). *The Quantum Self: Human Nature and Consciousness Defined by the New Physics* (in collaboration with N. Marshall). New York: Morrow.

INDEX

GLOSSARY

Solipcism

Ineffable